ALIEN ALBION: LITERATURE AND IMMIGRATION IN EARLY MODERN ENGLAND

Using both canonical and underappreciated texts, *Alien Albion* argues that early modern England was far less unified and xenophobic than literary critics have previously suggested. Juxtaposing literary texts from the period with legal, religious, and economic documents, Scott Oldenburg uncovers how immigrants to England forged ties with their English hosts and how those relationships were reflected in literature that imagined inclusive, multicultural communities.

Through discussions of civic pageantry, the plays of dramatists including William Shakespeare, Thomas Dekker, and Thomas Middleton, the poetry of Anne Dowriche, and the prose of Thomas Deloney, *Alien Albion* challenges assumptions about the origins of English national identity and the importance of religious, class, and local identities in the early modern era.

SCOTT OLDENBURG is an associate professor in the Department of English at Tulane University.

SCOTT OLDENBURG

Alien Albion: Literature and Immigration in Early Modern England

UNIVERSITY OF TORONTO PRESS
Toronto Buffalo London

© University of Toronto Press 2014
Toronto Buffalo London
www.utppublishing.com

Reprinted in paperback 2015

ISBN 978-1-4426-4719-0 (cloth)
ISBN 978-1-4426-3078-9 (paper)

Library and Archives Canada Cataloguing in Publication

Oldenburg, Scott K., 1969–, author
Alien Albion : literature and immigration in early modern England / Scott K. Oldenburg.

Includes bibliographical references and index.
ISBN 978-1-4426-4719-0 (bound). – ISBN 978-1-4426-3078-9 (paperback)

1. English literature – Minority authors – History and criticism. 2. English literature – Early modern, 1500–1700 – History and criticism. 3. England – Ethnic relations – History – 16th century. 4. Immigrants – England – History – 16th century. 5. England – Emigration and immigration – History – 16th century. I. Title.

PR120.M55O43 2014   820.9'92069120903   C2014-902896-2

University of Toronto Press acknowledges the financial assistance to its publishing program of the Canada Council for the Arts and the Ontario Arts Council, an agency of the Government of Ontario.

  Canada Council   Conseil des Arts
for the Arts   du Canada

ONTARIO ARTS COUNCIL
CONSEIL DES ARTS DE L'ONTARIO
an Ontario government agency
un organisme du gouvernement de l'Ontario

Funded by the   Financé par le
Government   gouvernement
of Canada   du Canada

Canada

Contents

Acknowledgments vii

Introduction: Forms of Multiculturalism in Early Modern England 3

Part One: Sectarian Inclusivity

1 From the Dutch Acrobat to Hance Beerpot: Multicultural Mid-Tudor England 23
2 The Rhetoric of Religious Refuge under Elizabeth I 45

Part Two: Provincial Globalism

3 Artisanal Tolerance: The Case of Thomas Deloney 75
4 Language and Labour in Thomas Dekker's Provincial Globalism 99

Part Three: Worldly Domesticity

5 The "Jumbled" City: *The Dutch Courtesan* and *Englishmen for My Money* 117
6 Shakespeare, the Foreigner 138

Conclusion: The Return of Hans Beer-Pot 173

Notes 185
Bibliography 245
Index 283

Acknowledgments

An earlier version of chapter 1 appeared in *English Literary History* 76.1 (2009) as "Toward a Multicultural Mid-Tudor England: The Queen's Royal Entry Circa 1553, *The Interlude of Wealth and Health*, and the Question of Strangers in the Reign of Mary I." An early version of chapter 5 appeared in *Literature Compass* 7.1 (2010) as "'Outlandish Love': Marriage and Immigration in City Comedies." In writing this book I am grateful for the support I have received at my home institution, Tulane University. Some of the research for this book was carried out under a Summer Fellowship from the Committee on Research at Tulane University, and this book was published with a generous subvention from the Dean of the School of Liberal Arts at Tulane University. I also want to thank my friends and colleagues at Tulane University, especially Dwight Codr (now at the University of Connecticut), Jean Dangler, Tom Frazel, Michelle Kohler, Mike Kuczynski, Adam McKeown, and Barb Ryan.

I began this project while a graduate student at SUNY Buffalo. I would like to thank University at Buffalo professors Barbara Bono, James Holstun, Scott Stevens, and Jim Swan for their advice and support during those early stages of development.

A special thanks goes to Suzanne Rancourt of the University of Toronto Press and the three outstanding readers she selected for the manuscript of this book. Their feedback has been invaluable.

Finally, I am especially thankful for the love and support of my children: Carlos (who offered to help me with capitalization throughout the manuscript) and Diego (who, upon learning the alphabet, volunteered to help me write an early draft of this book). Both have been there for all the stages of this book and their patience has been invaluable.

ALIEN ALBION: LITERATURE AND IMMIGRATION IN EARLY MODERN ENGLAND

"Our owne forefathers committing their works to writings, they seem aliens and strangers unto us."

– Godfrey Goodman, *The Fall of Man* (1616)[1]

Introduction: Forms of Multiculturalism in Early Modern England

Towards the end of *An Apology for Poetry* (1595), Sir Philip Sidney asks, "For what is it to make folks gape at a wretched beggar or a beggarly clown; or against law of hospitality, to jest at strangers because they speak not English so well as we do? What do we learn?"[2] By strangers, Sidney meant non-English peoples residing in or passing through England, most of whom were European immigrants seeking refuge from religious turmoil on the continent. Although even a cursory reading of Sidney's *Arcadia* will no doubt call into question Sidney's sincerity regarding laughter at "beggarly clowns," he seems to have followed his own advice on the tolerant treatment of strangers in his writing. In Sidney's lifetime there would have been no shortage of stranger-characters performed with thick accents from which he could derive his judgment: Hance Beerpot in *An Interlude of Wealth and Health* (1554–7), Colehazard in *A New Interlude of Impacyente Pouertye* (1560), Philip Fleming and Hance in *Like Will to Like* (1568), and Mercatore in *Three Ladies of London* (1581) are but a few that Sidney may have been thinking of as he wrote the *Apology*. Whatever Sidney's experience of these plays may have been, his defence of strangers in the *Apology* may have had a great deal to do with his witnessing the slaughter of French Protestants, the infamous Saint Bartholomew's Day Massacre in Paris on 24 August 1572, an event that, like so many of the acts of sectarian violence in early modern Europe, resulted in a massive influx of immigrants to England.[3]

The term *immigrant* is a fairly new addition to the English lexicon. The *Oxford English Dictionary* suggests that the word made it to print no earlier than 1792.[4] In the sixteenth century the terms *alien* and *stranger* were used interchangeably to refer to not only immigrants but also merchants passing through England, tourists, diplomats, and anyone else from outside the realm. In practical usage, however, the English did distinguish between strangers who settled in England and those who stayed in England for only a brief time. The Returns of Aliens, a careful record of the whereabouts of immigrants in London, was instituted by Henry VIII in 1523 and was carried out more frequently under Elizabeth. That The Returns do not account for ambassadors and their retinue, merchant strangers in England on business for a short time, and so forth, indicates that although the English lacked a specific word for immigrants, they nonetheless maintained the concept.[5] This book is about literature's contribution to an understanding of English-stranger relations from the 1540s through the 1600s with an emphasis on the 1590s when economic problems strained English-immigrant relations.

Immigration was a major issue during the early modern period: guilds routinely submitted petitions expressing their concerns about the influx of new labourers from the continent while Norwich, Maidstone, Halstead, and Colchester invited strangers to their areas so that new industries could be started.[6] In Norwich the stranger population sometimes reached close to 30 per cent of the total population;[7] statutes describing and sometimes limiting the rights of strangers were periodically issued while official stranger churches were built, affording Protestant refugees considerable freedom of religion. Issues of immigration were debated in the House of Commons and the House of Lords.[8] Most of the well-known portraits of the period (including the First Folio engraving of William Shakespeare) were made by Dutch artists.[9] As many as 50,000 Protestant refugees from the continent are estimated to have passed through London during Sidney's lifetime.[10] Many returned to the continent in due course, but even so, shortly before Sidney's death roughly 10,000 immigrants were counted as living in London.[11] That issues of immigration should work their way into a seminal text of early modern literary theory such as Sidney's should come as little surprise then. *Alien Albion* argues for the centrality of immigration to early modern English life and letters.

This book offers an alternative to the dominant ways in which literary scholars have understood the place of immigration in early modern life. Scholars have tended to emphasize moments of tension between the English and their immigrant neighbours, and typically conclude that the English were deeply xenophobic, that this xenophobia was foundational to English identity, and that the immigrant was invariably caught up in a self-other dynamic against which the English defined themselves.[12] Jean Howard and Phyllis Rackin suggest that the Tudor nation manifested itself in resistance to the French, in part because "the English were notoriously xenophobic." The "Other," argues Claire McEachern, "is an everpresent constituent of Englishness in this period."[13] Even Philip Schwyzer, who broadens and complicates the debate by defining the Tudor nation in terms of a complex British (rather than English) identity, places emphasis on "xenophobic impulses to which Tudor subjects were so notoriously prone."[14] These xenophobic impulses gave rise to a self-other paradigm essential to the construction of early English national identity.

Certainly, this process can be detected: the term *English* can scarcely exist without a recognition of something other than English. As Lloyd Edward Kermode's recent study of Elizabethan plays depicting English encounters with aliens has shown, Englishness itself is a fraught and contested concept, sometimes developing from a process of othering, but also at times incorporating the alien in its self-definition.[15] Whereas Kermode is primarily interested in mapping a complex ongoing formation of Englishness in relation to an idea of otherness, I examine the corollary, early English texts imagining a community that might accommodate the presence of immigrants in England.

No doubt some English at times took part in all too real anti-alien activities, but Andrew Pettegree cautions against an "assumption of xenophobia amongst sixteenth-century Englishmen."[16] While one may point to intermittent anti-alien activity, there are other moments of cooperation among English and immigrant, so much so that Nigel Goose has argued that for sixteenth-century Protestant refugees, early modern England "may have represented a veritable oasis of tolerance."[17] Goose's research, an important corrective to scholarly pronouncements about widespread English xenophobia, suggests that xenophobia is more evident in the eighteenth century with "the rise of English nationalism."[18] The *earliness* of the early modern period – the fact that what becomes modernity is only emergent in this period – opens up the possibility of locating other conceptions of community in competition with a culturally exclusive nationhood, ideas about community founded on something other than common birthplace.

Several scholars have argued that early English nationhood becomes apparent under Henry VIII, however. Andrew Hadfield begins his study of national identity in early English literature with an analysis of Henrician poet John Skelton, while Richard Helgerson and Claire McEachern see Henry VIII's break with Rome as a foundational act in the development of an English nation.[19] Although Elizabeth Sauer takes a longer view of the development of English nationhood, she also sees the break with Rome as a pivotal moment in the development of an English national consciousness.[20]

These critics see literature as integral to the formation of national identity, but they agree that the development of early English nationhood was neither uniform nor instantaneous but rather complex and contradictory, developing unevenly over time. McEachern finds in several canonical texts of the period assertions of an "ideal of social unity," while Andrew Escobedo sees similar texts evoking a sense of comradery indicative of national feeling.[21] None of these critics sees literature as perfectly reflective of society. Contradictions in the development of Englishness or Britishness, as Willy Maley explains, were often resolved through an appeal to "an origin-myth of 'national' unity" that marginalized opposition.[22] That is, the assertion of unity or comradery can often be seen as an attempt to occlude diversity and suppress alternative perspectives. Hadfield's linking of early English nationhood to the establishment of a public sphere is useful here, especially in light of Christopher Highley's exploration of Catholic writing of the English nation.[23] That is, throughout the early modern period, the nature of English identity was not singular but contested. Thus, within this public sphere one may find an English nation defined in a variety of ways. *Alien Albion* argues that amid these attempts to define a distinctly English cultural identity one may find texts that articulate a collective identity that is not recognizably national, but rather global or multicultural.

The Ditchley Portrait of Queen Elizabeth is a prime example of how an emphasis on nation obscures the complexities of early modern English culture. A gift from Sir Henry Lee to Elizabeth in 1592, this painting features Elizabeth hovering over a map of England, and seems so quintessentially English that it has been chosen as the cover of volume one of the *Norton Anthology of English Literature*.[24] In his landmark book *Forms of Nationhood* Helgerson reads the portrait as displaying the vain attempts of the monarchy to overshadow the claims of an early English nationhood; the queen covers the map and therefore trumps its power to define England independently of the monarch.[25] The most obvious relation between queen and map is that her toes point to Oxfordshire, the county of Lee's estate in Ditchley, but it is certainly possible that the painting represents a tension between the old dominant mode of group identity – monarchical power manifested in the image of the queen – and an emergent national consciousness becoming legible in cartography.

This focus on an emerging nation, however, occludes the painting's relation to immigration into England, the multiculturalism that pervades the painting. Elizabeth's richly patterned gown is almost certainly the work of French silk-weavers (there were few other silk-weavers in England at the time), and the large, puffed sleeves were a fashion brought over by Flemish immigrants.[26] The undergarment that allows Elizabeth's dress to fan out to cover (and symbolically encompass) England was known as a wheel farthingale, a fashion that came to England by way of France.[27] To Elizabeth's left is a sonnet, a form borrowed from Italian poets, inscribing her power not in English, but in Latin, a more global language than one might expect from this supposed token of Englishness. Finally, the painting itself is by the Dutch immigrant painter Marcus Gheeraerts, the Younger.

Here a symbol of Englishness – even if exemplary of the tensions between an emergent nationhood and a dominant dynastic rule – is riddled with signs not of native English traditions but of cosmopolitan innovation, a collaboration between Englishmen like Lee and England's immigrant communities. These multicultural collaborations, solidarities not grounded on shared birthplace, were emerging at the same time as and in tension with nationhood. That is, the nation and its definition of citizenship in a national community was only one of several ways to think about community in the wake of economic, religious, and political upheaval. These three major motors of change resulted in increased immigration. For centuries people had immigrated to England for economic opportunities, to offer skills scarce and therefore profitable in England. In the sixteenth century immigration increased as French, Dutch, Flemish, Walloon (French speakers from Spanish provinces), and Italian Protestants came to England seeking refuge from religious and political persecution and from the economic downturn that came with war and political instability.[28]

Alien Albion focuses on continental immigration to England rather than on the Scottish, Welsh, and Irish in England. The complex development of a shared British identity for the English, Irish, Scottish, and Welsh is substantially different from the Anglo-immigrant communities discussed here. As Colin Kidd points out, "in certain areas English and Welsh identities overlapped."[29] Thus, the discussion of the Welsh Parson in *The Merry Wives of Windsor* in chapter 6 examines the relationship between immigrants and *foreigners*, the term used to describe the many English and Welsh women and men who migrated from all parts of the realm to London and other English cities.[30] Somewhat similarly, with the accession of James I, the Scottish in England ceased to be officially counted as alien, and although the Irish residing in England were for the most part viewed by the English as fundamentally "other," as early as 1449 the law treated them not as aliens but as subjects of the monarch.[31] This is not to dismiss the topic of the Welsh, Scottish, and Irish migrations to England, but rather to suggest that the changing and contested nature of each group's status in the formation of Britain – what Willy Maley, Conrad Russell, and others refer to as "the British problem" –comprises a distinct, albeit related, field requiring one or more separate volumes.[32]

Immigration patterns were shaped by the political climate of England relative to that of the continent.[33] Whereas Protestant refugees were welcomed under Edward VI, Mary I sought their expulsion. Elizabeth I ushered in a cautious hospitality, supportive of immigration but not as open as Edward VI's reign had been. James I made a point of continuing Elizabeth's policies, but he was not averse to exploiting the position of strangers. Charles I was generally supportive of the economic rights of strangers, but Archbishop Laud's policies of uniformity led most strangers to side with the Parliamentarians in the English Civil War.[34]

Meanwhile events on the continent led to an uneven flow of immigrants to England. Although England had long hosted a Dutch community, the Duke of Alva's violent suppression of Protestants in the Dutch Provinces during the 1560s and the fall of Antwerp in 1585 led large numbers of Dutch Calvinists to seek refuge in England.[35] Ole Peter Grell estimates that between 1567 and 1590 approximately 100,000 Dutch Protestants fled the Netherlands, many settling temporarily and some permanently in England.[36] In the 1620s, at the outset of the Thirty Years' War, England again found itself host to an influx of refugees from the Low Countries.[37]

French immigration followed a similar pattern. As tensions between religious factions rose in the 1560s, many French Protestants immigrated to England, and the Saint Bartholomew's Day Massacre in 1572 marked a significant increase in the number of French Protestants fleeing sectarian violence.[38] When Henry III formally aligned himself with the Catholic League in 1585 another wave of French immigrants arrived in England. Between the Edict of Nantes of 1598 (France's formal policy of religious tolerance) and its revocation in 1685, French immigration slowed substantially and many Huguenots returned to France. In the 1680s Louis XIV's renewed hostility towards Protestants again prompted an exodus of Huguenots into England.

As Lien Bich Luu has emphasized, as in earlier centuries, economic motives also informed immigration to England. Practitioners of specific trades – those who worked in textiles, for instance – were more likely to see England as a desirable destination.[39] These causes of immigration – religion and craft – are also two of the three early modern forms of multicultural solidarity explored in this book. Although the Reformation fragmented a somewhat uniform Catholicism, the split led Protestants to see across geopolitical borders versions of themselves, members of the same Christian community; this is what I call "sectarian inclusivity," a term meant to emphasize one alternative to national consciousness. While birthplace never entirely disappears as a marker of identity (hence the use of the broad term "the English" throughout this book), the break with Rome opened the possibility of imagining a community founded on shared beliefs rather than shared birthplace. A degree of distrust might linger regarding more radical Protestant groups, but the English looked to the continent for much of their early inspiration in developing an English Reformation.[40] Henry VIII's break with Rome, however politically expedient and nationalist it may have been, led to the arrival of the first wave of Protestant refugees in England, even amid government activity against Protestant sects, including the burning of four Dutchmen suspected of Anabaptism.[41] Still, the importance of immigration from the continent in developing Protestantism in England is evident, especially in subsequent decades.[42]

Immigration increased with Edward VI's accession and the promise of a more genuinely Protestant state; by the end of his reign immigrants made up roughly 12.5 per cent of London's population.[43] Under the influence of several Protestant advisors, Edward granted a surprising amount of religious freedom to the Protestant refugees, and this no doubt fuelled the idea that England could serve as a real refuge from turmoil on the continent. In turn, it appears that Edward's advisors had hoped that the presence of continental Protestants would spark a more fervent Reformation in England. Edward's 1550 charter for the refugee churches instructed authorities to allow the strangers "freely and quietly to practice, enjoy, use and exercise their own rites and ceremonies and their own peculiar ecclesiastical discipline, notwithstanding that they do not conform with the rites and ceremonies used in our Kingdom."[44] Edward's charter indicates a remarkable respect for cultural difference, an early modern multiculturalism founded on common Protestant belief and marked difference from Catholicism.

This sectarian inclusivity is best theorized by Caleb Dalechamp in his 1632 tract, *Christian Hospitalitie Handled Common-place-wise*. Dalechamp, a Protestant refugee from Sedan, asserts that his immigrant experience gives him a certain degree of humble authority on the issue of hospitality. In his dedication to the Bishop of London, he writes, "so I being a stranger may speak and write of the entertainment of strangers."[45] He asserts that "It is an inhumane part for any Prince or Magistrate, to forbid strangers the coming or abiding in his Dominions," and he uses scripture to support this strong claim. "Christ's disciples," he explains, "thought the Samaritans unworthy to live, for not receiving him into a village of theirs" and "the Lacedemonians have been branded with the nickname of *Dirinoxeni, Injurious to strangers*, for not permitting strangers to dwell among them." He tempers this statement with two provisos: "That they [the strangers] be peaceable men and that the land be large enough for them."[46] That is, the host location must have sufficient resources to support additional people, and immigrants must be law-abiding members of the community. Dalechamp sets out four parts to public hospitality:

1 To suffer strangers to come into the land or countrey.
2 To defend them by good laws from injuries and wrongs.
3 To give them leave to exercise their lawfull calling, and to advance the ablest of them to some place of preferment.
4 To procure the relief of those that are in want and necessity.[47]

Dalechamp's broad charge to hosts is based on the idea of sectarian inclusivity: that all Christians participate in a community whose mandates supersede the maintenance of geopolitical borders. As Dalechamp explains, hospitality is to be extended to "strangers professing the true Religion, More specially strangers persecuted and banished for professing the true Religion; Most chiefly and above all, Ministers and Divinitie-readers persecuted for teaching and defending the same true Religion."[48] Although Dalechamp may assert that all strangers be met with hospitality – he goes on to say that hospitality should be given to "strangers of any Region or Religion" – a special sense of inclusivity exists among those of the Protestant faith. Chapters 1 and 2 explore in greater detail the dynamics of sectarian inclusivity from the 1550s through the early 1590s.

Sectarian inclusivity is but one mode of England's early modern multiculturalism. In general, early modern multiculturalism was a good deal different from current formulations of multiculturalism because it was largely Eurocentric. While the theatres of sixteenth- and seventeenth-century England frequently featured exotic characters representing distant cultures radically different from those in England, the immigrant communities of central concern to early modern England were French and Walloon, Dutch and Flemish, and to a lesser degree Italian, Spanish, and Portuguese.[49] The English, it should be noted, were not always precise in how they wrote about these groups: Walloons were often enveloped into the category of "French" while "Dutch" might cover Flemings and any number of nearby nationalities. Exotic theatrical characters enacted a variety of imaginary encounters that few playgoers would meet in real life, but the Dutch, French, and Flemish characters on the stage, however imaginary and stereotypical, approximated cultural encounters most of the audience experienced on a day-to-day basis in markets, workplaces, parish churches, taverns, and most of all in the liberties, an area densely populated by immigrant communities.[50]

Early modern English perceptions of these immigrant groups appears to have been informed by what Mary Floyd Wilson terms *geohumoralism*, the belief that climate significantly influenced humoral balances and therefore accounted for broad cultural differences between the English and their European neighbours.[51] Thus, while it may not have been involved with the prevalent current issues of race and post-colonialism, England's early modern multiculturalism was not unlike contemporary multicultural Britain: then and now England has had to address issues of immigrant rights, language barriers, and diverse cultural practices in order to overcome perceived differences. That being said, while contemporary multiculturalism aims at egalitarianism, early modern multiculturalism sometimes sought a community founded on models of hospitality and at other times strove to fit immigrants into a hierarchy that gave economic advantage to Englishmen.[52] Many studies of England's encounters with various cultures excavate a self-other paradigm where the encounter serves to consolidate a relatively coherent (and at times fragile) sense of Englishness;[53] *Alien Albion*, however, suggests that at least in their encounters with immigrants, many English men and women at times favoured communities based on something other than a shared sense of Englishness, that the encounter with strangers might, in some cases and for some individuals, redraw boundaries of self and other in ways that do not lead teleologically to modernity's premium on national identity. These solidarities founded on points in common other than birthplace, solidarities that overcame an English-Other paradigm, constitute what I am terming early modern multiculturalism.

Immigrants in early modern England were not usually valued for their Dutchness or Frenchness alone. More often, cultural differences were only one factor in English men's and women's attitudes towards their immigrant neighbours. Cultural differences were of course recognized – broad stereotypes abound in the period – but points of common interest and ways of collaborating often bridged the cultural and linguistic gap between native-born and immigrant to constitute the second form of early modern multicultural community explored in *Alien Albion*, a form of community I refer to as "provincial globalism." The early modern economy necessitated a global awareness, a sense of interdependence on not only foreign markets but also immigrant labour in England. As Sir John Wolley argued in a 1593 debate over the trade privileges of merchant strangers, "the Riches and Renowne of the City cometh by entertaining of strangers, and giving liberty unto them."[54] This early modern global conscience was tempered by a pervasive provincialism, a fairly conservative attitude that outsiders conform to local expectations in social relations. Thus Nicholas Fuller responded to Wolley, "It is no Charity to have this pity on them to our own utter undoing," and proceeded to complain that strangers "will not converse with us, they will not marry with us, they will not buy any thing of our Country-men."[55] Fuller called for greater integration into the economic and social fabric of English life, but like most of his countrymen, he also demanded that integration occur on English terms. The tension here between appreciating immigrants and at the same time insisting that they adapt to English social mores is emblematic of provincial globalism. While it is a far cry from a contemporary value of diversity, provincial globalism is clearly not xenophobia. On the contrary, the goal of provincial globalism seems to have been finding a mode of inclusion, albeit one that would be advantageous to the English and would minimize cultural differences.

I am not here pitting provincial against urban life, however. London may have been a cosmopolitan city, but many early modern Londoners still maintained a fairly narrow view of social and economic relations and expected substantial conformity from outsiders. Thus, English artisans could be tolerant and inclusive – even keen to learn the skills immigrants had acquired abroad – but they also demanded that strangers respect local guild ordinances and abide by local standards of fair play at the marketplace. Although intermittent anti-alien activity occurred in the period, on a day-to-day basis immigrants and their English hosts seems to have gotten along. Immigrants worked for English master craftsmen, and Englishmen apprenticed themselves to immigrant master craftsmen.

Dalechamp is again helpful in this respect. In the second half of *Christian Hospitalitie* he enumerates the three key responsibilities of strangers to their hosts: "Discretion, Modestie, and Thankfulnes." He explains that strangers should avoid "all singularity, and morosity in things indifferent, as diet, apparel, language, and matters of rites and ceremonies … The Law and Land, the custome and manner of the Region where we live must be the Rule and square of all lawfull actions."[56] Dalechamp calls for conformity to not only the law but also the manners, cuisine, and clothing of the host. In short, he calls for a degree of assimilation, not total surrender of cultural identity, but certainly a will to fit within the host culture.

Although from a modern perspective this premium on assimilation appears oppressive, even counter to the goals of multiculturalism, such behaviour, argues Dalechamp, shows not only discretion but also gratitude to the host culture.

While Dalechamp's insistence on cultural assimilation is not progressive, his mapping out of reciprocal obligations between immigrants and hosts comprises a genuine attempt at imagining a cooperative multicultural community. A failure of either the host or the immigrant could lead to less hospitable relations. One typical example of a breakdown in English-immigrant relations occurred in 1576 when London's Company of Founders discovered two immigrant craftsmen of the trade who "refuse to be sworne to observe and kepe Ordynances of theyre sayde Companye." The Founders took the case to the Court of Aldermen who authorized the company's wardens to arrest the two strangers if they continued to refuse participation in the guild structure.[57] The strangers may have been ignorant of the way the guild system worked, or they may have been trying to circumvent what they viewed as unnecessarily restrictive rules regarding their craft, or perhaps they could not afford the fees associated with joining the company. Regardless, the principle of provincial globalism called not for violence nor deportation, but rather a more thorough integration of the immigrants, an insistence on participation in the labour community. As Jacob Selwood demonstrates, however, even a high degree of integration could not guarantee protection from anti-alien activity.[58]

Anti-alien riots most often involved a magnification of a case similar to that of the two strangers in conflict with the Company of Founders. The English individuals violated the responsibilities of good hosts, and Dalechamp suggests that in such cases appeal must be made to the authority of the monarch.[59] More often than not, however, commoners took orderly steps of gradual escalation in dealing with potential breakdowns in English-immigrant relations and strove to find ways to collaborate with immigrants. Participating in the same craft could spark bitter competition or provide common ground between English and immigrant artisans. Chapters 3 and 4 explore further the dynamics of provincial globalism and the ways in which the English could forge a solidarity based on participation in a shared craft.

Immigrants and their English hosts could find a basis for collaboration in religion or trade, but strangers also appeared as integral parts of domestic life. Immigrants rented from Englishmen, and vice versa; immigrants worked in the households of the English, and vice versa; and immigrants and English married one another. Whether through formal agreements of landlord and lodger, bonds of service, or bonds of love, domestic life in England often included relations with those from other parts of the world. The third section of *Alien Albion*, "Worldly Domesticity," addresses this aspect of early modern multicultural community.

As with sectarian inclusivity and provincial globalism, worldly domesticity involves its own potential contradiction. Indeed, each of the modes of multicultural community described in this book contains internal tensions. In sectarian inclusivity there is both the establishment of a distinct religious identity and a question of how much doctrinal diversity is possible within that identity. With provincial globalism individuals value the unique skills and trade connections that come with immigration, but they also demand that the distinct culture that gave rise to those connections and skills adapt to English standards of economic and social activity. These are really early versions of contemporary cosmopolitanism, which, as Kwame Anthony Appiah notes, contains its own internal tensions in that the ethic of "universal concern" at times comes into conflict with the "respect for legitimate difference."[60]

With worldly domesticity, the premium of distinct cultural identities asserts itself most strongly, but oddly enough, the attempt at maintaining a distinct cultural identity was carried out most thoroughly by immigrants, rather than English hosts. In his study of the Dutch in Colchester, Nigel Goose finds uneven integration: the Dutch quickly integrated into Colchester's economy even though they were slow to attend English churches or marry into English families, especially before 1660.[61] This insularity was not limited to Colchester, but especially outside of England's urban centres, stranger churches appear to have fostered a sense of insularity to maintain congregation numbers.[62] The Dutch Church of Thetford had difficulty finding anyone among them who spoke sufficient English to communicate with the local Bishop, although their minister had lived in England for roughly fifteen years; even in bustling London one Dutch minister was found to speak almost no English.[63] Ministers may seem a special case since their vocation could be carried out almost entirely in their native languages, but English subsidy collectors also complained of a general lack of linguistic competence in English among strangers, evidence perhaps of the insularity of immigrant communities in early modern England.[64] Specific immigrant enclaves mostly in the suburbs of London and stranger churches throughout England helped immigrants adapt to life in England, but they also helped to create a tight-knit community resistant to assimilation.[65] By the 1590s the vast majority of London's refugees continued to attend French or Dutch churches; less than 15 per cent of strangers favoured the English church.⁶⁶ To a certain degree the stranger churches may have sheltered their congregations from contact with the English to maintain their own version of reform and foster the sense of a distinct community.

The English were not unaware of immigrant insularity. One 1571 petition to Queen Elizabeth complained that the strangers in London comprised "a common wealth within themselves," that "though they be denized or born here amongst us, yet they keep themselves severed from us in church, in government, in trade, in language and marriage."⁶⁷ According to this petition, the English-born children of strangers and even denizens – those strangers who had been granted a kind of permanent residency and more economic rights – kept well within the confines of their respective immigrant communities.⁶⁸ As with Fuller's complaint roughly twenty years later, economic considerations overlap here with issues of domesticity: both Fuller and this petition express a keen desire for immigrants to marry into English families. Despite such evidence, Pettegree qualifies the supposedly insular tendencies of the stranger churches, noting that examination of wills, marriage certificates, church attendance, and trade reveals that many strangers "slipped apparently effortlessly into English society"; Lien Bich Luu, in a survey of intermarriage and other forms of social contact suggests that "there was more social mixing" than one might expect given the reports of language barriers between immigrants and their hosts in England.⁶⁹ Chapters 5 and 6 examine this worldly domesticity in terms of private hospitality and marriage as they contributed to a greater degree of English-immigrant collaboration in household life.

These three types of multicultural connection in early modern England – solidarities based on religion, economic interest, and domestic life – correspond to the three main types of histories written about early modern immigration to England. In other words, discussions of early modern immigration have tended to focus on religious history, economic history, or individual genealogy. To be sure, several recent books – most notably Nigel Goose and Lien Bich Luu's collection, *Immigrants in Tudor and Early Stuart England* – bring these various types of history into conversation.⁷⁰ Similarly, in *Alien Albion* these three bases for solidarity overlap, sometimes to complicate, and sometimes to strengthen the bonds between English hosts and immigrants. The three forms of multicultural solidarity explored here involved emergent ways of thinking about community, and all three interacted with one another and competed with the emergent idea of English nationhood.

Moreover, this book progresses in a loosely chronological order beginning in the 1540s and ending in the 1620s, with the conclusion taking a longer but less detailed view of the late seventeenth century. Although successive waves of immigration complicate the picture, the chronological order here is not entirely coincidental. England was acutely aware that religious conflict led to the initial waves of large-scale immigration in the sixteenth century, and this important connection formed the first imagined multicultural community.[71] By the 1590s, however, economic problems in England could lead some to call into question this motive for immigration. As immigrants came to realize that they would not likely return to their places of birth, greater integration into the local economies of England brought new tensions between immigrants and their hosts, but also led to new forms of community founded on guild affiliation. As strangers established themselves in towns throughout England but especially in the urban centres, they forged personal relations with their hosts as neighbours, masters, servants, suitors, and potential spouses. Any of these modes of multicultural community could be active or called into question at any given moment. The concerns expressed in this book thus track this uneven development in immigrant-English relations.

Finally, the chapters of *Alien Albion* are focused on imaginative early modern writing: plays, pageants, ballads, poems, and prose fiction alongside religious, economic, and legal documents. All of these texts work in concert to give a sense of the emergent forms of early modern multiculturalism, but the focus throughout is literary. Literary texts contribute to the study of the effects of early modern immigration otherwise dominated by economic and religious historical scholarship in that they intervene imaginatively in society. These texts might reflect lived experience or suggest how things could be different. That is, plays, poems, prose fiction – the stories people tell themselves about immigration – are, like state documents, church records, and wills, important factors in the study of early modern immigration.

Chapters 1 and 2, for instance, explore literary and more generally cultural assertions of sectarian inclusivity. Chapter 1 juxtaposes Mary I's official positions on immigration with her coronation pageantry and the mid-Tudor interlude *Wealth and Health* to show how literature can manifest a Protestant solidarity in protest of the new monarch's anti-immigrant policies. Chapter 2 focuses on how Elizabethan literary texts such as Anne Dowriche's *The French Historie* (1589) and Christopher Marlowe's *The Massacre at Paris* (1592) show an awareness of Huguenot writing and counter a mounting anti-alien stance by narrating the Wars of Religion that led to increased immigration, justifying the presence of strangers by highlighting the hardships they experienced on the continent.

Anti-alien discourse of the 1590s moved from specific economic grievances to questioning the faith of Protestant refugees, weakening the bonds of a solidarity based on shared religion. Individuals interested in promoting the presence of immigrants in England responded by turning to the economic benefits of immigration, depicting the possibilities of peaceful coexistence through provincial globalism, an awareness of the economic interdependence of English commoners and their immigrant counterparts. Chapter 3 examines the ballads and prose fiction of Thomas Deloney and his vision of a multicultural community founded on class allegiances; chapter 4 amplifies this point through a reading of Thomas Dekker's pamphlets and plays.

The final section of *Alien Albion* moves from the workshops depicted in Deloney and Dekker to representations of multicultural households in the plays of William Haughton and William Shakespeare. Chapter 5 compares two city comedies in which Englishmen are attracted to immigrant women: Haughton's *Englishmen for My Money* (1598) and John Marston's *The Dutch Courtesan* (1605). In Haughton's play complex considerations of wealth, status, and birthplace lead to multicultural domestic spaces. Chapter 6 focuses on Shakespeare, not because his writing proves to be emblematic, but rather because it happens to deal with hospitality and its limits for immigrants and English migrants alike, highlighting another way in which strangers could find common ground with particular English men and women.

It might be noted that many of the texts under discussion in this book are today considered non- or semi-canonical. This marginality is to some extent an effect of the way canons of literature were formed in conjunction with the promotion of national identity.[72] It makes sense, then, that early English texts imagining an alternative to national identity might have been marginalized in the process, even though recent decades have seen a more flexible and inclusive approach to canonicity. Nonetheless, the texts discussed in this book were for the most part very popular in the period: Deloney's ballads and prose fiction went through numerous printings; Dekker's plays were performed at court; even *The Massacre at Paris*, a lesser known Marlowe play, was tremendously popular in its time.

The discussions in these chapters are, moreover, London-centric, not because there were no prominent immigrant communities outside of London but rather because London was the literary centre of early modern England. England hosted immigrant communities in Canterbury, Colchester, Halstead, Maidstone, Sandwich, Southampton, and elsewhere.[73] Having driven strangers from their town, citizens of Halstead soon found themselves petitioning for strangers to resettle to revive a failing economy.[74] Sandwich, Rye, and several other towns similarly found their economies bolstered by the Protestant refugees. These smaller immigrant communities faced distinct challenges, but the patterns of multicultural community appear to have run parallel to those of England's urban centres.

Despite the ways in which a literary lens leads to a focus on London, the discussion nonetheless touches on these other communities. Chapter 2 analyses the pageantry prepared for Elizabeth's 1578 visit to Norwich, which, after London, hosted the largest number of immigrants in early modern England. Like their London counterparts, immigrants in Norwich participated in literature broadly conceived. Dutch printer Anthony de Solemne briefly set up shop in Norwich where he oversaw the printing of *Certain Verses Written by Thomas Brooke* (1568) and a metrical translation of the psalms into Dutch in 1568.[75] Raised in Norwich, Dutch scholar Janus Gruter wrote verses while attending Cambridge.[76] The strangers of Norwich also participated in civic celebrations that often included a component of drama; for example, in October 1623 the Dutch and French of Norwich joined English drummers in celebrating Charles' return from Spain.[77] Chapter 2 also touches on the immigrant communities in Canterbury and Cambridge as well as the smaller communities in the West Country. Along similar lines, Deloney's *Jack of Newbury* (1597) and *Thomas of Reading* (1600), discussed in chapter 3, represent English-immigrant relations in Berkshire. Ultimately, however, *Alien Albion* analyses texts centred on London, host to early modern England's largest immigrant community.

My focus on the positive side of English-immigrant relations is not an attempt to paint a rosy picture of English tolerance. The modes of multicultural community I describe have anti-alien violence and discrimination as their backdrop, and with provincial globalism in particular one must note the way in which immigrants are included in the economy but also treated unequally. Still, it is possible to see how some early modern subjects overcame animosities and collaborated in church, shop, and home. These cross-cultural solidarities are indicative of the earliness of the early modern period. Once nationhood pervaded the way people imagined their sense of community, such solidarities became more difficult to prioritize. The value of examining these early modern social formations is not to merely observe what Peter Laslett described as "the world we have lost."[78] Certainly knowing more about immigration enhances our understanding of early modern life, but noting the way various emergent communities competed with the idea of nationhood also draws attention to the constructed nature of the cultural borders that define us. We would not want to revive early modern England's insistence on assimilation, but just as people in sixteenth-century England tried to see beyond the divide of English and alien to perceive shared interests and common goals, so we too might learn to see that borders merely get in the way of our recognizing how much we have in common with those we deem alien.

PART ONE

Sectarian Inclusivity

"Now we are no more stranger and forreiners but fellow-Citizens with the Saints, and of the household of God."
       Thomas Adams, *The Happiness of the Church* (1619)[1]

Chapter One

From the Dutch Acrobat to Hance Beerpot: Multicultural Mid-Tudor England

The first two chapters of this book focus on "sectarian inclusivity," multicultural communities founded on common religious beliefs. In his discussion of how Mary I's reign attempted to institute its own version of English national identity, Christopher Highley argues that, contrary to what seems to be a scholarly consensus, English nationhood need not be framed as an outcome of Protestantism, that Mary and Catholic English writers can also be seen to assert their particular version of Englishness.[2] This chapter builds on Highley's observation, focusing on the way an embattled Protestantism led to the forging of a community based not on language or birthplace but rather on shared beliefs. Mary's articulation of a Catholic English national identity necessarily marginalized some in the realm, producing a diverse community in opposition to her agenda, a community made up of English Protestants in solidarity with the sizeable Protestant refugee community in England and an either Protestant or tolerant portion of the merchant stranger community.

At the start of Mary's reign the immigrant communities in England amounted to as much as 12 per cent of the population.[3] An examination of the cultural dynamics of immigration during the Marian regime shows that although many English subjects could have taken the opportunity of Mary I's reign to scapegoat strangers, they more often seem to have valued and protected their immigrant neighbours. Solidarity between the English and the immigrants founded on a shared Protestantism often trumped concerns about the "otherness" of strangers. In this sense Protestantism can be seen to institute a sense of comradery based not on national feeling but rather on a shared religious identity. The Reformation introduced a schism with the Catholic Church, but the result was not a massive fragmenting of religious identity; the Reformation instead led subjects to look beyond the immediate confines of town or even realm to recognize that conscience crosses political borders. This sense of a community above state authority and beyond geopolitical borders is exemplary of sectarian inclusivity, and it is essential in understanding the way in which religious identity could form the basis of early modern England's multiculturalism. Comradery or unity may be signs of nationalism, but in this case comradery extended beyond concerns of birthplace and unity crossed national or proto-national borders and countered mid-Tudor England's significant Catholic regime.

Abroad, sectarian inclusivity might lead the English to support the United Provinces' battles against Spain; at home it fostered an ethic of protection and tolerance of immigrants, an ethic opposed to the oft-cited xenophobia of the English. The reign of Mary I provides a sound starting point for a study of English-immigrant solidarity, as it was a crime to be a stranger without denization papers, and Protestant refugees, whether denizens or not, were encouraged to leave the realm. Much of Mary's antipathy towards strangers stemmed from her dislike of the Protestantism with which many were associated, but her anti-alien proclamations tended to be more general in their animosity. One of the earliest described the recently arrived strangers as "evil-disposed persons" who had fled their places of birth to avoid punishment for a variety of "horrible crimes."[4] Another proclamation claimed that French strangers were "ministering just occasion of murmur and discontentation," stirring up rebellion among the Queen's "natural and loving subjects."[5] Of course, Mary married a stranger, but the state propaganda argued that Philip was really English even though he could barely speak the language. Among the adornments of the royal wedding was a book revealing that Philip was descended from John of Gaunt, a point reiterated by Mary's chaplain John Christopherson in *An exhortation to all menne to take hede and beware of rebellion*.[6] Regardless of how much English ale Philip consumed to compensate for the little English he could speak, Robert Tittler points out that popular antipathy towards Philip had less to do with his status as a stranger and more to do with his reputation as an oppressive ruler.[7]

What follows, however, is not an examination of Philip's dubious Englishness, but rather a close look at two much-neglected theatrical works performed for Mary. The first constitutes the earliest theatrical performance of her reign: the pageants presented by London residents during her royal entry to London on 30 September 1553, as a prelude to her coronation ceremony. The second text, *The Interlude of Wealth and Health*, has been described as "[i]nnocuous and difficult to date."[8] The play was entered in the Stationers' Register by John Waley between 1557 and 1558, and revised for publication in 1565, but these dates have not satisfied scholars, who suspect that the play was written and performed somewhat earlier than the registration date.[9] Although some suggest the play was written as early as 1506, T.W. Craik and C.F. Tucker Brooke offer substantial internal evidence situating it in the latter part of Mary's reign.[10] Thus, the two texts under consideration in this chapter span Mary's short reign and suggest a general trend in the period. Like the pageants created for Mary's 1553 royal entry to London, *Wealth and Health* was more than likely performed for the Queen.[11] Both the pageant series and the interlude deal with the fate of England; both performances draw the monarch's attention to the issue of immigration and reveal that, despite her best attempts, England could not follow her anti-alien designs. That is, both texts resist the notion of a xenophobic England and emphasize instead a multicultural mid-Tudor England founded on Protestant solidarity that scarcely resembles Mary's vision of a Catholic English nation exclusive of strangers.

Mary I's Coronation Pageantry

Between 22 August and 30 September 1553 Londoners took down the scaffolds that had borne the bodies of the supporters of would-be Queen Jane (John Dudley, Duke of Northumberland, Sir John Gates, and Sir Thomas Palmer) and replaced them with stages and fanfare for Queen Mary I's royal entry. Having survived a fairly peaceable but nonetheless anxiety-provoking succession crisis, Londoners now needed to put together an entertainment worthy of royalty.

Royal entries afforded London the opportunity to both entertain and instruct, to impress the new monarch through the speeches, spectacle, and theatrics that made up the pageants preceding the coronation ceremony.[12] For Elizabeth I's entry the city showed the new queen the "[c]auses of a ruinous commonweal" and the "[c]auses of a flourishing commonweal." For James I's entry Londoners exhorted their new king to maintain "MUTUIS COMMERCIIS" or balanced trade.[13] It should be kept in mind, however, that although the royal entry was a kind of street theatre authored and performed by the city as a whole, the plans for the festivities were usually submitted to the crown for approval. The official texts of Elizabeth's and James's entries were, after all, carefully crafted pieces of royal propaganda. Perhaps because of the ease with which she defeated Jane Grey's supporters, Mary I did not feel the need to publish an authoritative text of her accession for use as propaganda. To uncover London's initial message to

26 Sectarian Inclusivity

the new queen, then, we must look to a small collection of first-hand accounts: those by Giovanni Francesco Commendone, Thomas Lanquet, Henry Machyn, Edward Underhill, Charles Wriothesley, and the anonymous author of *The Chronicle of Queen Jane, and of Two Years of Queen Mary and Two London Chronicles*.[14] These accounts tend to privilege spectacle over speech, but an examination of them nonetheless sheds light on the relationship between Mary's court, which would demand a uniform culture of Catholic revival, and London, a city increasingly aware of its cosmopolitanism.

To get at the unique character of Mary's entry, I will begin by comparing the Fenchurch Street pageants of several early modern royal entries. Fenchurch Street was the site for the first pageant in many sixteenth-century royal entry pageant sequences. In 1547 Edward VI was welcomed at Fenchurch Street by "dyverse singing men and chyldren."[15] When Elizabeth I arrived there in 1559, she was greeted by a young English child, who delivered the first oration of the sequence.[16] Likewise, when James I came to Fenchurch Street in 1604, he was welcomed by two English actors: one was from the Children of Her Majesty's Revels; the other was the famous Edward Allen.[17] When Mary I arrived at Fenchurch Street, however, she was treated to a pageant prepared by the Genoese merchants. A boy actor delivered a speech that was unfortunately not recorded in any accounts of the pageant, and it is not known whether this child was Genoese or English. We do know, however, that the architects of this first pageant wanted to make sure that it was understood as a tribute to the new queen from London's Genoese community; one of the arches bore the following inscription:

> "Marie Reginae inclytae constanter piae coronam britanici Imperii et palman uirtutis accipienti Genuenses publica salute laetantes cultum optatum tribuunt"

> ["For Mary, renowned and ever pious Queen, upon her acceptance of the crown of the British Empire and the reward of virtue, the Genoese, with public acclaim, do joyfully offer this most excellent tribute"].[18]

Thus, before and after Mary's reign, Fenchurch Street served as the point at which the new monarch was given a properly English greeting, but in 1553 London's Mayor and Aldermen chose to begin Mary's entry with a greeting from strangers.

After the Genoese pageant, Mary and her entourage moved on to the corner of Gracechurch Street where she was again presented with a pageant by strangers, this time the "Easterlings" or Hanse merchants who occupied the Steelyard nearby.[19] At the end of Gracechurch Street Mary observed yet another entertainment by strangers, the Florentine pageant that featured verses claiming to speak not only for the Florentine community but "Omnes Publica" (all the people).[20] Of the nine pageants celebrating Mary's London entry and coronation, these first three were explicit in their stranger patronage and were described as the "myghtyest": the first featured several giants; the second, a fountain flowing with wine; the third featured a mechanical angel and presented an interesting set of parallels between Mary and not only Judith but also Tomyris, for, as Sydney Anglo notes, both of these had decapitated their oppressors just as Mary had beheaded Northumberland a month earlier.[21]

It was not until reaching Cornhill Street, the fourth stop on the way to Westminster Abbey, that Mary had the opportunity to observe a pageant put on explicitly by the English.[22] This pageant and the two that followed, at the little and great conduits in Cheapside, were probably the exclusive products of native-born Londoners, as was the pageant at Fleet Street. Judith M. Richards claims that "there were no purely English pageants" in the series;[23] she may well be right and such information would highlight my point, but while I have found nothing that explicitly contradicts Richards' claim, there appears to be no evidence to support her statement either. Nonetheless, what I take to be the exclusively English pageants were apparently much less spectacular – they receive scant attention in the first-hand accounts that provide the only memories of the royal entry. The pageants in honour of the new queen were clearly dominated by the presence of strangers.[24]

In fact, the first mention of a display of the arms of the city of London occurs in a description of Peter, a "Dutchman," who performed a variety of acrobatics, "triumphing and dancing" as Edward Underhill described it, on the weathercock of Saint Paul's Cathedral.[25] *The Chronicle of Queen Jane and Mary* explains that the Dutchman's acrobatics were "to the great mervayle and wondering of all the people which behelde him, because yt was thought a mattyer impossyble," and one spectator wrote,

> A man stoode on the wether cock of Paules. The pageantes in all places accustomed beyng moste gorgiously trimmed: And as her grace passed by Poules, a certain dutche man stode vpon the wethercock with an enseigne in his hande, flouryshyng with the same, and vnder hym vpon the crosse, a scaffold garnished with enseignes banners and streamers, and vnder that vpon the holle an other scaffolde with enseignes & streamers, very strange to ye beholders.[26]

The same pageant featured an oration by John Heywood, but his speech was so overshadowed by Peter's antics that no one recorded even the gist of it. Thomas Lanquet wrote of Peter's performance that, "among other strange sights there set foorthe, this was moste to be had in memory." Indeed, with the exception of Machyn and Commendone, every first-hand description of the pageant series mentions the Dutch acrobat, and other than Heywood himself, Peter is the only performer named in the entire sequence from the Tower to Westminster Abbey.[27]

Not much is known about Peter except that he was very agile. According to *The Chronicle of Queen Jane and Mary*, Peter constructed scaffolds on Saint Paul's roof, and in November of the same year Charles Wriothesley saw him repairing the weathercock.[28] These details indicate that he was an artisan, perhaps in either the building trades or, given the banners and streamers he used, the textile industry. In any case, he did not disdain physical labour. More importantly, his was the only entertainment we know of that featured the city arms: Peter reportedly waved a flag bearing a sword and red cross, identifying himself with the City of London.[29] Nearly every sixteenth-century royal entry to London included one or two pageants put on by stranger communities (originally to help fund the lavish spectacle), but the fact that a stranger waved the banner bearing the city's arms and that the first three pageants were performed by strangers indicates that the city's mayor and aldermen wanted to showcase London's immigrants; they wanted to communicate to Mary that London was made up of not only the English nobles, merchants, and artisans who lined the streets, but also merchant strangers and alien artisans.

Just six weeks earlier French and Flemish preachers had been forbidden from preaching, and two weeks prior to the royal entry, Mary had sent letters to Dover and Rye ordering, according to John Foxe, "all French Protestants to pass out of this realm."[30] At that time London was host to a sizeable immigrant population that was integral to the city's economic and social life. Catching wind of Mary's intention to deport immigrants, especially Protestant refugees, London's leaders seem to have decided that the pageants could entertain Mary while sending the message that Londoners were inextricably linked with the strangers living among them. The use of strangers in the pageants was, in a sense, an oblique petition, a challenge to the new queen: would it not seem ungracious for Mary, having accepted the greetings of the Genoese, Easterlings, Florentines, and Dutch, to request their deportation, as she had already done in other cities?

In September 1553 Mary had hardly even begun to rule and had not yet started the fires at Smithfield. For the moment the new monarch's monocultural ambitions were placed in check by London's theatrical lobbying. Oddly enough, Sir Thomas Wyatt's failed rebellion, in which he claimed that Mary was allowing strangers (here Catholic diplomats rather than Protestant immigrants) to take control of the realm, rekindled Mary's interest in eliminating immigrants from England even as some commoners criticized Wyatt for his stance on immigration, stating, for example, "we know most certnly that there is ment no maner of evil to us by those strangers."[31] In the aftermath of Wyatt's rebellion, new anti-alien legislation was put forth to expel strangers from the realm. On 18 August 1554, when London celebrated Philip's royal entry and coronation, Peter, the apparent star of Mary's first royal entry as queen, was nowhere to be found; he may have left England, or he may have been keeping a low profile given Mary's now clear hostility towards Dutch and French immigrants, particularly of the artisan class. The popular acrobatics at Saint Paul's were instead performed by a Spaniard (probably from Philip's retinue) who was not, unfortunately, up to the task; Foxe records that he lost his life as a result of one of his stunts.[32] By this time Mary and her council had renewed their interest in targeting English and immigrant Protestants in England. London did not then have the courage to renew its protest against a movement towards a homogenously Catholic England: the only one of Philip's royal entry pageants that was explicitly sponsored by strangers was that of the Hanse merchants, who were not at all offensive to Philip and his retinue. Still, if Wyatt's appeal to xenophobia was insufficient to garner enough widespread support for his rebellion, Mary's anti-immigrant stance also failed to homogenize English culture: the debate over monocultural England was not over. While Londoners may have opted out of another audacious display of support for strangers in Philip's royal entry, many continued to live, work with, and at times protect London's strangers.

In early 1554, for example, Mary issued a sweeping proclamation against strangers stating that,

> All and every such person or persons born out of her highness' dominions, now commorant or resident within this realm, of whatsoever nation or country, being either preacher, printer, bookseller, or other artificer or of whatsoever calling else, not being denizen, or merchant known using the trade of merchandise, or servant to such ambassadors as be liegers here from the princes and states joined in league with her grace, shall within 24 days after this proclamation avoid the realm; upon pain of most grievous punishment by imprisonment and forfeiture and confiscation of all their goods and

movables, and also to be delivered unto their natural princes or rulers against whose persons or laws they have offended.

The proclamation further required "all mayors, sheriffs, bailiffs, constables, and other her ministers, officers, and good subjects" to participate in the apprehension of any strangers remaining in the realm beyond the specified twenty-four days.[33]

A few days after the capture of Wyatt and one week prior to the 1554 anti-alien proclamation, Simon Renard, Imperial Ambassador to England, wrote to the Emperor: "[a] new revolt is feared because the people say so much noble blood ought not to be shed for the sake of foreigners. Many foreigners have departed, because marks were found on their houses."[34] While there was some anti-alien activity on the streets, it seems to have been on a small scale, since only Renard mentions these events. David M. Loades notes that Renard had a tendency to exaggerate tensions in the realm as a way to justify his presence in London and make his successful interventions in English politics seem especially triumphant.[35] Perhaps Mary issued the proclamation to placate some of Wyatt's anti-alien followers and to show that she could be just as xenophobic as Wyatt, but given the proclamation's exemptions – denizens, merchant strangers, and servants to ambassadors – and the targeting of specific occupations – "preacher, printer, bookseller" – it is clear that this proclamation marks the beginning of Mary's efforts to do away with traces of Protestantism and to revive Catholicism and the old traditions that had been suppressed during England's Reformation. The merchant strangers and ambassadors' servants were a mix of Protestants and Catholics, while the strangers who worked as preachers, printers, and booksellers were for the most part Protestant, as were many immigrant artisans. Foxe includes the proclamation in his *Acts and Monuments* because, he explains, "it chiefly and most specially concerned religion and doctrine, and the true professors thereof."[36] Shortly after the proclamation was issued, Peter Delenus of the Dutch Church and thirty of his congregation made their way to Hamburg to join the few hundred who had left England a few months earlier in anticipation of persecution.[37] Still, a number of strangers living in England for reasons other than religion were nonetheless ordered to leave.

One week after the proclamation, Renard wrote to Charles V, "[s]ince the publication of the edict on the expulsion of foreigners which I sent to Your Majesty, the people have behaved much better here."[38] But Pettegree estimates that about 10,000 immigrants, most of whom were not denizens, were living in London at the beginning of Mary's reign, and that while we have descriptions of small groups of strangers leaving London and arriving in cities of refuge on the continent, no reports of masses of Protestant strangers leaving England or arriving elsewhere in the 1550s have materialized.[39] Many must have stayed in defiance of the proclamation: at the beginning of Elizabeth's reign there were still roughly 6,000 strangers apparently living in London, and the denization rate was certainly not high enough to suggest that the majority of those remaining were denizens.[40]

Given the large numbers of strangers remaining in the realm, it is difficult to imagine that the "good subjects" entreated to help enforce the proclamation did not know the whereabouts of many strangers; if Londoners were truly xenophobic, we should expect numerous records of mass round-ups, strangers being detained, and Londoners actively informing on strangers, but there are very few instances of Londoners informing on their stranger neighbours and no instances of mass detentions and deportations by local authorities.[41]

Mary was not unaware of the large number of non-denizen strangers remaining in the realm. In 1558 she issued a proclamation reiterating the 1554 proclamation and noting that "notwithstanding there remaineth to this hour, as well within the city of London as elsewhere in sundry other parts of the realm, no small number of the said Frenchmen which be no denizens at all and yet not avoided hence according to the tenor of the said proclamation." Realizing that her subjects were not as fervently xenophobic as she had thought, Mary provided an incentive for turning in strangers: "[I]t shall be lawful for any of her said loving subjects not only to take the said Frenchmen not being denizens and every of them prisoners, and so to use them, but also for their apprehension and taking of them in that sort shall enjoy to their own proper use all such goods and chattels as the said French or any of them had or possessed at the time they were taken."[42] This renewed concern with strangers was sparked by two factors: the increased tensions with France and the more long-term concern that strangers were an important part of the Protestant underground. Indeed, some Protestants continued to enter the realm: Christopher Vitch, precisely the kind of stranger the 1554 proclamation sought to expel, came to England during Mary's reign and appears to have moved about relatively freely as he spread the word of the Family of Love.[43] The only individual who seemed especially interested in harassing strangers was Bishop Stephen Gardiner, who made it his personal mission to enforce the proclamation, but his animosity stemmed from religious fervour rather than a generalized dislike of immigrants.[44] Indeed, he never bothered Catholic strangers in the realm, suggesting that Catholics participated in their own brand of sectarian inclusivity. There is little other evidence to indicate that the English welcomed the proclamation or helped to enforce it, despite promise of rewards for doing so. Lack of evidence for vigorous anti-alien activity, however, reveals only part of the story of sectarian inclusivity.

Throughout Mary I's reign, committed Protestants participated in underground congregations, reading and discussing the Bible and other tracts, listening to sermons, and gathering money to administer to prisoners and the poor. As early as 1554 Mary clearly suspected the involvement of strangers in such congregations; she says as much in the anti-stranger proclamation discussed above. We know a good deal about one such underground congregation because Foxe included not only a narrative of the martyrdom of the congregation's leaders, John Rough and Cutbert Symson, but also letters and testimonies of the martyrs and records of Edmund Bonner's examinations of witnesses, including several members of the congregation.[45] One witness described the congregation as "a certain company of Frenchmen, Dutchmen, and other strangers, and amongst them Englishmen" who referred to one another as "brother" and ended their meetings by contributing to a fund for poor relief.[46] Three other witnesses note that the congregation's meetings were occasionally held at the house of a Dutch shoemaker named Frog, in Saint Katherine's, an area known for its dense immigrant population.[47] Some of the strangers in the underground congregation may have held denizen status and were therefore exempt from the proclamation, but a good many of the congregation's stranger-members probably were not denizens, as denization was costly; only the well-to-do or the well-connected could obtain papers.[48] In any case, Frog and the other strangers in the congregation were very much the people Mary targeted in her proclamations, but despite their apparent visibility, the congregation was not investigated until late 1557, and even then, the strangers in the congregation seem not to have been apprehended.[49]

There are three points to be gleaned from this episode of Mary's reign. First, the English Protestants operating underground had close relationships with the Protestant refugee community in the realm: similarities in religion outweighed considerations of linguistic and cultural difference. Second, the strangers seem to have had considerable influence on the practices of the underground congregation: descriptions of the congregation's gatherings indicate strong similarities to the Dutch Church's practice of "prophesy," a forum in which questions could be raised by the members of the group.[50] Third, Londoners were not particularly interested in causing problems for this group: for all its covert activity, the congregation was not invisible to Londoners, yet it was not until one congregation member betrayed the group to Bonner that anyone informed on them, and then only after some intimidation: Alice Warner, whose tavern hosted at least two congregation meetings, knew that the group included Protestant strangers but only thought to reveal this information after she had been detained and interrogated. Londoners saw strangers among them and even observed them participating in actions contrary to the crown's wishes, but did not inform on them until cornered by the authorities. Protecting strangers, emulating their religious practices, hosting and being hosted by them, all comprise varying degrees of sectarian inclusivity. The English do not seem to have been xenophobic enough to take advantage of the compromised position of their stranger-neighbours. Protestant solidarity trumped allegiance to the monarch or an abstract sense of Englishness.

The examples of Londoners actively defending strangers are even more telling. Pettegree has described two such instances.[51] A few months after Mary's 1554 proclamation was issued, two Dutch shoemakers were arrested for loitering after dark. When it was discovered that they were non-denizens they were detained, but after nine days they were released. It seems that allies in the Cordwainers' Company had intervened. The state and city authorities could have taken action against the strangers but decided against it, and the two shoemakers were apparently permitted to remain in London despite their violation of the anti-alien proclamation. Similarly, in 1556 when strangers were prohibited from being employed within London (with the exception of several trades including brewers, and a variety of occupations related to the cloth trade), the Dyer's Company successfully petitioned on behalf of their alien members.[52] As with Rough's underground congregation, when opportunities to harass or deport aliens arose, the supposedly xenophobic English did not act, and at times even protected strangers. Unlike the strangers in Rough's congregation, however, these tradesmen appear to have been protected primarily out of guild solidarity, a phenomenon that will be examined in chapters 3 and 4. As with nearly all events involving strangers in early modern England, complex considerations of religion, economy, and the traditional rights of the city trumped the more facile consideration of immigration status or supposed national identity.

We have, on the one hand, anti-alien legislation and the enthusiasm of Bonner and Gardiner for eradicating Protestant refugees from the realm. On the other hand we have examples of Londoners working with and helping strangers, examples of strangers playing prominent role in Mary's entry, the maintenance of a Protestant underground, and the economic well-being of the city. The idea of a homogenous, xenophobic England highlights the all-too-real tensions between immigrants and some native-born English throughout the early modern period, but it also obscures conflicts over right religion, city versus state authority, economic rights, and political power, all of which usually seemed more important to the English than differences between themselves and their stranger-neighbours. Rather than evoking a homogenous English culture defending itself against diversity in the name of some national "collective solidarity," the pageants for Mary's royal entry and the anecdotes described above demonstrate that many Londoners tried to maintain early modern England's immigrant populations and cosmopolitan character in the name of local guild solidarity or pan-Protestant alliance.

Wealth and Health

Sometime between Mary's two anti-alien proclamations, perhaps around the time that Bonner was interrogating Rough's underground congregation, *Wealth and Health* was performed for the queen. Although often interpreted as an anti-immigrant text, this play can also be seen as an attempt to open up discussion on the fate of strangers in the realm and to call into question any simplistic approach to the issue. The play begins with the characters Wealth, Health, and Liberty debating their relative importance to the realm. Eventually they reconcile themselves to one another, surmising in the end that they are interdependent. The characters Ill Will and Shrewd Wit enter, reveal their plot to exploit Wealth, speak with a Fleming named Hance Beerpot, and are hired as servants to Health and Wealth, specifically to manage their household. Good Remedy enters, explains that he speaks "for the comen welth," and warns Health and Wealth about their servants.[53] After Good Remedy discusses the importance of material wealth and spiritual health to England, he meets Ill Will and Shrewd Wit. Good Remedy exits, and Wealth and Health meet with Ill Will and Shrewd Wit, who inform their masters that they have allowed "revel and rout," "every knave and drab" to overtake the household, and yet Ill Will and Shrewd Wit are able to convince Wealth and Health to maintain their employment and reject Good Remedy (678–9). Good Remedy then argues with Hance Beerpot about the whereabouts of Wealth and orders Hance to leave. Health enters with a handkerchief on his head, explaining to Good Remedy that Ill Will and Shrewd Wit have infected him in "both body and soul," forced Wealth into "decay and necessitie," and imprisoned Liberty (807). Good Remedy and Health hide as Ill Will and Shrewd

Wit enter rejoicing in the damage done to Wealth, Health, Liberty, and Hance. Good Remedy interrogates Ill Will and Shrewd Wit, sends them to prison, and then tends to Wealth, Health, and Liberty. The play ends with a direct address to and prayer for the queen and her council.

In terms of Englishness, Lloyd Edward Kermode points to the way Ill Will and Shrewd Wit appear as the "aliens within" the realm, figures who exist to embody vices and to be banished or contained for the sake of constructing a sense of English identity.[54] This analysis works well within the allegory. Ill Will, after all, appears to have no geographical identity so it is natural that he poses a challenge to a sense of Englishness. When asked who he is, he responds, "I am your evil will / your will, & your will, & your will" (299–300), a claim that puzzles Liberty, who notes that each individual's will is different. Later, when confronted by Good Remedy, Ill Will impersonates a Spaniard, apparently a sign that he imagines preferential treatment for Spanish Catholic strangers, and perhaps an appeal to a Catholic sectarian inclusivity in Marian England.[55] Although his impersonation is not convincing enough to fool Good Remedy, it nonetheless underlines Ill Will's protean nature. In this sense, Ill Will participates in the tradition from which he is drawn. Vice figures often emphasize their ubiquity through descriptions of travel or connections to a variety of distant locales; Health's pronouncement that "the devyl and Yl Will is of one complexion" (923), if taken literally, further connects Ill Will to the precedent of medieval vices who appear with a mask or in red or black face.[56] At the abstract level of the civic allegory, what threatens Wealth and Health in the realm is the impulse to choose private gain over the needs of the commonwealth. As Kermode puts it, something "close to exorcism" occurs as the vices are contained in an effort to clearly delineate between a positive Englishness and a dangerous Otherness.[57]

Wealth and Health is not, however, purely allegorical. C.W. Wallace describes the development of Marian drama as a variety of hybridizing experiments mixing humanism, classicism, and native morality plays, "the classicization of the morality [play] and the Anglicization of the classic."[58] *Wealth and Health* certainly fits this description: like native morality plays, *Wealth and Health* concerns itself with spiritual matters in the figure of Health, but like many humanist texts the play also reflects on social ills and the management of the commonwealth. The opening scene presents a static dialogue that is not unlike the interludes of John Heywood, but the plot also includes a good deal of dynamic action characteristic of narrative drama. As for Anglicization, the play is without a doubt focused on England as its setting and central concern and it bears a number of native traits, but the text is also decidedly multilingual, featuring passages in French, Spanish, Latin, as well as the mix of Dutch, German and English spoken by the realistic rather than allegorical alien, Hance Beerpot. This multilingualism and the Flemish Hance Beerpot, who is largely superfluous to the main plot, confront the audience with the fact of England's diversity and force them to think about what value to assign that multicultural element of the realm. Darryll Grantley, summarizing the main point of the play, explains that it "argues for the importance of wealth to the well-being of the commonwealth at large, and advocates its proper management."[59] The fact that Hance is a minor character who could be edited out without doing damage to Grantley's summary of the play's argument makes his presence all the more conspicuous.

In his discussion of *Wealth and Health*, David Bevington explains that Hance Beerpot is the object of "traditional hostilities" towards strangers.[60] As we have seen, however, the commoners of the 1550s do not seem to have participated in such a tradition, despite ample opportunity and state approval. In addition to relying too heavily on the idea of a tradition of xenophobia, Bevington fails to take into account the courtly audience of *Wealth and Health*.[61] Popular traditions could be represented in courtly entertainments, but an appeal to a generalized xenophobia seems strained. The queen, after all, married a stranger, and Loades notes that the French-born Simon Renard was, up to 1555, one of Mary's closest confidants in court.[62] Philip, Renard, and any number of ambassadors and their retinues may have been audience to *Wealth and Health*. This play should be read, then, not through the lens of xenophobia, but within the context of tensions between the state's position on immigration and the relative failure of the proclamations due to the general population's lack of enthusiasm for anti-alien activity, that is, within the context of a complex set of social relations which at times prompted some to feel animosity towards aliens but at other times encouraged protection of and sympathy for immigrants. If Hance Beerpot indeed represents antipathy towards strangers, that antipathy must be understood in terms of differences in class as well culture and religion. If Hance is intended to be unlikeable, it is not because he is not English, but rather because he is neither English nor connected to the ruling class.

Unlike many mid-Tudor plays, *Wealth and Health* provides a curious blend of allegory and narrative drama.[63] As an allegory about the social and economic troubles facing England, the play participates in a morality play structure; the virtues Good Remedy, Health, Wealth, and Liberty and the vices Ill Will and Shrewd Wit supply the main action and argument. Hance Beerpot appears in two scenes and although he has little involvement in the main argument of the play, he is unique in that he has a proper (though stereotypical) name, a personal history, and even a "local habitation" in Saint Katherine's (where the Dutch shoemaker Frog sometimes hosted John Rough's underground Protestant congregation). Shrewd Wit suggests that Hance's real name is War (399, 826), but aside from Hance's claim that he can "scote de culveryn" (414) – that he is a gunner – Hance does not fulfil the role of War very well. Brooke has suggested that his presence refers to the conflicts with Flanders of 1557–8, but Craik sees "considerable difficulty" in Brooke's interpretation specifically and in Hance's role as War in general.[64] Hance does not fight, bring about conflict, or inspire warlike aspirations among the characters.[65] Moreover, according to Health, Wealth is harmed "by wast and war, thorow Yll Will and Shrewdwit," not through Hance (808). Finally, the *dramatis personae* lists Hance, not War, and it is worth remembering that the only character to refer to Hance as War is the consistently dishonest Shrewd Wit.

It is tempting, however, to read into Hance's inebriated state traces of a stock vice character of morality plays. Might he be a thinly disguised Sloth or Pride? True, his name suggests a love of drink, and at times he expresses a pride in his skills and his native country that exacerbates his status as an alien, but he has at least two jobs and a personal history. He tells Good Remedy, "ic myself be en scomaker" and "Ic myself cumt from Sent Katryns' dore mot ic skyne de can beer" (755, 753), and he offers himself up for more work: "Ic can skote de culverin, and ic can be de beare broer" (768). In addition to being a shoemaker and tapster, he can shoot a gun and brew beer: he is clearly not Sloth; instead of doing nothing, he can do anything. He brags, but perhaps he does so because he is trying to impress those around him so he can find more and better work, and his pride in his abilities is tempered by a subservient attitude to those he speaks with and his general appreciation of his host country. He has lived in England for thirteen years, he says, and has come to "love de Englishman" (774), but he also demands recognition for his contributions to the realm. He insists, "Ic best nen emond!" (401) – "I am somebody!"

Unlike the strangers' performances in Mary's royal entry, however, the character of Hance is mediated by an English author and actor. Always inebriated and only barely intelligible, Hance fulfils a certain stereotype, and his résumé is a composite of various aspects of the immigrant population in England at the time: he lives in an area and performs several of the jobs associated with mid-Tudor strangers. Because Hance mentions helping transfer wealth to Flanders, Kermode suggests that his name may refer to the Hanseatic League.[66] Even his place of origin is composite, since he is referred to as both Flemish and Dutch.[67] Rather than representing an abstract concept of vice or virtue, Hance stands outside the allegory as a character conspicuously grounded in London life, and his presence confronts the play of virtues and vices in *Wealth and Health* with the practical benefits and problems arising from immigration.

Just as Hance is generically different from the other characters in *Wealth and Health*, so the characters' attitudes towards him seem to trouble the allegory. Throughout the play Wealth, Health, and Liberty are subjected to the conflicting influences of Ill Will and Shrewd Wit on the one hand and Good Remedy on the other. As one might expect, Good Remedy differs greatly from Ill Will and Shrewd Wit. Good Remedy advises Health, Wealth, and Liberty to "take hede / Of excesse and prodigalitie" (709–10), while Ill Will and Shrewd Wit manage their masters' household with "revel and rout" (678), and are, according to Good Remedy, "full unthrifty" (641). Shrewd Wit brags about his ability to "flatter and lye" (439) while Good Remedy prides himself on the fact that he can "speake w[ith]out blame" (589), that is, freely and honestly as an advisor.[68] Good Remedy tells Health, Wealth, and Liberty that he works "to promote this realme / That you thre may prosper" (567–8), whereas Ill Will and Shrewd Wit seek to exploit Wealth by encouraging "brybry, theft, and prevy pyking" (442). The advice and actions of the virtue, Good Remedy, and the vices, Ill Will and Shrewd Wit, form binary sets: frugal/wasteful, honest/dishonest, lawful/lawless, selfless/selfish. As should be expected in such an allegory, Good Remedy is opposed in nearly every way to Ill Will and Shrewd Wit.

The one thing Good Remedy, Ill Will, and Shrewd Wit agree on is the status of immigrants: none of these characters speaks respectfully to Hance, despite his professed love of Englishmen and his offer to buy each a beer. In his first appearance on stage, Hance sings a Dutch song and then speaks with Ill Will and Shrewd Wit, who ask him where he has come from and what he is doing in their presence. After he announces his skill with guns, Ill Will sounds the note of an outraged xenophobe: "Nay, ye shall walke a Fleming knave, wyl ye not see / We have English gunners ynow, there is no rome empty" (415–16). Ill Will then dismisses Hance, but he remains, explaining that he is looking for work (421). Ill Will tries to use Hance to get at Wealth by suggesting that he ought to "go to the court, and for welth inquire" (422). Hance explains that Wealth is in Flanders, not England. His line, "It myself brought him dore," is understood by Ill Will as a reference to foreign wars resulting in the relocation of wealth (424–6). Ill Will becomes enraged and again dismisses him.

A similar conversation occurs when Hance meets Good Remedy, who asks where he comes from and what he is doing; Hance answers, and Good Remedy then dismisses him, but Hance continues to talk about his work as a shoemaker. Exasperated, Good Remedy says, "There is to many aliaunts in this realm; but now I, / Good Remedy, have so provided that Englishmen shall lyve the better dayly" (760–1). When Hance states his love of Englishmen, Good Remedy accuses him of flattery and of exporting England's wealth; Hance explains that he has lived in England thirteen years and brought with him many skills.

At this point there seems to be a printer's error, in which one line and a speech heading have been lost. From line 760 through to Hance's exit at line 778, Hance and Good Remedy exchange rhyming couplets; the first line of each couplet has a speech prefix (naming the character who is speaking) and is also indented. Between Hance's description of his contributions to the English labour market and his declaration that wealth is to be found elsewhere, there is a single line ("trust see so provide that welth from you have I shall" [769]) that has no speech heading; it also does not rhyme with Hance's lines before and after, and it is not characterized by Hance's stage dialect. It seems that the preceding line (that is, the first line of the couplet) is missing. If this missing line fits the dialogue pattern it would rhyme with "shall" and the couplet would be spoken by Good Remedy.[69] This assumption makes sense, since the next line is Hance's objection to the idea that wealth can be had from him: "Ic seg to you dat wealth is lopen in an ander country" ["I say to you that wealth dwells or runs about in another country"] (770). Good Remedy becomes enraged and tells Hance to leave.

Hance's conversations with Ill Will and Good Remedy follow the same pattern. They begin by questioning Hance's whereabouts and make a first attempt to dismiss him, move on to an attempt to get at wealth through Hance, express outrage at Hance's belief that wealth resides elsewhere, and end with a second, effective dismissal. Although Good Remedy is diametrically opposed to Ill Will and Shrewd Wit, his exchange with Hance is remarkably similar to theirs. What is more striking about Good Remedy's conversation with Hance is that Good Remedy echoes Ill Will (and to a lesser degree Shrewd Wit) throughout. Both Ill Will and Good Remedy describe Hance as "drunken" (397, 776), and Shrewd Wit and Good Remedy call him a "knave" (399, 765). When Hance enters, Ill Will asks, "Wherefore comest thou hither" and Good Remedy asks, "Thou Fleming, from where comest thou …?" (412, 752). Upon Hance's exit, Ill Will asks, "Is he gone, farewel Hanijkin bowse / I pray God give him a hounded drouse" (429–30); Jasper Platt Jr. explains that in this context "drouse" means "devil."[70] Good Remedy sounds surprisingly like Ill Will when Hance exits after the second exchange: "Is he gon? I pray God the devyl go with him" (779). Both Ill Will and Good Remedy express the same sentiment and use many of the same words. Charles Baskerville thinks that the line, "Is he gone?" comes from a popular ballad trope of the period; if Baskerville is correct, Good Remedy and Ill Will may even sing the same tune.[71]

Whether Baskerville is right or not, in the exchanges with Hance Good Remedy acts and sounds like Ill Will. The allegorical dichotomy of *Wealth and Health* breaks down precisely where the play breaks with the genre of allegory, that is, where the multigeneric plot runs into early modern England's multicultural reality. To suggest that the play subtly condemns Good Remedy would be reading too much into a moment that is superfluous to the overall plot; to suggest that the moment therefore does not matter, however, would be folly. There is a real paradox surrounding Hance. For example, Good Remedy, as noted above, expects to extract wealth from Hance's labour, but his statement, "Get thee hence, dronken Fleming! Thou shalt tary no lenger here" (776) is generally read as Hance's expulsion from the realm.[72] How can Good Remedy expel Hance and at the same time exploit his labour? Similarly, when Hance says that he helped transport wealth to Flanders, it is never really clear whether he is speaking of the allegorical figure Wealth, or the real wealth that circulates unevenly throughout the world. Hance's statements about wealth may be especially vexing to the allegorical figures because he talks about the complex reality of the circulation of wealth while the allegorical plot requires simple absolutes.

Craik and A.J. Hoenselaars think that Hance should be seen negatively and that Good Remedy's attitude towards Hance reflects an enthusiastic endorsement for Mary's policy of expelling strangers from the realm. But the vices Ill Will and Shrewd Wit relish Hance's deportation. Shrewd Wit endorses Hance's expulsion with a pun – "That horson Fleming was beshitten for feare / Because he should voyde so soone" (826–7) – but is the audience to laugh along with Ill Will and Shrewd Wit? Vice and Virtue awkwardly unite around Hance's expulsion, leaving the audience to sort out the complexity of immigration into England.

Craik lists Hance as one of several "comic and sinister foreigners" to appear in Tudor drama; Hoenselaars doubts Hance's comic potential and suggests that his drunkenness was intended not to add comedy to the morality but "to arouse the audience's aversion."[73] I believe Craik is right that Hance's drunkenness was intended for comic relief, but even if we agree with Hoenselaars that Hance is not very comical, it is difficult to see him as sinister.[74] Hance is not involved in Ill Will's and Shrewd Wit's exploitation of Wealth, Health, and Liberty. He does, however, confront the audience with a complex set of opposites. He is drunk but industrious, honest but sometimes offensively so. Although he is proud of himself and his homeland, there is no reason to doubt his sincerity when he declares his love for the English. He offers England a number of valuable skills, including military protection from foreign powers, but confesses that he is partly responsible for carrying wealth to Flanders. His contributions to the realm resist an easy fit with either Good Remedy or Ill Will, and Good Remedy cannot expel Hance without somehow becoming implicated in Ill Will's schemes. Thus *Wealth and Health* presents an allegory of England in which detrimental elements in the realm can be contained so that, as Health puts it, "Welth, Helth, and Liberty may continue here alway" (954), but the play also portrays the multicultural reality of England, and this troubles the simplicity of the allegory.

The presentation of an immigrant in the realm may have been intended to suggest that Mary needed to renew her anti-alien proclamation or intensify efforts to enforce it. Indeed, Ill Will's and Good Remedy's first dismissals of Hance, which Hance ignores, could very well be read as alluding to the ineffectiveness of the 1554 proclamation. But the play presents Ill Will and Shrewd Wit, rather than the immigrant artisan, as the source of harm to the realm. One would expect an allegory to portray the actions of Ill Will as bad and those of Good Remedy as good, but both characters dismiss Hance. Good Remedy and Ill Will differ, however, in their respective intentions. Ill Will dismisses Hance out of self-interest and a general delight in the misfortunes of others, while Good Remedy dismisses him for the sake of the commonwealth. In this sense, *Wealth and Health* seems to confront the audience with the question of means and ends regarding Mary's policy towards strangers. The play seems to ask, "To what degree does expelling strangers improve or deteriorate the health, wealth, and liberty of the realm?" Early in the play Health, representing spiritual well-being, argues for his pre-eminence above Wealth by advocating for a decidedly Catholic and predictably Marian, theology: "Grace, heaven, nor cunning cannot be bought," he says, "Without great paine, and good dedes wrought; / Els man cannot them have" (121–3); but when Wealth asks, "May not men buy heaven with richesse, / As to byld churches and make bye wayes?" (125–6), Health responds affirmatively.[75] Thus, Health and Wealth begin their reconciliation in the opening debate, but the issue of intent and the ambiguity implied by the agreement between Ill Will and Good Remedy regarding strangers introduces an unspoken problem for that reconciliation.

As demonstrated above, Mary's anti-alien proclamation was issued primarily to eliminate foreign Protestant influence from the realm, to disrupt Protestant sectarian inclusivity and thereby further her goal of creating a thoroughly re-Catholicized England. There are no hints, however, concerning Hance's religious beliefs. Since he arrived in England thirteen years earlier (towards the end of Henry VIII's reign?) he may well have been intended to be Protestant, but if he were the source of malignant false doctrine, we should expect his expulsion to coincide with Health's revitalization rather than his demise. Hance has already left England when the withered Health appears with a handkerchief on his head. Hance's expulsion seems to have no relation to the spiritual well-being of the realm: if anything, it corresponds to the wounds to spiritual Health. Two things happening in sequence does not necessarily imply cause and effect, but it is worth noting that the sequence of Hance's expulsion followed by Health's wounds is reiterated as Shrewd Wit and Ill Will discuss the outcomes of their misdeeds (825–32).

Moreover, *Wealth and Health* presents Hance, despite his insobriety and claim to have helped enrich Flanders, as a potential source of material wealth and military protection for the realm. The audience must wonder, then, if it is more than a coincidence that after Hance is exiled, Wealth falls into "decay, and necessitie / By wast and war" (807–8). What if strangers were good for material wealth by generating taxable income and bringing new skills to the realm, but bad for Catholicism in England because they introduced Protestant theology? In this sense, Hance's expulsion recalls and implicitly reopens the debate about whether Health or Wealth deserves more pre-eminence in England, and by extension whether decisions about strangers ought to be considered in light of the material or the spiritual interests of the realm. One may argue, as Jane Griffiths does, that despite the two statements that wealth can be got at through Hance, the Dutchman is nevertheless depicted as bad for the economy.[76] Shrewd Wit suggests that his many jobs could be filled by Englishmen, but we should be suspicious of anything Shrewd Wit says. The fact is that in the 1550s there were not very many capable English gunners and even fewer English brewers. Moreover, from the state's point of view, stranger-artisans were a greater source of revenue than their English counterparts. At the same time that the state insisted that stranger communities take care of their own poor relief, it taxed strangers at twice the rate imposed on their English counterparts in the Lay Subsidy and included the children of strangers in the poll tax.[77] The precarious position of immigrants in early modern England made them easier to exploit; perhaps this exploitation is what Good Remedy refers to when he speaks of getting wealth from Hance.

Exploitation, of course, is not a multicultural value, but it does offer one of the ruling class's motivations for sometimes advocating on the behalf of strangers. Still, as the episodes discussed in this chapter have shown, although some harboured ill will towards aliens in the form of exploitation or expulsion, others lived, worked, and worshiped side by side with these strangers and, when times got tough, had the courage to lobby for their protection against onerous employment restrictions and to hide them from religious persecution. *Wealth and Health* hints at the existence of such allies when Ill Will tells Hance, "But goe thy way, they be not here that promote thee can" (420). Perhaps few if any members of the audience of this performance had in fact advocated on the behalf of aliens, but throughout the realm, and especially in London, there seems to have been a reasonably large percentage of the population who tolerated and even valued the presence of strangers in the realm.

Around the time *Wealth and Health* was performed, John Christopherson, in *An exhortation to all menne to take hede and beware of rebellion*, attacked anti-alien sentiment directly by debunking the myths of seditious aliens and drawing attention to the Christian call to the acceptance of strangers:

> As for straungers we nede not to feare. For yf they do any injury to any subjecte of hers, they shalbe punyshed by the lawes of thys realme, as we be. And yf they behaue them selfe gentlye, as it is very lyke that they will, we shall haue cause to love them to ioyne frendship with them, and to make muche of them. For so shall we deserue thankes both of them & at goddes hand to, who wylleth us that we offende not, or hurte anye straunger.[78]

Christopherson's main goal in *An exhortation* was to show that there were no valid motives for rebellion. For example, he advises the poor to understand that poverty is God's will and perhaps punishment on them; the poor should, he claims, "patiently suffer their pouertie, & thanke God hartelye for it" rather than openly resist exploitation.[79] His advice concerning strangers was designed specifically to argue against Wyatt's rebellion and any objections to Mary's marriage, but unlike his advice to the poor, his view of immigrants seems fairly progressive. In many respects he advocates the same conception of hospitality that Dalechamp would promote almost eighty years later. Christopherson objects to xenophobia as an irrational fear, asks that strangers be treated equally under the law, and turns acceptance of strangers into a virtue. What place might these multicultural sentiments have had in Mary's vision of England as a realm in which strangers were *de facto* criminals, heretics, and rebels? Christopherson, despite his close ties with the Protestant persecutions that dominate discussions of the Marian period, does not fit well into histories that emphasize English xenophobia in the service of nation formation any more than Mary's royal entry fits into a model of early modern English literature that emphasizes homogeneity and consensus. Mary's royal entry, *Wealth and Health*, and Christopherson's *An exhortation* all emphasize precisely what is effaced in claims about the role of xenophobia in the development of Englishness: England has been multicultural and has wrestled with the central questions of multiculturalism for centuries.

To be sure, *Wealth and Health's* questions about the relative merits of expelling strangers are put forth with a number of safeguards. Unlike the pageants of the royal entry which celebrated the coronation of the new queen alongside an open celebration of London's diversity, *Wealth and Health* presents early modern England's multicultural reality ambivalently in the subplot through the comic figure of Hance Beerpot rather than in the main plot with its allegorical absolutes, and it frames the issue of immigration in terms of economic advantage rather than mutual respect. *Wealth and Health* simply suggests that immigration is too complex an issue for a clear-cut allegory. In allowing immigrants to stay in England the commonwealth might gain or lose wealth; by the same token the expulsion of strangers might be carried out for good or ill. The ambiguity concerning immigration is precisely the point. Like Christopherson and the royal entry, however, *Wealth and Health* portrays strangers as a relatively harmless and ultimately integral part of England. Mary I expressed fears about the influence of immigrants, but these fears were not the sentiments expressed by her chaplain in *An exhortation* or by her London subjects in her royal entry; moreover *Wealth and Health* treats the vices of the play as distinct from the immigrant. Mary Tudor may have sought a homogenous national identity for England, but all around her were signs of early modern England's multicultural reality.

Chapter Two

The Rhetoric of Religious Refuge under Elizabeth I

The ascension of Elizabeth I to the throne in 1558 naturally resulted in a return of Protestant refugees who had fled to the continent, but Elizabeth's policies were not nearly as liberal as those of her brother Edward. Leaders of the stranger churches entered negotiations on their return, amid the so-called Elizabethan Settlement of 1559, under which the stranger churches would not be granted the latitude they had previously enjoyed. Under Elizabeth stranger churches were under the purview of the Bishop of London, Edmund Grindal. Thus, Austin Friars, which had been taken from the strangers under Mary, was turned over not to Dutch ministers but to the Bishop who then turned it over to the Dutch; the French occupied the church at Threadneedle Street under similar circumstances. The central concern seems to have been the regulation of doctrine, and indeed, in 1560, the Bishop excommunicated Dutch minister Adrian van Haemstede for refusing to recant his sympathy for a group of Anabaptists.[1]

Despite the Bishop of London's control over the affairs of the stranger churches, the fact that he had been a refugee himself during Mary's reign meant that he did have a sincere desire to see the churches flourish with little interference. Even with Haemstede, Grindal had made several attempts at a less dramatic resolution to the doctrinal dispute.[2] While Elizabeth's attitude towards the stranger churches was cautiously positive, her regime seemed especially conscious of the economic advantages of immigration. In 1561, for example, she provided for the relocation of some strangers in London to Sandwich "for the help, repair, and amendment of our said town and port of Sandwich by planting in the same men of knowledge in sundry handy crafts, as also for the relief of certain strangers now residing in our city of London."[3] The intention was to reduce the stranger population in London while jumpstarting crafts in Sandwich, where the economy had begun to stagnate. Thus, the early years of Elizabeth's reign saw a positive but guarded reintegration of Protestant strangers into England.

Redefining England

Early in Elizabeth's reign it became possible to re-imagine the cultural borders of England to include immigrants. Printed in 1573, *A New Interlude No Lesse Wittie than Pleasant, Entitled New Custom* featured a disgruntled Catholic named Perverse Doctrine, exclaiming, "For since these Genevian doctours came so fast into this lande, / Since that time it was never merie with Englande."[4] The complaint is not to be taken at face value; it is directed at Light of the Gospel, a character who, from a Protestant point of view, embodies right religion in England but who evidently comes from the continent. Perverse Doctrine emphasizes this later attitude as he rails,

> For nowe of late that slave, that varlet, that heretique, Light of the Gospell
> Is come over the sea, as some credibly tell,
> Whom New Custome doth use in all matters as a staie,
> The most enemie to us in the worlde alway;
> Whose rancour is suche, and so great is his spite,
> That no doubt he will straightway banishe us quight.[5]

Here the English Catholic rather than the immigrant theologian worries about expulsion. When the English Protestant minister New Custom thanks the immigrant Light of Gospel for frightening away Ignorance and Perverse Doctrine, Light of Gospel replies, "Nay, they be my enemies also, that be enemies to you."[6] This passage redefines the boundaries of community so that English Catholics become outsiders to the realm. Much of the play is devoted to theological debate in which Perverse Doctrine recasts himself as Simplicity while New Custom explains that he is really not "New," and that he also goes by the name Primitive Constitution. In the end, rather than contain or otherwise vanquish the vice figures, New Custom and Light of the Gospel convince Perverse Doctrine to convert to Protestantism, and he is christened Sincere Doctrine. The English and immigrant Protestants of the play collaborate to establish a new criterion for inclusion in the community, and the solidarity between English and immigrant Protestants is strengthened by their exclusion of Catholics (here the vices Ignorance, Avarice, and Cruelty). In an instance of politics imitating art, a few years after *New Custom* was published, Parliament seriously considered taxing known Catholics as if they were strangers.[7] Thus, solidarities formed around Protestant identity could configure community in ways that denied the importance of shared birthplace; some immigrants could be seen as central symbols of the community while some English could find themselves excluded.

The experience of immigration was nonetheless trying. The displacement and isolation experienced by early modern immigrants to England can be seen in some of the poems of Huguenot Jacques Grévin, a poet, dramatist, and physician who spent some time in London during the 1560s. Passing his time along the Thames, he writes,

> Mais l'onde qui est sourde et la Pierre muette,
> Les Bestes sans raiso ne me font qu'ennuyer
> Depuis qu'il me souvient de ceulx que je regretted.
>
> [But the deaf waves, the mute stones,
> And the brute beasts only sadden me
> As I remember those that I sorrow for.][8]

The incommunicative landscape reflects not only the distance of those the poet misses, but also the linguistic isolation Grévin and his fellow refugees must have felt in England. Indeed, Grévin's own place in the refugee community may have been somewhat estranging. Kathryn J. Evans suggests that Grévin was likely wrestling with his faith around this time, and unlike most of his fellow French refugees, he was not fully committed to Calvinism.[9] Still, as Simon Mealor points out, the poem speaks to a general refugee experience in early modern England. Grévin writes of a sense of security in a peaceful England compromised by ambivalent feelings of desperation:

> Et ainsi, de Vulcob, je suis désesperé,
> Puisque de mes malheurs la deliverance est mise
> Sur les vens et les eaux, qui n'ont rien d'assuré
>
> [And thus, de Vulcob, I am in despair[10] –
> Because deliverance from my unhappiness
> Is in the hand of the winds and the waters, who have no certainty].[11]

The immigrant experience, even for someone only temporarily in exile, was fraught with conflicting feelings: the relief of refuge, the shock and isolation of displacement, uncertainty about the possibility of return, and concern for those left behind. The experience must have been more challenging for artisan-class strangers who had more struggles to meet needs than Grévin. The stranger churches were instrumental in fostering a sense of community for these exiles, providing charity for those in need, and generally helping them adjust to life in England, but shelter could also insulate and stunt integration.

The number of French immigrants increased in England drastically as the Wars of Religion intensified in the 1560s, especially after the Saint Bartholomew's Day Massacre in 1572, when more than 3,000 Protestants in France were slaughtered over the course of three days.[12] Spanish repression of the Dutch Revolt, especially in the late 1560s, resulted in similar waves of immigration to England. As John Strype notes, "England was now very hospitable to such of the religion as could escape, and had got over hither."[13] He also notes, however, a divergence of attitudes towards strangers at this time.[14] "The better sort of the queen's subjects," he writes, "were very kind unto these poor protestants; and glad to see them retired unto more safety in this country. But another sort (divers of the common people and rabble, too many of them) behaved themselves otherwise towards these afflicted strangers, men and women, who grudged at their coming hither, and would call them by no other denomination than *French dogs*."[15] If the anti-alien texts of this period contribute to a sense of Elizabethan national identity, the texts discussed in this chapter can be said to participate in a counterdiscourse imagining a community of English and immigrant based on shared faith rather than nationality. This chapter explores the various themes in Elizabethan texts that evoke sectarian inclusivity, especially the status of exile and the meaning of persecution, as well as the limitations of the rhetoric of co-religionists.

After lamenting the anti-alien sentiment of some in England, Strype describes Archbishop George Abbot's thoughts on the rapid immigration of Huguenot refugees to England: noting the poor treatment they received from many in England, Abbot explains that those

> that were wise and godly, used those aliens as brethren: considering their distresses with a lively fellow-feeling; holding it an unspeakable blessedness, that this little island of ours should not only be a temple to serve God in for

ourselves, but an harbour for the weatherbeaten, a sanctuary to the stranger, wherein he might truly honour the Lord; remembering the precise charge which God gave to the Israelites, to *deal well with all strangers;* because the time once was, when themselves were strangers in that cruel land of Egypt: and not forgetting, that other nations, to their immortal praise, were a refuge to the English in their last bloody persecution in queen Mary's days: and in brief, recounting, that by a mutual vicissitude of God's chastisements, their case might be our case. Which day, he prayed, the Lord might long keep from us.[16]

Strype's claims about Abbot's recollection of the 1570s highlight some important patterns of thought regarding immigration into early modern England. Those who appear to be anti-alien are spoken of negatively, whereas the welcoming of strangers appears as a sign of godliness. As with nearly all post-Marian defences of hospitality towards immigrants, the experience of English exile to the continent provides for a sense of sympathy, a sense that there is a common experience that comprises the multicultural community of Protestantism, a solidarity that permeates borders.[17] The allusion to the Israelites is also more than a mere platitude. Time and time again, Protestant writers connected their refugee experience to the Jewish exiles of the Old Testament.[18]

The use of the Jewish experience in the Old Testament pervades the sectarian inclusivity of English Protestants and their Protestant refugee neighbours. Of course, Catholics too had recourse to the Old Testament, but it seems to have held a special place among early modern Protestants. This is in part due to their interest in the Old Testament, but may also be related to actual contact with Jewish migrants. Lucien Wolf records instances of *Marranos* (Portuguese Jews) assisting Reform efforts on the continent and migrating with Dutch Calvinists into England.[19] In any case, allusions to Old Testament figures occur often in the rhetoric of Protestant inclusion. In 1578, as part of the pageantry surrounding her visit to Norwich, Queen Elizabeth was presented with speeches by Debora, Judith, and Hester, three powerful Old Testament women introduced by "Dame Norwich."[20] Michelle Ephraim has argued Elizabeth was at times compared to these Jewish heroines because they function "as a figure of the scripture itself."[21] Appropriating the Jewish woman, then, is akin to having exclusive ownership of the Old Testament. Furthermore, in terms of sectarian inclusivity, this appropriation of the pious alien redraws boundaries of insider and outsider in the realm even as it draws parallels between Protestant and Jewish exile.

This pageant, closed by Martia, "sometime Queene of England," is followed by a speech from Norwich's Dutch minister, Herman Modet, a charismatic ex-monk who, a little over ten years earlier, could be found leading iconoclastic raids on churches in Brussels and elsewhere.[22] He begins with a Protestant encomium to Elizabeth, "the nourse of Christ his church, whose minde obedient to Gods worde, the spirite of Christ, and zeale of Godlinesse."[23] Modet contextualizes the presence of strangers in Norwich: "the verie calamitie of Godly men, and teares of the afflicted, the teares, I say, of faithfull Christians have throughly moved thee to defende and protect the miserable and dispersed members of Christ objecte to every kinde of injurie, before beeten in peeces by a thousand deathes with the safetie and preservation as well of minde as bodie."[24]

What is telling here is that the minister then summarizes the Genesis "history of the innocent and most godly Josephus," the son of Jacob who is betrayed by his brothers who sell him into slavery. The stranger's version of the story is told in such a way that its resonance with Protestant refugees cannot be missed. Joseph has the anachronistic "godlinesse of a Christian heart," and God's mercy saves Joseph from "the bloodie conspiracie of his brethren" and casts him "in a strange kingdom unto the providence of God."[25] Elizabeth was then presented with a monument featuring the story of Josephus and a verse that compares his tribulations and eventual rise with Elizabeth's own imprisonment at the hands of her sister and ascension to the throne.[26] Protestant refugees and Queen Elizabeth herself are connected via the story of Josephus. Given the status of Jews in England, it is almost as if all Christians are recast as aliens, participating in the initial scriptural connection created by comparisons between Elizabeth and Old Testament heroines. The connection casts the contemporary experience of displacement as part of an ongoing story of right religion in the face of oppression.

In the next pageant, featuring Roman Gods, Apollo refers to his own alien intrusion on the pageantry while also alluding back to the refugees, declaring, "It seemeth straunge, to see such strangers here, / Yet not so straunge, but straungers knows you well."[27] Of course, Apollo and his fellow Gods are indeed strangers in Norwich, but the lines serve to highlight the motif of unifying the multicultural Protestant community around the idea of a shared experience of alienation. The idea that all Christians are in essence strangers was articulated throughout the period; for instance, John Whitgift, the Archbishop of Canterbury, concludes his 1573 sermon before the queen at Greenwich with the statement, "We are but strangers in this world, and therefore we must so behave ourselves as those that are in a strange country."[28] As with *New Custom*, the rhetoric of inclusion carried with it a new corresponding exclusion. When Elizabeth left Norwich at the end of the entertainments, her council remained to begin a much slower journey home. In each county, beginning with Norfolk, they were to hear the cases of accused recusants in an attempt to bring about acceptance of Protestantism. Some conformed, while others were fined or imprisoned.[29]

As Strype's descriptions show, however, although the English were prepared to accommodate immigrants in the name of Protestant community, the large numbers of immigrants entering England following theviolence of 1572 created tensions. In George Wapull's *The Tide Tarrieth No Man* (1576) Courage (a vice figure), Hurtful Help, Painted Profit, Feigned Furtherance, and Greediness plot to corrupt the realm. One of their first capers involves helping No Good Neighbourhood, who hopes to purchase a lease from a landlord currently renting to an Englishman, Tenant Tormented. No Good Neighbourhood explains that the tenant is so notoriously good that the landlord will likely be "unwilling to put him out, / And I but a stranger among them God wote" (333–34).[30] No Good Neighbourhood, the allegorical figure of failed communal feeling, is portrayed as a foreign influence, a stranger to the realm. As Kermode shows, this play (and several like it) attempts to make the moral problems of the realm material in the form of the alien.[31] Hurtful Help, who has chosen to drop his given name and go by the name of Help alone explains,

> Marry sir, it is much the better for that,
> For among us now, such is our country zeal,
> That we love best with strangers to deal.
> To sell a lease dear, whosoever will,
> At the French or Dutch Church let him set up his bill. (338–42)

Hurtful Help is more than happy to help the immigrant No Good Neighbourhood. The plot highlights a very real pattern of strangers in London either paying more for leases or rent (usually because they violated statutes on the number of individuals permitted to occupy a single dwelling) and thereby displacing English tenants, or otherwise competing too successfully in the market.

But *The Tide Tarrieth* is not a wholesale indictment of immigrants. As Kermode points out, the play presents a dizzying world of alienation where allegorical characters pass as their opposites (for example, Hurtful Help and other vice figures pass as their unqualified surnames) precisely because they invite the alien "disease" of greed.[32] At the core of the play is an excessive focus on the acquisition of material wealth contrasted with Christian charity. The evicted English tenant laments the lack of genuine Christianity in the realm. The culprit here is an English willingness to forego Christian kindness in favour of profit, to confuse (to use Kermode's term) conscience ("our country zeal") and economic interest ("To sell a lease dear"). The vices are eventually defeated by Christianity who declares, "Riches is no perpetual shield, / But the shield of Faith, shall ever remain" (1429–30). Christianity even carries a shield with the word "Riches" on one side and "Fayth" on the other. Presumably Christianity flips the shield at these lines, thereby emphasizing that while the two are important, conscience takes precedence over economic concerns and redefines "riches" in terms of spiritual wealth. Christianity is accompanied by Faithful Few, and together they right the wrongs of Hurtful Help, Courage, Greediness, Painted Profit, and Feigned Furtherance. The Faithful Few represents a Reformed community, no doubt, and one would presume that while No Good Neighbourhood was in England for economic advantage, other strangers might well be part of the "faithful few" under Christianity's shield, not unlike the underground communities described in chapter 1. Indeed, the main culprit in No Good Neighbourhood's case was, as Hurtful Help suggests, the landlord who prizes the stranger's money over his reciprocal obligations to his tenant. That being said, the fact that the stranger No Good Neighbourhood passes as simply Neighbourhood draws attention to an anti-alien anxiety that strangers might not be what they seem, that they enter the realm in the name of a pan-Protestant alliance, a communal feeling among the reformed, but might actually be Catholic spies or Anabaptists seeking to corrupt Christian neighbourhoods.

A more pointed complaint about the overcrowding caused by strangers and their children is registered in *The Pedlers Prophecie*, a play sometimes attributed to Robert Wilson. Printed in 1595 but possibly written and performed as early as 1561,[33] the play features an artisan, who complains,

> But, Aliants chop up houses so in the Citie,
> That we poore craftsmen must needs depart.
> And beg if they will, the more is the pittie.[34]

According to the artisan, rent is more expensive and work scarcer because of the increase in immigration to England. Rightly or wrongly, the artificer represents a portion of the English population that was ready to attribute the cause of economic hardship to the newcomers.

The titular peddler then blames a mariner for facilitating immigration. The mariner counters, "Thou beliefst, we bring in none but Gospellers, / And such as we know to be very good Christians."[35] That is, the mariner expects the common ground of shared faith to override concerns of nationality. The peddler argues that many come merely "under the pretence of the Gospell." This exchange reveals the limits of sectarian inclusivity: inclusion ends at the perceived border of shared faith. In the end, however, the many claims about social ills in England are somewhat ambiguous. In the final scene a Judge and an Interpreter discuss the peddler. The Interpreter explains that while "many thing be out of frame," the peddler's criticism of the realm is full of "so much untruth and mutuall hate" that many of the realm's problems can be attributed to "The enterprise of base medlers," like the peddler.[36] *The Pedlers Prophecie* then, like *Wealth and Health,* is ambivalent in its presentation of immigration as a problem. A number of other plays from the 1570s and 1580s voice similar complaints about immigration's effect on rent and economic opportunity.[37]

Persecution on the Continent and Hospitality at Home

The passages from Strype illustrate that this anti-alien attitude was of great concern to some in England, and that these divergent attitudes demonstrate competing notions of community in Elizabethan England. The anti-alien stance – due to a sense of economic competition, shifts in political and religious situations on the continent, or a general distrust of outsiders – fed a sense of Englishness as defined against a linguistic and cultural Other. Those who were more tolerant defined their community in terms of religious conviction, taking seriously the commandment in Leviticus that "the stranger that dwelleth with you, shall be as one of your selves, &

thou shalt love hym as thy selfe."[38] Indeed, both attitudes to strangers fed a sense of Englishness: rather than xenophobia, Felicity Heal finds that some English writers differentiated England from its neighbours by emphasizing the hospitality of the English.[39]

Among those who imagined a community of believers regardless of birthplace, publicizing the causes of immigration – intolerance on the continent – became all the more important. Calling for greater reform in the English church, one pamphlet emphasized solidarity with the Huguenots, referring to "the bloude of our breathren in Fraunce."[40] In the early 1570s François Hotman's pamphlet *De furoribus gallicus* appeared in England in numerous editions in Latin and French and in English under the title *A True and Plaine Report of the Furious Outrages of Fraunce*. This pamphlet was reprinted in 1574 as Book Ten of Jean de Serres's *The Three Partes of Commentaries Containing the Whole and Perfect Discourse of the Civill Warres of Fraunce* (translated into English by Thomas Timme). Henri Estienne's *Ane Mervaylous Discourse Upon the Lyfe, Deedes and Behaviours of Katherine de Medicis,* recounting her involvement in the massacre, appeared in English translation in 1575.[41] In 1576 Arthur Golding, better known today as a translator of Ovid and Calvin, translated two pamphlets on the events in France.[42] The 1579 Richard Robinson collection of poems, *A Poore Knight, His Pallace of Private Pleasures*, included an epitaph for humanist scholar Peter Ramus, who was killed during the massacre, and in the same year Andrew Maunsell printed Thomas Churchyard's verse account of the Wars of Religion, "The Calamatie of Fraunce."[43] Arthur Dickens counts more than 200 texts on the events in France printed in England during Elizabeth's reign.[44] More than mere interest in foreign affairs, these texts emphasize the dangers to England and the need for commitment to a pan-Protestant solidarity. Of course, Protestants also carried out mass violence against Catholics, but these English texts attempted to evoke sympathy for Protestants in France and, by extension, tolerance for French Protestants seeking refuge in England.[45] A similar mass printing of texts about the Wars of Religion occurred in the 1680s when Louis XIV's policy of forcing Huguenots to convert to Catholicism, and specifically his revocation of the Edict of Nantes (France's formal policy of religious tolerance issued in 1598), resulted in yet another mass migration into England.[46] That is, the publication in England of texts about persecution on the continent not only fed a desire for news from abroad, but also served to explain demographic changes at home.

Such seems to be the case for the 1575 translation of Theodore Bèze's *A Tragedie of Abrahams Sacrifice*, a closet drama written around the time Bèze came under the influence of Calvin and left Paris to teach in Lausanne, Switzerland, and first printed in 1550. The play is in part about Bèze's experience of exile. As he explains in the epistle to the reader, "God graunted me the grace to forsake the countrie where he is persecuted, to serve him according to his holy will."[47] Although he could not predict the level of violence that would ensue, the play reflects his awareness of intensified conflict between Catholics and Protestants in France. A little more than a decade later, Bèze himself would fail in an attempt at brokering some form of reconciliation at the Colloquy of Poissy.[48]

Engaging in anti-Catholic polemic, the opening monologue speaks to the isolation of the new convert, but after the events of 1572 the play's appeal certainly must have been the way it articulated the general experience of exile among Protestant refugees. During the 1570s it was printed and translated numerous times, no doubt because it resonated so clearly with the plight of Protestants in France at that time. The English translation was carried out by Golding and printed by Huguenot printer Thomas Vautrollier a year before the pair would collaborate on the pro-Huguenot pamphlets discussed above.[49] The play opens with Abraham's lament,

> Alas my God, and was there ever any,
> That hath indurde of combrances so many,
> As I have done be fleeting to and fro,
> Since I my native countrie did forgo?
> Or is there any living on the ground
> Of benefits that hath such plenty found?
> Loe how thou makest mortall men to see,
> Thy passing goodness by calamitie.
> And as of nought thou madest everything:
> So out of ill thou causest good to spring.
> Was never wight so blessed at thy hand,
> That could thy greatnes fully understand.[50]

Abraham here announces a central theme of the drama: as in Foxe's *Acts and Monuments* or Strype's *Annals*, the experience of suffering – "calamatie" – is part of God's plan for the righteous. Good coming from ill is a reflection of the crucifixion and the suffering of any number of Old Testament figures. Exile, here, gives faith meaning, and in the 1570s this must have been a special consolation for the Huguenots in England and Antwerp.

The song that Sara and Abraham sing similarly amplifies the theme of exile as part of the experience of the chosen:

> So long a time from all the wicked rowtes
> In towne and country where we come throughouts
> Thou of thy goodnes drewest us away,
>   from places that are given
> To serve false gods: and at this present day
>   hast wandringly us driven
> To travell still among a thowsand daungers,
> In nacions unto whom we be but straungers.[51]

While the song works to emphasize the background of Abraham's exile, the phrase "at this present day" serves to doubly emphasize the patterns of refuge sought by Protestants. It speaks specifically to the French protestant diaspora and tries to frame their suffering in terms of a broad typological pattern: the righteous have always been strangers. Although Abraham is ostensibly referring to his Jewish faith, he soon evokes "the true and living God," sounding rather like a persecuted Protestant.[52] Like the pageantry at Norwich, this song implicitly recasts the story of faithful Jews among pagan idolaters as the history of Protestants among Catholics.[53]

To amplify the point, Bèze interpellates Satan, who appears at this moment. This addition fits a general pattern in Protestant writing found in, for example, de Serres's *Commentaries*, in which Satan is the instigator of intolerance. Bèze's Satan, however, comes anachronistically disguised "in the habite of a Monke," a point emphasized in various woodcuts in the text.[54] Satan plots to undermine God's plan by dissuading Abraham from sacrificing Isaac, but the sight moves Satan, and he flees: "Of God and nature enmie though I bee: / Yit is this thing so hard a cace to see, / That even almost it is a greef to mee."[55] The detail highlights Bèze's intention of reinterpreting the Old Testament story in terms of the persecution of Protestants. The fact that this play was printed in England in 1575 suggests how invested Huguenot refugees and their allies were in not only advocating for English intervention on behalf of their fellow Protestants, but also advertising the causes of immigration into England and developing a rhetoric that promoted sectarian inclusivity.

The idea that the English needed to understand events abroad in order to continue their relatively open policy regarding Protestant refugees is especially apparent in Anne Dowriche's 1589 poem *The French Historie.* The author, a member of the powerful West Country Edgecombe family, had married Hugh Dowriche, a prominent rector with Puritan leanings.⁵⁶ *The French Historie* begins with a dedication to Anne's brother, Pearse Edgecombe, who served several times as a member of Parliament during Elizabeth's reign, a detail that leads Elaine Beilin, Susanne Woods, and Margaret P. Hannay to suspect that the poem is related to the Protestant agenda of Edgecombe's and Dowriche's circle.⁵⁷ Dowriche cites her "remembrance of your former courtesies" as justification for presuming to dedicate her book to her brother and vacillates between praising her work as "most excellent and well worth the reading" and disparaging it as "scarce worth the seeing."⁵⁸

Dowriche's participation in this example of what critics have come to describe as the modesty topos may have had to do with not only her status as a woman writer, but also, as Beilin points out, her otherwise bold entry into the public discourse of Tudor historiography.⁵⁹ Following an epigram encoding the names of the poet and her dedicatee and an acrostic poem again spelling out her brother's name,⁶⁰ Dowriche addresses the reader, explaining that "The noble Martirs of England are knowen sufficientlie almost to all; these excellent French Histories were seene but of few, being in worthinesse nothing inferior unto the other."⁶¹ She thus emphasizes a shared history of religious intolerance, the idea that narratives of persecution of Protestants in France should be read alongside those found in Foxe's *Acts and Monuments.*⁶²

As with Bèze's closet drama and Elizabeth's entertainments in Norwich, Dowriche uses Old Testament references to develop a model of an inclusive community of the Reformed that crosses political borders.⁶³ The narrative of the French Wars of Religion begins with numerous references to the travails of Old Testament figures including a paraphrase on idolatry from Deuteronomy: "For they that Idols serve, and from the Lord doo shrinke, / They shal be fed with bitter gall, & wormwood water drinke."⁶⁴ Later, the narrator refers to the fates of particular persecutors recalling God's judgment of Cain and Esau, the fall of the Pharaoh who held Moses and his followers in captivity, the fall of Saul, who "did persecute Gods chosen Prophet long," and so on.⁶⁵

The poem itself covers three episodes in the Wars of Religion in France designed to garner sympathy for the Protestant cause: "The outrage called the winning of S. James his Streete, 1557" recounts the discovery of a Huguenot meeting (not unlike the underground meetings under Mary I), ultimately resulting in the arrest and torture of several Huguenots; "The constant Martirdome of Annas Burgeus one of the K. Councell, 1559" describes the trial and execution of Huguenot senator Annas Burgaeus; and "The bloodie Marriage of Margaret sister to Charles the 9, Anno 1572" narrates the Saint Bartholomew's Day Massacre and the events that led up to it.[66]

Although much has been said about Dowriche's poetics as described in the epistle, her role as historiographer, and her use of sources, the framing device of the poem, often overlooked, is important in understanding the poem's relation to immigration and the Wars of Religion. An Englishman describes how, as he wandered in the woods, "In shrilling voyce and mournfull tunes, / Methought I heard one crie," and explains, "A thousand thoughts opprest my fearfull wavering braine, / In musing what amid the woods that fearfull voice shuld mean." Here the "fearfull voice" is echoed in the narrator's "fearfull wavering braine," emphasizing a kind of empathy in the Englishman. The narrator searches for the source of the cries and finds "Alone, no peril nigh, within a bushie dale, / A stranger" who takes over the vast majority of the narrative, recounting events in France.[67]

Although critics have seen in this framing device yet another example of Dowriche's strategy of self-effacement as she enters public discourse,[68] it is important to note that among the many ways such a strategy might be achieved, Dowriche chose to put a dialogue between Englishman and immigrant at the forefront of her poem. The figure of the immigrant and his painful narrative is specifically designed to evoke the feel of an eyewitness account and to elicit sympathy. The English narrator exists not only as a layer of distance between the female poet and her public, but as a model of an ethical response to those displaced by the persecution of Protestants abroad. By the end of the poem, the French immigrant narrator apologizes for keeping the Englishman so long; the Englishman responds,

> Not so, good frend, but if with me thou wilt remaine,
> I shall not think it anie charge, nor count it anie paine
> To heare and keepe thee still: but if thou wilt depart,
> For thy discourse take this reward, & thanks from frendlie hart.

The English narrator not only offers a sympathetic ear but models for Dowriche's readers the ethic of hospitality whereby the stranger is offered some "reward" and invited to remain. Insofar as the Englishman is a representative of an appropriate response to this narrative, the poem advocates that all Protestant refugees should be welcomed in England. In fact,

Dowriche's poem mediates several foreign Protestant voices. The main source material for *The French Historie* is clearly Timme's translation of de Serres's *The Three Partes of Commentaries Containing the Whole and Perfect Discourse of the Civill Warres of Fraunce*, but Dowriche also draws on other Huguenot texts including François Hotman's *A True and Plaine Report of the Furious Outrages of Fraunce* and Innocent Gentillet's *Contre-Machiavel*.[69]

French Historie is not merely a versification of these sources, however. As Megan Matchinske points out, Dowriche carefully selected and rearranged details from de Serres' lengthy tract, and although *The Commentaries* attributes some agency to Satan, several critics note the way in which Dowriche greatly expands this role.[70] Each of the three events recounted by the immigrant narrator involves the envy and fear Satan feels at the spread of Protestantism. In the first section Satan starts vicious rumours about the supposed impropriety of the underground reformed congregations.[71] In the next section Satan convinces the king to distrust Protestant advisors like Burgaeus.[72] In the third section, when Satan sees that some princes are prepared to defend the Protestant cause, the narrator explains, "It galde him to the heart, that where he did devise / To choake the word, that even there the more it arise.[73]

In her epistle to the reader, Dowriche explains that she has amplified the role of Satan to make "more lively" the description of "all the subtleties, villainies, cruelties and policies that were devised, and by divelish meanes put in practice against the godly," while not denying that persecution nonetheless comes from Satan's "spirite."[74] Her use of Satan may also owe something to Jacob Acontius, an Italian Protestant refugee in England whose *Stratagematum Satanae (Satan's Stratagems)* was widely circulated in Latin from the 1560s on.[75] Like Dowriche's immigrant narrator, Acontius sees Satan as primarily focused on those who, as he puts it, "enjoy the Light of Truth."[76] Dedicated to Queen Elizabeth but printed abroad until 1631, Acontius' work circulated in Puritan circles such as Dowriche's; for instance, William Ames's 1610 Latin translation of William Bradshaw's *English Puritanism* includes an allusion to Acontius's book.[77] In any case, that both texts feature Satan as a figure for intolerance and error speaks to the shared world view of English and continental Protestants at the time. This shared perspective on persecution as a sign of godliness is in part Dowriche's central thesis. The emblem on the cover of her pamphlet features a naked woman with a whip accompanied by the motto "Virescit Vulnere Veritas," or "Truth grows from a wound." Lest there be any confusion, "All that will live godlie in Jesus Christ, shall suffer persecution," a line from the Book of Timothy, is written above the emblem.[78] As with the story of Josephus presented in Norwich, persecution is not God's condemnation of the victims but rather a sign of the inevitable trials of a chosen people.

Somewhat unusually, *The French Historie* was printed by Thomas Orwin simultaneously for two different booksellers: Thomas Man in London and William Russell in Exeter, near where Dowriche and her extended family lived.[79] Micheline White has emphasized the importance of the West Country in Dowriche's writing, finding that she was part of a circle of Protestant women writers with Anne Locke and others in and around Cornwall and Devon.[80] One might imagine that the West Country provided the imaginary landscape of *The French Historie*. Taunton and Bristol hosted longstanding Flemish communities, and under Elizabeth, Walloon and Flemish immigrants established a settlement in Devon.[81] While the area was not host to a sizeable Huguenot community until the 1680s,[82] in 1574 there were plans afoot to relocate part of the London immigrant population to the West Country, specifically to Stonehouse, Devon, very near Anne Dowriche's birthplace.[83] The invitation, extended to the French, Dutch, and Italian churches of London, describes available plots of land and grants the use of a house, located near the river, that could hold 100 individuals, presumably for worship or as temporary accommodation during the construction of homes. The letter was signed by none other than Pearse Edgecombe, Anne Dowriche's brother and the dedicatee of her poem. Dowriche's reference to Edgecombe's "former curtesies" might refer to some unknown act of sibling kindness, and the use of the French refugee might be a strategy for entering public discourse, but it is very likely that both relate to Dowriche's support for her brother's hospitable attitude towards England's French, Dutch, and Italian exiles.

Attention to the framing device of the poem and its connection to Edgecombe's letter thus reveals the importance of immigration as a central issue. The poem's description of atrocities abroad and the figure of the distressed Huguenot as narrator ultimately serve to promote tolerance of immigration in England. Advocacy on behalf of Protestant refugees seems to have been a part of the Dowriche and Edgecombe families' belief system. On several occasions in the late seventeenth century the Edgecombe family assisted the French settlement at Stonehouse, and in 1691–2 a merchant named Nathaniel Dowrich (perhaps a descendent of Anne Dowriche) defied local laws by employing refugees living in the town to work on his ship.[84]

The Englishman of the poem may in fact be a veiled portrait of Pearse Edgecombe, or at least a figure modelled in part on him. Like Edgecombe, the Englishman of the poem sympathizes with the stranger and ultimately invites him to stay in England. *The French Historie* thus builds on Edgecombe's project, asserting a rationale for providing refuge to Protestant strangers. When the French exile introduces himself to the Englishman in the poem, he explains,

> I am a stranger wight, and France my native soyle,
> From which, of late, by luckles chance, & need, am forst to toyle.
> Such troubles and such warres of late have there befell,
> That such as feare the Lord aright no suretie have to dwell
> Within that wofull Land: so God me hether sent
> To live with you in happie state, which he this Land hath lent.[85]

As Dowriche's narrator puts it, the inclusive "happie state" described here is part of God's plan; by extension, to support the inclusion of strangers in England is to participate in divine providence.[86] As if to amplify the "happie" state of Anglo-immigrant relations founded on religious affinity, the Englishman immediately responds,

> Oh happie then am I: my frend I thee desire
> Come goe with me, for of these warres I greatly long to hear.
> And if that thou wilt staie, as long as thou wilt crave
> My house as thine, and all therein thou shalt be sure to have.[87]

Offering his house, just as Edgecombe offered a house in his letter to the stranger churches of London, the Englishman embodies Dowriche's ideal for English attitudes towards Protestant strangers; the rest of the poem, narrating the martyrdom of French Protestants, is designed to elicit similarly sympathetic responses from her readers in London and the West Country.

Dowriche's epistle to the reader is dated 25 July 1589. One week later Henry III of France was assassinated by Jacques Clèment, a Dominican friar and agent of the Catholic League who worried that Henry might develop a policy of tolerance towards Protestants. This event may have sparked special interest in Dowriche's timely poem, and indeed, it seems likely that the poem was printed in anticipation of increased immigration to England in the wake of the assassination.

Not much later Christopher Marlowe wrote his play on the Wars of Religion, *The Massacre at Paris*. Like Dowriche, Marlowe presents a highly selective version of events, but whereas Dowriche provides the exemplary moments culminating in the Saint Bartholomew's Day Massacre, Marlowe begins with the event that precipitated the massacre: the marriage of the Protestant Henry Navarre to the Catholic Margaret of Valois, Catherine de Medici's daughter. The play depicts the massacre, the assassination of Gaspard de Coligny in 1572, the crowning of the Duke of Anjou as Henry III in 1575, the Battle of Coutras between Henry of Navarre and Anne, Duke of Joyeuse in 1587 (in which the Huguenot forces overwhelm the Catholic royalist army), the battle between Henry III and the Duke of Guise and the murder of the Guise in 1588, and finally the assassination of Henry III in 1589. Rather than a "Satan" figure, Marlowe presents the Duke of Guise and Catherine de Medici as Machiavellian villains; these characterizations led Randall Martin to conclude that Marlowe was influenced by Dowriche's *The French Historie* as he wrote both *The Massacre at Paris* and *The Jew of Malta*.[88] Unlike Dowriche, Marlowe appears to have consulted the Catholic League pamphlets of Jean Boucher, but much of Marlowe's material, like Dowriche's, seems to have been drawn from Huguenot sources: Jean de Serres, François Hotman, Henri Estienne, Nicolas Barnaud, Michel Hurault, Antony Colynet, and Simon Goulart.[89] Moreover, Marlowe's depiction of the murder of French Protestant humanist Peter Ramus in *The Massacre* suggests a deep familiarity with Ramus's work on logic and rhetoric.[90]

In addition to his reading, Marlowe's connections to actual immigrants may have informed some of his thinking as he developed the play. His father, John Marlowe, was apprenticed to Gerard Richardson, an immigrant shoemaker living in Northgate Ward in Canterbury; in the year Christopher Marlowe was born, John Marlowe was involved in a suit lodged by Hermann Verson, an immigrant who resided near the Marlowe home in the parish of St George in Canterbury.[91] Both Richardson and Verson had arrived in Canterbury before the establishment of stranger churches there: Verson married Katherin Mason in Canterbury in 1552, and Richardson received his letter of denization in 1550.[92] John Marlowe's interactions with the two immigrants took place before his son could have any recollection of them (Richardson died a few weeks after Christopher Marlowe was born), but these relations illustrate how common it was for English inhabitants of Canterbury to come in contact with their immigrant neighbours. Such contact would naturally increase with the establishment of a larger immigrant population in Canterbury.[93]

In 1567, the then impoverished city of Canterbury attempted to follow the economic model of neighbouring Sandwich and Maidstone by inviting strangers to settle there and practice their trades. In 1568 about eighteen immigrant families, mostly French-speaking Walloons, joined the immigrant community in Canterbury. In 1575 a large wave of Protestant refugees found their way to Canterbury where they were given use of Saint Alphege Church (located in the Ward where Richardson had lived), and due to a dramatic increase in population they eventually came to occupy the western crypt of Canterbury Cathedral.[94] As antiquarian William Somner put it in 1640, the strangers comprised "a congregation for the most part of distressed exiles, growne so great and yet daily multiplying, that the place in short time is likely to prove a hive too little to contain such a swarme."[95] Somner wrote this nearly a half a century after Marlowe's death, but as early as 1582 city authorities were similarly alarmed by the growth of the immigrant community in Canterbury, which at that time accounted for more than 15 per cent of the population there.[96] Despite the concern about the size of the population, Anne M. Oakley's study of English-immigrant relations in Canterbury suggests a relatively peaceful coexistence and economically beneficial interdependence.[97]

David Riggs suggests that the young Marlowe would have been aware of the sudden increase in population around him and argues further that the events of 1572 had a profound impact on Marlowe, that Marlowe would have encountered refugees in Canterbury and heard about their plight. Given his father's connections to Canterbury's immigrant community, this suggestion seems at least possible. Indeed, Riggs argues that the French word *massacre*, brought to England via news of the slaughter in France, held a special resonance for Marlowe: *The Massacre at Paris*, *The Jew of Malta*, and both parts of *Tamburlaine* all feature massacres.[98]

Even if Marlowe was too young to appreciate the changes happening around him before he left Canterbury to study at Corpus Christi College, Cambridge, he would surely have noticed such changes on his return to witness the will of Katherine Benchkin in 1585, just three years after city authorities began to be concerned by the growth of the immigrant community around them.[99] Marlowe would also likely have been aware of Protestant refugees in Cambridge. During his time there John Copcot of Calais rose from university teacher to vice-chancellor of Cambridge, and he was appointed Master of Corpus Christi College the year Marlowe received his MA.[100] French theologian Peter Baro was Lady Margaret Professor of Divinity at Cambridge from 1574 to 1596, and in 1581, while Marlowe was working on his BA, Baro drew attention to himself by breaking with Calvinist thought on free will and predestination. Constance Kuriyama suggests that Marlowe would have been aware of the debates and may have listened to Baro's lectures.[101] Apart from these high profile refugees, well-to-do families from Norwich and Colchester are known to have sent their children to Cambridge for study at this time, and Marlowe may well have met several of these individuals.[102]

In addition to his reading for *The Massacre at Paris* and his probable encounters with Huguenot exiles, Marlowe likely had an interest in the writings of Theodore Bèze. John Gresshop, Marlowe's schoolmaster at King's School, owned copies of books by Bèze, among other reformers, and several critics suggest that Bèze, in addition to Calvin and Baro, informed Marlowe's understanding of predestination and the rights of individuals in relation to the state.[103] It is tempting to hear in Doctor Faustus's command that the demon Mephistophles "Go, and return an old Franciscan Friar; / That holy shape becomes a devil best" (1.3.26–7) an echo of Bèze's closet drama with Satan disguised as a monk.[104] Although both Bèze and Marlowe may have been drawing on the German folkloric tradition of Friar Rush (Frere Rausch), a devil in friar's robes who terrorizes a monastery, there is the likelihood that Marlowe had read Bèze's play.[105] Marlowe was certainly familiar with Nicholas Grimald's translations of Bèze's poetry in *Tottel's Miscellany*, and Anne Lake Prescott has shown Bèze's pervasive influence on Elizabethan poetry in general.[106]

By the time Marlowe wrote *The Jew of Malta* he had already clearly taken an interest in the plight of the Huguenots. The character of Machiavel in *The Jew of Malta* provides a way of understanding *The Massacre at Paris*. As he explains in the Prologue,

> Albeit the world think Machiavel is dead,
> Yet was his soul flown beyond the Alps,
> And, now the Guise is dead, is flown from France
> To view this land and frolic with his friends. (Prologue, 1–4)

The Machiavellian figures of *The Jew of Malta* are of a type with the Guise who instigates much of the anti-Protestant violence in *The Massacre at Paris*. By "this land," Machiavel may mean the fictive world of Malta he is introducing, but the phrase also clearly refers to dangers to England, the potential for the disorder depicted in Malta or the Wars of Religion dramatized in *The Massacre at Paris* to erupt in England. *The Massacre at Paris*, moreover, explains the presence of French refugees in England and argues for a sympathetic attitude towards them, even as some of Marlowe's fellow dramatists, Robert Wilson and George Wapull, for instance, attempted to capitalize on emerging feelings of animosity towards immigrants. *The Massacre at Paris* furthers anti-Catholic sentiment, but does so by suggesting that Catholicism is in actuality a screen for ambition, a "childish toy" in the hands of the Guise and Catherine de Medici.

The manipulation of religion is alluded to early in the play, as Henry Navarre declares,

> But he that sits and rules above the clouds
> Doth hear and see the prayers of the just,
> And will revenge the blood of innocents
> That Guise hath slain by treason of his heart
> And brought by murder to their timeless ends. (1.42–6)

It is not religious fervour but a rebelliousness against nature itself, the "treason of his heart," that spurs the Guise to his covert scheming and overt violence; this pseudo-Catholic position is contrasted with that of "the just" and "innocents," that is, the French Protestants, some of whom would soon escape to England.[107] More to the point, in keeping with the Protestant use of the Old Testament, Navarre's allusion to Jeremiah 19:4 ("the blood of innocents") casts the Guise as an oppressive idolater and Navarre himself as the last prophet of Judah.

Moreover, the play intermingles piety and brute force in a way that highlights the gratuitous violence against Protestants. When the Admiral requests, "O, let me pray before I die," Gonzago presents his sword and quips, "Then pray unto our Lady; kiss this cross" (5.28–9). Gonzago's sadistic joke turns the hilt of his sword into a cross and the Virgin Mary into a female figure of revenge. The macabre humour is even more pronounced when Anjou and the Guise murder the Protestant preacher Loreine. Just before stabbing the preacher, the Guise mocks, "'Dearly beloved brother' – thus 'tis written," and Anjou continues the mockery of the Protestant service joking, "Stay, my lord. Let me begin the psalm" (7.8–9).[108] The cavalier attitude towards slaughter here does not evoke the "cruel laughter" Stephen Greenblatt imagines such depictions of violence elicited for readers of Sidney's *Arcadia*, but nor does it necessarily invite the audience to take the aggressors' perspective, as Julia Briggs suggests.[109] Instead, the sadistic lampooning of Protestantism by the agents of violence would seem to emphasize the callous nature of the killing and elicit repugnance on the part of the audience.

Less humorous but along similar lines, Catherine asserts that although she shows Navarre considerable tolerance, "our difference in religion / Might be a means to cross you in your love" (1.15–16). The "cross" here could refer to a hope of possibly converting Navarre to Catholicism, but it also refers to Catherine's potential to interfere with Navarre. Since the audience knows what is about to happen, the image of a crucifix here is a double cross, an ominous sign of the violence to come. Indeed, the word "cross" echoes throughout the play as a sign of enmity rather than peace.

The pun on cross further points to the play's depiction of religion as both sincere faith and tool to manipulate others. Marlowe presents Catholicism as especially entangled with the corrupt politics of the play. Upon placing her son Henry III on the throne, Catherine confides to the Cardinal her plan,

> To plant ourselves with such authority
> As not a man may live without our leaves.
> Then shall the Catholic faith of Rome
> Flourish in France and none deny the same. (13.50–3)

Taken in isolation these final two lines might resound with a sincere promotion of faith, but the passage ties Catholicism to Catherine's Machiavellian ambition. As the Cardinal worries about difficulty in manipulating Henry III, Catherine suggests that she will arrange for his death as she had arranged for Charles IX's death earlier, surmising, "Tush, all shall die unless I have my will" (13.66). Such pronouncements lead one to see the Wars of Religion as the result of base manipulation and usurpation of political order rather than sincere battle over belief.

Briggs cautions against too simplistic a reading of both Henry III's character and the play as a whole. Interpreting *The Massacre at Paris* alongside Catholic League pamphlets, she presents a somewhat heroic Guise and a subtly cruel Henry III. Given *The Jew of Malta*'s allusion to the Guise, his overtly Machiavellian speeches, and the massive violence he perpetrates, it is hard to see him sympathetically. In his first soliloquy he describes his intention to use religion to serve his all consuming ambition: "My policy hath framed religion." In case the point is lost, he pauses on the word: "Religion! O Diabole!" (2.65–6). At his death, the Guise declares,

Vive la messe! Perish Huguenots!
Thus Caesar did go forth, and thus he died. (11.86–7)

Briggs reads this speech, especially the reference to Caesar, as evidence of the Guise's "personal courage," but as Alan Shepard points out, the reference to Caesar also hints at the Guise's hollow self-aggrandizement as well as his poor judgment.[110] Perhaps even more hollow is his last ditch effort to "frame religion" for his own ends, here to pose as someone who fought for his faith when he has already explained that he manipulates religious fervour. Still Briggs' point that Henry III also manipulates, murders, and desecrates is well taken. In some ways, Marlowe's play seems to dramatize the Wars of Religion as a kind of revenge tragedy in which each act of violence begets only more violence.

Amid all this, Henry of Navarre functions as a kind of Protestant chorus, commenting on the violence of the play. He soliloquizes on the "wicked Guise" who "takes vantage on religion" and "basely seeks the ruin of his realm" (19.22–31), underlines the Guise's manipulation of religion, and frames his own piety as a kind of patriotic resistance to the foreign influence of "popelings." Even Briggs ultimately surmises that the play approves of Navarre over Guise. Navarre's earlier lament, "How many noble men have lost their lives" (17.9), indicates how the audience is to view the massacre, and he goes on to sound a patriotic note that resonates with pan-Protestant solidarity:

But God we know will always put them down
That lift themselves against the perfect truth,
Which I'll maintain so long as life doth last,
And with the queen of England join my force,
To beat the papal monarch from our lands,
And keep those relics from our countries' coasts. (17.12–19)

Navarre's vision of the suffering of Protestants as part of God's larger plan to put down oppressors is not unlike the depiction of suffering in Dowriche's *French Historie* or Bèze's *A Tragedie of Abraham's Sacrifice*. Moreover, the evocation of "truth" leads to a solidarity with England, a movement from Navarre's "I" and "my" to an emphasis on "*our* lands" and "*our* countries' coasts." Many English may not have been thrilled at the prospect of further involvement in the Wars of Religion, especially in the wake of John Norreys's dubious expedition into Brittany, but the vision of victory through solidarity must have been appealing to some

Protestants in the audience.[111] To highlight this point, after Henry III has had the Guise assassinated, he reflects on the political problems the Guise had caused, linking the fate of Protestants in France to the political stability of England:[112]

> I ne'er was King of France until this hour.
> This is the traitor that hath spent my gold
> In making foreign wars and civil broils.
> Did he not draw a sort of English priests
> From Douai to the seminary at Rheims,
> To hatch forth treason 'gainst their natural queen?
> Did he not cause the King of Spain's huge fleet,
> To threaten England and to menace me? (20.99–106)

As with Navarre's speech, Henry III evokes both a common cause between himself and England and a corollary to Protestant sectarian inclusivity in England – English Catholics in France – but this cross-cultural solidarity is presented as a danger to England's stability. The potential treason against Elizabeth mentioned here highlights one of the key concerns of most contemporary documents on the Wars of Religion: it could happen in England.

By displaying behind the scene motives of the atrocities, *The Massacre in Paris* demystifies the way in which authorities manipulate masses into irrational anger. That English audiences of the early 1590s needed some clear explanation of French immigration to England seems clear, judging by a libel produced in 1593 which complained, "and you, fraudulent father, Frenchmen, by your cowardly flight from your own natural countries, have abandoned the same into the hands of your proud, cowardly enemies, and have, by feigned hypocrisy and counterfeit show of religion, placed yourselves here in a most fertile soil."[113] The phrase "feigned hypocrisy" reveals the convoluted logic of the author, but the tract itself also shows how easily the events on the continent could be misunderstood. Who, after watching *The Massacre at Paris*, could blame the Huguenots for fleeing? For an English audience wondering why so many French families were residing in London, the play makes the answer clear: they are victims of circumstance and overarching ambition, commoners caught in the crossfire of political manoeuvring.

The Massacre at Paris, like *The French Historie*, is an antidote to texts that ignore the contexts of French immigration to England and merely scapegoat the French. Ernest Varamund, the Scottish translator of the play's main source for the events of 1572, notes that, in addition to emphasizing the martyrdom of the French Protestants, he undertook his translation "for our good neighbors the Englishmen ... to serve their understanding."[114] The portrayal of these particular events abroad had a special importance to the English, for, as Varamund explains, "all Christendome hopeth for charitable assistance" from the English.

While some of Marlowe's fellow dramatists sought to foment distrust and resentment of strangers, *The Massacre at Paris* focuses on sympathy for and understanding of them. Just as Dowriche asserts a connection between English and French martyrs, so Marlowe's Navarre rhetorically joins French and English Protestants in a battle against Catholic forces. That the Protestant version of the Wars of Religion needed to be promoted is evident in anti-alien activity in the early 1590s. The aforementioned libel, for instance, may have singled out the French, but also railed against "beastly Brutes, Belgians, or rather Drunken Drones, and faint-hearted Flemings," and ended with the threat that, "And all the Apprentices and Journeymen will down with Flemings and strangers."[115] A second libel, posted to the door of Austin Friars on 5 May 1593, addressed similar themes, but in more graphic detail. The document, known as the Dutch Church Libel, warned, "Weele cut your throtes in your temples praying."[116] The majority of the text is aimed at economic issues: that the typical merchant stranger "Forestalls the markets," that artisans practice "three trades at least," and that the increased immigration has raised rent in the city. Like its predecessor, however, the Dutch Church Libel alleges that many strangers used religious persecution as a mere pretence to enter England, and that strangers were actually Catholic spies. Interestingly, just as the rhetoric of sectarian inclusivity often alluded to a certain degree of philo-Semitism, so the breakdown of a community founded on shared religion evokes anti-Semitism: the libel alleges "like the Jewes, you eate us up as bread."[117] No doubt, strangers were being figured as scapegoats for every failing of the Elizabethan state, and for those who bought into the false dichotomy of inclusion or stability, the latter may have seemed the only choice.

The Dutch Church Libel further stands out because it so obviously appropriates Marlowe for its agenda.[118] The libel states, "Not paris massacre so much blood did spill / As we will doe iust vengeance on you all" (40–1), and in case the allusion to Marlowe's play was missed, the author used the unlikely pseudonym of "Tamburlaine," Marlowe's infamous alien conqueror. The Privy Council objected to the threat of sedition and the anti-immigrant sentiment, claiming that among the anti-alien libels to appear that year, it "excead[ed] the rest in lewdness."[119] The few who attempted to answer the call of the Dutch Church Libel were imprisoned, and on 11 May – just six days after the discovery of the Libel at Austin Friars – the Council ordered officers to "search in anie the chambers, studies, chestes, or other like places for al manner of writings or papers that may geve you light for the discoverie of the libellers."[120] Further, the officers were granted the authority to interrogate and torture any suspects so as to "draw them to discover their knowledge concerning the said libels."[121] Marlowe and his roommate Thomas Kyd were called in for questioning, and both died soon afterward. In the months to follow, *The Massacre at Paris* was performed more than ten times, proving a popular and profitable play, emphasizing the martyrdom of the many at the hands of manipulators, not unlike the peddler as "base medler" in *The Pedlers Prophecie*.

As Kermode has shown, echoes of the Dutch Church Libel can be seen in not only Marlowe but also plays such as *The Pedlers Prophecie*.[122] The threat "Weele cut your throtes" (39) inverts the Peddler's warning that aliens "shall cut our throats."[123] The Libel's complaints about overcrowding and "Raysing of rents" was also prevalent not only in *The Pedlers Prophecie* but also in Wapull's *The Tide Tarrieth No Man* and, as Kermode has shown, in Robert Wilson's *Three Ladies of London*.[124] In the latter play, the character Artifex further complains that he is losing employment to aliens whose work is of deceptive quality:

> I am almost quite undone,
> But yet my living hitherto with good Conscience I have wonne.
> But my true working, my early rising, and my late going to bed,
> Is scant able to find myselfe wife and children dry bread:
> For there be such a sort of straungers in this cuntry,
> That worke fine to please the eye, though it be deceitfully,
> And that which is slight, and seemes to the eye well,
> Shall sooner than a piece of good worke be proffered to sell.
> And our English men be grown so foolish and nice,
> That they will not give a penny above the ordinarie price.[125]

Kermode notes that at this point Fraud convinces Artifex to embrace the "alien" practice of developing faulty goods that are pleasing to the eye.[126] The strain on the economy in the 1590s, here perceived as the result of immigration, complicated sectarian inclusivity and led many to reexamine the tensions between spiritual and economic health raised several decades earlier in *Wealth and Health*. To resolve the tension, individuals petitioned the state to maintain a registry to keep track of strangers in the realm. The state responded with the Returns of Aliens in 1593, and such surveys were repeated intermittently throughout the early modern period, almost always in response to English anxieties.[127] Another approach to the problem was to imagine other types of multicultural community. Though never losing sight of shared religion as a foundation for community, the texts that promote these other types of inclusivity focus on shared craft or common economic interest. The second and third sections of this book address these more specific modes of English-immigrant solidarity in the wake of the 1590s when economic problems and English relations with France and the Netherlands required something more than an appeal to shared religion and shared enmity with Catholicism.

PART TWO

Provincial Globalism

Nihil humani a me alienum puto
[Nothing human is alien to me.]

– Terence qtd. as Karl Marx's maxim.[1]

Chapter Three

Artisanal Tolerance: The Case of Thomas Deloney

Despite attempts to use narratives of Protestant persecution to keep sectarian inclusivity active in England, by the 1590s tensions between some English subjects and their immigrant neighbours had intensified, rendering religious affiliation less important to social cohesion. England's involvement in continental affairs – for instance, Leicester's loss of support in the Netherlands in 1586–7 and Essex's failed expedition in support of Henri IV in 1591 – led some to feel that their immigrant neighbours were perhaps less committed than the English in the continental conflicts.[2] The author of the Dutch Church Libel complained,

> And our pore soules, are cleane thrust out of dore
> And to the warres are sent abroade to rome,
> To fight it out for Fraunce & Belgia,
> And dy like dogges as sacrifice for you.[3]

A similar sense of resentment can be seen in Sir Francis Walsingham, who in response to complaints about the increased stranger population in Rye, suggested that the able-bodied strangers there be sent to war in France and the Netherlands.[4] Such sentiments were not uncommon, as Englishmen were wounded or killed on the continent confronting the forces that the refugees had fled.

Tensions were further exacerbated by domestic troubles: severe inflation and increased unemployment from the late 1580s through the 1590s stretched the bonds of shared religion close to the breaking point.[5] As early as 1571 and certainly from the late 1580s through the early part of the seventeenth century, many immigrants in England faced intermittent disruptions in their lives due to the activity of informers, individuals who received fees for successful allegations against others.[6] The harassment was such that in the summer of 1592, Lord Treasurer William Burghley ordered a stay of proceedings against Dutch candle-makers in London until such time as the informers could be questioned.[7] The need to question the informers was not merely a ploy to slow the wheels of local justice. Although informers proved to be indispensable to the enforcement of local laws, they were also often suspect in their dealings. Sir Edward Coke, for instance, urged that the "vexatious informer" be "well regulated and restrained," and noted that that informers were generally motivated by "malice or private ends, and never for love of Justice."[8] One petition from the Dutch Church complained that, "many poore Strangers being members of the said Dutch Church, be daily troubled and vexed by sundrie Informers, and especially by one Clement Banke."[9] The petition makes the specific accusations – that individual immigrant artisans had not completed an apprenticeship in London, and that non-denizens did not have the right to practice their trade in the city – and details the strangers' defence: that Queen Elizabeth had granted strangers the right to practice their trades in London. In response, Elizabeth appointed William Burghley and John Puckering, Keeper of the Seal, to hear all such cases brought by informers, but this did not, evidently, put a stop to the harassment. In 1595 Puckering wrote to Lord Mayor Stephen Slanye, "I doe now understand ... that the Informers doe still prosecute with all earnestness against some of the Dutch men,"[10] and then reiterated the Queen's policy that they, not the local authorities, should hear such cases.

Strangers were not the only targets of informers. Thomas Middleton satirized informers in *A Chaste Maid in Cheapside* (1613), and the general unpopularity of informers is evidenced by Elizabeth's 1594 proclamation demanding an end to mob violence against them.[11] In 1599–1600 and again in 1606, however, the molestations in London became so serious that the Dutch and French Churches joined together in listing grievances against specific informers.[12] By 1611 the Dutch and French Churches of London had assessed the situation and surmised that the conflicts arose neither from the state nor from a general sentiment but rather from individual informers preying on individual immigrants who saw payment of fines as a more viable and affordable option than legal defence.[13] Payment rather than resistance only encouraged informers, observed the church elders, so the churches resolved to raise what amounted to a legal defence fund for their members should they again be harassed by informers.[14] This tactic seems to have reduced the number of informers harassing strangers, but by 1616, amid new economic troubles, King James I was prompted to issue a statement against the activities of "sundry troublesome Informers."[15]

As the economy stabilized, so too did Anglo-immigrant relations, but the proceedings brought by informers opened up a debate about what exactly constituted Englishness. In 1591 some English-born children of denizens were compelled to petition Burghley to argue their rights as native-born subjects, and in 1600, among those informed on were the English-born sons of a French immigrant, accused of retailing cloth.[16] Cultural differences between English and immigrant families evidently rendered even English-born children of immigrants vulnerable to accusations of informers. Most children of early modern immigrants to England would likely have had a bilingual and bicultural upbringing. By the 1590s the vast majority of refugees were still attending the French or Dutch churches, while less than 15 per cent of strangers favoured the English church.[17] Whatever church they attended, the children of Protestant refugees were for the most part raised in households that were more strictly Calvinist than those of many of their English counterparts; their immigrant parents may have continued to dress differently from their English hosts and would likely not have mastered the English language.[18] Luu finds that subsidy collectors complained of a general lack of linguistic competence in English among strangers, all evidence of the relative insularity of the immigrant communities.[19]

Still, the fact that children of immigrants could often pass as English indicates that English culture had permeated immigrant communities.[20] The ability to pass as English suggests an awareness of the host culture, but there was no single homogenous English culture to which one might assimilate; instead there was a variety of early modern multicultural communities characterized, as I shall argue, by a paradoxical mix of provincial and global elements. By provincial I mean that early modern communities, even urban communities, were grounded in local ideas of reciprocal relations: some were enshrined in statutes and ordinances of guilds and towns and at times the central government: others were implicit in daily practices. Although some regulations of trade and conduct were legislated by the central government, such communities often differed from region to region so that the norms of a rural community could not be taken for granted in a more urban community like London or Norwich; even between urban communities, social and economic obligations could vary widely.[21] At the same time, these communities had a global awareness of economic interdependence that extended beyond England's shores, and a sense of the way events on the continent could impact their lives.

Immigrants posed a unique challenge to the delicate balance of provincialism and globalism and the balance between local and central government. To get at the place of immigrants in early modern England's provincial globalism, this chapter will explore the provincial yet global community of artisans as manifested in the literary texts of Thomas Deloney, who was very likely a descendant of strangers and thus would have been acutely aware of the pressures of cities and towns built on traditional reciprocal relations and the dependence of those cities and towns on an increasingly global economy.

Although some scholars have noted Deloney's probable immigrant heritage, little has been said about its effect on his literary output, the way he negotiated the provincial and the global elements of immigrant life. Deloney wrote popular literature – primarily ballads and prose fiction – and he seems to have passed as English; none of his contemporaries refer to a "French Deloney," for example, and even today scholars rarely take into account his probable immigrant heritage in interpreting his texts. As will be seen, the vision of England found in Deloney's writing is informed by an acute awareness of the experience of sixteenth-century immigrants to England. This chapter will examine how his prose fiction and ballads addressed, and to some degree resolved, the problems of exile, immigration, and integration through an appeal to the provincial globalism of early modern England's artisanal communities. Deloney, it would seem, had a vested interest in such a project, but no more or less than the authors of anti-alien tracts. Moreover, the popularity of his writing in the early modern period suggests that his vision of an England founded on local customs but global connections appealed to many readers.

Despite speculation about the place and date of Thomas Deloney's birth,[22] it seems fairly certain that he was the descendant of French or Walloon immigrants. His unusual surname, Deloney, looks like an Anglicization of the more common French forms Dalaune, Dalenne, or D'Lanoy.[23] As might be expected of the son or grandson of French-speaking immigrants, he knew French: Francis O. Mann and O.R. Reuter have emphasized that in his ballads and prose fiction he drew on French sources not yet translated to English, and his second known publication, a translation of *Les contes ou les nouvelles récréations et joyeux devis,* reveals an understanding of French unusual for someone with neither a university education nor the means to travel to the continent.[24] Deloney's previous publication, a translation of correspondence between the Archbishop of Collen and Pope Gregory XIII, is the first of several militant Protestant texts by Deloney: some of these texts deal with exile, and all are described by Max Dorsinville and Walter Davis as having a "Calvinist background," more Puritan or Huguenot than that of the Church of England.²⁵

Moreover, although Deloney is known today as a writer of ballads and popular prose fiction, during his life emphasis was laid on his status as a silk weaver, a profession dominated by immigrants in Norwich and London, the two centres scholars propose as Deloney's place of birth. Records in Saint Giles, Cripplegate, for instance, list the 1586 christening of "Richard Delonie sonne of Thomas Delonie, silk-weaver,"²⁶ and even in 1596, at the zenith of Deloney's ballad-writing career, Thomas Nashe nonetheless referred to him as "the Balletting Silke-weauer," and goes on to suggest that the mood of Deloney's writing is inextricably linked to the success of the cloth trade:

> whereas his Muse from the first peeping foorth, hath flood at liuery at an Alehouse wispe, neuer exceeding a penny a quart day nor night; and this deare yeare, together with the silencing of his looms, scarce that; he being constrained to betake him to carded Ale: whence it proceedeth, that since Candlemas or his Iigge of Iohn for the King, not one merrie Dittie will come from him, but The Thunder-bolt against Swearers, Repent England repent, & The strange iudgements of God.²⁷

Good times for the cloth trade, argues Nashe, result in Deloney's jigs and frolicsome ballads, while an economic downturn leads him to compose much gloomier material. This description, from Nashe's pamphlet *Have with you to Saffron Walden*, was printed two years before Deloney's bleak poem *Canaan's Calamity, Jerusalem's Misery* was entered in The Stationers' Register.²⁸

Passing as English

George Unwin, Eric Kerridge, and Lien Luu all agree that silk weaving was introduced to England by immigrants during the second half of the sixteenth century and that Englishmen only gradually adopted the craft. There were few native master silk weavers in England before 1615, and it was not until 1638 that the London Weavers' Company was granted authority over all silk weaving in and around London.²⁹ A French-speaking Calvinist silk weaver was unusual among the English, but typical enough among the French immigrant communities of early modern England; approximately one-third of the members of the French Church in London were involved in silk weaving. By 1593 roughly 18 per cent of all stranger households in London – more than 500 male strangers and perhaps an equal number of their wives and children – worked in some aspect of the trade. Cripplegate Ward, where Deloney appears to have lived for some time, was home to an estimated 10 per cent of all stranger silk weavers in and around London,[30] yet Deloney seems to have been taken as an Englishman, facing none of the employment restrictions or harassment imposed on strangers and their descendants.

What would it take for the descendant of a French silk weaver to pass as fully English? Linda Schlossberg has described passing as "a form of storytelling,"[31] a skill that Deloney had in spades. One would need an English sounding name (Deloney, not D'Lanoy) and would need to attend carefully to the nuances of spoken English; indeed, critics had praised Deloney's skilful sensitivity to dialogue. Ernest Baker describes him as the writer of "the best dialogue that has been seen yet in an English prose tale."[32] Similarly, Merritt Lawlis notes his sensitivity to regional dialect, using just enough dialect to indicate a character's birthplace and upbringing without compromising the overall intelligibility of the dialogue. Eugene P. Wright observes that Deloney was "tuned to the use and misuse of English by foreigners."[33] Finally, to pass as English one would need to break from one's immigrant family and integrate fully into the various "worlds within worlds," to use Steve Rappaport's phrase, the wards, precincts, parishes, and livery companies that made up London. Deloney, more than any other early modern writer, was closely associated with the culture of London's livery companies, which Rappaport describes as "apart from the family the most important form of social organisation in sixteenth-century London."[34] Deloney dedicated *The Gentle Craft, Part One* (1597), to "all the good Yeomen of the Gentle Craft" of shoemaking and its sequel to "the Master and Wardens of the worshipfull company of the Cordwaynors."[35] An active member of the London Weavers' Company, in his dedication for *Jack of Newbury*, Deloney wrote, "TO ALL FAMOVS Cloth Workers in England, I wish all happiness of life, prosperity and brotherly affection."[36] The phrase, "brotherly affection," highlights the importance Deloney placed on his membership in the Weavers' Company.

Attention to the nuances of English, a name change, and a strong connection to English institutions would help one to pass as English and become fully immersed in the provincial elements of London life. It may be, however, that Deloney did not have to try very hard to pass as English. His family may have integrated so thoroughly that many of these requirements were already in place for him. While he seems to have had a more militant Protestant upbringing than many of his English neighbours, he may have naturally identified with various aspects of early modern English artisan culture: drinking English ale (rather than the hopped beer of the continent), a strong belief in the importance of traditional rights afforded to commoners, and a deep respect for the monarch may all have come naturally to the young man. Still, these cultural aspects are also provincial requirements of local life; strangers were especially beholden to the monarch, since they viewed their stay in England as contingent on the crown's sympathy with their plight on the continent.[37] Brought up in England from an early age, Deloney would not have had trouble hurdling the linguistic barrier that prevented most immigrants from passing as English. Aside from his translation from French, he seems not to have drawn much attention to his connections to French Protestant culture.

Deloney seems always to have been considered English, not only by his contemporaries but also by scholars. For example, Roze Hentschell sees him as a writer of nationalist prose; Louis B. Wright notes that his ballad on the Peasant Revolt ends "Patriotically enough from the citizen's point of view"; and Dorsinville writes of Deloney's "close affiliation with the Elizabethan middle class."[38] Mann, more knowingly, describes Deloney thus: "A strong patriot and Protestant, he hated Spain and the Catholic Church with an honourable virulence, while his pride in substantial aldermen and civic corporations bespeaks him a typical Elizabethan Londoner, by adoption if not by birth."[39] These four interpretations provide different shades of the same reading of Deloney as quintessential London patriot. There is not, however, complete consensus in Deloney criticism: some critics see him as a propagandist for the state[40] while others call him a "bourgeois propagandist,"[41] and still others see in Deloney an avid critic of the Elizabethan state and the voice of an emergent proletariat.[42] Some depict him as an entrepreneurial spirit, the voice of emergent capitalism, or the rising middle class, while others see in him a supporter of traditional local economies, a critic of profiteering, and an advocate for the poor.[43]

As will be seen, I am dubious of a capitalist Deloney, although he depicts several characters that rise to wealth within the confines of traditional economies. The at times contradictory readings noted above, however, indicate the need for a more complex understanding of Deloney than has hitherto been offered. Rather than placing him as a thoroughly English author of state propaganda or an artisanal critic of state policies, it makes more sense to identify Deloney both as a stranger's son – an identity he seems to have hid but that nonetheless left an imprint on his writing, most notably in his fervent Protestantism – and as a member of the guild culture – an identity that encompasses not only the poor apprentices and yeomen celebrated and sympathized with in Deloney's prose fiction but also the wealthy masters and gentry whose proper conduct those same books depict and implore. This complexity explains some of the differing interpretations of Deloney's texts: he supported the state and was willing to promote its causes when it appeared to empower guilds or further the Protestant cause at home and abroad. He was critical of Catholics and those who ignored the authority of the guild system and other local institutions. There was sometimes tension between these two identities, one local, placing a high premium on stability, the other global and intent on disrupting Catholic authority and tradition.

In his identification with London's guilds, Deloney seems profoundly provincial, emphasizing the importance of local custom and a closed society anxiously guarding the secrets of the craft; at the same time, however, Deloney often depicts as heroes those who defy authority and deviate from local custom or abandon their local province when it seems contrary to their vision of the primitive church. This, I think, is due in part to the dominance of Protestantism and the accompanying conviction that Reform must occur globally among artisans in general, and in part to Deloney's own Protestant refugee heritage. In this sense, his immigrant heritage was in harmony with London's provincial globalism, but such harmony sometimes turned to discord. A case in point is Deloney's involvement in the relationship between native English and Protestant refugee weavers.

The London Weavers' Company and the Complaint of the Yoeman Weavers

The relationship between the London Weavers' Company, of which Deloney was an active member, and the immigrant weavers, of which Deloney was a perhaps closeted member, is a complex one. Edward VI and Elizabeth I both encouraged the influx of immigrant weavers so that native weavers could learn specialized skills.[44] The introduction of new materials and techniques (too numerous to list here) along with the surplus of labourers that came with immigration helped London and Norwich, the two largest hosts of immigrants, to dominate the clothing trade, but as Frances Consitt points out, the situation tended to benefit employers rather than employees.[45] Rather than seek the exclusion of the strangers from the city, several companies, including the London Weavers' Company, sought the inclusion of immigrant weavers by admitting them to the guild as "foreign brethren" or "admissioners."[46] This strategy was founded on a reciprocal arrangement: the strangers legitimated their place in the economy and presumably received protection from informers while the guilds expanded their regulatory powers and received the income from the increase in membership. Outdoing all other trades, between 1577 and 1583 the London Weavers' Company reported admitting 153 strangers to the company as masters and journeymen.[47] This large number reflects not only the massive number of strangers involved in the craft, but also the London Weavers' Company's commitment to the new strategy of controlling competition from strangers through greater integration: "foreign brethren" were admitted only in specific categories, none of which was equal to "freeman."[48] Moreover, the price of admission to the guild and to mastership for the "foreign brethren" was about four times that of the native weavers' six-shilling entry fee.[49]

In 1589, to ensure that strangers did not outdo their native brothers in the Weavers' Company, the guild issued ordinances limiting the number of foreign journeymen and looms that a stranger could maintain, and in 1595 the company further limited the number of apprentices that a stranger could keep.[50] These overly restrictive regulations stemmed from a fear that unconditionally welcoming Protestant refugees would lead to economic decline for the English. The existence of immigrant weavers working outside the guild system significantly compromised the longstanding authority of the livery company. The solution was to insist on a degree of economic integration, but it was nowhere near the assimilation as imagined by Dalechamp as part of the strangers' responsibility in the mutual obligations of hospitality. Such was the nature of early modern multiculturalism: it was inclusive but neither pluralistic nor egalitarian; it was global but that globalism was viewed through a narrowly provincial lens.

By the 1590s the wardens and bailiffs of the London Weavers' Company were apparently either not particularly interested in the regulation of immigrant weavers, or they found the task of enforcing ordinances too overwhelming. In 1595 a group of company yeoman produced a long list of strangers who maintained many more looms than allowed.[51] Although these strangers were brought into compliance with company regulations, the problems of enforcement continued, in part because the largely indifferent company leadership had become set on consolidating its power and preventing entry into its upper ranks. The strangers were, after all, involved in profitable practices covertly used among the company's leaders.[52] Joseph P. Ward notes that the company officers benefitted from the surplus of skilled weavers in need of employment, and that these leaders "willingly undermined the livelihoods of English weavers by allowing aliens unfettered participation in the metropolitan economy."[53] Frances Consitt describes the rift between the rank and file of the London Weavers' Company, who were interested in enforcing the traditional rules of the craft, and the company's indifferent leadership as a division between traditional modes of production and an emergent laissez-faire capitalism. "Artisan weavers," writes Consitt, "frequently suffered from capitalist exploitation and from unemployment due to new factors, like sudden fluctuations of the market."[54] The yeomen weavers, when faced with a violation of their vision of a properly functioning local economy, located the individuals thought to be responsible and sought to hold them accountable. Here, the yeomen weavers were trying to bring the newcomers into compliance with guild ordinances including limitations on the ability of individual shop owners to expand production or to deviate too wildly from set prices.

Facing indifference from those whose role it was to enforce the company's regulations, the poorer weavers sought other means to bring strangers into compliance with guild ordinances. In 1595 an allegedly inebriated weaver accosted the Mayor with the complaint and a litany of epithets; a group of apprentice weavers rescued their fellow weaver as he was hauled off to Bedlam, but on 1 June 1595 the ministers of the stranger churches were agitated by a petition from the "Yeomanry of the Company of distressed Weavers." The petition had been printed by Gabriel Symspon in an edition of 40, and was intended for delivery to the ministers and elders of the stranger churches as well as the Mayor and Aldermen.[55]

The fifteen yeoman weavers involved in the petition complained that alien weavers in the churches' congregations exceeded limits on keeping apprentices and looms, failed to maintain the secrets of the craft,[56] sold their products too far below market price, and sold goods made by strangers in Norwich, Canterbury, and Sandwich, again undercutting the local market. In all, the weavers were complaining that the strangers were undermining the London Weavers' Company by flooding the market for goods and labour; Consitt infers that the weavers took these issues to be the cause of one central grievance: low pay for valuable labour.[57] The weavers requested the assistance of the stranger churches: "In regard of all theis wronges long sustaynd," wrote the petitioners, "we thought it good to write theis our Letters unto you, that according as it becometh the Minister and Elders of soe Christian [a] Congregacon, we might intreate you to call those men before you and exhort them to be obedient to good Orders, which are made for a generall benefitt to all men that use this trade."[58] Instead of resorting to informers, the yeoman weavers, recognizing the central role of the church in the immigrant communities, sought the assistance of the strangers' religious leaders in enforcing regulations.

Mihoko Suzuki has described this petition as an example of the characteristically xenophobic activity of Londoners in the 1590s, linking it to the anti-alien May Day riot of 1517.[59] Ward, however, points out that the petition praises the policies of Geneva, Flanders, and France for placing restrictions on the economic activity of English émigrés working there. While Ward acknowledges xenophobia as an element in some of the anti-alien activity that preceded the petition, he rightly asserts that, "only the oddest sort of xenophobes would have praised foreign governments while criticizing the policies of their own."[60] Moreover, the petition lacks many of the stock inflammatory accusations of most anti-alien libels. It does not, for example, question the faith of strangers (as did the several anti-alien texts discussed at the end of chapter 2).[61] The statement, "If you aleadge that Straungers ought to be Cherrished and well intreated, we knowe it," is hardly the kind of comment expected from anyone harbouring anti-alien sentiments. More importantly, the petitioners are emphatically against expulsion: "It is not our intentes," wrote the weavers, "to drive awaye or expell any distressed Straungers out of our land, but to have them live here, that wee might be able to live with them, and that they should live under government and to be obedyent to good orders."[62]

Perhaps this petition has been misunderstood because of its provincial globalism: it seeks inclusion of immigrants but demands that they conform to "good orders," here the guild ordinances. It hopes for inclusion of immigrants but also demands that those included fit into the hierarchy of the local economy. Finally, it is worth noting that rank and file weavers were also exerting pressure on English silk weavers for similar violations. Around this time English silk weaver and button maker Robert Whyte complained of harassment by fellow weavers who accused him of keeping too many apprentices.[63] That is, the petition was part the weavers' overall effort to enforce rules that the guild's officers were failing to enforce.

Despite the flattery and the rather simple request that strangers follow the laws – albeit laws designed to monitor the economic activity of immigrants – the church leaders complained to the Mayor; three of the "distressed Weavers" were promptly arrested along with the printer of the petition, indicating that at least part of the objection had to do with the number of copies that were printed.[64] It was relatively easy for the authorities to locate the three weavers, for they apparently made no secret of their identities: all three – Willington, William Muggins, and Thomas

Deloney – signed the petition.[65] From prison the weavers contacted Sir John Popham, the Lord Chief Justice of England, who sympathized with them, procured their release, and encouraged the Aldermen to intervene in the guild's enforcement of its ordinances.[66]

Jack of Newbury

Many scholars mention Deloney's French background, and many more are intrigued by his involvement in the "Complaint of the Yeomen Weavers," especially as he alludes to the episode in one of his works of prose fiction, *Jack of Newbury*, but no one has tried to resolve or even draw attention to the rather obvious tension between Deloney's purported immigrant background and his role in the petition to the stranger churches. Deloney's connections to the French immigrant community, however weak at the time he signed the petition, may have led him to help ensure the generally respectful tone of the complaint, but had he revealed his immigrant lineage, he would have risked losing his hard-earned status as freeman of the city. For Deloney, the stakes of passing were high indeed, but the decision to complain to the stranger churches seems not to have troubled him. Twelve of the fifteen weavers involved were against the mass printing of the petition, but Deloney was one of the three who supported printing the complaint, supposedly to save time copying the document out multiple times, since the weavers intended to deliver copies to each Elder of the stranger churches, each Alderman, and the Lord Mayor.

Critics generally agree that Deloney alludes to the petition and his subsequent imprisonment in *Jack of Newbury* (1597) – a prose narrative of the life of John Smallwood (aka John Winchombe), a prominent member of the cloth trade – that combines chronicle history, legend, and jest-book material.[67] In *Jack of Newbury* Deloney explains that during Henry VIII's reign – when international relations had apparently so deteriorated trade that cloth was sold at such a low price "that the money scarcely paide for the wooll, and workemanship" – Jack and his fellows of the clothing trade decide to encourage the king to allow merchant strangers to again enter England and to mend trade relations with France so that English merchants could trade there, but then Lord Chancellor Wolsey is offended by Jack, and the lot of them are imprisoned.[68] Just as Deloney, Muggins, and Willington were eventually freed and their petition taken seriously, so these clothiers are eventually released from prison and their petition granted. The chapter ends with a banquet held by the merchant strangers of the Steelyard for the clothiers who had procured the resumption of their commerce.

Rather than the dominance of one group over another, Deloney here depicts the happy interdependence of native clothiers and strangers. It may well be that Deloney and his fellow weavers sought a similar resolution in addressing the Elders of the French and Dutch congregations. Roger Manning describes various disturbances in London in 1595, particularly in June of that year, as "the most dangerous and prolonged urban uprising in England between the accession of the Tudor dynasty and the beginning of the Long Parliament."[69] Rather than go the route of riot or informing, the weavers tried to resolve their conflict through appeals to law and order. While they could not broker an entirely peaceful resolution between natives and strangers in 1595, Deloney was able to depict such a resolution in his historical fiction. Schlossberg has pointed to the sometimes "fundamentally conservative" nature of passing[70] – passing necessarily involves conformity – but here Deloney's unique position as an immigrant in the role of a native silk weaver led him to seek a peaceful resolution to the type of conflict that in the 1590s had resulted in small outbreaks of violence between native craftsmen and immigrants.

Despite the attempt to broker a peaceful resolution between English and alien weavers and, in *Jack of Newbury*, a recasting of that hoped-for resolution as a banquet for native weavers and merchant strangers, several scholars see signs of xenophobia in Deloney's writing. For example, although Eugene P. Wright affirms that Deloney was probably descended from Huguenots, he later states, "the influx of refugees into sixteenth-century England was one of the causes of the social and economic problems central to Deloney's writings. Deloney, who had been jailed for complaining about unfair business practices [of French weavers], was not kindly disposed toward even those foreigners who could speak English fluently."[71] Wright feels no compulsion, apparently, to remind his readers that he believes Deloney's own parents or grandparents were among the refugees he suspects Deloney disliked. Of course, it is entirely possible for descendants of immigrants to so thoroughly reject the culture of their parents and so intensely adopt the dominant host culture that they display a degree of xenophobia (from the host culture's perspective), but this does not seem to be the case for Deloney.

Wright's assessment is based in part on a cursory reading of the "Complaint of the Yeomen Weavers" that is not exactly vitriolic in its stance regarding immigrant weavers, and in part on his reading of an episode in *Jack of Newbury* in which Master Bennedicke, a young Italian merchant, woos

Jone, one of Jack's maidens. Bennedicke, unfortunately enough, "could speak but bad English," so in his flirtations he remains "tonguelesse."[72] When he finally does try to speak, his lack of linguistic competence undermines all the progress he had made silently with Jone; he implores her, for example, to "come to my chamber, beshit my bed, and let me kisse you." After many such malapropisms, Jone laughed at his speech and "wild him not to trouble her anymore."[73] When Ian, Jone's kinsman, says of Bennedicke (Wright erroneously assumes Ian's statement is addressed to Bennedicke), "Mee thinkes he should forbeare to love, or learne to speake, or else woo such as can answer him in his language," word gets back to Bennedicke, who vows revenge on Ian.[74] Bennedicke plans to woo Ian's wife, Gillian, promising her cash and fine silks. Bennedicke is nearly successful but Gillian's conscience gets the better of her; she confesses to her husband who arranges to lure Bennedicke to lie with a hog by telling him that Jone is waiting for him in the dark. The bed trick ends with a confrontation between Bennedicke and Ian who exclaims, "Barkeshire maids will bee no Italians strumpets" as Bennedicke flees in shame.[75] This episode is somewhat similar to the "racialized bed-tricks" analysed by Virginia Mason Vaughan, in which Moors are put in the place of an expected lover, avoiding miscegenation but nonetheless playing with the forbidden desire. Here, however, the tantalizing tryst is the near consummation of Italian merchant and Englishwoman.[76] Both Wright and Suzuki relate this tale to Deloney's supposed xenophobia.

Wright states that "the fact that Benedick is a foreigner is important" and proceeds to relate Bennedicke's status to that of the Protestant refugees he thinks Deloney dislikes.[77] But it is a mistake to think all immigrants would be equal in Deloney's eyes. On the English stage, notes Lara Bovilsky, "Italy represented a nation among whose most famous identity-effects were popery, atheism, sodomy, murder and poison, deceit, 'practice,' erotic obsession and sexual promiscuity, and a preternatural propensity for revenge."[78] Michael Wyatt warns of "how problematic it is to generalize about the Italian 'community'" in England, but Deloney may well have intended Bennedicke to be read in terms of the stereotypes enumerated by Bovilsky: Bennedicke's Catholicism may be implicit, but his inclination to revenge and sexual promiscuity is apparent, and the bed trick renders him a potential sodomite. Deloney's attitude towards Italians may have been shaped by the theatre or it may relate to the decline in Anglo-Italian commerce during the sixteenth century.[79] Thus, we might modify Wright's claim and more accurately say that "the fact that Bennedicke is *Italian* is important."

Bennedicke's malapropisms, moreover, signal his refusal or inability to adapt linguistically to his host country. A commemorative poem from 1600 for Italian merchant Horatio Pallavacino, cited by Michael Wyatt, illustrates the premium placed on immigrant assimilation:

An Englishe man Italianate
Becomes a devill incarnate.
But an Italian Anglyfide
Becomes a Saint Angelifide.[80]

The first two lines are proverbial, expressing anxiety about cultural influence on England.[81] An immigrant who adapts to English ways, however, is supernaturally good, better than merely English. At the same time, this praise is oddly chauvinistic: what makes the hybrid Italian so "saintly" is his validation of Englishness. This odd mix of patriotism and inclusivity exemplifies provincial globalism. Whereas sectarian inclusivity often presented itself as an absolute acceptance of immigrant coreligionists, provincial globalism's concern with conserving local norms meant that inclusion of immigrants came with a number of demands designed to minimize the economic and social impact of immigration.

Between Jone's rejection of Bennedicke and the bestial bed trick, Deloney offers a lengthy description of the Italian merchant pining for Jone: "As a certain spring in Arcadia," writes Deloney, "makes men to starve that drinke it: so did poore Bennedicke, feeding his fancie on her beautie."[82] Bennedicke takes numerous unnecessary trips to be nearer to Jone and laments his inability to communicate in English. True, the malapropisms render Bennedicke laughable, but his plight is not without its pathos. Perhaps Deloney intended the punishment of the forlorn Italian to be a parody the Petrarchan lover in this work that owes more to middle class ballads and popular jest books than to courtly sonnet sequences and prose romance.[83] Moreover, Bennedicke's Petrarchan pose, like his malapropisms, is a sign of his Italian disposition, his resistance to being "Anglyfide." As will be seen, however, Bennedicke is punished not only for his status as a stranger, his inability to communicate well, and even his stance as hyperbolic forlorn lover, but also for his desire to disrupt Ian's family unit.

Similar to Wright, Suzuki reads the ending of this episode – Ian's slogan, "Barkeshire maids will bee no Italians strumpets" – as "a xenophobic and nationalist 'moral' that affirms the constitution of the English nation as the sum of its various parts."[84] There is little reason, however, to connect the regional identity of "Barkeshire maids" to the emergent idea of an

English nation. To do so would involve an examination of other incidents in Deloney's texts in which English women reject strangers because of xenophobia.

In *The Gentle Craft, Part One*, Deloney's first collection of legends about shoemakers, when Simon Eyre rises to the position of Lord Mayor, his journeymen shoemakers, John Denevale, Haunce, and Nicholas, compete to marry Florence, one of the English maid servants in Eyre's household. Florence accepts the courtship of John, a French shoemaker famed for introducing the "low cut shoo with the square toe" to London fashion.[85] The courtship continues until the Dutch Haunce, jealous of the favour Eyre shows to John, arranges to undermine the romance by telling lies about each to the other. Later, Haunce courts Florence, and even after she discovers Haunce's trickery in defaming John, she confesses, "hee is a kind-hearted and as loving a fellow as ever professed love to any." Even as the English Nicholas tries to woo her away, the narrator explains, "Haunce had her heart still."[86] Eventually Florence and Haunce arrange to marry, and it is only through the combined machinations of Nicholas and John that the marriage is prevented; John tries to take Haunce's place in the wedding, but as he speaks to her, his wife, recently immigrated to England and thought deceased, interrupts. Florence surmises that Haunce, as a fellow stranger, may too have a spouse abroad and so resolves to avoid matches with strangers. Eyre intervenes, matching Florence with Nicholas, and subsequently "shewed himselfe a good Master" to not only Nicholas but to Haunce and John as well.[87]

Julia Gasper describes this episode as "distinctly xenophobic" because "it suggests that foreigners are malicious, deceitful, or even bigamous,"[88] but to make such a supposition is to slide down the slippery slope Florence constructs. Haunce is not bigamous as far as we know; John is not intentionally bigamous, unless we guess that he is lying about his belief that his wife has died; and the English suitor Nicholas is involved in just as much dishonesty, deceit, and malice as Haunce and John.[89] If readers observe xenophobic or otherwise flawed views among the characters, it seems likely that Deloney intended us to notice their fallible thinking. That being said, there are a number of stereotypes in the episode: John is unusually choleric and Haunce is easily enticed to drink too much, but if there is "a xenophobic and nationalist 'moral'" here, it is that strangers are sometimes rejected for ungrounded suspicions: Florence accepts John's overtures and only rejects him because she has been told a number of falsehoods about him; she falls in love with Haunce and only rejects him out the fear that he may already be married, though this appears to be nothing but a suspicion.

"Barkeshire maids" may reject strangers, but London maids come rather close to marrying them; note that in *Jack of Newbury* neither Jone nor Gillian reject Bennedicke immediately for his Italianness. Far from being phobic about strangers, the women in Deloney's texts often flirt with strangers or are at least open to them as suitors. Chapter 5 deals specifically with the issue of marriage between English and strangers in city comedies, but for now it is worth noting that such marriages signal both a degree of assimilation among strangers and a kind of cosmopolitanism among the English.

To return to Berkshire, however, both Wright and Suzuki note that Bennedicke's punishment is similar to that of Will Summers, the king's jester, who, in an earlier episode in *Jack of Newbury*, attempts to woo Jack's maids with a promise of money, much as Bennedicke does with Gillian. Like Bennedicke, Will Summers's punishment is spending time with hogs; in this instance he is forced to feed and then eat with them.[90] The similarity should have drawn both critics to conclude that the two punishments are related to similar transgressions – attempts at treating the working women of Jack's household like prostitutes, trading, as Will Summers puts it, "everye kisse at a farthing."[91] The punishments may be rendered comic by the quips of the court jester and the malapropisms of the Italian merchant, but they are, like the "Complaint of the Yeomen Weavers," more closely aligned with the enforcement of traditional values, with ensuring that outsiders abide by the standards of the local community. These two shaming rituals – Deloney's skimmingtons – are instigated for and in part by women in defence of the standards of the local community and they mark a provincial threshold on global influence, whether the outsider hails from the continent or the court.

The provincial nature of Deloney's *Jack of Newbury* is tempered by the episode that directly precedes it, in which, as noted above, native weavers and merchant strangers celebrate their reunion. It may be that Deloney juxtaposed the two episodes to depict the tension between an expanding economy, embodied in the merchant strangers, and dangers to the maintenance of local custom, represented by Bennedicke's intrusion on the family unit, a tension, that is, between individual greed and communal standards. As if to further the point, in the next episode a local gossip convinces Jack's wife to amass more spending money by decreasing the quality of food for Jack's employees.[92] As with the previous episodes, attempts to exploit those who work for Jack – threats to the delicate balance of the reciprocal obligations of Newbury – leads to public humiliation: the servants intoxicate the gossip and cart her around town.[93] Will Summers tries to trade farthings for kisses; Bennedicke tries to lure Gillian to bed with a promise of cash and fine clothing; the gossip attempts to upset household custom by cheapening servants' food so her host can save twenty pounds a year. All three are humiliated because they presume to disrupt local practices: they see social relations in terms of money rather than in terms of the reciprocal obligations that make up the society of Berkshire, and specifically Jack's household. The status of Italian, or jester, or gossip marks these characters as potential threats to the local, patriarchal community, but they are punished not for their status but rather for their disruptive acts. Critics who see Deloney as an advocate for a rising middle class should note the moments in which Deloney seems to argue against maximizing profits. In all three episodes, commodification is punished with a shaming ritual.

This emphasis on the maintenance of local communal standards, rather than a self-other paradigm that edifies a national consciousness, seems to account for at least part of the England Deloney depicts in his writing. Note, however, that in *The Gentle Craft*, although Haunce and John do not win Florence's hand, both men remain integral parts of the local community, and that the community, while narrowly defining proper conduct so as to ensure a particular hierarchy, is inclusive of people who hail from beyond the realm. I agree, in part, with Hentschell who, following Helgerson, describes Deloney as constructing a "narrative of 'inclusion,' which 'works to broaden the national community.'"[94] Where I differ is in the emphasis on the "national," because the communities Deloney tends to portray are often inclusive of strangers: Richard Casteler in *The Gentle Craft, Part Two* (1598), marries a Dutch woman, Haunce and John continue to work happily in Eyre's shop, and merchant strangers feast with weavers; in the "Complaint of the Yeomen Weavers" the immigrant weavers are implored to integrate themselves into rather than leave the realm. If this is a nation, it is one whose borders are imagined as extremely porous. At the same time an English jester, an English gossip, and an Italian merchant are lumped together as intrusive or marginal to the imagined community.

Strange Histories

To examine Deloney's conception of England and Englishness further, we can look to Deloney's ballads, especially those that recount major events in English history. Although, as Mann points out, many of these ballads are simply versifications of Holinshed's *Chronicles*, Deloney's choice of which events to recount and his occasional deviations from his sources reiterate what is already apparent in his prose fiction: an England that is both provincial in its varied local communities and global in its inclusiveness. But these ballads also reveal another element in Deloney's vision of England: the centrality of exile in English history. The earliest extant edition of Deloney's second collection of ballads, *Strange Histories,* covers English history from the Norman invasion to the accession of Queen Elizabeth, drawing heavily on Holinshed with some passages taken from Foxe's *Acts and Monuments.* The earliest known edition of this collection was printed in 1602, although an earlier edition almost certainly existed. Unlike Deloney's first ballad collection, which brought together many previously published broadsides, the ballads of *Strange Histories* appear to have been written specifically for the collection.[95]

To a certain extent, *Strange Histories* reinforces the importance of communal rights and privileges already seen in the "Complaint of the Yeomen Weavers" and the punishments of Will Summers, Bennedicke, and the gossip, but there is additional emphasis on a multicultural ethic of inclusivity. The collection begins and ends with rebellions of the commons. The first poem deals with "The valiant courage and policie of the Kentishmen." When William the Conqueror takes over England, the Kentish commons cry,

> Let us not live like bondmen poore,
> to Frenchmen in their pride
> But keepe our ancient liberties,
> what chance so ear betide.
> And rather die in bloudie field
> in manlike courage prest:
> Then to endure the seruile yoake,
> which we so much detest. (33–40)[96]

Here, as with the "Complaint of the Yeomen Weavers," the emphasis is on "ancient liberties," English common law, and a sense of communal standards against changes that might be introduced from outside of England. Unlike the "Complaint," however, the French are here portrayed as particularly prideful rather than as coreligionists. When William the Conqueror is confronted by the armed commoners, he bargains,

> you shall have what you will:
> Your ancient customes and your lawes,
> so that you will be still:
> And each thing else that you will crave,

with reason at my hand,
So you will but acknowledge me,
chiefe King of faire England. (90–6)

The Kentish commoners agree, and so "those customes do remaine" (102), a kind of prequel to the Magna Carta and England's mixed government. As with the "Complaint," the issue is not foreignness per se – the rebels agree to recognize William as "King of faire England" – but the fear that the newcomers will ignore and thus erode customs and traditional rights. This is precisely the concern Deloney and his fellow weavers had with immigrant weavers infringing on the authority of their guild, a concern also manifested in *Jack of Newbury* when Will Summers, ignoring local standards of courtship, tries to purchase favours from the maids of Jack's household.

The final ballad of *Strange Histories*, "The rebellion of Wat Tyler and Iacke Straw," recounts the Peasant Revolt of 1381. This ballad expresses a measured sympathy with the cause of the rebellion, the imposition of the poll tax, and describes the rebels as "many a proper man" (2). When the king refuses to meet with the rebels, however, they wreak havoc on London. Deloney explains that the king pardons the rebels but "they his pardon did defie" (70) and continued their violence. Unlike their Kentish predecessors, these rebels exhibit little restraint. The king agrees to meet with them, and sends Sir John Newton to speak with Wat Tyler, "But the proud Rebel ... did picke a quarrel with the knight" (79–80). The Mayor of London intervenes, "arrests" Tyler, and kills him on the spot. "Thus," writes Deloney, "did that proud Rebellion cease, / and after followed a ioyfull peace" (94). Unlike the Kentish men, Wat Tyler, interestingly associated here with the pride of the invading French of the first ballad, refuses to recognize the king's authority, ignoring his pardon and attacking his messenger. For Deloney, doing away with a new tax is one thing; denying the authority of the king is quite another. The contrast in the portrayals of popular resistance in the first and last ballads of the collection suggests that Deloney advocates rebellion only for the purpose of maintaining the system rather than as a means for overthrowing it. This political position is reflected in "Complaint of the Yeomen Weavers" with its appeal to order rather than riot to achieve the goals of the artisans.

This reading of *Strange Histories* focuses on Deloney's selection of episodes from Holinshed, on how this choice – contrasting two rebellions – functions to insist on the importance of the rights of commoners while simultaneously asserting the ultimate authority of the monarch to keep order. The meaning of the rebellions emerges not from Deloney's treatment of them, for he does little but versify the accounts he found in Holinshed, but rather from his decision to begin and end the collection with these specific rebellions. More telling, perhaps, are the episodes from Holinshed and Foxe that Deloney altered to suit his purpose.

The ballad that most deviates from its sources is "The Dutchess of Suffolkes Calamatie," which begins by describing the persecution of Protestants during Queen Mary's reign, when "Smithfield was then with Faggots fyld" (13), laying special emphasis on the martyrdom of John Hooper, "good Hooper" (16), a close ally of the stranger churches. Deloney also pairs the martyrdom of Nicholas Ridley, Bishop of London, with that of Thomas Cranmer, the most instrumental of the stranger churches' allies.[97] Far from creating a versified *Acts and Monuments,* Deloney devotes the rest of the ballad to the Duchess of Suffolk, who "for the love of Christ alone / Her Land and Goods she left behind" (31-2). The Duchess and her family, along with their nurse, escape Mary's England and seek refuge in Flanders, where the exiles are robbed and beaten by a band of thieves. In the confusion, the nurse flees, and the Duchess, her husband, and their child find themselves "far from friends" and "succourless in a straunge land" (71-2). The travel begins to take its toll on the child and the Duchess turns to begging in the streets, but the language barrier prevents her from adequately relating her desperation and she receives no lodging for her family. Her husband then gets into a fight with a sexton who tries to drive the destitute family from the front of a church where they had sought shelter from the rain. The family is arrested and brought to court, where the Duchess is eventually recognized by a clergyman who had been to England. The clergyman advocates on her behalf and she and her family are given shelter by the governor of the town. After Mary's death the Duchess returns to England and her daughter is made Countess of Kent.

Unlike many of Deloney's historical ballads, this poem deviates substantially from print sources. Neither Foxe nor Holinshed mentions a nurse who abandons the family, though Foxe does list other servants brought on the voyage. In Foxe and Holinshed, the family is attacked by a captain who had a gripe with the Duke and at no time is the family driven to begging. In Foxe, the Duke finds people who speak Latin but in Deloney's version language barriers isolate the family until the court scene; in Foxe a number of powerful figures come to the family's aid throughout their period of exile. Teresa Watt points out that Deloney invents the role of the abusive sexton.[98] Whereas Mann disparages these deviations from the sources as based on "some garbled traditional version,"[99] it seems more likely that these changes were part of Deloney's design. The ballad consistently downplays Catherine Brandon's elevated social position, powerful connections, wealth, and linguistic capabilities. In place of these, Deloney emphasizes the family's anonymity, poverty, and linguistic isolation, thus making the unique story of the Duchess's flight resemble the flight of many religious refugees in the sixteenth century.

For example, Janus Gruter's English mother, who emigrated from Antwerp to Norwich with her Dutch husband and their child, writes of her family's many difficulties along the way: knowing no one, having no viable trade, losing their savings to an unreliable merchant, and so forth.[100] Dutch reformer Adrian van Haemstede describes similar hardships in his flight to England: the ship he travelled on nearly capsized, and when he arrived in England he and his fellow refugees were beaten and robbed.[101] Although "The Dutchess of Suffolkes Calamatie" describes an English family's exile to the continent, their trials and tribulations – flight, poverty, language barriers, and vulnerability to thieves or con artists – are apparently typical for refugees of the time; in downplaying the Duchess's unique status as a person of considerable importance in England, Deloney transforms her into a typical Protestant refugee, a heroic figure who risks everything and faces extraordinary hardships in the name of her faith. Her fortune is changed not by her court connections, but by her relationship with a Protestant minister who had been in England during the reign of Edward: for Deloney, pan-Protestant alliances can bridge the language and culture gap and save the protagonists. Such sensitivity to the refugee's plight recalls Deloney's insistence in the "Complaint of the Yeomen Weavers" "that Straungers ought to be Cherrished and well intreated," and his inclusion of relatively benign Dutch and French strangers in *The Gentle Craft*. There can be no mistaking that the story of the Duchess of Suffolk, as told by Deloney, was not unlike many stories he would have heard in his youth about his own ancestors and their countrymen coming across the channel to England. The similarities between the English men and women who, under Mary, travelled to the continent and the refugees from the continent who immigrated to an England under Elizabeth could not have been overlooked by either Deloney or his readers. Deloney Anglicizes the immigrant experience, putting, as it were, the immigrant in English clothing as a way of facilitating his readers' sympathies.

The ballads that make up *Strange Histories,* though varied, offer a fairly specific vision of England that is congruent with elements in Deloney's prose fiction. One might expect a collection of English ballads derived primarily from English chronicles to play a role in the construction of

Englishness, to present a fairly nationalist view of England. Instead the collection begins with a tale of inclusion on the part of the Kentish men followed by the Duchess of Suffolk's immigrant experience, in which her Protestant identity allows her acceptance in a foreign land; Deloney's consistent return to moments of exile and inclusion in English history renders exile a key element in his vision of Englishness. The immigration of Dutch and French Protestants appears to be part of a general pattern in English history, a pattern that, as the opening ballad suggests, need not disrupt local expectations and longstanding rights.

Throughout Deloney's writing, one can find stories of exile alongside accounts of traditional customs under attack. That these two themes emerge and at times are in tension with one another texts is no coincidence; these themes are Deloney's way of negotiating his unique experience of England's provincial globalism. Raised in England, among others of the artisan class, he was deeply rooted in provincial life and focused on his guild and parish; this focus manifests itself in his advocacy for the traditional rights of local communities against the disruptions of outsiders, whether they be French weavers, Italian suitors, English jesters, or even William the Conqueror. Deloney might render laughable outsiders who were thought to threaten social norms, but the same time, because his parents or perhaps grandparents had come to England as refugees, his writing reveals a profound appreciation for the global ethic of hospitality that is a paradoxical part of early modern English provincialism. For Deloney, the ethic of inclusion is important to not only economic well-being but also pan-Protestant alliance; he places a high value on those who, when faced with persecution, chose piety over allegiance to the state. When writing from the vantage of a local community, Deloney can make a joke of linguistic difference, but when engaged in a more global perspective he movingly describes the desperation of refugees facing linguistic isolation and hostility from locals.

Deloney revises stories of exile to render the refugee experience English, and even an essential feature of English history. When a conflict arose between native and immigrant weavers, Deloney sided with the English but he tried to navigate a middle road that avoided conflict and praised the piety of the Dutch and French refugees. In *The Gentle Craft* he managed a happy ending not only for Nicholas but for John and Haunce as well. Overall, Deloney tends to identify more strongly with England and the English customs he had found beneficial to his socio-economic class: he not only sided with the English weavers in their conflict with immigrants, but also tended to depict as heroic those who championed the cause of traditional rights so long as they did not deny the authority of the monarch: the Kentish rebels, Jack of Newbury, Ian all stand out as champions of the provincial. At the same time, refugees such as the Duchess of Suffolk are also treated as heroic, and Deloney seems especially intent on revealing to his readers that the Dutch Haunce and French John lived well despite losing Florence to Nicholas. Here then, we see Deloney negotiating between the provincial and the global, vacillating at times between English and immigrant, but usually trying to find a way of depicting in his fiction a peaceful coexistence, a banquet rather than a riot between English and stranger.

Chapter Four

Language and Labour in Thomas Dekker's Provincial Globalism

As an introduction to his discussion of canting in *Lanthorne and Candle-light* (1608) Thomas Dekker retells the story of the Tower of Babel. The relationship between cant (the supposed language of London's underworld) and the Biblical tale of linguistic diversity seems clear enough, but along the way Dekker digresses in a way that sheds light on his most well-known work, *The Shoemaker's Holiday* (1599), and its relationship to promoting a version of hospitality at once both provincial and global.[1]

Although Dekker follows Flavius Josephus in framing Nimrod as the hubristic sinner of the tale, Dekker's version has a decidedly artisanal focus.[2] Rather than using traditional images of God as a monarch, Dekker works with the hierarchy of the livery companies, referring to God as "the Master workman of this great universe"; Nimrod is a "saucy builder," and the spirit Confusion sent to prevent the completion of the tower is "the surveyor of those works."[3] Moreover, Dekker devotes considerable space to the plight of the workers at the loss of their mono-linguistic world. Described as a "strange linguist," the multi-tongued Confusion imparts different languages to different workers so as to interfere with their progress on the tower. When one labourer thinks he is being mocked by another, chaos ensues "so that the mason was ready to strike the bricklayer, the bricklayer to beat out the brains of his labourer" and so forth.[4] Dekker dwells on the way the existence of different languages – the primary marker of difference for early modern immigrants – creates animosity among labourers who would otherwise achieve great things together. Instead, "the workmen made holiday" and went their separate ways, joining anyone who spoke the same language. "And in this manner," writes Dekker, "did men at the first make up nations."[5]

This episode leads directly to the other important digression in Dekker's rendering of the Tower of Babel, his reflections on language before and after Babel. Dekker's vision of the world before its linguistic fall is nothing short of utopian. Conspiracies could not exist, and "A man could travel in those days neither by sea nor land but he met his countrymen and none others."[6] Dekker imagines a world without strangers, in which people could migrate without losing status or rights. This is a considerable expansion of the Biblical story, which simply states that "Then the whole earth was of one language and one speache."[7] After offering praise for the achievements of the various languages that resulted from the linguistic fall ("the rich and lofty Castilian" or "the sweet and amorous Tuscan"), Dekker laments the poverty of early English. According to Dekker, English "was but a broken language" that "dealt in nothing but monosyllables" and so "her eloquence was poorest, yet hardest to learn, and so, but for the necessity, not regarded amongst strangers."[8] Dekker explains that English was ultimately enriched by its global connections: over time "those noblest languages lent her words and phrases, and turning those borrowings into good husbandry, she is now as rich in elocution and as abundant as her proudest and best-stored neighbors."[9] English itself, argues Dekker, is a multicultural project.

Edmund Spenser famously asked Gabriel Harvey, "For why a God's name may not we, as else the Greekes, have the kingdome of our own Language?" This question in turn leads Helgerson to reflect on the way Elizabethan writers engage in a nationalist project around language.[10] Dekker's answer to Spenser's question is that England has a "kingdom of our own language," but the "our" is not exclusionist and national, but rather inclusive and multicultural. For Dekker, English, and by extension England, is not great in and of itself. It is English's interaction with and incorporation of other languages and peoples that accounts for its grandeur. In *Lanthorne and Candle-light* the opening focus on the centrality of labour and the value of cross-cultural connections presents another version of provincial globalism; an assertion of England's greatness coupled with an awareness that that greatness is founded on the collaboration with and influence of strangers.[11] The local is valued because of its interconnectedness with the global.

Like Deloney, Thomas Dekker was more than likely the son or grandson of immigrants to England. The name Decker seems common enough in England, but Thomas Dekker consistently spelled his surname with a double-*k* characteristic of the Dutch, and he appears to have had an intimate knowledge of Dutch language and literature, exemplified by the stage-Dutch he deployed in plays such as *Northward Ho!* and *The*

Shoemaker's Holiday, and in his use of untranslated Dutch and German sources.[12] Dekker's knowledge of nautical and military jargon has led some critics to suppose that he, like Ben Jonson, spent some time fighting in the Netherlands.[13] This latter theory is sometimes proposed as an alternate explanation for his knowledge of Dutch, but it seems just as likely that both his knowledge of Dutch and his commitment to the Protestant cause in the Netherlands are related to a Dutch heritage. He was raised, suggests Julia Gasper, by Dutch Protestants who fled to England in the 1560s, around the same time as the artists Martin Droeshout and Gheerart Janssen.[14] Whether or not Gasper is correct, it seems clear that Dekker had a reasonably strong connection to immigrants in England and specifically to London's Dutch community.

"The Prologue at Court"

The court performance of Dekker's *Old Fortunatus* given in 1599 featured a prologue and an epilogue in which two men, one English and one a stranger later revealed to be from Cyprus, make a pilgrimage to "the temple of Eliza" ("Prologue at Court," 1).[15] The play, a loose adaptation of a German legend, involves travel to Cyprus and Turkey, but much of the action happens in England.[16] The presentation of an amiable relationship between an Englishman and a stranger who describes himself and his fellows as "poore" (61) serves as a foil to the main plot in which two strangers die in the stocks because two English courtiers envy their magic purse. The English pilgrim of "The Prologue at Court" offers Elizabeth his "upright heart," while the stranger brings "That which all straungers doe: two eyes struck blind with admiration: Two lips (proud to sound her glorie:) Two hands held up full of prayers and praises" (12–16). In addition to expressing high praise, the stranger has brought with him "Old Fortunatus and his family" to entertain the queen (70). While the stranger may simply be thought to be passing through, not actually settling in England, the encomium to and entertainment of the monarch reflects well on strangers in general. Indeed, in the prologue the stranger has the longest and most flattering speeches to the queen (more than twice as many lines as the Englishman). After the stranger makes his offering to Elizabeth, the English pilgrim says to the stranger: "Now ile beg for thee too: and yet I need not: / Her sacred hand hath evermore been knowne, / As soone held out to straungers as to her owne" (57–9).

The English traveller offers to help the stranger, modelling a kind of solidarity apparently founded on their shared admiration for the monarch, though implicitly religion provides the immediate connection, even as Elizabeth herself is framed as the religious object: the travellers are "pilgrims," the court a "temple," Elizabeth's hand a "sacred hand." More importantly, Dekker's prologue praises Elizabeth's even-handed treatment of stranger and English alike.

The Whore of Babylon

In *The Whore of Babylon* (1605) this emphasis on a state policy of hospitality to strangers is amplified. Written in the wake of the Gunpowder Plot, the play features Titania, the queen of fairies (an allusion to the deceased Queen Elizabeth via Spenser's *Faerie Queene*), imagining a glorious future for her realm:

> The flowers we set, and the fruits by us sowne,
> Shall cheere as well the stranger as our owne.
> We may to strange shores once our selves be driven,
> For who can tell under what point of heaven
> His grave shall open? (1.2.56–60)[17]

Titania voices a familiar argument about hospitality: one must not only tolerate but welcome strangers because one might find oneself in a similar situation, in exile relying on the hospitality of others. Later in the play, the anticipated strangers arrive. Fideli announces to Titania,

> Neighbors, 'tis the nation
> With whom our Fairies interchange commerce,
> And by negotiation grown so like us
> That half of them are Fairies. (2.1.275–8)

The nation in question is the Netherlands, as the allegory makes clear, and the passage links the commerce between England and the Netherlands to their shared religion, here represented by their shared status as "fairies." The half of the Netherlands who are not "fairies" represent the Catholic faction. Titania welcomes the Dutch refugees: "In misery all nations should be kin / And lend a brother's hand. Usher them in" (2.1.300–1).

Here Dekker evokes the central tenet of sectarian inclusivity explored in chapter 2. Gasper describes *The Whore of Babylon* as "the definitive militant Protestant play," and indeed much of the allegorical plot presents an ideal of English intervention on behalf of the Netherlands, but Anglo-Dutch relations also involved hosting refugees in England, and Dekker can be seen to consistently represent such immigration in a positive light.[18]

"The Pageant of the Dutch-men"

Dekker's and Jonson's *The Magnificent Entertainment* celebrates the coronation of James I while, among other things, advocating for a stronger Anglo-Dutch alliance.[19] While it is not known which parts of the pageantry sequence can be attributed to which author in the collaborative effort, it is generally presumed that Dekker was very much involved in "The Pageant of the Dutch-men." Religion and kingship are predictably intertwined in this pageant, which includes Divine Providence pointing to heaven, a reference to James as Solomon, and a speech emphasizing the divine right of kings and the power of religion to bring about peace, quell rebellions, and maintain justice (530–40; 517–18; 625–705). The pageant's sermon renders the goal of the performance clear:

> Wee (the Belgians) likewise come, to that intent: a Nation banisht from our owne Cradles, yet nourced and brought up in the tender bosome of Princely Mother ELIZA. The Love, which wee once dedicated to her (as a Mother) doubly doe wee vow it to you, our Soveraigne, and Father, intreating wee may be sheltred under your winges now, as then under hers. (693–8)

Like several prior coronation pageants, the main point of the Dutch pageant was to secure the privileges afforded to strangers in London.[20] Along the way, however, Dekker focuses spectators' attention on Dutch contributions to England's economy. Marjorie Rubright has shown that the Dutch pageant in particular deconstructs distinctions of Dutch and English by placing its arch near the Royal Exchange, reminding spectators that the Exchange was a "copy" of Antwerp's *Nieuwe Beurs*.[21] As with *The Whore of Babylon*'s claim that the Dutch are "grown so like us," solidarity leads to a sense of community that blurs differences. One of the images in the middle of the arch – a Dutch fisherman singing – bore the following message:

> Quod celebret hoc emporium prudenti industria suos,
> Quovis terrarum negotiatores emittat, exteros
> Humaniter admittat, foris famam, domi divitias augeat. (599–601)

[This market, celebrating its people for their prudent industry, sends its merchants throughout the world, and humanely admits strangers here so that it may increase fame abroad and wealth at home.]

Along the top was an image showing "Marchants there being so lively, that bargaines seeme to come from their lippes" (575–8); nearby there was a placard imploring James to keep the ports open to merchants. Another image on the arch pictured "men, women and children (in Dutch habits) are busie at other workes: the men Weaving, the women Spinning, the children at their Hand-loomes &c." Still another showed "the Dutch countrey people, toyling at their Husbandrie: women carding their Hemp, the men beating it" (584–7, 570–1). Instead of a focus on religious affinities, which, as shown in previous chapters, were sometimes called into question, in lobbying for continued favour in England, the Dutch here emphasized their industriousness and their economic contribution to the realm.

Again and again Dekker used his role as a prominent London writer to lobby on behalf of strangers by emphasizing not only shared religion but also the value of labour and commerce as a point of common ground and solidarity, a point that could overcome resistance to linguistic or cultural diversity. Because labour was regulated locally through guilds, Dekker's particular form of multiculturalism quickly becomes a form of provincial globalism whereby the stranger is inducted into English institutions. The association of the local to the global is reiterated in several of Dekker's texts. In *The Magnificent Entertainment*, for example, the specific locale of the Royal Exchange conjures images of merchants abroad. In *The Whore of Babylon* an image of immigrants enjoying the fruits of England readily turns to images of English people living in exile on the continent. For Dekker, local sites naturally connect outward to the global and vice versa.

The Shoemaker's Holiday

Dekker's most popular play, *The Shoemaker's Holiday*, deals directly with his particular type of provincial globalism. Although Julia Gasper is right in seeing the play as motivated by England's relations with the Netherlands and developments on the continent (the backdrop of the play is a war in France and tensions over Anglo-Dutch trade), *The Shoemaker's Holiday* also relates pan-Protestantism to urban economic issues and follows the pattern of global and local sketched above.[22] Despite the political and commercial world without, Dekker focuses on the provincial: specific buildings, streets, and neighbourhoods in London.

A journeyman shoemaker is pressed to be a soldier in France and returns a disabled veteran, but the details of the war remain vague and the play focuses on the way England's global interactions affect the lives of people in London. The action takes place in a shoemaker's shop and on the streets of London. One of the main plots is Simon Eyre's self-fashioning transformation from a waggish master shoemaker to a populist Lord Mayor. But Dekker's provincialism, whether in *Lanthorne and Candle-light* or in this much earlier work, is always informed by his awareness of London's cultural diversity, represented not only by its merchant strangers but also the alien artisans living, working, and worshipping in London. In addition to a Dutch skipper, the main romantic plot of *The Shoemaker's Holiday* involves Hugh Lacy, a spendthrift gentleman who convincingly disguises himself as a Dutch shoemaker. That is, this play, like *The Magnificent Entertainment*, *The Whore of Babylon*, and other of Dekker's works, is acutely concerned with imagining what it means to be a multicultural realm, to participate in a global market, to be the host or the guest in England. In particular, the play focuses on what immigration means for artisans like those Dekker describes as forced to make "holiday" at the fall of Babel. Although *The Shoemaker's Holiday* deals specifically with strangers in London, its perspective on immigration is of a piece with *The Whore of Babylon*, *Old Fortunatus*, and *The Magnificent Entertainment*, all of which speak to immigration policy in England more broadly.

Loosely based on Deloney's *The Gentle Craft*, *The Shoemaker's Holiday* combines the story of Simon Eyre's rise to Lord Mayor of London with the tale of Sir Rowland Lacy's courtship of Rose, the daughter of Roger Oatley (Eyre's predecessor as mayor).[23] Both Oatley and Lacy's uncle, Hugh Lacy, earl of Lincoln, disapprove of the match on financial grounds. Lincoln offers the backstory during his conversation with Oatley: he explains that he had furnished his nephew with money, servants, and contacts on the continent, but Lacy spent all the money before he was halfway through Germany, and now broke, has become a shoemaker in Wittenberg. Despite his dislike of Lacy as a match for Rose, Oatley surmises from this that "yet your cosen Rowland might do well / Now he hath learn'd an occupation" (1.1.42–3). Although Oatley is not an especially sympathetic character – like Lincoln, he stands in the way of the young lovers – he does seem to announce an important theme: the rehabilitative nature of work. In addition, it is worth noting that Lacy's spending habits prevent him from going to Catholic Italy and instead strand him in Wittenberg, the birthplace of the Reformation. As anachronistic as it may seem (the historical Eyre was actually a fifteenth-century draper),

Protestantism and the reformative power of labour are linked in Lacy's role as an immigrant to Wittenberg: it is for this reason that, to circumvent Lincoln and Oatley, Lacy again takes on the role of artisan immigrant. Dekker uses Lacy's disguise as the Dutch Hans Meulter to pose his particular argument about provincial globalism: the paradoxical invitation to cosmopolitanism and the simultaneous demand that local mores be respected.

Written amid the economic tensions described in chapter 3, *The Shoemaker's Holiday* draws on Deloney's material to focus more intensely on artisanal solidarity. Pettegree notes that domestic troubles in England resulted in further attempts to limit the rights of immigrants in England, but when Hans Meulter (Lacy disguised as a Dutch shoemaker) is spotted by Firk, Master Simon Eyre's journeyman shoemaker, Firk declares, "hire him, good master, that I may learne some gibble-gabble" (1.4.44–5).[24] Although "Gibble-gabble" is a derogatory referral to a foreign language (and Firk does have fun at the expense of the Dutch language), linguistic difference is at least one factor that leads Firk to encourage his master to hire Hans. Moreover, Firk's line about learning Dutch anticipates the argument in *Lanthorne and Candle-light* that English is strengthened through its adoption of foreign words. At times Firk tries to repeat Hans's Dutch to comic effect, but the joke is as much about Firk's effort to quickly master a difficult language as it is about the sound of Dutch itself (1.4.81–6). As Marianne Montgomery notes, while Dutch might separate Hans from English shoemakers, the language of shoemaking bridges that gap.[25] Firk's fellow journeyman shoemaker poses a more serious argument in Hans's favour: "Fore God a proper man, and I warrant a fine workman: maister, farewell, dame, adew, if such a man as he cannot find worke, Hodge is not for you" (1.4.54–6). Hodge not only recommends Hans but threatens to quit should his master pass up the opportunity to hire the Dutch craftsman.

Andrew Fleck argues that *The Shoemaker's Holiday* mocks Dutch artisans, but if Firk's sincerity is in question, we need look no further than his later interaction with Lincoln and Oatley.[26] When asked to reveal the whereabouts of Hans, who is eloping with Rose, Firk declares that he knows where his co-worker is but cannot betray him, even when offered payment for the information: "No point: shal I betray my brother? No, shal I prove Judas to Hans? No, shall I crie treason to my corporation? No, I shall be firkt and yerkt then, but give me your angell, your angell shall tel you" (4.4.96–9). After receiving payment Firk does not, however, give the Mayor and the Earl correct information, but instead purposely misleads the two in order to protect Hans; remember also that while the audience knows Hans is an Englishman, Firk and his fellow shoemakers still believe him to be a Dutch shoemaker.

For all his madcap antics, Firk here makes a powerful political statement that should give pause to those who easily accept notions of pervasive English xenophobia in the service of English nationhood. As his use of the term "brother" and his reference to his "corporation" suggest, Firk places guild identity above that of birthplace, status, or language. He defies the authority of the city, represented by the Mayor, and the gentry, symbolized by the Earl of Lincoln, in favour of guild solidarity. Firk may have developed a friendship with Hans, but his argument for protecting him is based on the fact that he and Hans are both shoemakers, members of the Company of Cordwainers. As early as 1528 so many strangers had come to England to work as cordwainers that Henry VIII's administration sought to reduce their numbers.[27] By the 1590s the number had certainly grown, but rather than inspire greater competition and animosity, Firk argues for greater integration. Moments like these have led several critics to read *The Shoemaker's Holiday* as arguing against xenophobia: Peter M. McCluskey, for instance, sees a vacillation between pro-and anti-alien sentiment; Gasper reads the play as "replacing xenophobia with Protestant fraternity"; and Joseph P. Ward sees the play alongside other documents as displaying "limits to the popularity of xenophobia among London's artisans."[28]

Because the play questions xenophobia, David Scott Kastan reads *The Shoemaker's Holiday* as a conspicuous "fantasy of social cohesion and respect,"[29] a holiday from reality for sale in the marketplace of the theatre. "Social cohesion" is not evident, however, when the shoemakers confront Hammon, the Earl of Lincoln, and Mayor Oatley. Rafe's war wounds refuse aestheticization, and in the end, the newly married Lacy may find himself in the same unfortunate predicament as Rafe was at the beginning of the play – off to war. What is crucial to note is that Firk places great importance on his identity as a shoemaker, an identity much narrower than the nation yet inclusive of people from beyond its borders. The play works through tensions around immigration to imagine a community founded on local guild rather than national identity. In that sense, *The Shoemaker's Holiday* shares with Deloney's writings a recognition of London's global connections and an attempt to fit them into a local framework of institutions and reciprocal relations.

The play's provincial globalism is not limited to Firk's defence of his Dutch co-worker. Simon Eyre's rise to fame and power is made possible through his Dutch connection, Hans, and, as Christian Billing notes,

Dekker altered his source so that the Dutch are the single most important factor in Eyre's success.[30] In Deloney's *The Gentle Craft,* Eyre's French journeyman tells him of an opportunity to buy goods from a Greek merchant whose ship has sprung a leak.[31] In Dekker's hands, Lacy, disguised as the Dutch journeyman Hans, becomes acquainted with the Dutch skipper who is dealing on behalf of a Dutch merchant who "dares not shew his head" (2.3.14). The pressure on the merchant is not a leaking ship but probably an anachronistic fear of violating Queen Elizabeth's 1598 expulsion of Hanse merchants from the realm.[32] The Hanse merchants had occupied London's Steelyard since 1474 and retained special trade privileges in England, but throughout the sixteenth century English merchants worked with the state to reduce the competitive edge the Hanse merchants had in England.[33] By the 1590s the English merchants had become so prominent that they were competing with the Hanseatic cloth trade in German towns. Thus the Hanseatic League arranged for the expulsion of the English merchants, and Elizabeth was compelled to respond in kind.[34]

Indeed, when *The Shoemaker's Holiday* was performed for Queen Elizabeth, Dekker wrote a special prologue in which the speaker compares the actors to dejected sailors who have sunk "into the bottom of disgrace" through "mistrust and feare." Thus, the speaker explains, "On bended knees our sailes of hope do strike, / Dreading the bitter stormes of your dislike" (1–9). Since the speaker compares himself to a sailor, this prologue may have been spoken by the actor who also played the Dutch skipper, but in any case, the prologue serves to amplify the plight of merchant strangers as a context for the play.[35]

Insofar as Eyre's rise is to be admired, the allusion to the closing of the Steelyard may function as a subtle critique of the extreme measures each state had taken against merchants, a plea for resumption of negotiations to reinstitute trade.[36] In *The Shoemaker's Holiday* England profits from Eyre's dealings with the Dutch; such details argue that immigrants are a great benefit to the realm because they prove advantageous in England's inevitable economic interdependence with other nations.

The deal with the Dutch skipper and the Dutch merchant would not be possible without the participation of Eyre and Lacy in the gentle craft of the stage, the medium through which Dekker imagines his provincially global community. For the deal to go through, Eyre and Lacy must play the parts of alderman and Dutch immigrant respectively.[37] The actors – a gentleman and a citizen – play the parts of an alien artisan and a city authority so that Eyre can enrich himself and become sheriff and eventually Lord Mayor, promotions which, because of Eyre's magnanimity, benefit all of London. In this metatheatrical moment the theatre is seen as a model for London in general, a model that is not disruptive but beneficial to artisans and authorities alike, and is inclusive rather than xenophobic.

Hans is not an outsider but an integral part of London's economy. The profits made in the deal are predicated on Eyre's and Lacy's theatrical practice and their acceptance of the Dutch. Of course, the acceptance of Hans is predicated on the fact that the audience knows that he is English, but for the characters on the stage he is Dutch; to some extent the figure of Hans Meulter suggests the constructed nature of his stage-Dutch antecedents such as Hance Beerpot.[38] Whereas Eyre and Lacy play roles that make them the heroes of their respective plots, the least sympathetic characters of *The Shoemakers' Holiday* – Hammon, Lincoln, and Oatley – grossly misunderstand theatrical practice. Both Lacy and Hammon woo Rose. Lacy is successful in part because he embraces theatricality: he gains access to Rose only as Hans, and it is through playing that part that Lacy transforms himself from lazy prodigal to worthy gentleman with industrious hands.[39] Hammon, on the other hand, objects to such theatrics. When Rose rebukes his courtship, he rails,

> What, would you have me pule, and pine, and pray
> With lovelie ladie mistris of my heart,
> Pardon your servant, and the *rimer play*,
> Rayling on Cupid and his tyrants dart? (2.1.40–3, emphasis added)

Hammon objects to playing "the rimer," although, oddly enough, nearly all of his lines rhyme. Even more curious is the fact that while Lacy is seen as sincere in his act, Hammon, who rejects theatricality, is the least sincere character. He tells Rose, "I love thee dearer then my heart" (2.1.11), and immediately after Rose rejects him, he tries to woo Jane with similar language, "I love you dearely as I love my life" (3.4.50); in both scenes he swears by his hand (2.1.14; 3.4.115). His wooing of Rose begins to look like a rehearsal for his courtship of Jane, but unlike an actor, Hammon seems unaware of the theatrical elements of his life, and this makes him appear hypocritical. He claims that, "Enforced love is worse then hate to me" (2.1.51), but then tries to force Jane into marriage by taking advantage of her illiteracy and later by paying Rafe. In the end, the journeymen shoemakers call for a riot aimed at Hammon in order to wrest Jane from his grip and reunite her with Rafe.

While theatre is figured as inclusive, the most antitheatrical character also bears a name associating his antitheatrical stance with xenophobia.

Hammon is an allusion to Haman, the infamously xenophobic Biblical character who sought the extermination of the Jews. Hammon's largely unsympathetic role in *The Shoemaker's Holiday* supplies one reason for the acceptance of the shoemakers' rebellion. Whereas Edmund Tilney, Master of the Revels, demanded the removal of riot scenes from *Sir Thomas More* (and likely from other plays as well) this sedition scene was accepted as fit for the Queen because it is, in many respects, a righting and rewriting of anti-alien sedition in the 1590s.[40] Rather than basing the idea of community on birthplace, the shoemakers of Dekker's play imagine their community as one based on the artisans' shared experiences and adherence to local mores regardless of birthplace or class. Hammon, not Hans, is the outcast in this version of provincial globalism.

The point is further emphasized by the particularities of festivity. *The Shoemaker's Holiday* ends with a Shrovetide celebration, but as Frank Ardolino has shown, the Hammon plot in particular draws on Purim, a carnivalesque Jewish holiday celebrating Mordecai's and Esther's defeat of Haman.[41] To some degree this recalls the Protestant use of Judaism discussed in chapter 2, especially the Norwich pageant in which Elizabeth is compared to Esther, the Jewish queen who thwarts Haman's anti-Semitic plot.[42] As with his version of the Tower of Babel, Dekker may have drawn his knowledge of both Haman and Purim from Josephus, who describes the history and the festival memorializing it in *The Antiquities of the Jews*.[43] Dekker may also have gleaned the idea that Purim might be adapted to other cultures from a reading of Josephus who, especially in *The Antiquities of the Jews* and *Against Apion*, promoted the concept of Hellenistic Judaism, the idea that Judaism and Greco-Roman culture were ultimately commensurable.[44] Just as provincial globalism calls for the integration of immigrants into the customs and institutions of the host culture, so Dekker assimilates the Jewish festival to an English tradition.

Dekker further explores the relationship between xenophobia and anti-theatricality in the figure of Mayor Oatley, a thinly veiled portrait of John Spencer (Lord Mayor in 1594–5), who, like Oatley, sought to prevent his daughter's marriage to a spendthrift gentleman.[45] Spencer was one of London's most vociferously anti-theatrical mayors. In a 1594 letter to Lord Burghley, he complained that the theatres were "the ordinary places of meeting for all vagrant persons & maisterles men that hang about the Citie, theeves, horsestealers whoremoongers coozeners conny catching persones practizers of treason & such other lyke."[46] For Spencer, theatres not only drew audiences away from commerce and church but provided a forum for ordinary apprentices to meet "maisterles men" and seditious "practizers of treason."⁴⁷ Dekker takes Oatley one step further, however, by making the anti-theatrical mayor the most anti-Dutch character of *The Shoemaker's Holiday*. Only Oatley opposes Hans with the epithets "foul drunken lubber, swill bellie," and "fleming butter boxe" (4.4.52 and 43). There is reason for this characterization of Spencer: as an Alderman in the late 1580s, Spencer was twice involved in ordering that,

> all suche strangers as kepe anye shopes or shewes of anye wares, or marchan dizes within the Cittie or the fredome and Liberties of the same shall have there severall shopes windowes and dores made in suche sorte as people passinge by may not see them at worcke and so as their wares and marchandizes remayninge, and beinge within the same their shoppes or other places geve no open show to any people passinge by the same, levinge convenient lyght for them to worck.⁴⁸

Dekker gives the lie to xenophobia and antitheatricality by suggesting, in the figure of Oatley, that antitheatrical and anti-Dutch discourse go hand in hand while Dekker's theatre welcomes and protects early modern London's diversity just as Deloney figured the artisanal communities of England as both provincial and global.

It is Dekker's supreme stroke of irony that in the final scene of *The Shoemaker's Holiday* the anti-theatrical, anti-Dutch Oatley should see the marriage of his daughter to Lacy, the character most closely associated with actors and Dutch immigrants. In this scene Dekker distances the theatre from associations with sloth and seditious xenophobia. *The Shoemaker's Holiday* is not, however, a simple "fantasy of social cohesion" as Kastan puts it. Rather, it is a critique of anti-Dutch discourse and its association with the "imperfect pastimes" of riotous artisans and the theatre – it is an attempt to redefine the theatre as the "gentle craft" of cosmopolitanism. In *The Shoemaker's Holiday* Dekker divorces the theatre from anti-Dutch sentiment and remarries it to a London inclusive of citizen, stranger, and gentleman, an act symbolized in the final scene: when the King divorces and remarries Lacy to Rose, we see at one level the union of a gentleman-actor to a London citizen, and at another, the union of the Dutch Hans Meulter to the woman who happens to bear the name of the theatre in which *The Shoemaker's Holiday* was first performed, Philip Henslowe's Rose. And finally, the marriage of Hans and Rose may allude to the plea for resumed negotiations between the Hanseatic League and Elizabeth, as symbolized by the Tudor rose. That is, the marriage of Hans/Lacy and

Rose functions symbolically as a marriage between city and state, citizen and gentry, artisans and strangers.

Of course, Hans Meulter is not really Dutch. Underneath his Dutch disguise he is English, but as an Englishman, he is rather despicable: he is lazy and dishonest; he is a spendthrift; he takes money intended for his time as a soldier but deserts the war effort and spends the money as he wishes. As a Dutch shoemaker, however, he is hardworking, generous to his co-workers, helpful to his master, and true to his Rose. That is, he is more likeable as a Dutch artisan than as an English gentleman. There is, one hopes, a reforming quality to his role-playing as a Dutch shoemaker. Moreover, Dekker's use of Hans/Lacy is not unlike his use of the Tower of Babel story. Just as that tale suggests that people are really all one, divided only by a linguistic fall from grace, so the characters of *The Shoemaker's Holiday* come to find that their Dutch friend is really just like them, that the signs of difference are less important than the points of common interest.

The fall of the Tower of Babel may have divided people, but theatricality can help to restore that lost solidarity among workers. Balthazar, the protagonist of Dekker's *The Noble Spanish Soldier*, written sometime in the 1620s, declares the ideal version of this theatrical take on provincial globalism: when threatened with banishment, he retorts: "If I were [exiled], I lose nothing, I can make any Country mine: I have a private Coat for Italian Steeletto's, I can be treacherous with the Wallowne, drunke with the Dutch, a Chimney-sweeper with the Irish, a Gentleman with the Welsh, and turne arrant theefe with the English, what then is my Country to me?" (3.3. 100–4).[49] Balthazar evokes a number of stereotypes, but for an English audience, the final stereotype of the English as thieves undermines the others. What remains is Balthazar's assertion of himself as a potential immigrant whose improvisatory power allows him to adapt to the local culture. It is tempting to hear in Balthazar's final question an echo of Captain MacMorris in Shakespeare's *Henry V*, who asks, "Of my nation? What ish my nation?" (3.3.61), but the focus in Balthazar's speech is closer to that of Prince Henry in *1 Henry IV* who states that he "can drink with any tinker in his own language" (2.5.16–17). Prince Henry's claim provides a linguistic link between court and commons; in the words of Balthazar and the actions of Hans Meulter, Dekker extends these links across borders. If Dutch, French, Flemish are all personae that one can assume, if in exile one's fellow artisans are willing to take one in provided one somewhat adapts to local customs and institutions, "What then is my country to me?"

Early Modern England: Provincial and Global

I have argued that Deloney and Dekker, both sons or grandsons of strangers, passed as English subjects but infused their texts with a unique viewpoint that is narrower and yet more inclusive than the nation or realm. Connected to the immigrant communities through family ties, the two writers attempted to intervene in the breakdown of sectarian inclusivity by appealing to economic interdependence of labourers and merchants. The high premium Firk places on his identification with his livery company trumps all other possible identifications he might have had with the Earl of Lincoln and the Lord Mayor. Firk and his fellow shoemakers are provincial, narrowly defining their community as those who work as shoemakers, but at the same time, global, finding a common kinship with stranger shoemakers before recognizing a common cause with other Englishmen. Similarly, in Deloney's ballad "The valiant courage and policie of the Kentishmen" the rebels are not so much worried about a foreigner becoming king as they are about maintaining their local customs. The rebels from Kent, as rendered by Deloney, do not have a national or chauvinist outlook; that local customs might be lost elsewhere in the realm is none of their concern. Like Firk for Dekker, the Kentish rebels are heroes for Deloney not because they look forward to the agenda of an emergent nation but because they keep an eye on the preservation of local custom.

Neither Deloney nor Dekker are so provincial, however, as to ignore connections to the monarch. The king figures prominently as a guest of honour in both *Jack of Newbury* and *The Shoemaker's Holiday*. The monarch links the many local communities of the realm to one another, but that linking is not necessarily the same as national consciousness. "Barkeshire maids" are just that; they do not necessarily represent all women in the realm. Firk in *The Shoemaker's Holiday*, like Jack in *Jack of Newbury*, maintains a local identity grounded in a particular trade as well as a national identity based on birthplace, but the emergent national identity does not necessarily take precedence over the local identity.

What I see as a provincial mindset in Deloney and Dekker might be expected to bring with it the baggage of xenophobia, but as the above examples make clear, xenophobia is a rather muted issue. There are jokes about linguistic difference, but every anti-alien sentiment is coupled with more complex issues: the reciprocal responsibilities of guest and host in early modern theories of hospitality, and the maintenance of guild authority and communal expectations. The women in Dekker and Deloney's texts fall in love with strangers as easily as they fall for Englishmen. Deloney's

Bennedicke is Italian, but he is punished because he, like Hammon, attempts to disrupt the local community and family unit. It might be said that xenophobia lurks in the more repressive aspects of provincialism, but this is generally compromised by early modern subjects' awareness of economic interdependence with strangers.

There is, then, something of a paradox in these texts. The emphasis in Deloney and Dekker is almost always on a specific locale and the values of an even more specific local community: London shoemakers, Reading clothiers, Berkshire maids. At the same time, the local communities tend to include Flemish, French, Walloon, Italian, and Dutch strangers. This is the way some descendants of early modern immigrants dealt with their multicultural identities. Assimilated for the purposes of passing in the specific communities in which they worked, these descendants of strangers nonetheless had an eye to their immigrant heritage. The English towns seen through the eyes of these two descendants of strangers are neither national nor xenophobic, but rather provincial and global.

One nagging issue remains: What if Deloney and Dekker were not the descendants of immigrants to England? Although the cases for Dekker's Dutch and Deloney's French background appear to be quite strong, there is, nonetheless, the possibility that scholars will someday find definitive genealogical data confirming that Deloney and Dekker both hail from longstanding English families. Oddly enough, while such data would invalidate the premises of some of these chapters, the analyses of the texts would continue to stand: Deloney and Dekker remain committed to inclusion of immigrants in the realm. The specific connection these writers had to the immigrant communities would necessarily have to be reassessed: perhaps Deloney was apprenticed by a French silk-weaver; perhaps Dekker came to appreciate the Dutch during a stint in the Netherlands. Or perhaps the two inhabitants of London came to know and respect the immigrant communities of early modern England through inevitable contact. Regardless of such speculation, in their engagement with issues of immigration, both Dekker and Deloney seem paradoxically provincial and cosmopolitan. They both focus on the city as a primary site of political power but in their historical representations of the city, they recognize the ongoing presence of strangers, their positive contribution, and the generally multilingual, multicultural character of London and several other cities in the realm.

PART THREE

Worldly Domesticity

"They will not marry with us."
– Complaint at the House of Commons, 1593[1]

Chapter Five

The "Jumbled" City: *The Dutch Courtesan* and *Englishmen for My Money*

In the previous chapters amid the various relations between strangers and English men and women – solidarity based on provincial globalism or sectarian inclusivity – we have seen marriages or near marriages between English and strangers. The French shoemaker John Denevale and the Dutch shoemaker Haunce were entertained as credible suitors for Florence in Deloney's *Gentle Craft, Part I;* likewise, in *Gentle Craft, Part II,* among several potential mates, the prosperous Richard Casteler chooses to marry a Dutch woman. Beyond fictional matches or near matches, John Marston of Coventry, father to the dramatist of the same name, married Mary Guarsi, daughter of Andrew Guarsi, an Italian immigrant who was a surgeon.² By 1660 even the minister of the Dutch Church of Sandwich was apparently married to an Englishwoman.³

The insularity of the immigrant communities, however, was a formidable obstacle to such marriages. In 1574 Matthew Parker, Archbishop of Canterbury, wrote to the Dutch Church of London of his dismay at learning that the sacrament had been denied to a Dutch woman of their congregation for marrying an Englishman *"ac si atrox aliquid"* ("as if it were something terrible").⁴ As mentioned in the introduction, a 1571 petition complained about how difficult it was to marry into the immigrant community, and in 1593 the issue was raised in the House of Commons as one of several grievances about the insularity of England's immigrant communities.⁵ Andrew Spicer in his study of assimilation in the period writes, "Marriages outside the [stranger] community were indeed exceptional." Charles Littleton finds only twenty such marriages in the records of the French Church of London during the 1590s, but there are several records of Anglo-immigrant marriages in the archives of the Dutch Church in London. Many marriages between English subjects and immigrants took place in the English rather than the Dutch or French churches to avoid the censure of the stranger churches.[6]

It appears that the stranger community itself was the greatest obstacle to successful courtship of strangers. The motivations for maintaining their communities apart from the English were twofold. First, increased integration with their hosts might compromise the doctrinal integrity of the stranger churches. Second, with their change in status from churches of temporary refuge to apparently permanent Huguenot and Dutch Calvinist outposts, the stranger churches found that assimilation led to attrition in their community. Valerie Morant finds that assimilation of the Dutch community in Maidstone took roughly 200 years; the process sped up only with Archbishop Laud's insistence on uniformity, a policy that eventually led to the demise of the Dutch Church there.[7] Similarly, Judy Ann Ford finds that strangers in Sandwich tended to assimilate into the larger community through integration in local parish churches until the process was slowed down by the establishment of official stranger churches.[8] The relative infrequency of intermarriage was a result not so much of constructing a "pure" Englishness as an effort on the part of stranger churches to maintain their distinct refugee congregations.

Interest in marriages between English and strangers in the early modern period indicates not only an alternative mode to self-other dynamics prevalent in some parts of the population, but also an early English populace intentionally treating its cultural and ethnic borders as permeable, leading to a more thoroughly multicultural England. As shown in chapters 1 and 2, as fellow Protestants, the Dutch, French, and Walloon in England were viewed more positively, but Thomas Fuller, in his *Church History* (1655), offers a surprisingly economic rather than religious explanation for the interest in immigrant spouses. Recalling Dutch immigration into England in the fourteenth century, he writes,

> Happy the yeoman's house which one of these Dutchmen did enter, bringing industry and wealth along with them. Such who came in strangers within their doors soon after went out bridegrooms, and returned sons-in-law, having married the daughters of their landlords who first entertained them. Yea, those yeomen in whose houses they harbored soon proceeded gentlemen, gaining great estates to themselves, arms, and worship to their estates.[9]

At least part of this narrative can be attributed to Fuller's desire to anachronistically put Protestant refugees in a positive light, but his strategy would not work if his readers would not consider it plausible that a productive Dutch artisan might become an attractive match for their daughters. Indeed, he repeats the appeal: "the richest yeomen in England would not disdain to marry their daughters unto them."[10] Religion, economics, and status all coalesce in Fuller's view of marriage between English and strangers.

Marriage, as an official stamp on a personal relationship and as the means by which reproduction is labelled "legitimate," runs squarely into issues of gender, community, and the state. In that sense the operations here recall Gayle Rubin's explication of the sex/gender system in which particular societies construct women as "a domestic, a wife, a chattel, a playboy bunny, a prostitute, or a human Dictaphone in certain relations."[11] Literary texts of the early modern period vary in how they imagine immigrant women fitting into the sex/gender system, but texts that seek to construct Englishness against aliens, as will be seen, are more likely to portray immigrants as prostitutes, objects to be exploited and then resented. For other texts, home life, and specifically marriages between English and immigrants, could comprise what I call "worldly domesticity" – a tendency to shift from the guest-host dynamic of immigration to a situation in which immigrant and English merge as "one flesh" to manage the household economy.

The early English home is presumably a foundational aspect of Englishness and emergent nationhood, but as shown in this chapter and the next, the home was also already a site of multicultural interaction. To approach this site of early modern multiculturalism we must examine the relationship between community and gender relations. Linda Racioppi and Katherine O'Sullivan See have shown that gender, although not often addressed, underlies the dominant theories of nationhood, those of Benedict Anderson, Ernest Gellner, and Eric Hobsbawm (who see the nation as a distinctly modern formation) as well as those of Anthony D. Smith and John Armstrong (who see the nation emerging much earlier).[12] Women, according to Nira Yuval-Davis "reproduce nations biologically, culturally and symbolically."[13] The nation is reproduced symbolically through women in metaphors of the nation as a "mother-land" and in propaganda that links national territory to the female body. Biological and cultural reproduction of the nation overlap in women's roles as mothers. As frequent primary caregivers of their children, mothers play a central role in the cultural education of new generations. Elsewhere, Yuval-Davis and Floya Anthias emphasize that for nations invested in a particular racial make-up, mothers logically act as "reproducers of the boundaries of ethnic/national groups."[14]

Yuval-Davis's work is aimed at contemporary society, but even though gender roles have changed significantly since the 1600s, the particular relation between women and community holds true. For example, Linda Pollock has asserted that there is no evidence of a "significant change in the quality of parental care given to, or the amount of affection felt for infants for the period 1500–1900."[15] More recently, Patricia Crawford has demonstrated the high emotional investment poorer parents had in their children in early modern England.[16] Even Lawrence Stone, who emphasizes the relative remoteness of early modern parents to their children and an evolution in child-rearing practices culminating in the modern day, nonetheless states that "it would be a mistake to think that there was no affective bonding between parent and child."[17] Whether we agree more with Stone or with Pollock and Crawford, all three scholars argue that parents across all classes played major roles in their children's lives, for example advising them on choice of spouse and career.[18] Thus, it can be said that the importance of early modern women to early modern definitions of community is similar to the importance Yuval-Davis attributes to the relationship between women and the modern nation.

Although Yuval-Davis posits a variety of relations – biological, cultural, and symbolic – it is clear that women's role as mothers is especially important in the relationship between women and the nation. It is crucial to note that marriage is the means by which that role is legitimated, especially in early modern societies. Nancy Cott notes that mothering is intimately connected to marriage rites and that this connection explains much of the pressure nations place on the legal institution of marriage, on what counts, or does not count, as a valid union: "No modern nation-state," she writes, "can ignore marriage forms, because of their direct impact on reproducing and composing the population. The laws of marriage must play a large part in forming 'the people.' They sculpt the body politic."[19]

It is with a focus on the intimate connection to motherhood, marriage, and domesticity and their relation to collective identity that I wish to now approach immigration in early modern England through readings of two city comedies, William Haughton's *Englishmen for My Money* (1598) and John Marston's *The Dutch Courtesan* (1605), and in chapter 6, a selection of Shakespeare's plays. Given the relationship between women and the nation, the imaginative writing of the period might be expected to display a high degree of endogamy among the English, assuming, that the English had some form of pervasive national consciousness to protect from the influence of outsiders. As I have shown, however, national identity was only one of several emergent ways of thinking about and defining community. Some might place more importance on the inclusion of coreligionists or fellow artisans. Status often took precedence over birthplace and few could ignore issues of economic interdependence with strangers. Furthermore, immigrant spouses were not shunned but actively sought by many. Marriage and the needs of the home involved immigrants more than one might expect: the complex manner in which the domestic interacted with the global, so that the home became a site of multiculturalism, is what I term "worldly domesticity." We have moved, then, from the broad landscape of pan-Protestant alliance and sectarian inclusivity in England and the provincial globalism of the workshop to settle in a more domestic site of multiculturalism, the home and the marriage contract. As will be seen, some texts from this period offer a picture of emergent national identity while others provide the multicultural counter-discourse of worldly domesticity.

The Dutch Courtesan

The Dutch Courtesan, performed in 1605, is the first English play known to use an immigrant character for its title.[20] In the opening scene Freevill, a young gentleman, decides to break off his relations with the Dutch prostitute Franceschina, as he is soon to be married to Beatrice, the respectable English daughter of Sir Hubert Subboys. Freevill introduces Franceschina to his rigidly moralistic friend Malheureux, who, despite his insistence on abstinence and rational thought over base desires, instantly becomes infatuated with her. Franceschina, infuriated by Freevill's decision to leave her for Beatrice and noting Malheureux's attraction to her, promises to be his if he will kill Freevill and give her Freevill's ring, a love token he had received from Beatrice. Malheureux agrees, but upon consideration tells Freevill of the plot. The two men conspire to stage Freevill's death so that Malheureux can satiate his desire for Franceschina. Malheureux returns to Franceschina with the ring only to be arrested; Franceschina had contacted the authorities and arranged for them to overhear Malheureux's confession. Rather than free his friend immediately, however, Freevill continues to feign death, apparently to teach Malheureux a lesson about controlling his desires – an ironic motive since the first scene of the play features Malheureux instructing Freevill on sexual incontinence. As Malheureux mounts the scaffold, Freevill reveals all and Franceschina is imprisoned.

The subplot of the play involves Cocledemoy a citizen-jester who repeatedly plays tricks on Mulligrub, a London vintner. Mulligrub and his wife are highly acquisitive and many of Cocledemoy's antics are aimed at punishing them for their corrupt business practices; Jean Howard sees Mulligrub as an inversion of the kind of magnanimous citizen Dekker might stage.²¹ In the final scene Mulligrub faces death, confesses all his methods for swindling customers, and, like Malheureux, is saved at the last minute.

While a far cry from Dekker's generally positive portrayal of strangers, this representation of a Dutch immigrant in London is not entirely negative. As a courtesan (rather than a punk or whore), Franceschina displays a degree of continental sophistication not seen in the stereotypical prostitute of the early modern English stage. She sings, plays the lute, and can discourse on a variety of topics. Characters seem to be enchanted by her. Early in the play, even though Freevill is prepared to break off relations with her, he nonetheless describes her as "a pretty, nimble-eyed Dutch Tanakin; An honest soft-hearted impropriation; a soft, plump, round-cheeked frow, that has beauty enough for her virtue, virtue enough for a woman, and woman enough for any reasonable man" (1.1.147–51). At the prospect of meeting Franceschina, Malheureux exclaims, "Fie on't! I shall hate the whole sex to see her. The most odious spectacle the earth can present is an immodest, vulgar woman" (1.1.154–56), but he nonetheless becomes obsessed with her almost immediately. In short, the text indicates that Franceschina is to be seen as beautiful; this is perhaps the point. She seems to owe something to enticing vice figures such as Ill Will in *Wealth and Health,* characters who are associated not only with the spread of social ills but with travel.

The Dutch Courtesan does, however briefly, invite some sympathy for Franceschina. Dutch women were sometimes forced into prostitution as labour restrictions and life in the suburbs may have left destitute immigrants with few other vocations; her relentless and irrational devotion to Freevill also makes her seem a little tragic, not unlike Angelica Bianca in Aphra Behn's *The Rover*.²² Michael Scott notes that this possibility for sympathy troubles the plot, indicated by the awkward absence of Crispinella, Beatrice's outspoken sister, during the play's resolution. According to Scott, "if Marston had put words into her mouth her character would have demanded the right to criticize the whole unstable fabric of the plot's mixed conventions and dubious philosophy. She would have had to take up the cause of the wronged Franceschina."²³ Anne Haselkorn likewise finds that the play reinscribes male fantasies of domination over women by treating Franceschina "as if she were nothing more than an object" and contrasting her with the passive Beatrice and the ultimately subdued Crispinella.²⁴

Harry Keyishian, on the other hand, asserts that Marston wrote *The Dutch Courtesan* as a tacit attack on Dekker and his more sensitive treatment of prostitutes in *The Honest Whore*.²⁵ Perhaps part of this attack was the choice of a homicidal *Dutch* prostitute, an allusion to Dekker's heritage and Dutch-centric attitude in plays such as *The Shoemaker's Holiday*. In addition to being a prostitute, Franceschina is a member of the Family of Love, a Protestant sect that began in the Low Countries. Although Jean Dietz Moss notes the diversity of actual practices among the Family of Love, the sect was generally associated with an early modern communism, free love, and a form of moral exceptionalism based on the idea that once a member had experienced revelation, he or she need not fear God's final judgment, regardless of moral behaviour.²⁶ The Family of Love advocated simulation (appearing to be members of the dominant religion), which led to accusations of hypocrisy, and their alleged acceptance of adultery within the sect led to its association with licentiousness.²⁷ Coming on the heels of James I's denunciation of the Family of Love as "that vile sect" in the 1603 edition of *Basilikon Doron*, the negative ideas about Familists are emphasized in Marston's play to discredit Franceschina as lascivious and hypocritical.²⁸

As Philip J. Finkelpearl asserts, *The Dutch Courtesan* "shows the corrupting effect of an alien force, a Dutch prostitute, on the life of a young Englishman living in London."²⁹ That Franceschina is an immigrant prostitute need not, however, render her a corrupting force. In Thomas Middleton's *Anything for a Quiet Life* (1621), the French prostitute Margarita unwittingly helps Young Franklin to pass as French in order to avoid arrest by Camlet and the Barber, his creditors. There are linguistic jokes to be sure, but such jokes are mostly about the language gap rather than some risible stage dialect. For example, when Margarita finds herself translating Young Franklin's French to the authorities, she explains that his father sells *poissons*, which the Barber understands to mean poison until Margarita comes up with the English word, fish. Before she exits, Camlet pays her for her translation services stating, "Look, there is earnest, but thy reward's behind. Come to my shop, the Holy Lamb in Lombard Street; thou hast one friend more than e'er thou hadst" (3.2.146–9). Whereas Margarita produces amity, Franceschina pits Malheureux against his friend Freevill and betrays both men. Moreover, Franceschina's suspect religion appears to be spreading in the London of the play. Her bawd, Mary Faugh, is also a practitioner of the Family of Love, as are the Mulligrubs. Thus, the simulation advocated by the Family of Love is evident not only in Franceschina's commodification of love, but also in the Mulligrubs's business practices: Cocledemoy describes Mulligrub as a "spigot-frigging jumbler of elements" (3.2.38–9), that is, someone who adulterates drinks to increase profits.³⁰ Both sell illusions of a sort. Later, Cocledemoy jokingly rails against Mulligrub,

> For whereas good ale, perries, braggets, ciders, and metheglins was the true ancient British and Troyan drinks, you ha' brought in Popish wines, Spanish wines, French wines, *tam Marti, quam Mercurio*, both muscadine and malmsey, to the subversion, staggering, and sometimes overthrow of many a good Christian. You ha' been a great jumbler. O, remember the sins of your nights!" (5.3.105–11)

The term "jumbler" forges a strong link between Mulligrub and Franceschina, as it could refer not only to adulterating wine but also to engaging in illicit sexual activity. Just as Franceschina is associated with bringing an alien religion to England, so Mulligrub brings "Popish wines," drinks that undermine British identity (and it is British here; metheglin is associated with the Welsh). The jumbled nature of the Mulligrubs is especially clear here: earlier Mistress Mulligrub had lamented that "our wines are Protestants" (2.3.8–9), a line that, as David Crane notes, indicates the adulteration of wine and sets the Mulligrubs apart from the mainstream English religion.³¹

These details (and others), argues Marjorie Rubright, reveal a play that engages in "a cultural double vision, one that envisions the signifiers of Englishness and Dutchness as emerging always in relation to one another."³² I would add that Franceschina's frequent pronunciation of "will" as "vill" might further link Freevill to the Dutchness of the play. But the play itself is a bit of a cultural "jumble" throughout. Malheureux's French name, which means "depressed," links him semantically to the Mulligrubs, whose name refers to stomach aches, and by extension, depression.³³ As if to underline the connection, these two semantic cousins are both nearly executed. English, French, and Dutch all run into one another on the scaffold as they are reformed of their jumbled identities.

Franceschina, the apparent source of Dutchness in the play, also turns out to be a cultural "jumble." Although she is referred to as a "Dutch Tanakin" (1.1.146–8), Martin L. Wine describes her speech as "a helter-skelter of Germanic, French, Italian, as well as pure English pronunciation."³⁴ Hoenselaars has claimed that in Franceschina's jealousy and capacity for revenge there are traces of an Italian stereotype.³⁵ Andrew Fleck suggests that Franceschina is comical in part because of this "yoking of aurally discordant Dutch stage accent to Franceschina's alluring Venetian manners." Rubright suggests that the hodge-podge of stereotypes and epithets associated with Franceschina render her resistant "to stable national and ethnic categorization," and that this instability is part of the "capacious category of 'Dutch' that the theatre of the period was busy producing."[36] Following Wine, Jean Howard describes Franceschina as "cosmopolitanism rendered attractive and then monstrous."[37] Her name, moreover, indicates that she is to be taken as a variation on Francesquina, the coarse and often licentious stock character of the Italian *commedia dell' arte* tradition.[38] Thus, Marston infuses his London city comedy with traces of his own Italian heritage.

The "jumble" of identities that characterizes Franceschina parallels Cocledemoy's description of British drink as undermined by Mulligrub's Italian, French, and Spanish wines. Howard, however, argues that *The Dutch Courtesan* tempers anxieties about London cosmopolitanism by showing Cocledemoy to be a master of cultural difference. Cocledemoy impersonates a Scottish barber (2.3), a French peddler (3.2), an English sergeant (5.3), and a bellman (4.5), and he cites Cicero (2.1.163) and speaks garbled Greek (4.3.10–15). As Howard shows, Cocledemoy's improvisatory skills allow him to engage with and perform otherness without losing his Englishness.[39] This is in marked contrast to the Mulligrubs, who, Rubright suggests, seem to be "going Dutch" in religion and diet.[40]

Still, acting French or Dutch is one thing; being Dutch or embracing Dutchness, is quite another. *The Dutch Courtesan* presents actual immigrants as the source of a deviant religion and associates them, via Mulligrub, with defective products, allegations that echo the anti-alien libels discussed at the end of chapter 2. Franceschina is in many respects a scapegoat, a figure onto whom social ills are projected to be contained or exiled.[41] In the end she retreats to a Iago-like silence on all matters: "Ick vill not speak. Torture, torture your fill / For me am worse than hang'd, me ha lost my will" (5.3.56–7). There is potential here for a bawdy pun on *will*, as Franceschina's sexual appetite has been thwarted, but *will* also recalls her lost lover Freevill, and finally her own freewill as the play contains the immigrant as a figure of society's ills.[42]

As Franceschina loses her freewill, so Freevill's freedom from Franceschina empowers him to choose the ethereal Beatrice, whose name recalls not the popular *commedia dell'arte* but rather Dante's courtly love object from *La Vita Nuova*.[43] Freevill presents his decision in a soliloquy that is loosely based on Michel de Montaigne relativist "Of Custom."[44] "What man," asks Freevill, "would leave / The modest pleasures of a lawful bed, / The holy union of two equal hearts" (5.1.61–3). Freevill contrasts this scenario with "the unhealthful loins of common loves, / The prostituted impudence of things" (5.1.67–8). Although the choice seems rather simple, it should be remembered that Freevill was among Franceschina's best customers and he spends a good portion of the opening scene jovially defending prostitution from Malheureux's moralizing attacks: "Alas good creatures, what would you have them do?" demands Freevill, "Would you have them get their living by the curse of man, the sweat of their brows? So they do. Every man must follow his trade, and every woman her occupation ... They sell their bodies; do not better persons sell their souls?" (1.1.97–125).

Freevill's transformation owes something to the discovery that Franceschina is prepared to have him murdered for leaving her, but his rhetoric suggests other motives for rejecting her. His disdain for "common loves" is related not only to the way a prostitute holds her love in common, but also to class and to the Family of Love and their early communist beliefs; the line thus serves as a rejection of Franceschina on class and religious grounds as well. Alastair Hamilton states that adultery within the Family of Love was "sanctioned enthusiastically."[45] Whereas Janet E. Halley argues that this was only one interpretation of the Family of Love texts, it was a reading that, for their opponents, conveniently maligned the group.[46] The breakdown in English-immigrant relations is precisely on the point of religious difference, since sectarian inclusivity was the foundation for much of early modern England's multicultural attitudes and the classed solidarity of craft founded on provincial globalism.

Moreover, the phrase "common loves" with its appositive, "The prostituted impudence of things," hints at Freevill's vision of marriage as a form of ownership, in contrast to things held in common. Franceschina is reduced to the status of a "thing" whose will is therefore unnatural or "impudent." The view of marriage as a husband's ownership of a wife, while reflected in early modern England's theory of marriage, seems to be out of step with actual practice. Amy L. Erickson has demonstrated that from initial courtship and marriage settlements to the crafting of wills, women were much more active than marriage pamphlets suggest. In fact, Erickson shows that the place of women in the marriage process is to some degree based on class, noting that "strict settlements to preserve property in the male line were used only by the wealthy" and that more equitable arrangements were often instigated by "ordinary women."[47] Thus, Freevill's rejection of Franceschina may on some level involve different expectations of gender roles: the upper class Freevill seeks a passive female in Beatrice, while the working-class Franceschina demands but in the end is denied self-determination or will.

Marston's play was first performed at Blackfriars Theatre before a select audience of Inns of Court men, members of the gentry, and well-to-do professionals; roughly a decade later the play was revived at court.[48] Indeed, the "will" of Freevill's name implies both gender and class privilege. Freevill's choice of Beatrice rests on the idea that he will have "undoubted issues" (5.1.65), legitimate heirs. His rejection of "common loves" as impudent "things" may have more to do with status and securing wealth for himself and his descendants than with anything else, but *The Dutch Courtesan* uses the rejected immigrant to promote a national agenda of un-jumbling the realm: Freevill is to marry Beatrice Subboys, Malheureux and Mulligrub repent their flirtation with Franceschina's world view, and Franceschina is silenced. Here then is a play that represents the immigrant as "jumbled" and "jumbling," a threat to stable national identity, some "thing" (to use Freevill's wording) that needs to be exorcized from the realm. In contrast, Haughton's *Englishmen for My Money* dramatizes the allure of immigrant women in a way that valorizes worldly domesticity.

Englishmen for My Money

Unlike *The Dutch Courtesan,* William Haughton's *Englishmen for My Money* was written for Philip Henslowe's theatre, which catered to popular Elizabethan tastes.[49] Little is known about Haughton. He wrote plays for the Admiral's Men and was a frequent collaborator with Thomas Dekker and Henry Chettle, but he is best known for *Englishmen for My Money*.[50] Like *The Shoemaker's Holiday*, *Englishmen* is an early forerunner of city comedy, but unlike the Jacobean city comedies, Haughton's play avoids much of the satirical bite of Ben Jonson or Thomas Middleton.

The play, set in London, tells the story of three English gentlemen – Harvey, Ferdinand Heigham, and Ned Walgrave – who owe substantial amounts of money and all their land to Pisaro, a Portuguese immigrant merchant and usurer settled in London. By his now deceased English wife, Pisaro has three daughters – Laurentia, Marina, and Mathea – who, through encouragement of their English tutor Anthony, have fallen in love with Harvey, Heigham, and Walgrave respectively. When Pisaro discovers that his three greatest debtors have designs on his daughters, he objects, dismisses Anthony, and sends his servant Frisco to find a French tutor for his daughters. Anthony, privy to this plot, disguises himself as Monsieur Mouse, is promptly hired as the new French tutor, and continues advocating on the Englishmen's behalf. In the meantime, Pisaro has arranged to match his daughters with three merchant strangers: Delion, a Frenchman, Alvaro, an Italian, and Vandal, a Dutchman.[51] The complicated plot revolves around a number of jests and counter-jests and ends with the successful matches of Pisaro's daughters to the three English gentlemen, who in turn secure the land they owed to Pisaro. Pisaro ultimately gives his blessing to the matches and invites everyone to a wedding feast.

Because the English suitors triumph over their stranger adversaries, *Englishmen for My Money* has often been read as "patriotic," "jingoistic," and "nationalist."[52] At the same time, the play is notable for its attention to local detail that few outside of London would recognize. For example, Pisaro's servant Frisco refers to a number of very specific landmarks as he mischievously misleads the stranger-suitors through the London's dark streets: Ivy Bridge (3.3.50) "the Blue Boar in the Spittle" (3.3.60), the smell of pasties on Abchurch Lane (3.3.43–5), and so forth (2.2.7).[53] Kermode asserts that city comedies are intent on presenting London as representative of England as a whole,[54] and *Englishmen* may be seen to make gestures in this direction: Walgrave's and Heigham's names perhaps allude to parishes outside of London (the former in Northhamptonshire, the latter in Norfolk). But one could just as easily claim that this play presents London as containing the world, or at least Europe. The London that Haughton presents is a multilingual home to English, Dutch, French, Portuguese, and Italians. To be sure, the English are given pre-eminence, but in many ways the strangers of *Englishmen for My Money* embody the same productive economic values as those in *The Shoemaker's Holiday*, so much so that in his labour-focused reading of the play, Tom Rutter argues that Pisaro's values dominate the world of the play.[55] Indeed, of all the characters, Pisaro most embodies a humanist ideal, excelling in business but also speaking in verse and keen to promote his daughters' education in languages and moral philosophy.

Despite Pisaro's admirable qualities, several recent critics have focused on the cultural identity of Pisaro's daughters, usually to emphasize their Englishness. Working with a geohumoral model of the immigrant as always imperfectly adapted to his climate, Alan Stewart argues that these women "are shown as being perfectly, belligerently English-children of the maternal soil, not of the paternal seed."[56] Similarly, Edmund Campos, in his exploration of Pisaro as a "crypto-Jew," focuses on points in the text that emphasize "maternal inheritance."[57] Unlike most stage strangers, Pisaro's daughters, like Pisaro himself, speak perfect English, indicating a high degree of assimilation and perhaps the strong influence of Pisaro's deceased English wife. This "positive portrayal of the three daughters," argues Campos, "encourages a carefully constructed notion of miscegenation – one that allows access to the trade advantages of the Crypto-Jew, but one that will not compromise English national identity."[58] Pisaro's Jewish characteristics are not so cryptic as to go unnoticed by Walgrave, who, in his first speech, rants about Pisaro's "snout / Able to shadow Paul's, it is so great" (1.2.15–16). Walgrave's anti-Semitic stance should not, however, occlude Pisaro's important status as a merchant stranger and his connections with that community. More importantly, Haughton does not go out of his way to emphasize the English mother's influence as greater than the Portuguese father's; the mother is, after all, unnamed and absent while Pisaro is an ever present influence on his daughters' lives. He is their only living relative; he arranges for their education; he supervises them; he poses the greatest obstacle to the Englishmen's aspirations of marriage; and he supplies the material inheritance, the dowries that seem to be part of the young women's attractiveness to their English suitors. Walgrave declares,

> We'll work our lands out of Pisaro's daughters,
> And cancel all our bonds in their great bellies –
> When the slave knows it, how the rogue will curse! (4.1.113–15)[59]

Walgrave fantasizes that male virility can cancel debts and turn reproduction into the production of wealth. Like so many male lovers on the early modern stage, his interest in Mathea seems to be both romantic and economic.[60] While Pisaro's daughters seem fairly English, the play also makes it clear that part of their attractiveness comes from their father's financial skill, which, in the play, is intimately connected to the Royal Exchange in a scene that highlights the global nature of the English economy (1.3).[61]

It is also clear that Pisaro's daughters are well aware of their bicultural upbringing. When Mathea believes that Walgrave is really Delion impersonating Walgrave, she rails,

> No, no, it is the Frenchman in his stead,
> That Monsieur motleycoat that can dissemble.
> Hear you, Frenchman, pack to your whores in France.
> Though I am Portingale by the father's side,
> And therefore should be lustful, wanton, light,
> Yet goodman goose-cap, I will let you know,
> That I have so much English by the mother,
> That no base slavering French shall make me stoop.
> And so, Sir Dan-delion fare you well. (4.1.39–47)

Emma Smith takes the line "so much English by the mother" to indicate the dominance of the daughters' Englishness. Their father's side is here couched in a subordinate clause, and Mathea's point is to emphasize that in terms of stereotypes, her English chastity wins out over Portuguese licentiousness.[62] Moreover, she seems to have a low opinion of the French, associating Delion with fools and prostitution. Given these stereotypes, it makes sense that Pisaro's daughters would want to suppress their Portuguese heritage. Still, Elizabeth Schaffer rightly points the complexity and contradiction of this assertion of Englishness: Mathea only recognizes her English suitor when he mockingly speaks French.[63] Her attempt to highlight her Englishness does not necessarily efface her Portuguese background, and her description of her own mixed heritage prompts Walgrave to declare angrily,

> You Dan-de-lion, you that talk so well.
> Hark you, a word or two good mistress Matt.
> Did you appoint your friends to meet you here,
> And being come, tell us of whores in France,
> A Spanish jennet, and an English mare,
> A mongrel, half a Dog and half a bitch;
> With tran-dido, dil-dido, and I know not what?
> Hear you: if you'll run away with Ned,
> And be content to take me as you find me,
> Why so law, I am yours. If otherwise,
> You'll change your Ned, to be a Frenchmans trull?
> Why then, *Madame* Delion, *je vous lassera a Dio, et la bon fortune*! (4.1.50–61)

In the midst of this misunderstanding, Walgrave draws attention to Mathea's mixed parentage, calling her "a mongrel." For Walgrave, at least, the mere mention of her father's influence compromises her claim to be more English. Even if early modern England operated on the principle of *jus soli* (rule of birthplace), it would seem that at the level of character development Haughton wanted to show that this mixed heritage was important to Walgrave – the word "mongrel," and an accompanying series of bestial images is at hand the moment Mathea mentions her parentage.[64] Walgrave complains that she "talk[s] so well," the very characteristic that potentially masks her immigrant heritage, as if the illusion that she might be fully English were suddenly shattered by the words "Portingale by the fathers side." Critics may see Pisaro's daughters as essentially English, but their Portuguese father is an overbearing presence throughout the play and their immigrant heritage is at the fore in this scene.

It should be noted, however, that Walgrave's reactions are not shared by his fellow Englishmen. After his anti-Semitic entrance, when he complains that he is losing his land to Pisaro and rages, "He will be damned, the rogue, before he do't!" (1.2.32), Harvey responds, "Prithee, talk milder" (1.2.33). When an enraged Walgrave wants to pursue Pisaro, Heigham says, "Nay, prithee Ned Walgrave, let's bethink ourselves" (1.3.302). Reflecting on the fact that Mathea will have dinner with Delion, Walgrave declares, "'Swounds, I'll geld him first / Ere that infestious losel revel there," to which Heigham replies, "Come, let us leave this idle chat" (3.2.11–16). Over and over again, Harvey and Heigham find themselves trying to calm their intemperate companion. Twice Heigham and Harvey jokingly ask, "What, speechless, Ned?" (3.2.7; 4.1.48), apparently finding sport in their friend's choleric disposition. Walgrave even comments on his companions' efforts to calm him as he confronts Pisaro, telling Heigham, "Prithee me no prithees" (4.1.139). Kermode rightly suggests that in Walgrave Haughton portrays "the over-zealousness and unguardedness of English pride."[65] Although there are several jokes at the expense of immigrant speech, Walgrave's hyperbolic rage appears to be part of the humour of the play as well.[66] Critics see the script as patriotic and even nationalist, but the most jingoistic character, Walgrave, is also the most laughable of the Englishmen.

Englishmen for My Money, then, makes fun of the extremes of national identity. Jokes are made at the expense of both the stereotypical stranger-suitors and the virulently patriotic Walgrave. In this sense, the play embraces a London somewhere between English chauvinism and *The Dutch Courtesan*'s "jumble" of national identities. Emma Smith frames the three daughters as representing "the pure English nation," but also notes that, "the feminized symbol of the city is always and inescapably hybridized, as London simultaneously asserts an idea of the native while registering the complex diversity of its populace."[67] Similarly, drawing attention to the way in which usury compromises national pride and confuses English and alien in the play, Kermode ultimately concludes that Pisaro's "daughters are determined to incorporate themselves into the English body politic."[68] More can be made of the daughters' determination, however, for what they symbolize, as Smith points out, is not only a space but a people; they are not only incorporated by but incorporate the English. Importuning the three daughters, Walgrave promises, "And ere the morning, to augment your joys, / We'll make you mothers of six goodly boys" (4.1.99–100). Again, Walgrave's enthusiasm is joked about as Heigham cautions, "Promise them three, good Ned, and say no more" (4.1.101). This jovial negotiation emphasizes how all three gentlemen plan on creating heirs to the wealth they hope to regain from Pisaro through his daughters.

Whether they have six or three children, however, the inheritors of their land will be part English, part Portuguese (and if Campos is right, a little Jewish), the very "mongrels" Walgrave objected to just fifty lines earlier, and the Englishmen's father-in-law will be an immigrant. What seems like a bid for independence from strangers, wresting debts from Pisaro, turns out to be the creation of stronger ties to immigrants.

The scholarly emphasis on male will over female agency is perhaps an effect of later revision: today the play is known as *Englishmen for My Money, or a Woman Will Have Her Will*, but the main title appears to have been added when the play was prepared for print. The subtitle focusing on female will appears as the main title in the Stationer's Register and Henslowe's *Diary*.[69] The current title constitutes the frame through which the play is now read; today critics focus on *Englishmen*, often relegating a passive or purely symbolic role to Pisaro's daughters, but this play is equally concerned with immigrant women and their will, their machinations to gain the objects of their desires. The revelation of female desire is at least in part what upsets Walgrave. His rant about the mating of Spanish and English horses results in mongrels oddly defined as participating not in two cultures but in two genders: "half a Dog and half a bitch." This particular instance of hermaphroditic imagery stems from Walgrave's discovery of Mathea's sexual agency, an apparent subversion of the patriarchal myths of passive femininity with an active masculinity.

Walgrave's anxieties about Mathea's alien heritage seem tied up with fears of a female desire that undermines the perfect control of English patriarchs. Walgrave's "tran-dido, dil-dido," a common ballad refrain, further underlines his concerns about female sexuality.[70] "The Beautiful Shepherdess of Arcadia," a bawdy late sixteenth-century ballad (printed in the eighteenth century), uses this refrain for each of the sexual escapades of the knight's encounter with the shepherdess. Pauline Kiernan interprets Robert Greene's "Mulidor's Madrigal" – with its opening lines, "Dildido, Dildido, / O love, O love, / I feel thy rage rumble below and above!" – as a description of autoeroticism.[71] By the 1620s "trangdido" apparently referred to a person's backside: for example, in John Ford's *The Lover's Melancholy* (1628), Corax vaunts, "Let him come Trollio. I will firk his trangdido" (4.2.43), and in Ford's *Fancies Chaste and Noble*, Secco declares that to get revenge on those who have cuckolded him, "Nay, I will tickle their trangdidos" (4.1.165–66).[72] Similarly, "dil-dido" seems to have been suggestive of a substitute for a phallus: in Middleton's *A Chaste Maid in Cheapside*, Allwit rounds out his musings about how cuckoldry relieves him of his marital duties by singing, "La dildo, dildo la dildo, la dildo dildo de dildo" (1.257). The bawdiness of the ballad refrain may well have been Walgrave's intention, but the lines also provide a limit to his sexual knowledge, since he ends with "and I know not what."

The original title, then, amplifies a theme of female will, recalling the potentially bawdy pun in Franceschina's final lines.[73] Even in the printed title, *Englishmen for My Money*, "Englishmen" are the commodified objects rather than subjects of action.[74] The possessive pronoun "*My*" could relate to an imagined audience's approval of the Englishmen, but given the plot, it could also refer to Pisaro or his daughters, his money or their individual dowries. In either case, the seemingly patriotic title is possibly voiced by a member of London's prominent immigrant community drawing attention to the way the play portrays domestic alliances between English and immigrants.

Although courtship typically empowers young women, one need not assume that marriage brings an end to female agency. Erickson observes that "wives at all social levels … managed finances on their own behalf and jointly with their husbands."[75] We cannot know how Pisaro's daughters fared in their marriages, but an early modern audience would likely have projected a kind of social and economic partnership between the English husbands and their half-Portuguese wives, an arrangement in marked contrast to Freevill's vision of marriage as ownership. There is, at any rate, little reason to suppose that marriage would make the daughters significantly less Portuguese. They have already participated in a kind of provincial globalism, linguistically assimilated to England.

The central point of the title, however, is that the immigrant women are not only chosen (and therefore become passive objects enclosed or otherwise contained by the fictional Englishmen) but also choose and are therefore agents in the creation of a new cooperative multicultural domestic space. From the first scene of the play the three women declare their interest in the English suitors. That is, marriage is a victory for both the Englishmen and the immigrant's daughters. As the tutor Anthony urges their interest in the Englishmen by threatening to teach them philosophy, Marina says,

> Thy ever loving Harvey I delight it;
> Marina ever loving shall requite it.
> Teach us philosophy? I'll be no nun.
> Age scorns delight; I love it being young. (1.1.101–4)

Whether prompted by Anthony or not, the attraction between Harvey and Marina seems mutual, and the aforementioned female will is apparent in her speech: no philosophy, no nunnery, only Harvey. Similarly Laurentia states,

> Why was I made a maid, but for a man?
> And why Laurentia, but for Ferdinand?
> The chastest soul these angels could entice;
> Much more himself, an angel of more price.
> Were't thy self present, as my heart could wish,
> Such usage thou shouldst have, as I give this. (1.1.109–14)

Interestingly, like her suitor (and a little like her father), Laurentia combines an interest in romance with an interest in finance as she evidently kisses a coin in place of Heigham: the English suitors are "angels" enticing chaste souls, just as coins ("angels") attract flesh and blood individuals. Thus, Mathea echoes the play's original title in her declaration of love for Ned:

> I'faith I'll have thee Ned, or I'll have none./
> Do what they can, chafe, chide, or storm their fill,
> Mathea is resolved to have her will. (1.1.122–4)

Although the daughters entertain Pisaro's merchant strangers, they do so under duress. When the English suitors arrive, they are keen to meet with them. In the end, both the English suitors and the daughters get what they want: the women have their will, the Englishmen their money. The daughters thwart their stranger-suitors, and the final jest of the play, a cooperative effort between the daughters and their suitors, seems to reconcile Walgrave to his bride's agency. Rather than fixating on the triumph of the male suitors, the original title emphasizes the triumph of the women, while the later title chosen for publication balances female agency with the importance of the would-be grooms. Taken together the two titles emphasize their mutual interest in marriage, their collaborative courtship, a fantasy of mutually forging a worldly domesticity.

Collaboration between Englishmen and willing half-immigrant women is at the core of *Englishmen for My Money*. In his examination of emergent national identity in this play and *The Shoemaker's Holiday*, Andrew Fleck argues that "Foreign figures in English city comedies function in many ways, but typically they come to the stage to be used, mocked, gulled, and ultimately expelled, often to the advantage of good, native Englishmen."[76] To be sure, Vandal, Delion, and Alvaro are gulled, and the various jokes at their expense must have been satisfying for those in the audience who hungered for a simple scapegoating of strangers. From another angle, however, this treatment of the strangers highlights the issue of collaboration in the creation of a multicultural domestic space: had the merchant strangers been successful in their courtship, the play would reflect the insularity of London's immigrant communities. Instead, the play rewards the intermingling of English and immigrant by imagining a scenario in which Englishmen and immigrant women create new and more profitable family units. The daughters are, after all, the product of such a union and are now entering into a similarly multicultural marriage.

Rather than pariahs, Pisaro's daughters appear as highly sought after prizes, and they view their English suitors as desirable as well. Like the allegiance between native artisans and merchant strangers expressed in Deloney's *Jack of Newbury* and Dekker's *Shoemakers' Holiday*, the bond here between native and stranger seems mutual. Note also that like Deloney and Dekker, but unlike Marston, Haughton was writing for an audience with popular tastes, made up often of artisans and apprentices. As mentioned in the beginning of this chapter, the English complained of the difficulty had in securing marriages to strangers. Rather than consolidating some abstract sense of national identity, *Englishmen for My Money* plays out the fantasy of overcoming the obstacles of marrying into the stranger communities: here family, rival suitors from the immigrant communities, and the ability to afford a marriage in the first place are all overcome. Given the ways in which Yuval-Davis describes women reproducing the nation, however, such a fantasy also suggests that the community being reproduced was not entirely invested in an idea of Englishness grounded in what we now view as nation. Rather, the idea of England imagined here is distinctly multicultural, though predicated on the three daughters' assimilation. After all, if Haughton had wanted the three daughters to be seen as purely English, he certainly could have come up with a plot device to simply make them so. While I take issue with critics who actively try to diminish their Portuguese heritage, it is nevertheless true that the play wants it both ways: the daughters speak perfect English and take pride in their maternal inheritance, but Pisaro's presence reminds the audience that at some level these women are part Portuguese. Their Englishness makes them unproblematic spouses, but it is their inheritance from their father that makes them attractive to the Englishmen.

Such an interpretation, however, recalls the question with which the chapter began: why would the English clamour so for access to immigrant wives? The answer can be approached through a comparison between

Franceschina and Pisaro's daughters. Franceschina is an unsuitable bride for Freevill primarily because her class and occupation would compromise Freevill's own fairly high social status as a gentleman. Franceschina brings neither status nor an acceptable source of income to a marriage, and she adheres to a set of suspect religious beliefs. As Rubright has shown, however, *The Dutch Courtesan* depicts a similar process by which London's cosmopolitanism is replicated within the domestic sphere in the portrayal of the Mulligrubs "going Dutch," appropriating religious and dietary characteristics that blur the border between Dutch and English.[77]

Pisaro's daughters, on the other hand, stand to inherit not only the lands their suitors pawned to Pisaro but also the wealth he has accumulated from others as a merchant and a usurer. As daughters of a merchant stranger/usurer, Laurentia, Marina, and Mathea lack a secure status in London, but they have capital. Although Campos makes much of Pisaro's possible Jewish identity, his family's Judaism appears to be so cryptic that it is never mentioned as a complicating factor in marriage; this is in marked contrast to Franceschina, who is associated with the problematic Family of Love. By marrying three English gentlemen, Pisaro's daughters enter into an exchange of wealth for status to the mutual benefit of both immigrant brides and native grooms.[78] What is crucial is that the brides and grooms benefit from one another: the impoverished gentlemen regain their land, and the half-immigrant brides elevate their status. Had the daughters married the merchant strangers favoured by their father, they would have gained wealth but not status; this would have reinforced the idea of London's immigrant community as insular and apart from the English. These fictive marriages, then, appear to be based at least in part on economic interdependence between status-seeking strangers and money-seeking gentry, a form of solidarity in domestic space that crosses cultural and ethnic borders.

The Dutch Courtesan casts "will" as the dangerous trait of a Dutch prostitute, and passivity as the appropriate trait of Englishwomen; *Englishmen for My Money* presents its popular audience with a positive view of immigrant women's will. In this sense, the marriages of the three English gentlemen to the three daughters of the immigrant Pisaro are not unlike the marriage Fuller describes in *Church History,* in which English landlords and masters happily married their daughters off to Dutch artisans: the unique and profitable skills brought by many Protestant refugees made them attractive to some Londoners, and as Fuller suggests, the Dutch artisan's productivity might be great enough to augment his status to that of gentleman. Similarly, in Deloney's *The Gentle Craft, Part II,* Richard Casteler, the frugal but famous benefactor of London, does not marry the English maids who have made their interest in him apparent but rather chooses a Dutch maid who "could do diverse pretty feats to get her own living."[79] As David Cressy points out, the economic dimension of such marriages reveals not so much a coldly calculating populace but rather one of several prudent considerations in the courtship process.[80]

The marriages discussed here fit the larger pattern I have sought to delineate in this book. There was an emergent discourse of national identity that might scapegoat immigrants to consolidate a positive idea of Englishness, but there was also a counterdiscourse that imagined English hosts, especially Londoners, and their immigrant neighbours forming solidarities based on shared religion, on mutual interest in the welfare of their city, or on shared craft and the importance of interrelations between artisan producers and merchant strangers. As with those bonds between English and immigrant, the marriages reveal mutual interest and friendlier relations than most historians and literary scholars have attributed to early modern England. When xenophobic rhetoric is espoused, it often represents, as in Walgrave's vitriolic "mongrel," a moment at which mutual interest has disintegrated. That is, such rhetoric is usually used to express discontent with a breakdown in social relations, (for example, weavers complaints about guild ordinance violations) rather than as an expression of inherent dislike of immigrants because of where they came from or what language they spoke. The complaints about the insularity of the immigrant communities cited in the beginning of this chapter are a case in point. While these complaints express dissatisfaction with the Dutch and French living in England, they are aimed ultimately at closer and more interdependent relations with immigrants, at integration rather than deportation. *Englishmen for My Money* provides an "imagined community" in which such integration succeeds. Three Englishmen prepare to settle down with three half-immigrant women, their livelihoods made possible by Pisaro, who similarly maintains a multicultural domestic space in London. In the end the Englishmen are invited to feast at the immigrant's home to celebrate their marriages. This play presents a London inhabited by people from throughout Europe, and the plot aims to replicate that worldliness in the home.

Chapter Six

Shakespeare, the Foreigner

Every so often the authorship of the plays and poems attributed to William Shakespeare is called into question by someone claiming not only that Shakespeare was not the author of said works but that the real author was not even English.[1] In April 2000 *The Times* published an article arguing that Shakespeare was really Sicilian.[2] Sometime Oxfordian Sigmund Freud entertained the idea that Shakespeare was really French, and philosopher Kuno Fischer is said to have professed that Shakespeare must have been of German ancestry.[3] Although these claims never gain much of a sympathetic audience, they point to Shakespeare's status in world literature and his importance as a national symbol; that is, Italy, France, and Germany would like to lay claim to Shakespeare as one of their own.

As wild as such claims are, they are also symptoms of Shakespeare's odd fit as a national icon, for although his plays and poems are seen as quintessentially English, they are also often described as addressing universal themes and interpreted as offering the perspective of the "other" rather than that of a cultural insider. Current scholarship tends to avoid the idea of Shakespeare's potential universality, but we need look no further than *Post-Colonial Shakespeares* (1998) to see how Shakespeare's plays are interpreted as able to mediate distant and disparate national identities from the Kathakali in India to tensions over property rights in modern-day South Africa.[4] The emphasis on performance as a mediating factor effectively avoids questions of universality, but avoiding that issue has not resolved the tension; instead it manifests itself in the divergent interpretations of nationalism and globalization in Shakespeare's texts. That is, while Shakespeare's texts are frequently looked to as part of the story of the construction of early English nationhood, they are also analysed in terms of cross-cultural contact that sometimes reinforces but often undermines a sense of a stable national identity. The nationalist Shakespeare is necessarily involved in constructing and providing rationales for the political boundaries that differentiate one group from another, while the cross-cultural Shakespeare is portrayed as blurring and even de-legitimating those very boundaries and undermining our expectations of the relationship between character and culture.

For example, Claire McEachern, Richard Helgerson, Willy Maley, Philip Schwyzer, Jean E. Howard, Phyllis Rackin, and a host of other critics find one or all of the plays that make up the first and second tetralogies to be involved in English nation formation. McEachern points to the issue of a cohesive body politic and "common language," Helgerson, to an identification with the monarch, and Howard and Rackin to the use of gender in the construction of a nation.[5] Despite differences in how these literary histories write the nation and at what cost, there is a degree of consensus among these critics about the plays' (and by extension Shakespeare's) involvement in a discourse of emergent English nationhood.

Critics disagree, however, about Shakespeare's participation in a discourse of nationhood when they turn to his tragedies dealing with cross-cultural encounters. A number of readings of these plays (especially those of Leslie Fiedler and Jonathan Burton) support the idea of a nationalist Shakespeare by claiming that the "other," no matter how complex and sympathetically dramatized, is invariably cast out of the community.[6] Such readings are countered by critics such as Graham Bradshaw, who concludes that Shakespeare shows a great deal of sensitivity to diverse cultures, and Geraldo de Sousa, who reads Shakespeare as challenging "Eurocentric isolationism and feelings of ideological superiority."[7] More recently, Richard Wilson has shown that Shakespeare uses the figures of the Jew, the Moor, and the stranger to promote an ethic of tolerance and hospitality; B.J. Sokol asserts that, "What we will meet in Shakespeare's portrayals of tolerance is the celebration of those who can transcend rancour arising from human differences."[8] These readings of Shakespeare suggest a deconstruction of the stability of identity grounded in complexion, religion, language, political allegiance, and birthplace – precisely the attributes often said to ground national character.[9]

Given that these different Shakespeares tend to manifest themselves in different genres – nationalist Shakespeare in the history plays, cross-cultural Shakespeare in certain tragedies and comedies – it is not impossible for the two tendencies to coexist, but I would like to present another possible Shakespeare, one deeply rooted in the conditions under which he lived and wrote in London. A focus on Shakespeare's legal status and his relations with immigrants around him, and the way in which these factors shaped his living and working conditions can make sense of the divergent readings of Shakespeare in terms of nation and cross-cultural contact. This is not to say that Shakespeare is "our contemporary," to use Jan Kott's phrase. Shakespeare can be seen to be rather like Deloney: linguistic difference provided ample material for jokes, but both writers participate in an early modern ideal of hospitality, depicting communities that are inclusive but also guarded about the possible influence of outsiders.

This chapter begins with an exploration of some of Shakespeare's acquaintances in London, followed by readings of two plays tangentially related to the histories so frequently found to be involved in the formation of English nationhood: *The Merry Wives of Windsor* is a comedy inextricably connected to the second tetralogy; *Sir Thomas More* is a history play of sorts but does not feature the monarch as a central figure. What becomes clear in these two readings is a shared experience of an early modern ethic of inclusivity and its limits in domestic space.

Shakespeare among the Immigrants

It is not known precisely when Shakespeare made his way from Stratford-upon-Avon to London. The last reference to him in Stratford occurs in 1585 when his twins were baptized; the first reference in London is found in Robert Greene's *Groats-Worth of Wit* in 1592.[10] That Shakespeare had a high enough profile in London to merit Greene's disapproval suggests that he had been there for some time: Greene's invective alludes to *Richard Duke of York* (*3 Henry VI*), so Shakespeare must have been working in London at least long enough to compose at least two history plays and probably *The Two Gentleman of Verona*, estimated to have been written as early as 1591.[11] One striking element of Shakespeare's life in London that requires some emphasis is his connection to the immigrant communities in the city, and while I shall not argue that Shakespeare was really a Huguenot, I do believe that these connections are important in understanding *Sir Thomas More* and *The Merry Wives of Windsor* in particular, and much of his work more generally. These connections to immigrant communities seem to have begun soon after he came to London and persisted throughout his time there.

Whether Shakespeare arrived in London on his own or as part of the Queen's Men, as Samuel Schoenbaum speculates, most scholars agree that one of his first acquaintances there was almost certainly printer Richard Field.[12] Field was born in Stratford-upon-Avon in 1561. His father, Henry

Field, had done business with Shakespeare's father, John Shakespeare, and despite differences that led the elder Field to bring suit against the elder Shakespeare in 1556, they apparently resolved their differences, for in 1592 when Henry Field died, John Shakespeare was among those taking inventory of Field's goods. Richard Field left for London in the late 1570s and began an apprenticeship to London printer George Bishop; Bishop soon arranged for six years of Field's apprenticeship to be under prominent printer and French Protestant refugee Thomas Vautrollier, who in the 1570s had been involved in the printing of several pro-Huguenot pamphlets. A.E.M. Kirwood suggests that Bishop may have placed Field under Vautrollier because Bishop himself had no time to devote to his training, but Bishop had made a similar arrangement a year earlier, placing his apprentice William Hammond under French bookbinder Lewis Senior. Bishop may have been subcontracting his apprentices to strangers as a business deal whereby strangers could circumvent restrictions on the number of apprentices they were allowed to employ. At any rate, Richard Field, a young man from out of town, found himself in the employ of a stranger rather than a Londoner.

Vautrollier specialized in theological texts such as Jean Calvin's *Institutes* and John Knox's *The History of the Reformation*, but he also printed a number of books aimed at language learning, and it seems that his shop had had a reputation for handling texts that were difficult to print. In 1587, shortly after Field gained his freedom (having completed his final year under Bishop), Vautrollier died; the next year Field married his former master's widow, Jacqueline Vautrollier, and took over Vautrollier's shop in Blackfriars.[13] Field continued Vautrollier's printing of Protestant polemics and language texts (for example, several editions of Claudius Hollybrand's *The French Littleton*), but he expanded the shop's market by overseeing the printing of such literary landmarks as George Puttenham's *Arte of English Poesie* (1589), the first edition of John Harrington's *Orlando Furioso* (1591), the first complete edition of Edmund Spenser's *Faerie Queene* (1596), Sidney's *Arcadia* (1598), Thomas Campion's *Observations in the Art of English Poesie* (1602), and George Chapman's translation of *The Iliad* (1611). In the early 1590s Field printed the earliest known works of Shakespeare: the first several editions of *Venus and Adonis* (1593–96) and the first edition of *The Rape of Lucrece* (1594). Publishing these Shakespeare texts may make sense to modern readers, but it must have been a considerable gamble on Field's part; the fact that the poet was a fellow Stratfordian no doubt played a role in his decision to publish the then largely unknown poet.

Jacqueline Vautrollier seems to have been very much involved in the day-to-day operations of the shop; she ran it when Thomas Vautrollier was away in Scotland, and even after she married Field, her name continued to appear alongside his as printer of a number of texts. It seems reasonable to assume that Richard Field and his French wife, Jacqueline, were among Shakespeare's first friends in London. Stephen Greenblatt and Charles Nicholl note that much of Shakespeare's wide reading is attributable to his friend's publications – Field printed Thomas North's translation of Plutarch's *Lives* (1595), for example – and he no doubt possessed a number of books from his competitors, many of which likely found their way into Shakespeare's hands.[14]

Schoenbaum suggests that it was perhaps through Jacqueline Field, who attended the French Church, that Shakespeare came to lodge with the Mountjoys, a well-to-do Huguenot family living on Silver Street in Saint Olave's Parish.[15] Christopher Mountjoy was a prominent tire-maker (a maker of decorative headgear), and his wife, Marie, is known to have consulted astrologer and sometime playgoer Simon Forman on more than one occasion. We know from a deposition that Shakespeare definitely lived with the Mountjoys in 1604, but he had probably lived with them for some time before and certainly continued after that year; Charles Nicholl asserts that Shakespeare likely began lodging there between 1602 and 1603.[16] In any case, Shakespeare stayed with the Mountjoys long enough to have been entrusted with the important brokering of a marriage between the Mountjoys' daughter Mary and their apprentice Stephen Belott, whose mother was also a member of the French reformed community in London. That Shakespeare was entrusted with the task of arranging the marriage suggests that he had been on very good terms with at least one if not both of the parties in the marriage for a considerable time. In 1612 Shakespeare was called to testify as to the nature of the contract he had brokered, for Christopher Mountjoy had apparently never fulfilled his financial obligations to Bellot; the case was eventually referred to the French Church at Threadneedle Street.[17] E.A.J. Honigmann suggests that this episode may have formed the basis for go-betweens in *All's Well that Ends Well* and *Measure for Measure*, plays Shakespeare was likely composing around the time of the initial negotiations. Along similar lines, Nicholl suggests that the character of Constable Elbow in *Measure for Measure* may have been based on the French silk-weaver Anthony Elbowe, a neighbour from Shakespeare's time in Bishopsgate.[18]

Shakespeare's connections to London's stranger communities were not limited to the French Reformed community, however. The engraving on the

First Folio was made by Martin Droeshout. The Droeshouts were Dutch Protestant refugees who immigrated to London in the 1560s. There were two Martin Droeshouts: Martin Droeshout the elder and his nephew Martin Droeshout the younger. Scholars have assumed that the younger Droeshout was the First Folio engraver and from this have surmised that the artist never saw Shakespeare, since the younger Droeshout would have been only fifteen at the time of Shakespeare's death.[19] However, June Schlueter and Mary Edmond have shown that the engraving was more than likely done by the elder Droeshout. Why, asks Edmond, after all their expense, would Heminges and Condell employ an inexperienced engraver unfamiliar with Shakespeare's face?[20] Honigmann argues further that the elder Droeshout had sketched Shakespeare from life and that Heminges and Condell wanted to use that particular likeness either because it captured the image of the man they knew or because it was the only sketch from life available.[21] Along similar lines, Edmond theorizes that Droeshout's engraving was based on a lost portrait by Droeshout's fellow Protestant refugee and sometime associate Marcus Gheeraerts II.[22] Finally, the elder Droeshout may have been contracted as the engraver because he had had some form of contact with Shakespeare if not as the artist of a lost sketch, then as an acquaintance or business associate of another kind. Speculation could go on, but the point is that Shakespeare appears to have had some acquaintance with at least one of the aforementioned artists of the Dutch Protestant community.

Similarly, Honigmann argues that the stonemason Gheerart Janssen, who sculpted the Shakespeare funeral monument now located in Stratford-upon Avon and whose shop was located just down the street from the Globe Theatre, may well have known Shakespeare personally.[23] The shop location is right for the two to have met, and as with Droeshout, it is worth noting that Janssen immigrated to London from the Netherlands. Thus the two possibly authentic depictions of Shakespeare's physical likeness were created by immigrants who may have met Shakespeare at least once if not several times. The proximity of the Globe to Janssen's shop is of particular significance. As Steven Mullaney reminds us in *The Place of the Stage*, the theatre's surroundings are important to the overall experience of Shakespeare's plays.[24] While Mullaney is careful to contextualize the theatre in terms of bear baiting, prostitution, and leprosy, he does not mention that the Globe, like the Rose and the Swan, was located in an area that, according to the Returns of Aliens, 1593, was home to more than 300 immigrants.[25] On the way to the theatre audience members would hear and see strangers, and Shakespeare was no doubt aware of their presence, if not well acquainted with some as well.

Although a personal connection between Shakespeare and the artists and neighbours named above is probable rather than certain, there was a definite friendship between Shakespeare and Elias James, a second-generation immigrant from the Netherlands. Like many descendants of strangers, James had adopted an English sounding name: his grandfather Jacob van Hawstert came to England in the 1560s and Jacob's children took his given name and Anglicized it as their new family name. Elias James, like his father, uncle, and grandfather, was a successful beer brewer; his brewery, located at Puddle Wharf, near Blackfriars Theatre, was estimated to be worth just over £800 in 1590.[26] Leslie Hotson has shown that Elias James was related by marriage to John Jackson, one of Shakespeare's trustees in the purchase of the Blackfriars Gatehouse in 1613; Elias James died in 1610 and was buried directly across from Shakespeare's Blackfriars' property.

A friend of a friend of Shakespeare's would hardly be worth attention, were it not for the fact that a poem attributed to Shakespeare, entitled "An Epitaph on Elias James," was featured in the 1633 edition of Stow's *Survey of London*.

> When God was pleased, the world unwilling yet,
> Elias James to nature paid his debt,
> And here reposeth. As he lived, he died,
> The saying strongly in him verified:
> "Such life, such death". Then, a known truth to tell,
> He lived a godly life, and died as well.[27]

The fact that James' grave was so close to Shakespeare's property and that he was connected to Shakespeare via John Jackson only strengthens the attribution, and the evidence points to a reasonably close relationship between Shakespeare and James. As both a descendent of a Dutch family and as a brewer, a craft dominated by immigrants and their descendants, James would have maintained considerable connections with the Dutch community, and, as pointed out in chapter 3, children and grandchildren of strangers were often counted as strangers no matter how assimilated they had become. Moreover, the epitaph describes James as living "a godly life," suggesting that his connections to the Dutch community may have extended beyond distant relations and professional necessities to the church at Austin Friars. The epitaph itself testifies to a level of reverence like that of Shakespeare's epitaph for the Stanley family to which he had many close connections.[28]

Shakespeare interacted more regularly with Nichlas Tooley, fellow actor in the King's Men. Born in Antwerp of a Flemish mother and English father, Tooley was brought to London as a boy following his father's death. He was eventually apprenticed to Richard Burbage and like Shakespeare became a shareholder in the Lord Chamberlain's Men. Mary Edmond suggests that Shakespeare may have known members of Tooley's family in Warwickshire and been instrumental in introducing Tooley to the theatre.[29]

Scholars have long speculated that Shakespeare may have had some contact with poet Amelia Lanyer, the English-born daughter of Italian immigrant and court musician. Although the idea that Lanyer was the Dark Lady of Shakespeare's sonnets has generally fallen out of favour, Susanne Woods asserts that Shakespeare "could hardly have avoided several of her (male) Bassano musician cousins who were around court continuously through the 1590s and beyond."[30] Along similar lines, Jonathan Bate and Saul Frampton have claimed a relationship between Shakespeare and John Florio, the English-born son of Italian Protestant refugee Michaelangelo Florio.[31] Frampton goes on to theorize that Florio edited the First Folio of Shakespeare's works. If so, the First Folio, like the Ditchley Portrait discussed in the Introduction, is yet another example of an iconic object of Englishness bearing traces of multicultural England.

Nicholas Tooley, Elias James, Stephen Bellot, Christopher, Marie Mountjoy, Mary Mountjoy, Jacqueline Field, perhaps Martin Droeshout, Gheerart Janssen, and/or Marcus Gheeraerts II, and probably John Florio and the Bassano family – it is striking how many of Shakespeare's friends and acquaintances were strangers or sons and daughters of strangers. On one hand, this testifies to the prevalence of immigrants living in and around London. On the other, as Greenblatt notes, Shakespeare "seems to have had an affinity for neighborhoods – Shoreditch, Bishopsgate, Cripplegate, and the Clink in Surrey – inhabited by artisans, many of whom were émigrés from France or the Low Countries."[32] Focusing on Shakespeare's time in St Helen's Parish, Park Honan remarks on the numerous immigrants surrounding him and suggests that Shakespeare seems to have been comfortable living among strangers.[33] The neighbourhoods and company Shakespeare kept should give some pause to those scholars who suppose that Shakespeare was a closet-Catholic.[34] Would a Catholic be living with Huguenots, one of the most adamantly anti-Catholic Protestant groups in London? And why would he write an epitaph complimenting Elias James' Protestant piety? Perhaps this poem was the allegedly Catholic Shakespeare's cover, or perhaps he identified the repression of

Protestants abroad with that of Catholics in his own place of birth, and so lived sympathetically with them. Or perhaps scholars have been wrong about Shakespeare's deep faith in Catholicism. It may be that Shakespeare left his Catholic faith (if he ever had it) behind in Stratford-upon-Avon with his wife and children. Whether as a Catholic living among adamant Protestant refugees or as an Englishman who came to know well the intimate lives of immigrants, such relations likely led Shakespeare to some insight about what it might be like to be a stranger in Ephesus or Illyria, a Moor or Jew among Catholic Venetians.[35]

More than religion, Shakespeare probably had economic motives for his choice of residences in London. On his way from Warwickshire to London, he may have come across a popular ballad such as the seventeenth-century "London's Praise, or, the Glory of the City," which amid the encomia to the city features passages of warning to outsiders:

> Unto themselves a Charter free,
> this wealthy City holds,
> All that have freedom there to be,
> the Chamberlain enrolls.
> No Forraigner can set up there,
> their orders are so strong,
> In shop they must not sell no ware,
> least they the Free-men wrong.[36]

As noted in the Introduction, the term *foreigner* could refer to immigrants but more often denoted migrants from throughout the realm. As they did with strangers, the guilds restricted the economic and political participation of foreigners who failed to join one of the livery companies. Strangers or foreigners without the freedom of the city could only buy goods from a freeman and were prevented from running an open shop, selling wares, or participating in the city's governance in any meaningful way. Many guilds prevented strangers and foreigners from working even as low-wage labourers.[37] The coveted freedom of the city could be inherited from one's father but more often was granted only to those who had been admitted to one of the livery companies; the price of admittance was an apprenticeship and usually a gift to the company's wardens.[38] According to "London's Praise,"

> A countrey Boy comes up to town,
> perhaps no cloaths to his back:
> Nor to one creature there is known,

yet he need never lack:
If that he be just and true,
and have an honest face,
And willing any work to do,
he need not want a place.

The phrase "willing any work to do" suggests either irregular wage labour or an apprenticeship, the latter of which would lead to the freedom of the city. Shakespeare, however, was not a "countrey Boy" seeking to eke out a living. He was an adult in need of enough income to support himself in London and his family in Stratford. His family could ill afford his contracting as an apprentice for seven years before seeing any income, and occasional wage labour would not pay for food and lodging for himself and his family. That the outsider Shakespeare would have noted the premium Londoners placed on the freedom of the city as a marker of contrast with strangers and foreigners operating outside of the guild system is verified by John Michael Archer's study, *Citizen Shakespeare*, which explores discourses of citizenship in Shakespeare's plays.[39]

As with many non-denizen strangers, foreigners like Shakespeare tended to live in the liberties of London where they could practice a trade with minimal interference from the guilds. As discussed in chapter 3, such cracks in the authority of the guilds sometimes led to tension between, on one side, members of guilds, and, on the other, strangers and foreigners. Strangers and foreigners were often lumped together in petitions because the two groups made up a substantial proportion of the economically active non-free of London. That is, for these petitioners, participation in an apprenticeship system that provided cheap help and inducted individuals into the culture of the guild was more important than national identity. By 1606 agitation was such that an act of Common Council sought to limit the economic activities of "divers and sundry strangers borne, and likewise forreiners from the liberties of the said Cittie."[40] Competition from strangers and foreigners who worked outside of the guilds' authority made it difficult for young men to set up their own shops because the increase in population had inflated rent and flooded the market for goods and labour. Since neither foreigners nor strangers tended to join the guilds, apprentices in London considered them to be essentially the same.

Ian Archer has found in the 1580s and 1590s, around the time Shakespeare must have been establishing himself in London, a marked increase in livery companies taking legal action against strangers and foreigners.[41] When Shakespeare came to London it makes sense that he would live among immigrants. He no doubt experienced something of the difference guilds' members perceived between themselves and outsiders. In terms of economic freedom and political rights, Shakespeare would have had much more in common with immigrants than with Londoners. Helgerson too writes of Shakespeare's "social insecurity" in London and notes that this, in part, accounts for what he sees as Shakespeare's gradual spurning of clowns, the usually rustic figures who provide comic relief in earlier plays.[42] This argument provides the basis for Helgerson's analysis of Shakespeare's participation in the purging of "barbarism" from the theatre and the nation it constructed in history plays. The discourse of nationhood in the second tetralogy is perhaps due to the fact that Shakespeare's histories tend to contrast the high politics of kingship with the concerns of commoners. This dual nature of England, one part seemingly organized around the monarch and the other around a shared sense of belonging, is precisely the tension Helgerson finds lurking in numerous Elizabethan texts, most of which evince a certain kind of patriotism.

If the patriotism of Shakespeare's histories sometimes leads to an assumption of an early English nation, it is at least in part because of what counts as a history play: *King John,* but not *Cymbeline,* although both are set in England's distant past; *1 and 2 Henry IV,* but not *The Merry Wives of Windsor,* although the characters overlap and the locales are all grounded in a realistic depiction of England;[43] *All is True/Henry VIII,* but not *The Play Sir Thomas More,* although both depict events from the same decades. In each of these pairings one play is excluded from the histories, and each of those excluded plays complicates the readings of Shakespeare as a poet of national consciousness.[44] I shall examine the two plays that are most closely related to the histories: *The Merry Wives of Windsor,* a comedy intimately connected to the second tetralogy, and *Sir Thomas More,* a play partially written by Shakespeare representing the rise and fall of More as statesman. These two plays dramatize the potential for a more inclusive cosmopolitanism in England's urban centre, based on a willingness to participate in, rather than circumvent, local practices; both plays insist on social relations based on communal understanding instead of social exclusion based on an "othering" paradigm. Finally, both plays deal with the domestic, the demand for and limits of domestic hospitality in early modern England.

Staging Inclusion (1): *The Merry Wives of Windsor*

"When Hal banishes Falstaff," writes Helgerson, "both carnival and the clown feel the blow."[45] Helgerson aligns Henry V's banishment of Falstaff with the exclusion of clowns and the labouring class they tended to represent on the stage; this theatrical exclusion, he argues, is part of Shakespeare's valorizing of a distinctly monarchical form of nationhood.[46] Helgerson's position is not far from Anthony D. Smith's view that the artisans and peasants of England were not part of the early development of an English nation.[47] Helgerson is aware of the paradox here and suggests that self-alienation was an integral part of England's writing itself as a nation. More recently, he has found a similarly nationalist discourse at work in *The Merry Wives of Windsor* even though the play features the return of Falstaff.[48] Without denying the construction of Englishness in the play, I would like to suggest that *The Merry Wives of Windsor*, with its contemporary or near contemporary setting and its main plots revolving around two Windsor citizen families, the Fords and the Pages, also participates in a counterdiscourse of worldly domesticity whereby multicultural elements find their way into the English home. In one plot Sir John Falstaff, an outsider to Windsor, disrupts the order of the community, first by allegedly poaching deer, and second by attempting to woo Mistress Margaret Page and Mistress Alice Ford, the "merry wives" of the title. The play is punctuated by the various ways Mistress Ford and Mistress Page punish Falstaff for his transgressions. At the same time, at least some of the antics are intended to reform Frank Ford, Mistress Ford's overly possessive husband.

In another plot Abraham Slender (a timid citizen caught up in the politics of arranged marriage), Fenton (a misjudged gentleman), and Doctor Caius (a choleric French immigrant) vie for the hand of Margaret Page's daughter, Anne. Each is favoured by at least one character in the play: Fenton by the Host of the Garter Inn, Slender by Justice Shallow and Master George Page, and Caius by Margaret Page. When Caius discovers that the Welsh parson Hugh Evans is trying to enlist the Doctor's servant Mistress Quickly to help promote Slender's courtship of Anne, Caius challenges the parson to a duel; the Host of the Garter Inn turns the duel into a jest by sending each to a different appointed place; when the jest is discovered, Caius forgoes the duel and instead conspires with Evans to trick the Host into giving away his horses to three prominent Germans visiting Windsor. In the final scene the plots come together as the members of the Windsor community disguise themselves as fairies to frighten and abuse Falstaff who has wandered into the woods for a supposed rendezvous with the "merry wives." At the same time, Master Page has arranged for a secret wedding between Slender and Anne while Mistress Page has arranged for a secret wedding between Caius and Anne. However, Anne and Fenton fool all, and are happily married while Caius and Slender are left to wed two boys who were disguised as Anne. The play ends with an invitation to a banquet at the Pages' home.

While composition and performance dates are notoriously difficult to pin down, the Stationers' Register and publication dates are somewhat more straightforward: Falstaff may have been banished in *2 Henry IV* and is noticeably absent in *Henry V,* both registered in 1600, but he reappears in *The Merry Wives of Windsor,* entered in the Stationers' Register in 1602.[49] Part of Helgerson's argument, of course, is that artisans and clowns were relegated to the comedies, but it is significant that no other comedy rubs so closely to the material of the histories. *Merry Wives* features a number of characters from the *Henriad,* such as Fenton, who is referred to as a friend of the waggish Prince. Moreover, the play can be read as a comic rendering of the menacing figures of the *Henriad*: in place of the Dauphin and the French soldiers we have the comically choleric stranger, Doctor Caius; in place of the menacing Welsh Glendower, we have the laughable Welsh Parson Hugh Evans; the claims of Welsh witchcraft in *1 Henry IV* are domesticated as Falstaff takes on the guise of the witch of Brentford; and the brutality visited on English children in *Henry V* are nothing more than a comic lesson in Latin in *Merry Wives.* One cannot help but think of Karl Marx's opening to *The Eighteenth Brumaire,* in which he describes history as repeating itself as farce.[50] Here indeed the material of the histories is reworked as comedy. Is it any wonder, then, that Friedrich Engels wrote in 1873, "There is more life and reality in the first act of the *Merry Wives* alone than in all German literature"?[51] Taking the historical materialist at his word, *Merry Wives* would then seem to pose an argument about England as Shakespeare saw it, an England that involved local citizens like the Fords and Pages, foreigners like Evans, and strangers like Caius.

In her analysis of the folio and first quarto versions of *Merry Wives,* Leah Marcus shows that the latter text systematically avoids references to Windsor and has "an urban setting strongly suggesting London."[52] The folio, she argues, is the script of a royal performance with less biting attacks on the nobility and more references to specific Windsor locales. This in itself suggests that Shakespeare's company tailored the play to address issues pertinent to London. By muting the garter context of the play, the urban quarto of *Merry Wives* foregrounds the story of foreigners and strangers (Falstaff, Fenton, Evans, and Doctor Caius) attempting to integrate into the local community, and the rules by which they must do so.

With strangers comprising a significant percentage of London's population, Caius, the French doctor and suitor to Anne Page, would seem to fit Engels's and Marcus's belief in the verisimilitude of the play. Hoenselaars sees Caius as the product of English stereotypes of the French,⁵³ but it is likely that Shakespeare's relations with Jacqueline Vautrollier and the Mountjoys must have at least informed his portrayal of French immigrant doctor. The apparently cantankerous Christopher Mountjoy in particular may have influenced Shakespeare's characterization of Caius as especially quick-tempered. Mountjoy's dispute with his daughter and son-in-law suggests a somewhat stubborn personality, and his later excommunication from the French Church for "licentious living" only adds to the portrait of a flamboyant and difficult older man not unlike Caius.⁵⁴ Of course, this latter anecdote about Mountjoy refers to a time well after the composition of *Merry Wives,* but Shakespeare knew Mountjoy by the late 1590s (if not earlier) and there may well have been episodes that would lead Shakespeare to the same general picture of a crank.

Shakespeare's portrayal of Caius is not entirely negative, however. Jacqueline Vautrollier, the other Mountjoys, and any number of unrecorded acquaintances may have tempered Shakespeare's depiction of the French immigrant. Without a doubt, Caius is no romantic hero, but he is ready to duel with Evans (unlike the similarly combative but ultimately timid Sir Andrew Aguecheek in *Twelfth Night,* for example): Caius's bravado is not without some substance, and this lack of cowardice breaks with the stereotype of the choleric but cowardly Frenchman that Hoenselaars maps out.⁵⁵ When Caius discovers that the duel was the Host of the Garter's practical joke, he gets revenge through the horse-stealing caper, but his revenge does not escalate tensions: evening the score with the Host reconciles the two. Caius, then, is laughable but not so thoroughly stereotypical as to lack some dignity. Moreover, the fact that the jest and counter-jest occur between a stranger and a character known only as the Host suggests that the play is invested in exploring the value of and limits to hospitality between locals and strangers or foreigners in England.

Caius and Evans are ostensibly set apart from the local community through linguistic difference, but the play also seems to undermine language as the basis for defining insider and outside in Windsor. Caius and Evans, notes David Daube, are both laughed at for making, as Falstaff puts it, "fritters of English" (5.5.136).⁵⁶ The editors of the *Norton Shakespeare* likewise suggest that, "Windsor's sense of community depends on a cheerfully casual ethnocentrism" manifested in several allusions, but especially "in the fractured English of the French Caius and Welsh Evans."⁵⁷ Caius is not entirely a pariah, however, and his relative mastery of English is not necessarily a marker of absolute alterity. When Falstaff interprets Mistress Ford's body language as expressing interest in an affair with him, Pistol exclaims, "He has studied her well, and translated her will: out of honesty and into English" (1.3.42–3). English here is figured not as the accurate language of community but rather the errant language of illicit affairs and self-interest. Mistress Quickly, moreover, is no master of even her native tongue: she misunderstands Evans's question about the number of noun cases in Latin, and further reveals her confusion by insisting that the answer cannot be "two" as young William Page says, but three, since the number must be odd, as in the phrase "'Ods nouns" (4.1.17–20). Although this exchange comprises her intrusion in a Latin lesson, the inadvertent puns reveal her own lack of command of the English language.[58]

Similarly, Slender's speech is marred with malapropisms: at the prospect of the arranged marriage between himself and Anne Page, he muses, "I will marry her, sir, at your request. But if there be no great love in the beginning, yet heaven may decrease it upon better acquaintance, when we are married and have more occasion to know one another. I hope upon familiarity will grow more contempt" (1.1.206–10). With *decrease* for *increase*, *contempt* for *content*, Slender's mastery of his own language is perhaps less precise than Caius and Evans' mastery of English as a second language. Linguistic competence, then, can hardly be held up as the sign of one's membership in the Windsor community. Despite the gibes about his mastery of English, Mistress Page nonetheless favours Caius as a match for her daughter over the well-connected native-born citizen Slender and the gentleman Fenton.

It is, in fact, not the stranger Caius, but native English foreigner Falstaff who is treated as the outsider, the pariah of the Windsor community. When Falstaff is thrown into the Thames, Shakespeare dramatizes a well-known communal punishment reserved for those who had no place in the community. Many accounts of resistance to tax collectors and other unwelcome outsiders, for example, included a ritualistic disposal of the outsider in a nearby river, an act symbolically aligning the outsider with refuse.[59] Falstaff's other punishments have a similar symbolic meaning: he is dressed as the witch of Brentford and subsequently beaten for it, a punishment that not only feminizes him but connects him to the absolute outsider, the witch. And in the final scene the entire community conspires to dress him as Herne the hunter and to burn him with tapers. As Herne, Falstaff is forced to embody his violations of the community's values: his knightly courage is trampled on as he cowers before children dressed as fairies, and he wears horns that recall not only the cuckolds he tried to make out of Ford and Page, but also the deer he apparently poached from Justice Shallow at the outset of the play. The coordinated nature of

Falstaff's final punishment before he repents emphasizes that Caius and Evans are not outside the local community; they are included in the community's ritual shaming of Falstaff.[60]

Certainly the foreigner Shakespeare never faced at the hands of Londoners the humiliations Falstaff faces in Windsor, but Shakespeare's attention to the foreigner rather than the stranger as absolute outsider is telling. Fenton, too, is a foreigner to Windsor, but he is not thrown in the river or burned in the forest. The picture of community Shakespeare offers in *Merry Wives* is inclusive but demanding in its expectations of outsiders. Falstaff violates traditional property rights by poaching, and more importantly he violates the sanctity of the family (another kind of poaching, observes Jeffrey Theis) when he tries to seduce the wives of Ford and Page.[61] In the quarto, instead of Herne, Falstaff is dressed as "Home the Hunter," an interesting connection to his specific violation of the homes of Ford and Page. Moreover, when Falstaff meets with Mistress Ford, he consistently and conspicuously puts his status as a knight on display as though this status were inherently more valuable than that of master or freeman of the city to a citizen of Windsor: to Mistress Ford he announces, "I wish thy husband were dead: I'll before the best lord. I would make thee my lady," and of her beauty he states, "Let the court of France show me such another. I see how thine eye would emulate the diamond. Thou hast the right arched beauty of the brow that becomes the ship-tire, the tire-valiant, or any tire of Venetian admittance" (3.3.40–2; 45–8). Such affectations do not sit well in a community founded on bourgeois rather than aristocratic ideals, a community in which, for example, claims of inherited right are less important than an earned freedom of the city. Falstaff the foreigner is an outcast not because he comes from outside of Windsor but because he fails to participate in or even recognize the communal norms of Windsor. Caius, on the other hand, operates within Windsor's system of values, offering his services to the community, employing locals, and matching jest with jest.

In the end, however, Caius is among the dupes of the play, for Anne's will (like that of the daughters in *Englishmen for My Money*) wins out, and she marries not the Windsor insider Slender, but Fenton, the English foreigner to Windsor. Caius thinks he has married Anne Page, but upon closer inspection he discovers otherwise: "By Gar, I am cozened! I ha' married *un garçon*, a boy, *un paysan*, by Gar. A boy! It is not Anne Page, by Gar. I am cozened" (5.5.187–9), and a few lines later, "'Ay, be Gar, and 'tis a boy. Be Gar, I'll raise all Windsor" (5.5.191). Here many editors interpolate Caius's exit.[62] That Caius leaves the stage at this moment of discontent leads Hoenselaars to suppose that he makes a Malvolio-like exit, and that this departure figures Caius as the ultimate outsider in the play.[63] Malvolio's exit in *Twelfth Night* is also an editorial interpolation, but one with sound textual evidence: Orsino orders, "Pursue him" (5.1.367), and one can only assume that a need to pursue indicates an exit or near exit from the stage. But there is no such textual evidence for Caius's exit. Since none of the characters of *Merry Wives* suggests that he be pursued and no one comments on what some editors have taken as his absence, it seems logical enough that Caius remains on stage after expressing his displeasure. Thus, in the final lines of the play, when Mistress Page declares, "Good husband, let us every one go home, / And laugh this sport o'er by a country fire, / Sir John and all" (5.5.218–20), she is inviting not only Falstaff and Evans, but also Caius. Mistress Page, Caius's strongest advocate, is after all making a kind of peace offering to all those who had been gulled in the play's final jest. Caius is a stranger, but he is also in the end returned to the local community of which he is an integral part. There is no doubt that *Merry Wives* is intent on its depiction of Englishness, but the Englishness here is one defined by concepts of hospitality. To be English is to be a host.

One curious punishment in *Merry Wives* remains, and this one is meted out not by the fictional community of the play but by Shakespeare and his company: when Ford disguises himself so as to prove himself a cuckold, he uses the name Brooke, and the play not infrequently puns on the name Oldcastle. Oldcastle and Brooke were references to the Brooke family – Henry Brooke, Lord Cobham in particular – a family that prided itself in being descended from the Lollard Sir John Oldcastle. Shakespeare's company had already been censored for using the Oldcastle name for the "trunk of humours" renamed Falstaff (*1 Henry IV* 2.5.410), so why would they persist in braving the authority of the Brooke family? Some suspect that Lord Cobham was opposed to the theatre, or that Shakespeare maligned Oldcastle because he identified him with the kind of hypocrisy he observed in some Puritans.[64] I would like to suggest one other possible motive: as warden of the cinque ports, Lord Cobham was responsible for ensuring the enforcement of the Queen's will regarding foreign shipments into England. On several occasions, Cobham wilfully neglected his duties when it involved protecting immigrants from municipal statutes that ran contrary to the Queen's own favour towards merchant strangers. Only when mandated by the Privy Council would Brooke venture to prevent the exploitation of merchant strangers.[65] To what degree Henry Brooke had become notorious for his indifference to the exploitation of strangers is unknown. Nonetheless, it is important to note that in *The Merry Wives of Windsor*, strangers like Caius are constant members of the community while an Englishman like Falstaff is viewed until the end as an outcast. Of course, Falstaff is ultimately invited to the Pages, but only after undergoing a series of punishments to induct him into the community's system of values; it is agreement to this system of values, not birthplace or class, that earns one an invitation to the imagined community of Windsor.

Staging Inclusion (2): *Sir Thomas More*

While *Merry Wives* shows Shakespeare domesticating the material of the histories within the generic constraints of comedy, his hand in *Sir Thomas More* involves him in reworking or working against the genre of the history play as it has been defined by critics. Tracey Hill has shown how, by focusing on London as a collective protagonist, *Sir Thomas More* differs from most histories of the period, but most of the criticism of the play has focused on issues of authorship, date, and censorship, since the manuscript includes notes from Master of the Revels, Edmund Tilney.[66] Indeed, although *The Riverside Shakespeare* and *Norton Shakespeare* include complete versions of other Shakespeare collaborations, such as *Two Noble Kinsmen* and *Henry VIII*, these editions include only the portion of *Sir Thomas More* attributed to Shakespeare.[67] This is a real pity since *Sir Thomas More* has much to offer as an example of how many plays were likely written, as a play with substantial thematic connections to several plays in the Shakespeare canon, and as an interesting play in its own right.

The play depicts the rise and fall of Thomas More as a man of the people. Despite this fairly straightforward trajectory, the script features a wide variety of episodes from the May Day riot of 1517 to More as practical joker and impromptu actor, and to the end with More on the scaffold. It begins with the scenes attributed to Shakespeare, the events surrounding the ill May Day riot of 1517 giving More the role of peacemaker. This event, the play implies, results in More's initial rise from sheriff to member of the Privy Council and eventually to Lord Chancellor. In the aftermath of the riot, More even intervenes to save the majority of rioters from the gallows; only John Lincoln, the main instigator, is executed. What puzzles critics are the episodes that follow the riot: More saves a thief from death so that he can help in a jest to embarrass an over-zealous justice. Then More meets with Erasmus, but he does not engage in a humanist dialogue; instead he plays a practical joke on his friend. Then, a long-haired man arrested for brawling is given the choice between getting a haircut or going to jail. Later, More improvises a part in an interlude. All of this seems to critics to be fairly light-hearted material for a dramatization of the protagonist of *A Man for All Seasons*, but (with the exception of the haircut episode) they make More likeable, rather like Shakespeare's Prince Hal or Dekker's Simon Eyre. More then refuses to sign an unnamed document (presumably the Oath of Supremacy), he resigns the Lord Chancellorship, and retreats to his home where he is eventually arrested. He is imprisoned, even as the commoners come out to support him, and he is duly executed, as was Lincoln whom he could not save earlier. Despite the picaresque organization of the play, a recent performance at the Globe met with very positive reviews, confirming Georgio Melchiori's assertion that *Sir Thomas More* is more coherent than the collaborative authorship and censorship would seem to suggest.[68]

This is not to say that the bibliographic and stylometric analyses are less important than the studies of the play's coherence, theme, or cultural work. Clearly, an understanding of the sources, authorship, and dates of writing, revision and performance are crucial to a study of any play. Indeed, the determination of dates of composition and possible performance is an important and particularly vexing issue in interpreting this particular play: some evidence has led critics to believe that it was written as early as 1586, while others believe that the play was written around the turn of the century, and still others believe it was drafted at an early date and that Shakespeare involved himself in a revision of the work in the early seventeenth century.[69]

While collaboration has been an important topic in and of itself, I believe that it fits within the play's depiction of More. The very materiality of the play with its multiple "hands" making separate scenes suggests a decentring of *author*ity through its method of composition, which has more in common with the collective piece work of an artisan's shop than with the vision of the solitary genius leading his company of players. That is, the play's engagement with issues of inclusion is directly related to issues of economics and domestic space. It is likely that Tilney famously demanded that the insurrection against aliens be addressed "only by A shortt / reportt & nott otherwise" for precisely this reason.[70] I would like to defy the censor by examining the dramatization of the anti-alien sentiment as it relates to *Sir Thomas More* as a whole and to the play's cultural surrounds. First we must examine the material *Sir Thomas More* reworks.

The Evil (or Ill) May Day riot of 1517 stands out as emblematic of the dangers of revolt in the Tudor imagination. For several scholars it further functions as a dramatic example of the so-called tradition of xenophobia in early modern England.[71] However, although anti-alien sentiment certainly was the central issue in the May Day riots, G.R. Elton suggests that the anger of the May Day riots was "momentary and local," as opposed to the widespread and sustained anger one would expect from a tradition of xenophobia, and Rappaport similarly suggests that the Evil May Day riot may have figured "so prominently in Tudor London's history not for its representativeness but because of its *singularity*."[72] For this reason Pettegree warns against "[a]n assumption of xenophobia amongst sixteenth-century Englishmen, all too often evidenced by the single example of Evil May Day."[73] Three important aspects of the narratives of the riot should be noted.

First, although Hall describes the rioters as "ryotous," "misruled," and generally chaotic, the chronicles hint that the rioters were perhaps fairly well disciplined.[74] Apart from a small group of young Englishmen that reportedly struck strangers and threw them into nearby latrines on 28 April, no beatings or murders of immigrants have been recorded in any of the accounts of the Evil May Day riots.[75] This is surprising given that between 1,000 and 2,000 rioters roamed the streets that night.[76] The rioters were not exactly peaceful, however; the records indicate that they were primarily interested in damaging property. Even so, historian Thomas Wyatt writes, "although the London authorities promised restitution for damage to property, no very serious claims appear to have been made."[77]

Second, the May Day rioters appear to have been focused on specific targets: individuals who were suspected of having accumulated their wealth by violating ordinances and the community's sense of fair trade. John Stow explains that one group of apprentices attacked the house of "John Mutas (a Picarde) or Frenchman, who dwelled there, and harbored in his house many Frenchmen, that kalenedered wolsteds, and did other things contrarie to the Franchises of the Citizens."[78] It is not that the rioters accidentally stumbled upon this particular stranger – his notoriety indicates that he was quite definitely one of the prime targets. Another group of rioters, reports Hall, broke into houses "and threwe shooes and bootes into the street."[79] That the rioters were taking out their aggressions on random bits of footwear, that they should find enough shoes in select houses for chroniclers to take notice, should strike readers as odd: the rioters seem to have located the shops where strangers had been making and retailing shoes contrary to the laws that required guild membership, specific limits on the number of English apprentices and journeymen, and so forth. The rioters as represented in the contemporary accounts of May 1517 thus attacked property rather than people and focused on specific instances of immigrants infringing on the economic order of the city. This is not to say that the generalized anti-alien violence was justified, but rather to put this moment of xenophobia in a specific social and economic context.

Finally, the riot itself does not seem to have been prompted by a tradition of hostilities but rather, as Martin Holmes puts it, "the unfortunate coincidence of anti-alien tension on several levels at once." Stories of recent affronts to the status of individual Englishmen, grievances regarding merchant strangers forestalling the markets, and a general awareness of the preferment of several strangers at court all focused tensions on strangers whether they were cause of tensions or not.[80] The Evil May Day riot appears to have been prompted at least in part by economic concerns along with a perception that the authorities were not responding to grievances in a meaningful way. That the riots were understood to imply a critique of the state's handling of social and economic affairs in the city is made clear in the aftermath of the violence. Prisoners were found guilty of treason rather than riot, and several were hanged, drawn, and quartered, the customary punishment imposed when, as Susan Dwyer Amussen puts it, "the state saw itself threatened" and in need of reasserting its absolute authority over its subjects.[81]

Although the rioters appear to have been more restrained than many would suppose, it would be a mistake to discount anti-alien sentiment altogether. It seems unlikely that the riot would have occurred had the grievances been aimed at any number of the rioters' countrymen; identifying the offending groups would have been too difficult. Because the strangers were set apart culturally, linguistically, and in many cases geographically, living in particular neighbourhoods, they were easily identifiable targets, but the riot would not have occurred had local authorities taken action to redress grievances. The May Day riot is clearly an instance of English xenophobia, but that does not necessarily indicate that the English were predisposed to xenophobia. The riot emerged as a result of specific circumstances.

Sir Thomas More engages in a late Tudor/early Stuart interpretation of these early sixteenth-century events. Between More's execution and the writing of the play London had changed substantially. In 1517 there were relatively few strangers living in London, and most had come to London to prosper as merchant strangers, as highly sought after craftsmen, or as part of an ambassador's retinue; by the time *Sir Thomas More* was written, there were many more strangers living in London, most of whom had come for refuge rather than for economic advantage. In 1517 most strangers were wealthy and well connected, but by the 1590s strangers were present in all social and economic strata. In 1517 England was decidedly Catholic;

by the time *Sir Thomas More* was written Protestantism had been in place for several decades, and as we saw in the petition of the yeomen weavers in chapter 3, regardless of economic tensions, by the 1590s there was a sense of Protestant solidarity among the English and strangers. While drawing on earlier sources, *Sir Thomas More* nonetheless addresses the changes in immigration patterns that had occurred since 1517, revealing therefore not repetition of a "tradition of xenophobia," but precisely the complexity I think is involved in early modern immigration in England.

For example, Edward Hall, in his account of the events leading up to the Evil May Day riots, explains that "a lombard called Francis de Bard, entised a mans wife in Lombard street to come to his chamber with hir husbands plate, which thing she did."[82] When the cuckolded goldsmith appealed in Guildhall for the return of both his wife and his gold, de Bard released the wife but managed to force payment for the woman's board. Likewise, a carpenter named Williamson was imprisoned after an altercation with a French stranger over who had the right to purchase some doves. Finally, Hall describes how a group of French strangers scoffed at the punishment of one of their countrymen for murdering an Englishman. Each anecdote explains not so much Hall's initial claim – that "a great hartburning and malicious grudge amongst the Englishmen of the citie of London against strangers" developed out of economic competition – but rather his secondary claim: that Londoners were angry that the strangers "set nought by the rulers of the citie, & bare themselves too bold of the kings favor."[83] In the first two cases, strangers use their connections with the court to manipulate the justice system and thwart their English adversaries; in the third case the strangers express contempt for local justice.

Sir Thomas More draws on these anecdotes, but they resonate with more recent events, a noticeable increase in immigration, and occasional anti-alien activity, such as the June 1592 riot that broke out after Dutch candle-makers in violation of local statutes were protected from punishment by the Privy Council.[84] The play relates so clearly to contemporary events that Tilney insisted that the references to French strangers be changed to the more remote Lombards, no doubt in deference to the French refugee community in London.[85] The play begins with de Bard's attempts at "purchasing" Doll Williamson, the carpenter's wife who alludes to the first event described above: "Thou thinkst thou hast the goldsmith's wife in hand, whom thou enticedst from her husband with all his plate, and when thou turnedst her home to him again, mad'st him, like an ass, pay for his wife's board" (1.9–13).[86] The addition of yet another episode of a stranger attempting to disrupt a household and the fact that the second anecdote regarding the doves is taking place offstage between Caveler and Doll's husband, condenses Hall's account and emphasizes the humiliating impotence of the English: "How now, husband?" chides Doll, "What, one stranger take thy food from thee, and another thy wife?" (1.34–5). As with Mistress Ford's and Mistress Page's humiliation of Falstaff for literal and figurative poaching, here a wife protests an outsider's violation of the domestic order of the community.

Sir Thomas More also makes more of the indignities motivating the antagonism, defined largely in terms of class and status. In the Hall account, the stranger insults Williamson by calling him "a knave."[87] In *Sir Thomas More*, this comment is amplified. The stranger Caveler exclaims, "Beef and brewis may serve such hinds [as Williamson's]. Are pigeons meat for a coarse carpenter?" (1.24–5). And when fellow stranger de Bard threatens to use his connections at court to punish his English adversaries, Williamson reminds his allies this is no idle threat, that a stranger had previously procured his imprisonment when he "took the wall of a stranger" (1.47). The strangers here are associated with the ruling class who have the "right" to "take the wall" over artisans and apprentices, demean them as "hinds," claim privileges over citizens, and manipulate justice through connections to court. Whereas Hall describes the motives of the May Day riot as economic competition and a judicial conflict between rights of the city and those of the monarch and his allies, the play emphasizes these as signs of class conflict: artisan class English against wealthy, well-connected, upper-class strangers.

The class element of early modern xenophobia is not merely an interpretive move on the part of the authors of *Sir Thomas More* alone. In 1551 an anti-alien uprising appeared imminent; according to Jehan Scheyfve, "Evilly disposed persons have taken advantage of this [an inflated estimate of the number of strangers in England] to assert that prices would not go down unless all these foreigners were slaughtered."[88] Scheyfve explains that the wealthy English soon came to believe that the slaughter would extend to the upper classes:

> Though at first the English themselves, especially people of quality, paid little attention, they have since realised that the matter is of consequence, not only touching foreigners, but English merchants and rich burgesses, not forgetting the Council, who would not escape, especially my Lord of Warwick and Mr. (Sir John) York, master of the Irish mint (sic), the two men most bitterly hated by the people ... At the same time, some peasants at different places thirty or forty miles away from London had formed a project to get together

a force of 10,000 or 12,000, finish off all gentry of the neighborhood, and march to London to the assistance of the people of that city."[89]

Discontent with strangers was tied to dissatisfaction with the ruling class in mid-Tudor England. As with *Sir Thomas More's* representation of Evil May Day, Scheyfve links anti-alien sentiment to class antipathy. Rather than national unity born of a self-other dynamic, xenophobia here divides the realm into two groups: English artisans and poor peasants on one side, and other strangers and the rich on the other. The latter group is unified in its foreignness: the strangers come from other countries and the rich often participate in or advocate practices like enclosing and engrossing, which because new were often viewed as foreign. The "bitterly hated" Warwick, associated above with strangers, after all, would be remembered for his advocacy of enclosures, and his violent battle against the anti-enclosure rebels on Mousehold Heath during Kett's rebellion.[90] As will be seen, *Sir Thomas More* attempts to separate anti-alien sentiment from class antipathy and redirect concerns to the home.

John Lincoln, the catalyst of the Evil May Day riots in Hall and *Sir Thomas More*, emphasizes the economic objection to strangers. He describes himself as "a mean man" whose solidarity is with his "brethren," the shopkeeper George Betts and the "clown" Ralph Betts (1.90–4). While the events depicted in *Sir Thomas More* emphasize class-based indignities suffered by the English, Lincoln's bill, quoted almost exactly from Hall, articulates a broader phenomenon:

> "For so it is that aliens and strangers eat the bread from the fatherless children, and take the living away from all the artificers, and the intercourse from all merchants, whereby poverty is so much increased, that every man bewaileth the misery of the other, for craftsmen be brought to beggary, and merchants to neediness. Wherefore, the premises considered, the redress must be of the commons, knit and united to one part."[91]

According to Lincoln, the influx of immigrant artisans makes it hard for London's artisans to thrive, and merchant-strangers likewise outdo their English counterparts to the point that England's entire economic woes can be blamed on strangers – in many respects a staging of the anti-alien libels of the early 1590s discussed in chapter 2. Lincoln was undoubtedly mistaken to attribute the widespread poverty to a single group of people; Roger Manning suggests the general increase in population and the cost of war as the central causes of poverty in the period,[92] but by appealing to "the commons," to everyone from beggars to merchants "united to one part," Lincoln offers up a radical, albeit xenophobic and misguided proposal, a common struggle to feed the hungry and employ the unemployed. Lincoln comes close to articulating an early English nation as embattled collective.

Numerous critics have noted a similarity between the representation of Lincoln in *Sir Thomas More* and of Jack Cade in *2 Henry VI* (1591).[93] The comparison stems in part from the belief that the two plays were written around the same time. The theory that Georgio Melchiori and John Velz advocate is that Shakespeare was recruited to write these particular scenes for *Sir Thomas More* because of his success in dramatizing the rebellion in *2 Henry VI*. This comparison, as fruitful as it may be in theorizing Shakespeare's participation in the composition of *Sir Thomas More*, leads Melchiori to suggest "the ideological unfitness" of the riot scene to the rest of the play. More pointedly, Velz discredits Lincoln by comparing Cade's *non sequiturs* to Lincoln's reply to Sergeant Downes's offer of the king's mercy.[94] But the Cade-Lincoln connection suggests not the illogic of either character but the levelling tendencies of both. Indeed, what Velz labels an illogical *non sequitur* in Lincoln appears instead to be a case of Lincoln equivocating:

> DOWNES: What say you to the mercy of the King? Do you refuse it?
> LINCOLN: You would have us on th'hip, would you? No, marry, do we not. We accept of the king's mercy, but we will show no mercy upon the strangers. (6.22–6)

Accepting the king's merciful pardon is akin to admitting wrongdoing, so Lincoln separates the offer of mercy from the act it pardons, the attack on strangers. Rather than illogical, Lincoln appears to be engaged in a politically savvy moment of equivocation, carefully phrasing his speech so as to avoid an admission of guilt.[95] History has shown that a king's pardon of rebellion does not preclude execution.[96] At the same time, no one, I think, could defend the actions of de Bard and Caveler in the beginning of the play. It is Lincoln's generalization that seems objectionable. Lincoln may well have been intended as a foil to More: both are acutely aware of the economic hardships of their commoners, but one is misguided in his call for open rebellion against strangers. Shakespeare may have disapproved of the scapegoating while still sympathizing with the need for the commons to be "knit and united to one part" to deal with the economic and social ills apparent in the 1590s, the very ills that made relations between Londoners and foreigners like Shakespeare so tense.

Nonetheless, the Shakespeare scene in which More quells the May Day riot does not seem to be ideologically different from the previous scenes, as long as we note the class dimension emphasized in *Sir Thomas More* in the anti-alien riot and the fact that the play critiques, rather than applauds, anti-alien sentiment by drawing attention to the religious and economic differences between Henrician and late Elizabethan/early Jacobean England. Unlike the sergeant who appeals to the authority of the king, a decidedly bad rhetorical move given the anti-absolutist vein of the opening scenes with the strangers who refer to their connections at court, More appeals to the often overlooked moral convictions of the crowd. To be sure, there was a tendency for rebellious commoners to uphold the authority of the king while rejecting the place of the nobility, but here the indignant attitude of strangers connected to court only prefigures the larger problem of the play, Henry VIII's seemingly arbitrary exercise of royal authority, so More instead reverses the class indignities preceding the riot. More asks the rioters to,

> Imagine that you see the wretched strangers,
> Their babies at their backs, with their poor luggage
> Plodding to th' ports and coasts for transportation,
> And that you sit as kings in your desires,
> Authority quite silenced by your brawl,
> And you in ruff of your opinions clothed. (6.85–90)

The image of "wretched strangers" fleeing with their "poor luggage" is anachronistic. The passage depicts a fundamental difference between the strangers of the early sixteenth century and those of the latter half of the century. Strangers in England during More's lifetime were not generally poor: artisans immigrated because their particular trades were highly sought after; merchants were there because they could offer goods unavailable in England; and retinues of ambassadors were well connected.[97] Shakespeare's audience, however, would have been more familiar with the desperate strangers evoked in More's speech, refugees who fled to England without preparation or savings. There were, of course, successful strangers who made good livings in London – Vautrollier and Mountjoy among them – but the vast majority of strangers did not easily prosper and had less resemblance with the upper class de Bard and Caveler who begin the play than with the displaced poor More describes in his speech. In that speech, Shakespeare is able to deny his sources' contrast between rich stranger and impoverished Londoner by having More invert the roles: whereas earlier in the play strangers were wealthy and connected to court, it is now the Londoners who "sit as kings in [their] desires"; if strangers were full of pride, it is now a Londoner who wears a "ruff" of opinion; if Londoners were poor and degraded, it is now the strangers who are poor and exploited. In this inversion of the earlier scenes and the anachronistic depiction of the immigrants of London in the 1590s rather those of some eighty years ago, the speech resists the idea that the events of 1517 properly resonate with the discord of the 1590s.

What is important here is that More steps out of his time frame to emphasize a class of strangers who have more in common with the rioters than with upper-class Englishmen. Honigmann suggests that the image of displaced poor leaving with nothing but their children and "poor luggage" gives clues to the breadth of Shakespeare's reading as it echoes a passage from More's *Utopia* on the effects of enclosures:

> by one meanes therfore or by other, either by hooke or crooke they muste needes departe awaye, poore, selye, wretched soules, men, women, husbands, wives, fatherlesse children, widowes, wofull mothers, with their yonge babes, and their whole houshold smal in substance and muche in numbre, as husbandrye requireth manye handes. Awaye thei trudge, I say, out of their knowen and accustomed houses, fyndnge no place to reste in. All their housholdestuffe, which is verye litle woorthe, thoughe it myght well abide the sale: yet beeynge sodainely thruste oute, they be constayned to sell it for a thin of nought. And when they have wandered abrode tyll that be spent, what can they then els doo but steale, and then justly pardy be hanged.[98]

Beyond Shakespeare's reading, however, the allusion is relevant to the argument posed in *Sir Thomas More.* Even if they were unfamiliar with More's *Utopia,* an early modern audience may well have connected the image of homeless refugees displaced by political and religious upheaval to their English counterparts displaced from the countryside by economic innovation. The similarities between the two descriptions lump foreigners and strangers in the same category much as did the laws restricting their economic activity in London. In that sense, the allusion functions to further bridge the gap between London artisans and their migrant and immigrant counterparts.

More then emphasizes the common positions of the refugees and the rioters. Following the inversion of wealthy stranger and impoverished Londoner, he continues his argument:

> Say now the king,
> As he is clement if th'offender mourn,
> Should so much come too short of your great trespass
> As but to banish you: whither would you go?
> What country, by the nature of your error,
> Should give you harbour? Go you to France or Flanders,
> To any German province, Spain or Portugal,
> Nay anywhere that not adheres to England:
> Why you must needs be strangers. (6.138–46)

Here More introduces the threat of punishment, but more importantly he asks the rebels to imagine themselves as refugees – what Nina Levine aptly describes as More's appeal to a "common strangeness."[99] Paralleling Titania's vision of immigration in *The Whore of Babylon*, discussed in chapter 4, some audience members may well have been displaced from the countryside, and others could recall the exile of Protestants from England during Mary's reign; both groups could thus readily identify with the situation. A similar rhetorical move was made in Parliament on 21 March 1593 in an argument against a proposal to limit the ability of strangers to retail their wares: Master Finch argued, "In the days of Queen Mary, when our Cause was as theirs is now, those Countries did allow us that liberty, which now we seek to deny them. They are strangers now, we may be strangers hereafter. So let us do as we would be done unto."[100] Shakespeare thus stages one of the most prevalent arguments against xenophobia in the period. It may be that the play was intended to publicize this kind of argument in order to quell any dissatisfaction with the fact that this particular proposal passed in the House of Commons but not in the House of Lords.[101] Central to More's (and Finch's) argument is the idea that anyone, especially a Protestant in the sixteenth century, could be a stranger. The argument thus demystifies "strangeness" and replaces it with solidarity, here a bonding around the idea of home and homelessness. More's anti-xenophobia speech works within this play to draw a new line between "us" and "them." It intervenes in the early/mid-Tudor notion that the court and strangers comprised a coherent side and argues instead that strangers (late Tudor strangers) are part of the London community that suffers the abuses of the privileged.

This is a central point of coherence for the play, despite its several authors. In his first scene in the play, More allies himself not with Justice Suresby, a logical ally, but with the accused and appropriately named Lifter, "The only captain of the cutpurse crew" (2.8), a much less likely friend of the sheriff of London. In fact, More and Lifter are in league together to outwit Suresby, who feels for Lifter and has therefore raised on his behalf the lame defence that the victim of the pickpocketing was, in essence, asking for it:

> I promise ye, a man that goes abroad
> With an intent of truth, meeting such a booty,
> May be provoked to that he never meant.
> What makes so many pilferers and felons
> But such fond baits that foolish people lay
> To tempt the needy miserable wretch?
> Ten pounds, odd money; this is a pretty sum
> To bear about, which were more safe at home. (2.28–35)

More then arranges for Lifter to steal Suresby's purse. Although the episode is described as "a merry jest" (2.75), it is a jest instigated by More to show Suresby that one can be sympathetic with the accused without relying on sophistry. Contrary to the claim to discontinuity from hand to hand of the authors of the play, the More who sympathizes with prisoners and sees logic as the basis of law seems congruent with the More who quells the May Day riot through an appeal to reason. In both situations he applies rational thought rather than the letter of the law while tempering punishment with an understanding of the causes for transgression. More embodies justice tempered by equity.

While Melchiori argues that the play as a whole is an attempt to show "the abuses perpetrated under cover of the absolute power of the king," I think this insight can be broadened to suggest that the play protests any unwieldy application of power.[102] The king's insistence on More's signature, Justice Suresby's attempt to confound the jury, de Bard's use of court connections to overcome commoners' notions of justice, and the rioters who want to "sit as kings" all point to More's interventions in abuses of power. *Sir Thomas More* seems to say that many conflicts can be resolved through an understanding of the poorer, the weaker, or the less politically advantaged of the realm. Indeed, much more is made of More's amicable relationship with Lifter, the rioting crowd, and other commoners than is made of More's legendary friendship with Erasmus and his connections to Henry VIII. Further, this plea for an understanding of the poor is not unique among Shakespeare's histories. We are not, I think, meant to feel satisfied when in *2 Henry VI* the petitions of the commons are torn as a symbolic rejection of their request (1.3.1–45). Likewise, Henry V's "band of brothers" is mostly a band of commoners, and Hal expresses dismay at Falstaff's exploitation of his foot soldiers (*Henry V* 4.3.60 and *1 Henry IV* 4.2). There is a populist strain in many of Shakespeare's plays.

More's rise would seem to be the answer to the commoners' complaints about the application of justice for the poor that is at the root of the anti-alien sentiment. This is the implication of the scene in which the rebels are spared hanging for participating in the May Day riots. The scene departs drastically from its source. In Hall's account, the rebels are "executed in most rigorous maner."[103] Given that on May fourth "eleven paire of gallowes" were set up for the executions and that the king's stay of execution did not arrive until May seventh, one may assume that a large number of rebels were hanged. The gallows were not taken down until May 22nd when 411 "poore yoonglings and old false knaves […] everie one a halter about his necke" were gathered in front of the king to be granted a general pardon.[104] Leaving the gallows assembled throughout the city for more than two weeks may have been a symbolic move to remind Londoners of the punishment for rebellion, but the possibility that hangings continued over the two-week period cannot be ruled out: the "poor yoonglings" who were about to be hanged were surely not the first transgressors who would have been executed. In *Sir Thomas More*, although the new sheriff is rebuffed for "mak[ing] such haste with men unto their death" (7.137), the play makes it seem as though only Lincoln was executed. That More has procured the pardon of all the other rebels situates him as the link to the crown the city needed for a proper administration of justice.

More's presence reforms not only the justice system but also the rebels and their notion of insiders and outsiders. In Hall, Lincoln maintains his xenophobic stance even in his gallows speech: "My lordes, I meant well, for and you knew the mischief that is ensued in this realm by straungers, you would remedy it."[105] In *Sir Thomas More*, Lincoln comes to repent:

I must confess I had no ill intent
But against such as wronged us overmuch.
And now I can perceive it was not fit
That private men should carve out their redress

Which way they list. No, learn it now by me:
Obedience is the best in each degree. [...]
Henceforth be warned to attempt the like
'Gainst any alien that repaireth hither. (7.53–67)

Had the authors wanted to present a xenophobic play, they could have retained Lincoln's original speech resisting the typical gallows repentance. Instead, the pronounced line between "us" (commoners) and "them" (strangers) is blurred in that both are figured as victims of arbitrary and capricious justice. Lincoln further hedges his repentance by emphasizing, "Obedience is best in *each degree*": this statement would seem to be the voice of the contrite wrongdoer, but the emphasis on degree also introduces a sense of reciprocal obligations, redistributing complicity across classes. More's speech quelling the riot and Lincoln's repentance stage a kind of inclusion for strangers in the realm while emphasizing the roles individuals must play in the community. In terms of English-stranger relations, obedience in each degree recalls the scripted roles of hospitality that in 1517 both host and guest failed to fulfil. More's emphasis on the shared plight of stranger, foreigner, and English alike calls for a renewed inclusivity in England.

The multiple hands in the composition of the play parallels this theme of inclusion: Munday and Chettle, both freemen of the city, worked cooperatively on the play with Dekker, a descendent of Dutch immigrants, and Shakespeare, a foreigner. The authors depict More's rise as diffusing the xenophobia that was fomented by a state that too easily ignored the plight of the commons. More's rise opens a line of communication between city and court, and leads even Lincoln to trust that "Obedience is best," that the commons and strangers will be obedient, and so will the court. Lincoln's hanging, however, is problematized by More's fate: after his rise to Lord Chancellor, his meeting with Erasmus, and his interaction with the players, More refuses to sign the Oath of Supremacy, a refusal that leads him from exile to imprisonment, and ultimately, like Lincoln, to the gallows. The fact that the Oath is never specifically named, however, suggests that More's refusal is to be viewed as a division not between Catholic and Protestant but between an unwieldy exercise of power and the rights of subjects.

The scenes between Lincoln's execution and More's refusal to sign the Oath are for the most part light-hearted. More's refusal and subsequent execution returns to the domain of the complaints of the commoners regarding the king's arbitrary notion of justice. More, like the refugees he asks the rioters to sympathize with, is stripped of his status and possessions. More importantly, he is put in the position Lincoln had been. If More's death is ennobling, the culmination of a wise man's life and his adherence to ideals that supersede the crown's authority, is not Lincoln's sympathy for his fellow English women and men equally ennobling, particularly since in the play Lincoln renounces his anti-alien stance and thus echoes More? Had the play ended with More at the top of his career, the commoners would perhaps seem to be to blame for the violent opening scenes, but the final execution opens up what seemed to have been closed off. After witnessing highly sentimental scenes between More and his family, watching a brewer lament "Nor a wiser, nor a merrier, nor an honester" man had served the position of Lord Chancellor (15.15), hearing a horse-keeper declare, "he was too good a lord for us" (15.20), the audience must sense that a further injustice has taken place, an injustice that cannot be separated from the complaints that were first framed as anti-alien and then reconfigured by More as based on a common station in life – the potential for anyone to become an impoverished refugee. The status of outsider shifts throughout *Sir Thomas More* from strangers to rioters to Suresby and finally to More himself. Justice, the play argues, requires the knitting of the commons "united to one part," but that one part must include all of the commons – not only artisans and merchants but also strangers and foreigners – just as the composition of the play hinged on the cooperation of citizen, alien, and foreign writers. By the same token, those who execute an arbitrary or overly stringent form of justice become outsiders to the community. In *Sir Thomas More* injustice lies not at the door of a stranger's house, but at the feet of the monarch and his or her economic allies.

Both Caius in *Merry Wives* and the strangers of *Sir Thomas More* are in many respects victims of the communities in which they live, but the conflicts between them and their adversaries are ultimately resolved through a process of inclusion. Caius participates in Windsor's collective punishment of Falstaff and, like the rest of the Windsor community, is invited to the Fords' home. More stops the anti-alien riot by pointing to the similarities in social and economic circumstances between strangers and English, arguments that could not have been made until Elizabeth's reign. In both plays, too, that which marks one as an outsider is not birthplace but rather a failure to live up to communal standards of justice, especially standards that comprise what Dalechamp calls "private hospitalitie," the reciprocal obligations of individual hosts and strangers regarding the home. Poaching and the seduction of married women violate the host's home, and in *Sir Thomas More* a great deal of outrage stems from the attempted seduction of Doll Williamson, another violation of domestic space.

The inclusion of strangers and exclusion of whoever violates local values in Shakespeare's plays provides an alternative to nationalist Shakespeares. At times Shakespeare could bring the emergence of a discourse of nationhood into focus; at other times he could amplify the discourses of inclusion explored in this book. Shakespeare seems to have found himself in close quarters with strangers, and his status as a foreigner to London placed him under economic constraints similar to those imposed on strangers. As a member of the Lord Chamberlain's Men and then the King's Men, such restrictions would not have hampered him much, but he must have been acutely aware of the restrictions that applied to him in his status as one of the non-free of the city. Shakespeare did not experience a nation as we know it today: according to Anthony Smith, nations tend to have not only a collective history and myths, but also a sense of "us" and "them" grounded in national origin, a national, public culture, and standardized laws and customs that extend throughout the national territory.[106] Shakespeare's *Merry Wives* shows citizens actively enforcing their own sense of justice, and *Sir Thomas More* seems dubious about the unchecked power of the state. As we have seen in both plays, while there is an attempt at a collective memory, the sense of "us" and "them" does not seem to be based entirely on one's place of birth, and local customs are depicted as more important than the imposition of uniform national laws.

It may be said that *Merry Wives* and *Sir Thomas More* and their view of strangers as integral to English communities are not representative of Shakespeare's output. Helgerson points out, for example, that *Sir Thomas More* is part of Henslowe's repertory of plays that emphasized commoners rather than kings, that Shakespeare's contribution to the play may be atypical, as he had to adapt to "the Henslowe environment."[107] That there may have been such an environment to adapt to is in itself significant, however. It suggests that, in the period, there was room for other conceptions of community, conceptions that ran counter to a purely national identity. Moreover, *Sir Thomas More* and *Merry Wives of Windsor* are not the only Shakespeare plays that deal with issues of immigration and the place of strangers. For example, in *The Comedy of Errors* Luciana explains that Antipholus of Syracuse (mistaken for his brother of Ephesus) swears he is "a stranger here" (4.2.9), and the plot revolves around the vulnerability of strangers in the city; much of the humour stems from the interchangeability of the brothers and their servants, thereby emphasizing the arbitrary nature of defining a person as alien. In *Twelfth Night* Antonio worries about Sebastian because the neighbourhoods of Illyria "to a stranger, / Unguided and unfriended, often prove / Rough and unhospitable" (3.3.9–11). In *All Is True/Henry VIII* Queen Katherine appeals to an ethic of tolerance and protection of strangers when she pleads, "I am a most poor woman, and a stranger" (2.4.13). In addition to race and age, Roderigo emphasizes that Othello is "an extravagant and wheeling stranger" (1.1.137), and this is precisely what makes Othello vulnerable to Iago's supposedly insider information about the nature of Venetian women.

For an early modern audience fresh from a walk through the immigrant neighbourhoods of the suburbs, the term *stranger* would not only suggest "outsider" but also evoke the legal category familiar to Londoners. Indeed, in *The Merchant of Venice* it is in a legal rather than loosely cultural context that Portia reminds Shylock that he is an "alien" rather than a citizen (4.1.344). I am not suggesting that Shylock should not be understood as a Jew or that Othello was not a Moor, but rather that their legal status as strangers must have resonated with early modern audiences' experiences of strangers. These strangers are different from one another – some, like Othello and Shylock, are immigrants while others, like Sebastian and Antipholus of Syracuse, are merely visitors – but the prevalence of strangers in Shakespeare's plays suggests that the themes of immigration and integration addressed in *Merry Wives* and *Sir Thomas More* are a central rather than peripheral part of the Shakespeare canon. Moreover, in *Othello* and *The Merchant of Venice*, revenge is prompted by perceived failures of reciprocal obligations of hosts and strangers: Shylock is spurred on by the loss of his daughter to Lorenzo, and in *Othello* most of the revenge plots can be traced back to presumptions of infidelity. Both plays involve violations of domestic space, failures in "private hospitalitie."

In Shakespeare's plays the patriotically English and cross-cultural tendencies discussed above combine to reveal an England that values reciprocal obligations of hospitality. Insofar as worldly domesticity could pose a threat to domestic norms, both *Merry Wives* and *Sir Thomas More* focus on violations of the family unit as at the root of breakdowns in hospitality. The norms of hospitality can be restored, however, by the guest adapting to the community's expectations, or by the host imagining the possibility that anyone could be a stranger. In these two plays valuing the community means maintaining local rather than national customs, including rather than excluding immigrants, and recognizing anyone's potential to be a stranger. Contrary to the claims about Shakespeare being French, or Italian, or German, Shakespeare seems fully English, by which I mean he is thoroughly committed to the reciprocal obligations of host and guest in England's early modern multiculturalism.

Conclusion: The Return of Hans Beer-Pot

Despite the development of English national identity alongside anti-alien sentiment in the seventeenth century, writers throughout the period still appealed to the value of hospitality and the modes of imagining multicultural community explored in this book. In the Marian interlude *Wealth and Health,* discussed in chapter 1, Hance Beerpot is banished by Good Remedy, but the name lingered in the English imagination. In 1618 he reentered England in his own play, Dabridgcourt Belchier's *Hans Beer-Pot, His Invisible Comedie of See Me, and See Me Not.*[1] Although Belchier owned substantial land in Guilsborough, Northamptonshire, he wrote the play while in Utrecht, where he died a few years later.[2] The play is set in the Netherlands and is dedicated to the governor of Utrecht, Sir John Ogle, an Englishman who had fought in support of the Dutch Republic in the 1590s.[3] Shortly after the play was printed, Ogle was dismissed from the governorship, having been caught up in conflicting allegiances in the Calvinist-Arminian debates and their outcome at the National Synod of Dort; this issue is alluded to in the play when the tapster Flutterkin declares, "Here is small newes: Our Church-men disagree / About Opinions, which nere troubles me."[4] According to the title page, the play had been presented "In the Low Countries, by an honest Company of Health-Drinkers." Critics have generally presumed that this was actually the case, and that the play was likely performed to entertain soldiers who were stationed in Utrecht to quell violence related to the Calvinist-Arminian split in the region.[5] At any rate, the timing and dedication, signed by Belchier, "to be commanded," indicate that Belchier was in the Netherlands to lend military support.[6] *Hans Beer-Pot* emphasizes the need to keep the peace amid religious factionalism and the rising tensions towards the end of the Twelve Years' Truce between Spain and the Dutch Republic.[7] The English

Sergeant Goodfellow has a "troubled head" and "is so vext / With this worlds cares," and the elderly country gentleman Cornelius Harmants wants to join with his son among the soldiers in town.[8]

The play features Cornelius Harmants, his wife Hanneke, their son Younker (a soldier seeking advancement), Hans Beer-Pot (a sly but ultimately dutiful servant to the Harmants), Jaques Garland (a merchant married to Younker's sister), the aging Sergeant Goodfellow, his sentinel Pasquill Beermond, the tapster Flutterkin, and a moor named Abnidaraes Quixot (self-described as "A Spaniard, Moore, halfe Turke, halfe Christian").[9] With the exception of Quixot, who appears alone on stage to sing songs and remind the audience of the looming Spanish presence, the characters engage in conversations about drinking, military strategy and the merits of foot soldiers, nostalgia about the military exploits of Englishmen of the sixteenth century, and poetry (with special reference to "that famous learned Knight, / Sir Philip Sidney, Scholers, souldiers pride," and an allusion to Spenser's "Fayery Land").[10] As George Evans Light remarks, *Hans Beer-Pot* mixes English patriotism with a longing for improved Anglo-Dutch relations.[11]

Although set outside of England, the play makes much of the close ties between the English and the Dutch and reveals some of the pressing issues that came to bear on English-immigrant relations in the seventeenth century. Hans explains that he is well known among the soldiers, "But Serjeant Goodfellow, I love him best, / And why? Because he loves my masters sonne."[12] Echoing his namesake in *Wealth and Health,* who had declared "Ic love de Englishman," this more fluent Hans Beer-Pot describes the mutual amity among English and Dutch in the Netherlands and goes on to emphasize that his master, Cornelius, frequently gives the sergeant gold. In many ways, Cornelius is the figure of ideal Anglo-Dutch relations. Upon hearing his name, Flutterkin says,

> O theres a man lives bravely, keeps an house,
> Releeves the poore, his gates be never shut;
> His tables free, theres meat for honest men:
> He livde in England, learnt that countryes guise,
> For Hospitality, few such be here:
> Yet frugall too, was never prodigall.[13]

Rolf Soellner sees in this passage a description of idealized hospitality, a difficult balance of "frugality and generosity."[14] Although the Dutch gentleman is the host, hospitality is something he learned from the English. The play thus praises England for the hospitality it has shown Dutch exiles like Cornelius while suggesting that at least a few were prepared to reciprocate. Paralleling the invitations to multicultural feasting in Deloney's *Jack of Newbury*, Haughton's *Englishmen for My Money*, or Shakespeare's *The Merry Wives of Windsor*, Cornelius invites the English Sergeant Goodfellow and others to his home to eat venison "from England, baked in Rye paste."[15]

In addition to the depiction of Anglo-Dutch hospitality, the play evokes nostalgia for the kind of English militant Protestantism that Julia Gasper finds in Dekker's *The Whore of Babylon*. In conversation with his wife, Cornelius begins "To thinke upon times forepast," things he observed "In Englands Court so famous and renowmde (sic.) / Of great Elizaes blessed memory."[16] Cornelius praises the way England "ayded so these troubled Netherlands," and evokes the names of "those Worthies," Robert Devereux, Second Earl of Essex, Sir John Norreys, Sir Philip Sidney, and Sir Francis Vere, all of whom fought in France, the Netherlands, or both "Gainst hells foule mouth, and Spanish Tyranny."[17] Later Cornelius adds to the pantheon of Elizabethan legends recalling that they were "honoured more then other men": Sir Francis Drake, Sir Thomas Cavendish, Sir John Hawkins, and so on.[18] Glossing over any controversy associated with these figures, Cornelius ascribes a robust masculinity to Elizabeth's foreign policy, a nostalgia intended at least in part as a consolation to English soldiers in the Netherlands, most of whom were at this time essentially mercenaries, soldiers for hire working outside the policies of their monarch.[19] The play seems to lament that the days of English militant Protestantism seem past, but Sergeant Goodfellow explains that he tells his children about the wars of the sixteenth century so that they will "tread their Fathers steps; / To make them bold to banish servile feare."[20]

In contrast, as Cornelius prepares to join with the English soldiers, his wife, Hanneke, counsels, "Let us not meddle with the Magistrate, / But see, unseen, and hope for whats the best."[21] The play thus pits a highly idealized masculine martial past against a feminine, cautiousness about the present. Although Belchier could not have expected his little-known and mostly light-hearted play to have an impact on English foreign policy, the strategy of having Hanneke promote a passive foreign policy while much of the play applauds Elizabethan intervention seems to anticipate and feminize James's preference for peaceful diplomacy.

In response to such objections to James's policies, a month after the start of the Thirty Years' War, *The Peacemaker* (1618) – an anonymous pamphlet (actually by Thomas Middleton) authorized by James and in part posing as his in its Epistle addressed "To all Our true-loving and peace-embracing subjects" – equated peace with the ideal of moderate masculinity.[22] The pamphlet describes the various vices that threaten peace, specifically the drunkenness so pronounced in *Hans Beer-Pot*. Instead of the play's association of alcohol with manliness and male bonding, *The Peacemaker* describes drunkenness as "man unmanned," a failure of masculine self-discipline.[23] Interestingly, both *Hans Beer-Pot* and *The Peacemaker* extol the virtues of hospitality to immigrants. Amid its praise of peace in England, *The Peacemaker* commands, "let in strangers to behold and taste thy blessings."[24] Middleton cleverly weaves this positive attitude to strangers into the discussion of vice and virtue: while Drunkenness, the stereotype often attributed to Dutch immigrants, "is no stranger to the world," Peace "hath been a stranger" to England.[25] More important is the pamphlet's specific plea on behalf of strangers: "The disturbed French seek succour with thee; the troubled Dutch fly to thy confines; the Italian leaves his hotter climate. These and many more all seek shelter under the sweet shadow of thine *olive branches*."[26] Whether beating the drums of war or singing the praises of peace, many English writers continued to value the ideal of English hospitality fostering a multicultural England.

Early on, however, the Thirty Years' War put a clear strain on Anglo-Dutch relations. In "The Exiled Shepherd" (1622) Dutch poet Sir Constantijn Huygens describes "the chalk-white strand of Britain ... To which shores our Flemish lowlands / Were connected, long ago."[27] This lost geographic link is of little comfort to Huygens' titular "shepherd-boy of Holland ... by grief brought low."[28] Dedicated to Dutch scholar Lord Daniel Hensius, who had lived in exile in England as a boy, the poem describes Huygens' isolation and frustration during his extended diplomatic mission to England to gain support for the United Provinces in the Thirty Years' War.[29] The speaker of the poem seems desperate as he tells the "Ebb-tide" of his "silent grieving and real pain," which he contrasts with the typical pastoral pose of "sensual weeping." That is, rather than engaging in a kind of pastoral escapism, his "exiled mind runs over / Holland's battle-blooded fields." For Huygens the changing tide recalls not only the ships it carries to and from England but also "the spring-tide of his grief" and the instability of the times.[30]

Huygens arrived in England at a particularly bad time for Dutch strangers at court. Although Huygens was knighted by James, his poem attests to the difficulties he faced: James was banking on a proposed marriage between Charles and the Spanish Infanta, and was thus reluctant to enter into support of Spain's enemies. Robin D. Gwynn describes King

James and the Stuarts in general as "a source of anxiety, not support" for the stranger churches in England.[31] Grell agrees, recounting a 1619 Star Chamber case in which 160 merchant strangers were accused of illegally exporting bullion.[32] In the end only eighteen were prosecuted but they faced either severe fines (totalling £60,000) or imprisonment.

It is difficult to extrapolate from isolated cases a general attitude, however. At the outset of his reign, James wrote to the stranger churches that "if any molest you in your Churches, on your appealing to me I will avenge you."[33] Delegates from the French Churches met James at Greenwich in 1603 to praise him as embodying "the faith of Abraham, the discipline and foresight of Joseph, the goodness and faithfulness of Moses, the victories of Joshua and David, the wealth and wisdom of Solomon, and the sanctity of Hezekiah and Josiah."[34] As with the rhetoric of refuge discussed in chapter 2, here again strangers applied Old Testament icons to the English monarch as a way of creating a transnational bond. Bernard Cottret notes that this pantheon of manly Old Testament figures appears to have been carefully selected to reflect James's already well-established public persona and theory of kingship.[35] James also had personal connections to Huguenots. As a young man he expressed a special admiration for Huguenot poet Guillaume de Salluste Du Bartas: James translated that poet's *L'Uranie* in *The Essayes of a Prentise in the Divine Art of Poesie* (1584), and wrote a commendatory sonnet for Thomas Hudson's translation of Du Bartas's *The Historie of Judith*.[36] In 1611, following the successful treatment of Queen Anne, Sir Theodore Turquet de Mayerne, a Huguenot born in Geneva, became James's chief physician.[37]

James's generally positive attitude towards individual Huguenots need not be extended to Dutch Calvinists in general, but in 1612 James issued Letters Patent confirming for the Dutch in Colchester "all priviledges liberties immunities and freedoms contained as well in diverse former Orders, as used and tolerated unto them for many years in the raigne of our late deare sister Queen Elizabeth," and four years later, James formally reiterated the rights of all strangers in England to practice their trades.[38] At the very least, these instances and *The Peacemaker* articulate his desire to be perceived as welcoming of immigrants.

Still, the state's motive for issuing statements about strangers' rights to practice trades in England was prompted by complaints that "the said Strangers are daylye and grevouslye molested ... by sundry troublesome Informers."[39] Unlike Elizabeth's approach to informers, discussed in chapter 3, the Jacobean state was not wholly against such anti-alien activity. In response to a 1617 petition from the stranger churches again complaining about informers, the Privy Council suggested that while informers might be overstepping their bounds, the grievances against strangers seemed also to have merit and ordered that the cases be heard.[40] With several years of inflation and two years of bad harvests, England was once again facing economic hard times like those that gave rise to tensions in the 1590s. Grell and Luu agree that the economic troubles from 1615 to the end of James's reign fostered xenophobic attitudes, especially in England's urban centres.[41]

News from abroad did not help ease these tensions. As the English East India Company tried to expand its presence, it met with considerable resistance not only from Spanish and Portuguese merchants, but also from the Dutch. Within days of arriving at the Indonesian island of Tidore, Sir Henry Middleton found himself banished by the king of the island, who had been advised by Dutch merchants there. Middleton explains that as the English prepared to leave, the king's secretary, along with a Dutch merchant, delivered a letter addressed to King James with a merchant rather than royal seal. Following on the heels of their banishment, the lack of ceremony around the letter was naturally taken as an insult, and the English refused to deliver the letter even after the king confirmed it to be from him rather than the Dutch merchants. Middleton describes the seal as having "two letters, an H and a B, which stood for Hans Beerpot, with a merchant's mark between the letters."[42] However accurate the details of Middleton's narrative, it seems that he interpreted the initials as those of a stock stage character as a way of containing the insult within the confines of English stereotypes of the Dutch. Moreover, Belchier, who clearly took an interest in Anglo-Dutch relations, may have read about this incident and sought to use his play to recast the character of Hans Beer-Pot as benevolent servant rather than belligerent foe.

This insult to the English merchants is really minor compared to what would develop between the English and the Dutch in the East Indies. Although at times the two companies might join forces against the Portuguese and Spanish presence in the East Indies, a 1624 pamphlet depicted Englishmen brutally tortured by Dutch merchants in Amboina.[43] By this time James had abandoned the Spanish match and was pursuing a new Anglo-Dutch alliance against Spain, so he took a diplomatic approach to what was dubbed "the Amboyna Massacre." Nonetheless, such sensational images could only fuel suspicion of immigrants in England.[44] An anonymous poem from this period lamented that "While for their shares, of Indian wares, English & Dutch doe brawle, / The Spanyards watch, advantage catch, to seize on them & all."[45] The author worries that the competition in the East Indies has undermined Protestant solidarity and strengthened their common enemy, the Spanish.

Even in a context of rising trade tensions, the modes of imagining multicultural community explored in this book persisted in England. Edmund Bolton, for instance, ends his wide-ranging *Hypercritica* (1618–21) by enumerating the duties of anyone attempting to write a history of England. Before being "a Christian Patriot," writes Bolton, one must first be "a Christian Cosmopolite," a writer whose purpose extends beyond the narrow confines of national borders.⁴⁶ Bolton was a recusant, and it may be that a closet-Catholicism led him to value Catholic sectarian inclusivity, a sense of community that traversed borders, much like the Protestant sense of community discussed in chapters 1 and 2. Whether Protestant or Catholic, the main point is that the importance of inclusion based on religion could still take precedence over issues of patriotism.

As James I attempted to end divisiveness among Protestants, he reached out to Huguenot scholars in a gesture of sectarian inclusivity. Isaac Casaubon, a well-respected scholar who was born in Geneva and spent his final years in refuge in England, was often called to court to discuss theological matters with James and his bishops and was recruited to write treatises in defence of James's theological positions.⁴⁷ Casaubon was buried in Westminster Abbey in 1614, but his death did not end James's inclusive approach to sectarian issues. Huguenot pastor Pierre Du Moulin was in frequent correspondence with James and upon visiting him in 1614 was entreated to remain in Canterbury.⁴⁸ A frequent defender of James's policies, Pierre Du Moulin, encouraged by James, attempted to bring about a kind of consensus among the various Protestant factions in Europe. Although the project ultimately failed, the attempt is yet another sign of sectarian inclusivity at work in England and abroad even as religious factionalism became more pronounced.⁴⁹

This is not to say that sectarian inclusivity was pervasive under James. The prevailing image in George Benson's 1609 sermon at Paul's Cross is of strangers devouring goods, an image reminiscent of anti-alien libels of the 1590s.⁵⁰ Although Benson's sermon evokes the image as a spiritual metaphor, he also weaves his "devouring" motif into a critique of foreign travel, complaining that Englishmen "sucke up the infections of other countries, and returning home with stomakes fully charged, they vomit their poyson in their mothers lap; they practice in England, what they have unhappily learned abroad."⁵¹ Acknowledging the necessity of trade, Benson is primarily concerned with the way a popular fascination with foreign customs could lead to a loss of English identity: "men that should be meer English are not themselves; but compounded men, Spanish, Dutch, Italian and whatnot?"⁵² Such statements, much like Marston's depiction of the "jumbled" Franceschina, continued alongside evocations of hospitality and the idea of a common "strangeness" among coreligionists. In contrast to Benson's negative metaphor of devouring strangers, Thomas Adams continued to assert, "We are all in this world eyther strangers or straglers. The Godly are strangers," and in 1622 he implored "Domestickes" to not only "provide for their owne" but for strangers as well.[53]

Away from the pulpit, some Jacobean texts continued to imagine a community founded on provincial globalism. In *Christian Hospitalitie* (discussed in the introduction) Dalechamp appended to his conclusion – that "Christian demeanor in strangers is a good means to revive Christian hospitality" – a copy of James's 1616 speech demanding that the English "keep hospitalitie."[54] Although James was clearly advocating for the repopulation of the countryside and care for the poor there, Dalechamp's appropriation of this speech attempts to fit the general appeal to hospitality into his specific vision of reciprocal obligations between immigrants and their English hosts.

The premium Dalechamp placed on immigrants adapting to their host culture can be seen in the productive relationship between a Dutch merchant and Englishmen imagined in Middleton's *No Wit/Help Like a Woman's* (1611).[55] In that play, Sir Oliver Twilight's wife and daughter have been missing for several years, but he has recently been asked for a ransom. Sir Oliver sends his son Philip and his servant Savourwit to pay the ransom. Instead, the two waste the money, and Philip marries Mistress Grace Sunset. They tell Sir Oliver that his wife is dead and that Grace is his long-lost daughter; thus, during the day Philip must pretend that Grace is his sister. At this point a Dutch merchant delivers a message from Sir Oliver's wife inquiring about the ransom. Because of his movement from place to place, the Dutch merchant becomes a guarantor of truth from abroad, and he even recognizes Grace as a woman he once saw in Antwerp. As Marianne Montgomery puts it, in the figure of the Dutch merchant Middleton combines commerce and credibility.[56]

The play, moreover, illustrates the importance of a common language, a degree of assimilation indicative of provincial globalism. Although only a sometime resident of England, the Dutch merchant speaks perfect English, but his son has yet to integrate into English society. When the Dutch merchant leaves his son behind while he runs errands, Savourwit takes advantage of the boy's lack of English; he pretends to speak Dutch to the boy to clarify the story Sir Oliver has been told. The Dutch boy does not understand the Savourwit's nonsense syllables, but Savourwit claims that each of the Dutch boy's responses discredits the merchant's story. Savourwit further claims that the merchant's knowledge of English is a sign that he speaks with "a double tongue," that he is deceptive or, as Montgomery puts it, "double-dealing" (1.3.140).⁵⁷ The Dutch boy's lack of linguistic competence in English renders him, and the Dutch in general, vulnerable to Savourwit's misrepresentation.

Fortunately for Sir Oliver, the Dutch merchant reenters to debunk Savourwit's machinations. The complicated plot continues, and as with so many plays imagining a place for strangers in the community, this one ends with an invitation to a feast: "You're a stranger," says Sir Oliver to the Dutch merchant, "Your welcome will be best," and in case the point is missed, the widow Lady Goldenfleece reiterates the sentiment, speaking to the now returned Lady Twilight and the Dutch merchant, "Come, my long-wished for madam; / You and this worthy stranger take the best welcome" (8.157–8, 9.24–5). In this depiction of English life, the assimilated Dutch merchant provides a worldly perceptiveness that resolves problems in England, revealing the cruel plot to trick Sir Oliver and leave Lady Twilight a hostage. While the Dutch boy's lack of English makes Sir Oliver vulnerable to lies, the real problem in this community is the self-indulgence and unnatural indifference to others demonstrated by Philip and by Savourwit, whose name and attitude towards strangers recalls the character Shrewd Wit in *Wealth and Health*. Although the Dutch merchant is a minor character, his role promotes the importance of provincial globalism to England, and, as Christian Billing notes, his character seems to subvert stage stereotypes of drunken Dutchmen.⁵⁸

Similarly, in terms of the household and the family, a multicultural attitude can be seen to persist in the English imagination even in the context of the economic hard times during the second decade of the seventeenth century. In *A Fair Quarrel* (1615–16), a play by William Rowley and Thomas Middleton, Jane Russell, the daughter of a wealthy citizen of London, has a child by her betrothed, a gentleman by the name of Fitzallen. Jane gives birth in secret and she and her lecherous physician entrust the care of the infant to a Dutch nurse who declares, "ick sall do de best of tender nurses to dis infant, my pretty frokin" (3.2.13–14). Although her stage dialect sets her apart from the other characters of the play, the nurse is also very likely among the play's most consistently trustworthy characters. The main linguistic joke in the scene is merely Jane's own pun on the nurse's "de godimother" to which Jane self-deprecatingly says, "I am the bad mother" (3.2.20–1). The physician, Jane, and the physician's sister Anne all recognize the nurse's value and offer her payment for her trouble; thus Jane's honour and a major domestic duty are entrusted to the immigrant nurse. When Anne pays the nurse, she states, "I must be a little kind, too" (3.2.22), a statement that is at least rhetorically not the same as payment for services or charity. As Linda Pollock has shown, in the early modern period *kindness* was a complex "cluster concept" involving bonds of family, friendship, and patronage, an act of generosity or sympathy that still retained aspects of its etymological root *kin*.[59] Note also, at the risk of putting too much pressure on one word, that Anne's use of the word *kind* here appears to induct the Dutch nurse into a worldly domesticity. Later, the physician, frustrated at Jane's rejection of his advances, attempts to expose the scandal, but the nurse indicates that she believes the physician to be the father, "unwittingly embarrassing" him, as Hoenselaars points out, and temporarily thwarting his plan.[60] The Dutch nurse, like the Dutch merchant in *No Wit / Help Like a Woman's*, is a minor character, but she is presented as a positive addition to English domesticity.

David Nicol reads *A Fair Quarrel* as endorsing citizen values.[61] I would argue that acceptance of immigrants into the domestic sphere is a part of the citizen values the play promotes. There are counter-examples in the period, moments of xenophobia developing in tandem with an English national identity, but the modes of multicultural community examined in this book were durable enough to continue well into the seventeenth century. Economic conditions, doctrinal disputes, and events abroad might help or hinder Anglo-immigrant solidarities, and throughout the period there were changes in relations to specific immigrant groups. The economic rivalry between English and Dutch merchants, for instance, could cause resentment of Dutch immigrants in England, but as the examples from Middleton described above show, despite tensions abroad, writers could also continue to imagine a place for the Dutch in England. That place, as I have argued, was often contingent on religious affiliation, economic interdependence, and the degree to which strangers were willing to live and communicate on English terms. This is not contemporary multiculturalism – the emphasis here is one diminishing rather than valuing differences – but these modes of solidarity do represent early attempts at forging more positive Anglo-immigrant relations.

Although strangers had long appealed to the authority of the monarch during breakdowns in Anglo-immigrant relations, Archbishop Laud's animosity towards the diversity of worship represented by the stranger churches led strangers to increasingly identify with English Puritans; indeed, they found common cause with the Parliamentarians during the Long Parliament and the English Civil War.[62] Strangers played an important part in military training during the 1640s in London, Norwich, and Colchester.[63] As a show of support for strangers, in 1643 Parliament cited the original charter of Edward VI, and reinstated the stranger churches' "Libertie and Exercise of their Religion and Discipline as it is used beyond the Seas, in the Reformed Churches of severall Nations."⁶⁴ Laud's suppression of strangers and Puritans alike only strengthened the bond between the coreligionists so that even during the Anglo-Dutch Wars, the Dutch in England led a fairly peaceful existence.⁶⁵

This is not to say that tensions in Anglo-immigrant relations disappeared, however. Daniel Statt has charted an intense debate over immigration that spanned the entire eighteenth century.⁶⁶ Following the Great Plague of 1665–6 some saw immigration as a way of quickly repopulating the country. As one anonymous pamphlet put it, "There is nothing so much wanting in England as People."⁶⁷ In the 1680s another wave of Huguenots immigrated into England, fleeing Louis XIV's renewed persecution of Protestants. By 1688 the half-Dutch William of Orange had become king of England, bringing with him a retinue of Dutch courtiers, and the first decade of the eighteenth century saw an influx of German immigrants.⁶⁸ While some in England advocated a policy of inclusion of and solidarity with them, others, notes Statt, expressed disdain, describing immigrants as a "swarm with outlandish faces," "frog-landers," "scum," and "vermin."⁶⁹

It is in response to this climate of hostility to immigrants that Daniel Defoe wrote his satire, *The True-Born Englishman* (1701). As Statt notes, Defoe's consistent support for immigrant rights is evident in such texts as *Lex Talionis* (1698), *Giving Alms no Charity* (1704), and his *Brief History of the Poor Palatine Refugees* (1709).⁷⁰ In the preface to *The True-Born Englishman* Defoe explains that while his main goal is to expose the "Vanity" of those who "value themselves upon their Pedigree," he felt prompted to write the satire having seen "the Town all full of Lampoons and Invectives against Dutchmen, Only because they are Foreigners, and the King reproached and Insulted by Insolent Pedants, and Ballad-making Poets, for employing Foreigners; and for being a Foreigner himself."⁷¹ Defoe thus surveys English history to trace the alleged pedigree of the "true" Englishman. He concludes between conquests and waves of immigration, that the true Englishman is a "Het'rogeneous Thing," "a Contradiction," and, drawing attention to the constructed nature of national identity, the Englishman is "in Fact a Fiction" (335, 372–3).

In his historical survey Defoe pays special attention to the period covered in this book, linking it to immigration in the late seventeenth century:

Dutch, Walloons, Flemings, Irishmen, and Scots,
Vaudois and Valtolins, and Hugonots,
In good Queen Bess's charitable reign,
Supplied us with three hundred thousand men. (259–62)

The term "charitable" in this context seems to refer to Elizabeth's reputation for allowing Protestant refugees to settle in England. Although Defoe never loses sight of economic issues – the immigrants are "of every trade" (265) – the focus here is on religious persecution. He specifies "Hugonots" rather than simply referring to the French, for instance. The "Vaudois" (or Waldenses) were a longstanding Reformed sect whose persecution in 1655 prompted John Milton's poem "On the Late Massacre in Piedmont"; the term "Valtolins" refers to sectarian violence in the northern Italian Valtelline valley during the Thirty Years' War.[72] Following this stanza, Defoe describes Scottish migration into England under James I. As in Deloney's depiction of England in *Strange Histories*, Defoe's satire frames conquest and migration as essential aspects of English history.

"The offspring of this miscellaneous crowd," writes Defoe, soon "grew Englishmen" (269–70).[73] That is, over time the various modes of multicultural community described in this book – sectarian inclusivity, provincial globalism, and worldly domesticity – led to a level of integration that established them as English even as that process redefined Englishness. Defoe's central point is that Englishmen who spurn immigrants are ultimately hypocrites. Describing the more recent influx of Huguenots, Defoe predicts that their

> Children will, when riper Years they see,
> Be as Ill-natur'd and as Proud as we: /
> Call themselves English, Foreigners despise,
> Be surly like us all, and just as wise. (330–3)

By "just as wise," Defoe, of course, means "not very wise at all." Underlying the vehemence of xenophobia, he argues, is an ignorant desire to distance one's self from one's own immigrant past. The texts discussed in this book – those that, like Mary I's coronation pageantry, bear traces of immigrant participation in English life, or like Belchier's *Hans Beer-Pot*, Middleton's *The Peacemaker*, Dowriche's *The French Historie*, and so many others, embrace the idea of hospitality to strangers – are then especially English because they recognize what Defoe's "Englishman" does not. Immigration is and always has been a part of English culture.

Notes

Introduction: Forms of Multiculturalism in Early Modern England

1 Godfrey Goodman, *The Fall of Man, or the Corruption of Nature, Proved by the Light of Our Naturall Reason* (London: Felix Kingston for Richard Lee, 1616), 294–5.
2 Sir Philip Sidney, *An Apology for Poetry* (Indianapolis: Bobbs-Merrill Educational Publishing, 1970), 79–80. I am here listing the publication rather than estimated composition date.
3 Katherine Duncan-Jones suggests that Walsingham was Sidney's implied reader for the *Apology*. Is it a coincidence that Sidney first met Walsingham in France shortly before the massacre? Could it not be said that the passage on strangers refers to the men's shared experience of the massacre? The Huguenot context for Sidney's thinking has not gone unnoticed. Responding to a paper on the riot scenes in the *Arcadia*, Robert Quinn speculated that the Helots may be a veiled reference to the Huguenots. See Katherine Duncan Jones, *Sir Philip Sidney, Courtier Poet* (New Haven: Yale University Press, 1991), 234; and Robert Quinn, Respondent, "What's New in Arcadia? Property, Dissonance, and Naming," *41st Annual International Congress on Medieval Studies*, Kalamazoo, MI, 5 May 2006.
4 The verb *immigrate* is considerably older, dating back to 1623.
5 Chapter 1 revisits this issue as regards legal discourse in mid-Tudor England. For The Returns, see R.E.G. Kirk and Ernest Kirk, eds., *Returns of Aliens Dwelling in the City and Suburbs of London, 1525–1571*, Huguenot Society of London, Quarto Series 10 (Aberdeen: University Press, 1908). See also Irene Scouloudi, *Returns of Strangers in the Metropolis 1593, 1627, 1635, 1639: A Study of an Active Minority*, Huguenot Society of London, Quarto Series vol. 57 (London: Huguenot Society of London, 1985); and William

Durrant Cooper, *Lists of Foreign Protestants and Aliens Resident in England, 1618–1688, from Returns in the State Paper Office* (Westminster: Camden Society, 1862).

6 On the economic motive for stranger settlements, see Nigel Goose, "Immigrants and English Economic Development in the Sixteenth and Early Seventeenth Centuries," in *Immigrants in Tudor and Early Stuart England*, ed. Nigel Goose and Lien Bich Luu (Brighton: Sussex Academic Press, 2005), 136–60; and Luu, *Immigrants and the Industries of London, 1500–1700* (Farnham: Ashgate, 2005), 109–21. See also Bernard Cottret, *The Huguenots in England: Immigration and Settlement c. 1550–1700* (Cambridge and New York: Cambridge University Press, 1991), 55–7; Ronald Pollitt, "'Refuge of the Distressed Nations': Perceptions of Aliens in Elizabethan England," *The Journal of Modern History* 52.1, on demand supplement (1980): D1004; Laura Hunt Yungblut, *'Strangers Settled Here among Us': Policies, Perceptions and the Presence of Aliens in Elizabethan England* (London and New York: Routledge, 1996): 30, 52, 57; and Valerie Morant, "The Settlement of Protestant Refugees in Maidstone during the Sixteenth Century," *Economic History Review* 4 (1951): 210–14.

7 Cottret, *Huguenots in England*, 62.

8 Simonds D'Ewes, *A Compleat Journal of the Votes, Speeches, and Debates, Both of the House of Lords and House of Commons throughout the Whole Reign of Queen Elizabeth* (London: Paul Bowes, 1693), 504–5.

9 For a brief discussion of this portrait, see E.A.J. Honigmann, "Shakespeare and London's Immigrant Community circa 1600," in *Elizabethan and Modern Studies, Presented to Professor Willem Schrickx on the Occasion of His Retirement*, ed. J.P. Vander Motten (Gent: Seminarie voor Engelse en Amerikaanse Literatuur, R.U.G., 1985), 143–53.

10 Andrew Pettegree, *Foreign Protestant Communities in Sixteenth-Century London* (Oxford: Clarendon Press, 1986), 299.

11 See Ole Peter Grell, *Calvinist Exiles in Tudor and Stuart England* (Farnham: Ashgate, 1996), 4–5. On numbers of immigrants in England, see Luu, *Immigrants*, 91–100; and Jacob Selwood, *Diversity and Difference in Early Modern London* (Farnham: Ashgate, 2010), 24–30.

12 See, for example, A.J. Hoenselaars, *Images of Englishmen and Foreigners in the Drama of Shakespeare and His Contemporaries* (Rutherford, NJ: Farleigh Dickinson University Press, 1992). Gillian E. Brennan also finds xenophobia ubiquitous in sixteenth-century English literature; see Brennan, "The Cheese and the Welsh: Foreigners in Elizabethan Literature," *Renaissance Studies* 8.1 (1994): 40–64.

13 Jean Howard and Phyllis Rackin, *Engendering a Nation: A Feminist Account of Shakespeare's English Histories* (London: Routledge, 1997), 49; Claire McEachern, *The Poetics of English Nationhood, 1590–1612* (Cambridge: Cambridge University Press, 1996), 25.
14 Philip Schwyzer, *Literature, Nationalism and Memory in Early Modern England and Wales* (Cambridge: Cambridge University Press, 2004), 2.
15 Lloyd Edward Kermode, *Aliens and Englishness in Elizabethan Drama* (Cambridge: Cambridge University Press, 2009).
16 Pettegree, *Foreign Protestant Communities*, 282. See also C.W. Chitty, "Aliens in England in the Sixteenth Century," *Race* 8 (1966–67): 142.
17 Nigel Goose, "'Xenophobia' in Elizabethan and Early Stuart England: An Epithet Too Far?" in *Immigrants in Tudor and Early Stuart England*, ed. Nigel Goose and Lien Bich Luu (Brigthon: Sussex Academic Press, 2005), 129.
18 Goose, "'Xenophobia,'" 129.
19 Andrew Hadfield, *Literature, Politics and National Identity: Reformation to Renaissance* (Cambridge: Cambridge University, 1994); Richard Helgerson, *Forms of Nationhood: The Elizabethan Writing of England* (Chicago: University of Chicago Press, 1992), 4; McEachern, *Poetics*, 1. Also see Liah Greenfeld, *Nationalism: Five Roads to Modernity* (Cambridge: Harvard University Press, 1992), 29–31.
20 Elizabeth Sauer, "The Peculiar Status of Early Modern England," in *Reading the Nation in English Literature: A Critical Reader*, ed. Elizabeth Sauer and Julia M. Wright (New York: Routledge, 2010), 144–5. Sauer asserts that nationhood was nascent prior to the early modern period. Of course, some scholars see English nation formation occurring in the premodern period; see, for example, Anthony Hastings, *The Construction of Nationhood: Ethnicity, Religion and Nationalism* (Cambridge: Cambridge University Press, 1997), 47–51; Michael T. Clanchy, *England and Its Rulers, 1066–1272* (Oxford: Blackwell, 1998), 173–89; and R.R. Davies, *The First English Empire: Power and Identities in the British Isles, 1093–1343* (Oxford: Oxford University Press, 2000), 158.
21 McEachern, *Poetics*, 1, 19–20; Andrew Escobedo, *Nationalism and Historical Loss in Renaissance England: Foxe, Dee, Milton* (Ithaca: Cornell University Press, 2004), 11.
22 Willy Maley, *Nation, State and Empire in English Renaissance Literature* (New York: Palgrave/Macmillan, 2003), 26
23 Hadfield, *Literature*, 5–8 passim; Christopher Highley, *Catholics Writing the Nation in Early Modern Britain and Ireland* (Oxford: Oxford University Press, 2008).

24 On Sir Henry Lee, see Roy Strong, *The Cult of Elizabeth: Elizabethan Portraiture and Pageantry* (Berkeley: University of California Press, 1977), 129–40, 154–5. On the portrait specifically, see Louis Montrose, *The Subject of Elizabeth: Authority, Gender, and Representation* (Chicago: University of Chicago Press, 2006), 127–33; Kevin Sharpe, *Selling the Tudor Monarchy: Authority and Image in Sixteenth-Century England* (New Haven: Yale University Press, 2009), 383–8; Strong, *Cult of Elizabeth*, 154–5; and Roy Strong, *Gloriana: The Portraits of Queen Elizabeth I* (London: Thames and Hudson, 1987), 135–43.
25 Helgerson, *Forms*, 114. For an analysis that complicates the relationship between identity and early modern cartography, see Christopher Ivic, "Mapping British Identities: Speed's *Theatre of the Empire of Great Britain*," in *British Identities and English Renaissance Literature*, ed. David J. Baker and Willy Maley (Cambridge: Cambridge University Press, 2002), 135–55.
26 Arnold J. Fleming, *Flemish Influence in Britain*, vol. 1 (Glasgow: Jackson, Wylie, 1930): 230–1
27 The term farthingale was a borrowing from Spanish; see Janet Arnold, *Queen Elizabeth's Wardrobe Unlock'd* (Leeds: W.S. Maney and Sons, 1988), 194–200.
28 For immigration in the medieval period, see Sylvia L. Thrupp, "A Survey of the Alien Population of England in 1440," *Speculum* 32.2 (1957): 262–73; James L. Bolton, *The Alien Communities of London in the Fifteenth Century: The Subsidy Rolls of 1440 and 1483–4* (Stamford: Brepols, 1998); Keechang Kim, *Aliens in Medieval Law: The Origins of Modern Citizenship* (Cambridge: Cambridge University Press, 2001); Raymond Fagel, "The Netherlandish Presence in England before the Coming of the Stranger Churches, 1480–1560," in *From Strangers to Citizens: The Integration of Immigrant Communities in Britain, Ireland and Colonial America, 1550–1750*, ed. Randolph Vigne and Charles Littleton (Brighton: Sussex Academic Press, 2001): 7–16; and Justin Colson, "Alien Communities and Alien Fraternities in Later Medieval London," *The London Journal* 35.2 (2010): 111–43.
29 Colin Kidd, *British Identities before Nationalism: Ethnicity and Nationhood in the Atlantic World, 1600–1800* (Cambridge: Cambridge University Press, 1999), 186–7. Philip Schwyzer likewise describes what he calls "a Welsh paradox," a tendency for the Welsh to simultaneously develop and resist the idea of Britishness; see Schwyzer, *Literature, Nationalism and Memory*, 76–96, especially 95. For more on Anglo-Welsh relations, see Glanmor Williams, *Wales and the Reformation* (Cardiff: University of Wales Press, 1997); J. Gwynfor Jones, *Wales and the Tudor State* (Cardiff: University of Wales Press, 1989); Peter R. Roberts, "The Welsh Language, English Law and Tudor

Legislation," *Transactions of the Honourable Society of Cymmrodorion* (1989): 19–75; and Willy Maley and Philip Schwyzer, eds. *Shakespeare and Wales: From the Marches to the Assembly* (Farnham: Ashgate, 2010).
30 The term "foreigner" often carried this definition though the modern denotation of someone from another country also existed throughout the early modern period: "foreigner, n." in *OED* Online, December 2012, Oxford University Press. For more on Anglo-Welsh relations, see Lloyd Edward Kermode, *Aliens and Englishness in Elizabethan Drama* (Cambridge: Cambridge University Press, 2009), 85–118.
31 Lien Bich Luu, *Immigrants*, 100; J.L. Bolton, "Irish Migration to England in the Late Middle Ages: The Evidence of 1394 and 1440," *Irish Historical Studies* 32.125 (2000): 1–21; Marc Caball, "Faith Culture, and Sovereignty: Irish Nationality and Its Development, 1558–1625," in *British Consciousness and Identity: The Making of Britain, 1533–1707*, ed. Brendan Bradshaw and Peter Roberts (Cambridge: Cambridge University Press, 1998), 112–39. See also, Michael J. Braddick, *State Formation in Early Modern England c. 1550–1700* (Cambridge: Cambridge University Press, 2000), 340–97.

On the Scottish presence in England, see James A. Galloway, "Scottish Migration to England, 1400-1560," *Scottish Geographical Magazine* 112.1 (1996): 29–38; J.A.F. Thomson, "Scots in England in the Fifteenth Century," *The Scottish Historical Review* 79.207 (2000): 1–16; Keith M. Brown, "Scottish Identity in the Seventeenth Century," in *British Consciousness and Identity: The Making of Britain, 1533–1707*, ed. Brendan Bradshaw and Peter Roberts (Cambridge: Cambridge University Press, 1998), 236–58.

There is an ever-growing body of research on early modern Ireland. On Anglo-Irish relations in the early modern period, see Ciaran Brady and Jane H. Ohlmeyer, eds., *British Interventions in Early Modern Ireland* (Cambridge: Cambridge University Press 2005); Sean J. Connolly, *Contested Island: Ireland, 1460–1630* (Oxford: Oxford University Press, 2007); John McGurk, *The Elizabethan Conquest of Ireland: The 1590s Crisis* (London: St Martin's Press, 1997); Brian Mac Cuarta, ed., *Reshaping Ireland, 1550–1700: Colonization and Its Consequences* (Dublin: Four Courts Press, 2011); and Alexandra Walsham, *The Reformation of the Landscape: Religion, Identity, and Memory in Early Modern Britain and Ireland* (Oxford: Oxford University Press, 2011). For literary studies of Anglo-Irish relations, see Brendan Bradshaw, Andrew Hadfield, and Willy Maley, eds., *Representing Ireland: Literature and the Origins of Conflict, 1534–1660* (Cambridge: Cambridge University Press, 1993); Andrew Hadfield, *Edmund Spenser's Irish Experience: "Wild Fruite and Savage Soyl"* (Oxford: Oxford University Press, 1997); Andrew Hadfield and John McVeagh, eds., *Strangers to That Land:*

British Perceptions of Ireland from the Reformation to the Famine (Gerrards Cross: Colin Smythe, 1994); and Patricia Palmer, *Language and Conquest in Early Modern Ireland: Renaissance Literature and Elizabethan Imperial Expansion* (Cambridge: Cambridge University Press, 2001).

32 Willy Maley, *Nation, State and Empire*, 7–29 passim; and Conrad Russell, "The British Problem and the English Civil War," *History*, 72.236 (1987): 395–415.

33 For useful overviews of these patterns, see Luu, *Immigrants*, 104–12; Cotrett, *Huguenots*, 8–17.

34 Grell, *Calvinist Exiles*, 42–5, 74–97.

35 On the Dutch Revolt, see Alistair Duke, *Reformation and Revolt in the Low Countries* (London: Continuum Press, 2003); Jonathan I. Israel, *The Dutch Republic: Its Rise: Its Rise, Greatness, and Fall, 1477–1806* (Oxford: Oxford University Press, 1995); Geoffrey Parker, *The Dutch Revolt* (Ithaca: Cornell University Press, 1977); Andrew Pettegree, *Emden and the Dutch Revolt: Exile and the Development of Reformed Protestantism* (Oxford: Oxford University Press, 1992); and James D. Tracy, *The Founding of the Dutch Republic: War, Finance, and Politics in Holland, 1572–1588* (Oxford: Oxford University Press, 2007).

36 Grell, *Calvinist Exiles*, 4–5.

37 On the Thirty Years' War, see Geoffrey Parker, *The Thirty Years' War* (New York: Military Heritage Press, 1988); Jason White, *Militant Protestantism and British Identity, 1603–1642* (London: Pickering and Chatto, 2012); Ronald G. Asch, *The Thirty Years War: The Holy Roman Empire and Europe, 1618–48* (New York: Palgrave/Macmillan, 1997); and Richard Bonney, *The Thirty Years' War, 1618–1648* (Oxford: Osprey, 2002).

38 On the French Wars of Religion, see Denis Crouzet, *Dieu en ses royaumes: Une histoire des guerres de religion* (Seyssel, France: Champ Vallon, 2008); Stuart Carrol, *Martyrs and Murderers: The Guise Family and the Making of Europe* (Oxford: Oxford University Press, 2009); and Mack P. Holt, *The French Wars of Religion, 1562–1629* (Cambridge: Cambridge University Press, 2005).

39 Luu, *Immigrants*, 111–12 passim.

40 On the limits of tolerance among Protestants, see Alistair Duke, "Martyrs with a Difference: Dutch Anabaptist Victims of Elizabethan Persecution," *Nederlands Archief voor Kerkgeschiedenis* 80 (2000): 263–81; and Alexandra Walsham, *Charitable Hatred: Tolerance and Intolerance in England, 1500–1700* (Manchester: Manchester University Press, 2006), 236–8. On the degree of tolerance among Protestant exiles, see Ole Peter Grell, "Exile and Tolerance," in *Tolerance and Intolerance in the European Reformation*, ed. Ole Peter Grell and Bob Scribner (Cambridge: Cambridge University Press,

1996), 164–81; and Jesse Spohnholz, *Strangers and Neighbors: The Tactics of Toleration in an Early Modern German Town* (Newark: University of Delaware Press, 2010).
41 Pettegree, *Foreign Protestant Communities*, 20–2.
42 See Patrick Collinson, *Godly People: Essays on English Protestantism and Puritanism* (London: Hambledon Press, 1983), 245–72.
43 Luu, *Immigrants*, 92; see also Pettegree, *Foreign Protestant Communities*, 20, 78.
44 Qtd. in Johannes Lindeboom, *Austin Friars: History of the Dutch Reformed Church in London, 1550–1950* (The Hague: Martinus Nijhoff, 1950), 202.
45 Caleb Dalechamp, *Christian Hospitalitie Handled Common-place-wise* (Cambridge: Thomas Buck, 1632), A4. On early modern hospitality theory in general, see Felicity Heal, *Hospitality in Early Modern England* (Oxford: Clarendon Press, 1990).
46 Dalechamp, *Christian Hospitalitie*, 11.
47 Ibid., 11. For a discussion of possible tensions between "public hospitality" and "private hospitality" in Dalechamp, see Kermode, *Aliens*, 67–8.
48 Dalechamp, *Christian Hospitalitie*, 24–5.
49 On Italians in England, see Michael Wyatt, *The Italian Encounter with Tudor England: A Cultural Politics of Translation* (Cambridge: Cambridge University Press, 2005); M.E. Brachtel, "Regulation and Group-Consciousness in the Later History of London's Italian Merchant Colonies," *Journal of European Economic History* 9.3 (1980): 585–610; Alan Haynes, "Italian Immigrants in England, 1558–1603," *History Today* 27.8 (1977): 485–534; John Tedeschi, "Italian Reformers and the Diffusion of Renaissance Culture," *Sixteenth Century Journal* 5.2 (1974): 79–94; and Stefano Villani, "The Italian Protestant Church of London in the Seventeenth Century," in *Exiles, Emigrés and Intermediaries: Anglo-Italian Cultural Transactions*, ed. Barbara Schaff (New York: Rodopi, 2010), 217–36. On the Spanish immigrants in early modern England, see, Paul J. Hauben, "A Spanish Calvinist Church in Elizabethan London, 1559–65," *Church History* 34.1 (1965): 50–65. On the Portuguese, see Edmund Valentine Campos, "Jews, Spaniards, and Porintgales: Ambiguous Identities of Portuguese Marranos in Elizabethan England," *English Literary History* 69.3 (2002): 599–616; Edgar Samuels, "London's Portuguese Jewish Community, 1540-1753," in *From Strangers to Citizens: The Integration of Immigrant Communities in Britain, Ireland and Colonial America, 1550–1750*, ed. Randolph Vigne and Charles Galton Littleon (London: Huguenot Society of Great Britain and Ireland, 2002), 239–46; and Lucien Wolf, *Jews in Elizabethan England* (London: Spottiswoode, Ballantyne, 1929), 2–10 passim.

50 There were some Africans in early modern England, but commoners seem to have been consistently concerned about European immigrants rather than the small number of Africans among them. On Africans in England, see Imtiaz Habib, *Black Lives in the English Archives, 1500–1677* (Farnham: Ashgate Press, 2008). On the demographics of early modern England, see William Cunningham, *Alien Immigrants to England*, 2nd ed. (London: Frank Cass, 1969; 1st ed. 1897), 144–6; Pettegree, *Foreign Protestant Communities*, 21; Irene Scouloudi "Notes on Strangers in the Precinct of St. Katherine-by-the-Tower c 1500–1687, and on the 'Flemish Cemetery,'" *Proceedings of the Huguenot Society* 25.1 (1989): 75–82; and Scouloudi, *Returns of Strangers*, 77.
51 For more on geohumoralism, see Mary Floyd-Wilson, *English Ethnicity and Race in Early Modern Drama* (Cambridge University Press, 2003).
52 On contemporary multiculturalism, see Tariq Modood, *Multiculturalism: A Civic Idea* (New York: Polity Press, 2007).
53 See for example, Ania Loomba, *Gender, Race, Renaissance Drama* (Manchester University Press, 1989); Daniel Vitkus, *Turning Turk: English Theater and the Multicultural Mediterranean, 1570–1630* (New York: Palgrave, 2003). Kermode's *Aliens and Englishness* provides a recent example of a highly nuanced version of this approach.
54 D'Ewes, *Compleat Journal*, 506.
55 Ibid.
56 Dalechamp, *Christian Hospitalitie*, 105–6.
57 William Meade Williams, ed., *Annals of the Worshipful Company of Founders of the City of London* (Privately printed, 1867), 66.
58 Selwood, *Diversity and Difference*, 126–7.
59 Dalechamp, *Christian Hospitalitie*, 13–15.
60 Kwame Anthony Appiah, *Cosmopolitanism: Ethics in a World of Strangers* (New York: W.W. Norton, 2006), xv.
61 Nigel Goose, "The 'Dutch' at Colchester: The Economic Influence of an Immigrant Community in the Sixteenth and Seventeenth Centuries," *Immigrants and Minorities* 1.3 (1982): 261–80.
62 See for example Andrew Spicer, "A Process of Gradual Assimilation: The Exile Community in Southampton, 1567–1635," in *The Strangers' Progress: Integration and Disintegration of the Huguenot and Walloon Refugee Community, 1567–1889, Essays in Memory of Irene Scouloudi*, ed. Randolph Vigne and Graham C. Gibbs, 186–98 (London: Huguenot Society of Great Britain and Ireland, 1995); and Morant, "Settlement of Protestant Refugees," 210–14.
63 Joannes Henricus Hessels, *Ecclesiae Londino-Batavae Archivum*, 3 vols (Cambridge: Typis Academiae, 1887–97), 3.1, 573–5, 710–11.

64 Luu, "Assimilation or Segregation: Colonies of Alien Craftsmen in Elizabethan London," in *The Strangers' Progress: Integration and Disintegration of the Huguenot and Walloon Refugee Community, 1567–1889, Essays in Memory of Irene Scouloudi*, ed. Randolph Vigne and G. Gibbs (London: Huguenot Society of Great Britain and Ireland, 1995), 167.
65 For a map of the concentration of immigrants throughout London, see Yungblut, *Strangers Settled*, 26.
66 Luu, "Assimilation," 168; Scouloudi, *Returns of Strangers*, 147–21.
67 Qtd. in Luu, "Assimilation," 160.
68 Patents of Denization from the crown and Acts of Naturalization from Parliament afforded two ways for immigrants in the period to circumvent some of the economic restrictions placed on strangers. It is difficult to make generalizations about these documents, however, as each one specified different rights and privileges. On denizen status, see, Scouloudi, *Returns of Strangers*, 3–13; Luu, *Immigrants*, 142–6; and Selwood, *Diversity and Difference*, 38–41.
69 Pettegree, *Foreign Protestant Communities*, 302–5; Luu, *Immigrants*, 152–3. In a later article Pettegree compares immigrants' wills from the 1560s to those of the 1590s and asserts that "even among the less well-off the growing number of children born in England suggested that the process of peaceful assimilation would quicken as time went on"; see Andrew Pettegree "'Thirty Years On': Progress toward Integration amongst the Immigrant Population of Elizabethan London," in *English Rural Society, 1500–1800: Essays in Honour of Joan Thirsk*, ed. John Chartres and David Hey (Cambridge: Cambridge University Press, 1990), 309. For further discussion of gradual assimilation of immigrants in early modern England, see Grell, *Calvinist Exiles*, 122; Ephraim Lipson *The Economic History of England*, vol. 2 (New York: Barnes and Noble, 1959): 57; Charles Galton Littleton, "Geneva on Threadneedle Street: The French Church of London and Its Congregation, 1560–1625," Dissertation (University of Michigan, 1995), 163.
70 Nigel Goose and Lien Bich Luu, eds., *Immigrants in Tudor and Early Stuart England*, (Brighton: Sussex Academic Press, 2005). Jacob Selwood's *Diversity and Difference in Early Modern London* combines economic and cultural history, and is one of the few books on early modern immigration by a historian to engage in the literary discourse of the period. Grell's earlier *Calvinist Exiles in Tudor and Stuart England* also balances religious, economic, and political history.
71 I am here consciously appropriating Benedict Anderson's phrase, "imagined community," which he develops in describing the formation of national consciousness; see Benedict Anderson, *Imagined Communities: Reflections*

on the Origin and Spread of Nationalism, rev. ed. (London and New York: Verso, 1991), 1–9.

72 See, for example, Jonathan Brody Kramnick, "The Making of the English Canon," *PMLA* 112.5 (1997): 1088.

73 On the various immigrant communities outside of London, see Nigel Goose, "The Dutch in Colchester"; Robin D. Gwynn, *Huguenot Heritage: The History and Contribution of the Huguenots in Britain* (London: Routledge, 1985), 26–41; Andrew Spicer, *The French-Speaking Reformed Community and Their Church at Southampton, 1567–1620* (London: Huguenot Society of Great Britain and Ireland, New Series, 1997); Marcel Backhouse, *The Flemish and Walloon Communities at Sandwich During the Reign of Elizabeth I, 1561–1603* (Brussels: Koninklijke Academie voor Wetenschappen, Letteren en Schone Kunsten, 1995); Anne M. Oakley, "The Canterbury Walloon Congregation from Elizabeth I to Laud," in *Huguenots in Britain and Their French Background, 1550–1800*, ed. Irene Scouloudi (Totowa, NJ: Barnes and Noble, 1987), 56–71; Morant, "Settlement of Protestant Refugees in Maidstone"; Beate Magen, "The Administration of the Walloon Settlement in Canterbury 1576–1599," *Proceedings of the Huguenot Society of London* 22 (1970–76): 307–17; Raingard Esser, *Niederländische Exulanten im England des späten 16. und frühen 17. Jahrhundert: Die Norwicher Fremdengemeinden* (Berlin: Duncker & Humblot, 1996).

Some of Raingard Esser's invaluable work has been published in English: see Esser, "News across the Channel: Contact and Communication between the Dutch and the Walloon Refugees in Norwich and their Families in Flanders," *Immigrants and Minorities* 14.2 (1995): 31–46; Esser, "Germans in Early Modern Britain," in *Germans in Britain since 1500*, ed. Panikos Panayi (Hambledon: Continuum, 1996): 17–28; and Esser, "Social Concern and Calvinistic Duty: The Norwich Strangers' Community," in *Het Beloofde Land, Acht Opstellen Over Werken, Geloven en Vluchten Tijdens de XVIe en XVIIe Eeuw, Bijdragen tot de geschiedenis van de Westhoek*, ed. Jaak Decaestecker (Dikkebus, Westhoek, 1992), 172–84.

See also Christine Vane, "The Walloon Community in Norwich: The First Hundred Years," *Proceedings of the Huguenot Society* 24 (1984): 129–37; W.J.C. Moens, *The Walloons and Their Church at Norwich: Their History and Registers, 1565–1832* (Lymington: Huguenot Society of London, 1887–8); Matthew Reynolds, *Godly Reformers and their Opponents in Early Modern England: Religion in Norwich c. 1560–1643* (Woodbridge: Boydell Press, 2005), 39–63; Douglas Rickwood, "The Norwich Strangers 1565–1643, A Problem of Control," *Proceedings of the Huguenot Society of London* 24.2 (1984): 119–28.

One should also consult earlier work on these communities: C.W. Bracken, "The Huguenot Churches of Plymouth and Stonehouse," *Report and Transactions of the Devonshire Association for the Advancement of Science, Literature and Art* 66 (1934): 163–79; Thomas Dorman, "The Foreign Element in the Parishes of St Peter, Holy Cross and Canterbury, 1575–1684," *Proceedings of the Huguenot Society of London* 2 (1886–87): 197–204; Dorman, "Notes on the Dutch, Walloons, and Huguenots at Sandwich in the Sixteenth and Seventeenth Centuries," *Proceedings of the Huguenot Society of London* 2 (1886–87): 205–62; William J. Hardy, "Foreign Refugees at Rye," *Proceedings of the Huguenot Society of London* 2 (1886–7): 406–27; Hardy, "Foreign Settlers and Colcheser and Halstead," *Proceedings of the Huguenot Society of London* 2 (1887–8): 182–96. Charles E. Lart, "The Huguenot Settlements and Churches in the West of England," *Proceedings of the Huguenot Society of London* 7 (1901–4): 286–303; H.J. Cowell, "The French-Walloon Church at Glastonbury 1550–1553," *Proceedings of the Huguenot Society* 13 (1923–9): 483–515; F.W Cross, *History of the Walloon and Huguenot Church at Canterbury*, Publications of the Huguenot Society 15 (London: 1898); V.B. Redstone, "The Dutch and Huguenot Settlements of Ipswich," *Proceedings of the Huguenot Society* 12 (1917–23): 183–204; R.A. McCall, "The Huguenot in Kent," *Proceedings of the Huguenot Society of London* 12 (1924–9): 18–36.

74 *Calendar of State Papers, Domestic Series, of the Reigns of Edward VI, Mary, Elizabeth, 1547–1580*, ed. Robert Lemon (London: Longman, 1856), 120/22; Hardy, "Foreign Settlers at Colchester and Halstead."
75 Thomas Brooke, *Certayne Versis Written by Thomas Brooke, Gentleman* (Norwich: Anthony de Solemne, 1570; Petrus Dathenus, *De C.L. Psalmen Dauids. Wt den Francoyschen dichte in Nederlantschen overghesett door Petrum Dathenum* (Norwich: Anthony de Solemne, 1568, (STC / 2322:04).
76 Leonard Forster, *Janus Gruter's English Years: Studies in the Continuity of Dutch Literature in Exile in Elizabethan England* (London: Oxford University Press, 1967).
77 David Galloway, *Norwich: 1540–1642*, Records of Early English Drama 5 (Toronto: University of Toronto Press, 1984), 179–80.
78 Peter Laslett, *The World We Have Lost: England before the Industrial Age* (New York: Charles Scribner's Sons, 1965).

1. From the Dutch Acrobat to Hance Beerpot

1 Thomas Adams, *The Happiness of the Church* (London: G.P. for John Grismand, 1619), 137–8.
2 Highley, *Catholics Writing*, 12–20.

3 See Luu, *Immigrants*, 92.
4 Paul L. Hughes and James F. Larkin, eds., *Tudor Royal Proclamations* (New Haven: Yale University Press, 1964–9), 2: 31.
5 Hughes and Larkin, eds., *Tudor Royal Proclamations*, 2: 83.
6 John Christopherson writes, "the Prince of Spayne is vnto vs no straunger, but one of the bloude royall of Englande, by reason that his father the emperours Maiestie, that nowe is, bothe by hys father syde & mothers cometh of the Kinges of Englande." Christopherson, *An exhortation to all menne to take hede and beware of rebellion wherein are set forth the causes, that commonlye moue men to rebellion, and that no cause is there, that ought to moue any man there vnto* (London: John Cawood, 1554), M5r.
7 See Robert Tittler, *The Reign of Mary I* (London: Longman, 1983), 23.
8 Frank Percy Wilson, *The English Drama, 1485–1585* (New York: Oxford University Press, 1969), 34.
9 Like many printers, Waley, a founding member of the Stationers' Company, apprenticed several strangers; see Edward Arber, ed., *A Transcript of the Registers of the Company of Stationers of London, 1554–1640*, vol. I (London, 1875), 22. For John Waley, see Kirk and Kirk, *Returns*, 1: 169 and 3: 344; and Ernest James Worman, *Alien Members of the Book-Trade during the Tudor Period* (London: Blades, East and Blades, 1906), 69.
10 Mark Hunter disagrees and suggests a date prior to 1506, but the basis for his dating is flimsy at best; he claims that the play's affinities with the early sixteenth-century play *Youth* and the reference to the Flemish character Hance Beerpot as a mercenary (a gunner to be precise) and to wealth being transported to Flanders indicate that it was composed prior to 1506. See Hunter, "Notes on the Interlude of *Wealth and Health*," *Modern Language Review* 3.4 (1907): 366–9. While *Wealth and Health* may be fruitfully compared to *Youth*, more critics have found telling similarities between *Wealth and Health* and the Marian interlude *Respublica*. In part because of these similarities, critics argue that the two plays were written and performed at around the same time; see Thomas Wallace Craik, "The Political Interpretation of Two Tudor Interludes: *Temperance and Humility* and *Wealth and Health*," *The Review of English Studies*, new series 4.14 (1953): 98–108; A.J. Hoenselaars, *Images*, 30; and Ranier Pineas "The Revision of *Wealth and Health*," *Philological Quarterly* 44 (1965): 560–62.

As for the reference to wealth being transported to Flanders, David M. Loades notes that Mary began her reign in considerable debt and chose to increase foreign debt in her first year as queen. Much of that debt was owed to bankers in Antwerp, which had been annexed to Flanders since 1365, so a loss of wealth to Flanders could well signal a 1550s composition date. See

Loades, *The Reign of Mary Tudor: Politics, Government and Religion in England, 1553–58* (London: Longman, 1991), 129–33 and 232–9. It is well known that Mary employed foreign mercenaries occasionally. Historian Thomas Wyatt, for example, writes, "Most of the gunners in the Tower were Flemings, Italians and fewer Englishmen"; "Aliens in England before the Huguenots," *Proceedings of the Huguenot Society of London* 19 (1953): 85. See also C.V. Malfatti, ed. and trans., *Two Italian Accounts of Tudor England: A Journey to London in 1497; A Picture of English Life under Queen Mary* (Barcelona: Itinerarium Britanniae, 1953), 56; William Page, Preface to *Letters of Denization and Acts of Naturalization for Aliens, 1509–1603*, in Publications of the Huguenot Society of London, vol. 8 (Lymington, 1893), iv–xcviii; Ralph Sadler, *The State Papers and Letters of Sir Ralph Sadler* (Edinburgh: James Ballantyne, 1809), 1: 393; and Cunningham, *Alien Immigrants*, 142. While Hunter is right to focus on the character Hance Beerpot, Flemings were not closely associated with beer brewing in England, as Hance Beerpot is, until after 1524, and the word "berepot" did not enter print until well after Hunter's proposed date of composition. Thus, I agree with C.F. Tucker Brooke, Craik, and Darryll Grantley that *Health and Wealth* was written and performed sometime between 1553 and 1557. See Brooke, *The Tudor Drama: A History of English National Drama to the Retirement of Shakespeare* (Boston: Houghton Mifflin, 1911); and Grantley, *English Dramatic Interludes, 1300–1580: A Reference Guide* (Cambridge: Cambridge University Press, 2004), 363–5.

11 See Craik, "Political Interpretation," 30.
12 There is a substantial body of scholarship on the royal entry as a genre. See, for example, Malcolm Smuts, "Public Ceremony and Royal Charisma: The English Royal Entry in London, 1485–1642," in *The First Modern Society: Essays in English History in Honour of Lawrence Stone*, ed. A.L. Beier, David Cannadine, and James M. Rosenheim (Cambridge: Cambridge University Press, 1989), 65–93; David M. Bergeron, *English Civic Pageantry, 1558–1642* (London: Edward Arnold, 1971); and Alice Hunt, *The Drama of Coronation: Medieval Ceremony in Early Modern England* (Cambridge: Cambridge University Press, 2008).
13 Richard Mulcaster, *The Queen's Majesty's Passage*, in *Renaissance Drama: An Anthology of Plays and Entertainments*, ed. Arthur F. Kinney (Malden, MA: Blackwell, 2001), lines 658 and 664; Thomas Dekker, *The Dramatic Works of Thomas Dekker*, vol. 2, ed. Fredson Bowers (Cambridge: Cambridge University Press, 1953), line 591.
14 See Giovanni Francesco Commendone, "Events of the Kingdom of England Beginning with King Edward VI until the Wedding of the Most Serene

Prince Philip of Spain and the Most Serene Queen Mary," in *The Accession Coronation and Marriage of Mary Tudor as Related in Four Manuscripts of the Escorial*, trans. Malfatti (Barcelona: published by C.V. Malfatti, 1956); Thomas Lanquet, *An Epitome of Chronicles Conteyninge the whole discourse of the histories as well of this realme of England, as al other cou[n]treys, with the succession of their kinges, the time of their reigne, and what notable actes they did* (London: William Seres 1559), STC, 2nd ed. / 15217.5, Early English Books Online, http://eebo.chadwyck.com (accessed 5 April 2006); Henry Machyn, *The Diary of Henry Machyn, Citizen and Merchant-Taylor of London from A.D. 1550 to A.D. 1563*, ed. John Gough Nichols (Camden Society New York and London: AMS Press, 1968), series 1, 42; Edward Underhill, "The History of Wyatt's Rebellion" in *Tudor Tracts, 1532–1588*, ed. Alfred F. Pollard (New York: E.P. Dutton, 1903), 170–98; Charles Wriothesley, *A Chronicle of England during the Reigns of the Tudors from A.D. 1485 to 1559*, vol. 2, ed. William Douglas Hamilton (London: Camden Society, 1877); *The Chronicle of Queen Jane, and of Two Years of Queen Mary, and Especially of the Rebellion of Sir Thomas Wyat*, ed. John Gough Nichols (London: Camden Society, 1850); and vol. 12, *Two London Chronicles from the Collections of John Stow*, ed. Charles Lethbridge Kingsford, Camden Miscellany (London: Camden Society, 1910).

On Mary's failure to effectively use printing as a tool to assert her authority see David M. Loades, "The Press Under the Early Tudors: A Study of Censorship and Sedition," *Transactions of the Cambridge Bibliographic Society* 4.1 (1964): 29–50. Note, in contrast, the relative dominance of the printing trade by Protestant refugees: see, for example, Colin Clair, "Refugee Printers and Publishers in Britain during the Tudor Period," *Proceedings of the Huguenot Society of London* 22 (1970–76): 115–26; Fleming, *Flemish Influence*, 254–61; and Worman, *Alien*. Mary was undoubtedly aware of the power of the press, especially in its capacity to promote Protestantism – see, for example, her proclamations against printing related to doctrine in Hughes and Larkin, eds., *Tudor Royal Proclamations*, 2: 5–8 and 57–9 – but she seemed to believe that a simple removal of Protestant propaganda would ensure her subjects' obedience.

15 Quoted in Sydney Anglo, *Spectacle, Pageantry, and Early Tudor Policy*, 2nd ed. (Oxford: Clarendon Press, 1997), 283.
16 See Mulcaster, *Queen's Majesty*, 65–130.
17 See Dekker, *Dramatic Works*, 304–10.
18 Commendone, "Events," 32; my translation.
19 On the Hanseatic League, see Phillippe Dollinger, *The German Hansa*, trans. and ed. D.S. Ault and S.H. Steinberg (Stanford, CA: Stanford University

Press, 1970); T.H. Lloyd, *England and the German Hanse, 1157–1611* (London: Macmillan, 1991); and Raingard Esser, "Germans in Early Modern Britain," in *Germans in Britain Since 1500*, ed. Panikos Panayi (Hambledon: Continuum, 1996): 17–28.
20 Commendone, "Events," 32.
21 *Two London Chronicles*, 29. See Anglo, *Spectacle*, 320–21; and *The Chronicle of Queen Jane*, 29.
22 See Machyn, *Diary*, 45.
23 Judith M. Richards, "Mary Tudor as 'Sole Quene'?: Gendering Tudor Monarchy," *The Historical Journal* 40.4 (1997): 899 n. 20.
24 *Two London Chronicles* makes no mention of the pageants at Cheapside and Cornhill, focusing instead on the Dutch entertainer at St Paul's and the three stranger pageants. Commendone ("Events," 31) claims that of all the pageants, "only two of them [were] worth noticing, one by the Genoese, the other by the Florentines." *The Chronicle of Queen Jane* devotes little attention to the English pageants. Machyn devotes more description to the strangers' pageants, but applies the adjective "goodly" even-handedly (44–5). Charles Wriothesley describes the whole series but devotes considerably more attention to the strangers' pageants. Edward Underhill mentions only the Dutch entertainer at St Paul's; See Underhill, "Wyatt's Rebellion," *Chronicle*, 182.
25 Underhill, *Wyatt's Rebellion*, 182.
26 *Chronicle of Queen Jane*, 55; *Two London Chronicles*, 235.
27 Lanquet, *Epitome*, 327. Some letters do not mention Peter, but all the letters and chronicles that give details about the pageants (beyond simply mentioning that the royal entry occurred) include a description of the acrobatics at Saint Paul's.
28 See *Chronicle of Queen Jane*, 55; and Wriothelsey, *Chronicle*, 104.
29 See *Chronicle of Queen Jane*, 30. It is worth noting that, like Peter, the authors of Florentine pageant presumed to represent all of London.
30 John Foxe, *Acts and Monuments*, 12 vols (Albany, OR: Hartland Publications, 1997), 10: 737. See *Calendar of Letters, Despatches, and State Papers Relating to the Negotiations between England and Spain*, ed. Royall Tyler, vol. 11 (London: Hereford Times, Limited, 1916), 173.
31 John Proctor, *The historie of wyates rebellion with the order and maner of resisting the same, wherunto in the ende is added an earnest conference with the degenerate and sedicious rebelles for the serche of the cause of their daily disorder* (London: Robert Caly, 1555), 27–28 (STC, 2nd ed. / 20408, Early English Books Online, http://eebo.chadwyck.com [accessed 5 April 2006]). Proctor here quotes Sir Robert Southwell, Sheriff of Kent, as he dissuaded a

crowd from supporting Wyatt by focusing on Wyatt's appeal to xenophobic impulses. Of course, Wyatt's anti-alien battle-cry protested the plans for Mary to marry Philip and therefore give a stranger authority over English subjects, but his rhetoric seems to have been generally received as an attack on all strangers. Later, Proctor writes that the commoners felt that accusations of treason were unwarranted, "calling to their remembrance how Wyat in al apparance made his whol matter of styr, for strangers, & no waies against the quene" (55). Christopherson claims that there were two motives for Wyatt's rebellion: "One, to delyuer our countrie from the oppression of straungers, as it was reported, and another to restore agayne Luthers lewde religion" (*An exhortation,* 82). Chronicles tend to emphasize xenophobia as a motive in rebellions. Claire Valente suspects that this emphasis was a way of discrediting and distracting from the main grievances of many rebellions; see Valente, *The Theory and Practice of Revolt in Medieval England* (London: Ashgate, 2003), 59, 133.

32 See Foxe, *Acts,* 10: 1033.
33 "Proclamation for the Driving Out of the Realm Strangers and Foreigners," Hughes and Larkin, eds., *Tudor Royal Proclamations,* 2: 32.
34 Simon Renard, in *Calendar of Letters,* 11: 96.
35 See Loades, *Reign,* 25.
36 Foxe, *Acts,* 10: 803.
37 See Pettegree, *Foreign Protestant,* 117.
38 Renard to Charles V, in *Calendar of Letters, Despatches, and State Papers Relating to the Negotiations between England and Spain,* ed. Royall Tyler, vol. 12 (London: His Majesty's Stationery Office, 1949), 126.
39 See Pettegree, *Foreign Protestant,* 78, 118; Pettegree, "The Stranger Community in Marian London," *Proceedings of the Huguenot Society* 24.5 (1987), 391; and Luu, "'Taking the Bread out of Our Mouths': Xenophobia in Early Modern London," *Immigrants and Minorities* 19.2 (2000): 1–22, esp. 9.
40 By 1593 most of those who had remained in the realm throughout Mary's reign would have died, but the Returns of Aliens for 1593 lists some non-denizen strangers who were present as early as 1539; see Kirk and Kirk, *Returns,* 218. See also Luu, "'Taking the Bread,'" 9.
41 See Pettegree, *Foreign Protestant,* 120.
42 Mary I, "Order Deporting French Aliens," in Hughes and Larkin, eds., *Tudor Royal Proclamations,* 2: 83.
43 See Page, "Preface," xxxi.
44 See Pettegree, *Foreign Protestant,* 115–6; and *Calendar of Letters,* 11: 217.
45 See Foxe, *Acts,* 11: 769–99.
46 Ibid., 11: 256–63.

47 Ibid., 11: 796 and 10: 793–95. Little is known about Frog, but his hosting the meetings indicates that he was clearly a prominent figure in this particular congregation. The Lay Subsidies, taken on 14 May 1559, records three strangers with the surname Frogge living in Saint Katherine's: Martyn and Gover Frogge, who were servants to William Jonson, and John Frogge, a resident of Saint Katherine's as far back as 1540 and as late as 1571 when he was listed as a denizen. See Kirk and Kirk, *Returns,* 251–2, 20, 457. On the immigrant population in Saint Katherine's, see Irene Scouloudi, "Notes on Strangers in the Precinct of St. Katherine-by-the-Tower c. 1500–1687, and on the 'Flemish Cemetery,'" *Proceedings of the Huguenot Society* 25.1 (1989): 75–82.
48 Much less than half the total stranger population at the time were denizens. See Page, "Preface," lii–liii.
49 Foxe records only one execution of a stranger during Mary's reign: Lyon Cawch, a Flemish merchant; see Foxe, *Acts,* 11: 256–63.
50 For a discussion of this practice, see Pettegree, *Foreign Protestant,* 63–5.
51 See Pettegree, *Foreign Protestant,* 123.
52 Page notes that the Mayor was compelled to issue the regulations against aliens because Mary's 1554 proclamation had been such a failure; see Page, "Preface," xxx.
53 *The Interlude of Wealth and Health,* ed. W.W. Greg, Malone Society Reprints (London: Chiswick Press, 1907), line 590.
54 Kermode, *Aliens,* 36–40.
55 See Hoenselaars, *Images,* 41. Kermode argues that Ill Will is here to be taken as Spanish or implicated in Spanish identity; see Kermode, *Aliens,* 38–9.
56 See, for example, Francis Hugh Mares, "The Origin of the Figure Called 'the Vice' in Tudor Drama," *Huntington Library Quarterly* 22.1 (1958): 19–20.
57 Kermode, *Aliens,* 39–40.
58 Charles William Wallace, *The Evolution of the English Drama up to Shakespeare* (Port Washington, NY: Kennikate Press, 1968), 101.
59 Darryll Grantley, *Wit's Pilgrimage: Drama and the Social Impact of Education in Early Modern England* (Farnham: Ashgate, 2000), 152–3.
60 David M. Bevington, *Tudor Drama and Politics: A Critical Approach to Topical Meaning* (Cambridge: Harvard University Press, 1968), 133–4.
61 See Hoenselaars, *Images,* 30; and Craik, "Political Interpretation."
62 See Loades, *Reign,* 25.
63 I can find no other mid-Tudor play that intermixes characters as *Wealth and Health* does. The Marian plays *Respublica* and *Love Feigned and Unfeigned,* for example, do not intermix allegorical and realistic characters. See W.R. Streitberger, *Court Revels, 1485–1559* (Toronto: University of Toronto Press, 1994), 206.

64 Craik, "Political Interpretation," 106. See also Brooke, *Tudor Drama*, 107.
65 C.S. Lewis discusses the proper function of the allegorical figure of War in the Thebaid, for example; see Lewis, *The Allegory of Love: A Study in Medieval Tradition* (London: Oxford University Press, 1973), 50–1.
66 Kermode, *Aliens*, 34–5.
67 This composite may simply be indicative of the dramatist's imprecision. Dutch and Flemish, like French and Walloon, were frequently used interchangeably.
68 For all Shrewd Wit's bragging about being a great deceiver, he and Ill Will turn out to be horrible liars; much of the comedy emanates from their habit of saying precisely what they are doing and then falling over themselves to cover up the truth they have just revealed to their masters. See, for example, *Wealth and Health*, 499–510.
69 Greg and Holthausen agree with my attribution of this line: see Greg, ed., *Interlude of Wealth and Health*, vii, x; and Ferdinand Holthausen, ed., Einleitung to An Interlude of Welth and Helth: *Eine Englische Moralität des XVI. Jahrhundrets* (Kiel: Universität Kiel, 1908), 34. See also John S. Farmer's decision regarding this line: Farmer, ed., *Recently Recovered "Lost" Tudor Plays* (London: Early English Drama Society, 1907), 300.
70 Jasper Platt Jr., "'Drowse'=Devil," *Notes and Queries* 116 (6 July 1907), 6. Prior to Platt's suggestion, Greg had declared the word "unintelligible" ("Notes on the Society's Publications," *Collections* 1 [London: Malone Society, 1907], 1). A.E.H. Swaen agrees with Platt; see Swaen, "*Wealth and Health*," *Englische Studien* 41 (1910): 456. St. Swithin disputes Platt's gloss, but I find Swithin less persuasive; see Swithin, "'Drowse'=Devil," *Notes and Queries* 116 (27 July 1907), 73. Even if Platt were wrong, there remain a considerable number of echoes of Ill Will reverberating in Good Remedy's speech during his encounter with Hance. Platt also suggests "hounded" as "hundred." The epithet "bowse" in these lines interestingly combines Hance's handling of guns (as in harquebus) and drinking: see "bouse | bowse, n.1," *OED Online*, December 2012, Oxford University Press.
71 See Charles Read Baskerville, *Elizabethan and Stuart Plays* (New York: H. Holt, 1934), 180 n. 3.
72 See Craik, "Political Interpretation," 106; and Hoenselaars, *Images*, 41.
73 Craik, *The Revels History of Drama in English*, vol. 2 (New York: Barnes and Noble, 1977), 197; Hoenselaars, *Images*, 40.
74 Holthausen also finds humour in Hance's inebriated speech; see "Einleitung," 65.
75 This representation of Catholic theology is admittedly crass. This part of the play may have been revised for publication by someone interested in

writing into the play a bit of Protestant polemic. Nonetheless, it is clear that in the course of the debate Wealth and Health resolve their differences, and the argument that follows regarding Hance withstands hints of Elizabethan revision.
76 Jane Griffiths, "Counterfeit Countenance: (Mis)representation and the Challenge to Allegory in Sixteenth-Century Morality Plays," *Yearbook of English Studies* 38.1–2 (2008): 30.
77 See Scouloudi, *Returns*, 17–18.
78 Christopherson, *An exhortation*, Q1r–Q2v.
79 Ibid., C6r.

2. The Rhetoric of Religious Refuge under Elizabeth I

1 For an overview of the restoration of stranger churches under Elizabeth, and the circumstances of Haemstede's excommunication, see Patrick Collinson, *Godly People: Essays on English Protestantism and Puritanism* (London: Hambledon Press, 1983) 227–35. See also Pettegree, *Foreign Protestant Communities*, 133–81; Cottret, *Huguenots in England*, 45–78; John Strype, *Annals of the Reformation* (Oxford: Clarendon Press, 1824), 1: 8.
2 Grindal's formal letter of excommunication may be found in Hessels 3.1, 142–3.
3 R.H. Tawney and Eileen Power, *Tudor Economic Documents*. 3 vols, (London: Lowe and Brydone, 1924; 1963), I: 297. On immigrant settlements for economic purposes, see Nigel Goose, "Immigrants and English Economic Development in the Sixteenth and Early Seventeenth Centuries."
4 *A New Interlude No Lesse Wittie Than Pleasant, Entitled New Custom* (London: William How for Abraham Veale, 1573), 2.1, C3r. Little scholarly work has been done on this adamantly Protestant play. Frederick G. Fleay suggests that it was written around 1562–3; Martin Wiggins offers 1570–3 as the likely date of composition, the latter date being the date of the play's first printing. Paul Whitfield White argues that the play's interest in vestments indicates a date in the mid-1560s and speculates that it was part of the repertoire of the Earl of Leicester's Men. See Frederick Gard Fleay, *A Chronicle History of the London Stage* (London: Reeves and Turner, 1893), 64–5; Martin Wiggins in association with Catherine Richardson, *British Drama, 1533–1642: A Catalogue, Volume II: 1567–1589* (Oxford: Oxford University Press, 2012), 96; Paul Whitfield White, "Patronage, Protestantism, and Stage Propaganda in Early Elizabethan England," *The Yearbook of English Studies* 21 (1991): 51–2.
5 *New Custom*, 2.3, C4v.
6 Ibid., 3.1, D1v.

7 Cottret, *Huguenots in England*, 67.
8 Qtd. and trans. in Simon Mealor, "*O Belle Tamise*: The Development of a Huguenot Pastoral Mode in Elizabethan England," in *Archipelagic Identities: Literature and Identity in the Atlantic Archipelago, 1550–1800*, ed. Philip Schwyzer and Simon Mealor (Aldershot, UK: Ashgate, 2004), 182. Grévin's poems from England appear in Jacques Grévin, *Jacques Grévin, 1538–1570*, ed. Lucien Pinvert (Paris: Ancienne Librairie Thorin et Fils, 1899), 370–86.
9 Kathryn J. Evans, "Jacques Grévin's Religious Attitude and The Family of Love," *Bibliothèque d'Humanisme et Renaissance* 47.2 (1985): 357–65.
10 Vulcob refers to Jean de Vulcob, a Huguenot sympathizer and nephew to the then French Ambassador to England. An acquaintance of Sidney's, Vulcob was in fact at the English court around this time. Later he would become Ambassador to the Holy Roman Emperor. See *Calendar of State Papers: Spanish: Calendar of Letters and State Papers Relating to English Affairs, Vol. II: Elizabeth, 1568–1579*, ed. Martin A.S. Hume, (London: Eyre and Spottiswoode, 1894), 71–2; Sir Philip Sidney, *The Correspondence of Sir Philip Sidney*, vol. 1, ed. Roger Kuin (Oxford: Oxford University Press, 2012), lxi.
11 Mealor, "*O Belle Tamis*," 182–4.
12 Foxe claims that the slaughter in Paris alone amounted to 10,000 and that the subsequent attacks outside of Paris reached 30,000. Although these numbers no doubt fail sound statistical demographics, they do give a sense of the horrific picture painted in the minds of the English as regards the plight of Protestants abroad; see Foxe, *Acts*, 8: 1215. For a cogent summary of the events surrounding the Saint Bartholomew's Day Massacre, see Barbara Diefendorf, "Memories of the Massacre: Saint Bartholomew's Day and Protestant Identity in France," in *Voices of Tolerance in an Age of Persecution*, ed. Vincent P. Carey (Washington, DC: Folger Shakespeare Library, 2004), 45–62. See also Donald R. Kelly, "Martyrs, Myths, and Massacre: The Background of St. Bartholomew" *American Historical Review* 77.5 (1972): 1323–42. For an overview of the events leading up to the massacre, see Robin Gwynn, *Huguenot Heritage: The History and Contribution of the Huguenots in Britain* (London: Routledge, 1985), 6–19.
13 Strype, *Annals*, 3: 239.
14 On the general divergence of Elizabethan attitudes toward strangers, see Yungblut, *Strangers*, 28–45.
15 Strype, *Annals*, 2, part 1: 241.
16 Strype, *Annals*, 2, part 1: 241.
17 On the Biblical discourse of hospitality, see Heal, *Hospitality*, 122–40, 169–78.
18 See, for example, discussions of this motif in Menna Prestwich, "Calvinism in France, 1555–1629," in *International Calvinism 1541–1715* (Oxford:

Clarendon Press, 1985), 95. On the importance of Jewish texts to early Reformers, see Sharon Achinstein, "John Foxe and the Jews," *Renaissance Quarterly* 54.1 (2001): 86–120. See also Anthony Grafton and Joanna Weinberg, *"I Have Always Loved the Holy Tongue": Isaac Casaubon, The Jews, and a Forgotten Chapter in Renaissance Scholarship* (Cambridge, MA: Harvard University Press, 2011).

19 Wolf, *Jews,* 3–4, 8–9. See also, C.J. Sisson, "A Colony of Jews in Shakespeare's London," *Essays and Studies* 23 (1938): 37–52; Roger Prior, "A Second Jewish Community in Tudor London," *Jewish Historical Studies* 31 (1988–90): 137–52; James Shapiro, *Shakespeare and the Jews* (New York: Columbia University Press, 1996); and Janet Adelman, *Blood Relations: Christian and Jew in Merchant of Venice* (Chicago: University of Chicago Press, 2008), 4–5.

20 Debora was also featured in Elizabeth's coronation pageantry. The accounts of the Norwich pageants may be found in David Galloway, ed., *Norwich,* 243–330. For a discussion of this pageant in the broader context of immigrant contributions to royal pageantry, see Raingard Esser, "Immigrant Cultures in Tudor and Stuart England," in *Immigrants in Tudor and Early Stuart England*, ed. Nigel Goose and Lien Bich Luu (Brighton: Sussex Academic Press, 2005): 166–7. On the figure of Debora in early modern England, see Michelle Osherow, *Biblical Women's Voices in Early Modern England* (Farnham: Ashgate, 2009), 77–110.

21 Michelle Ephraim, *Reading the Jewish Woman on the Elizabethan Stage* (Farnham: Ashgate, 2008), 5.

22 For more on Modet, see Moens, *Walloons,* 7–10; 43–4; and James Aitken Wylie, *The History of Protestantism* 3 (London: Cassell, Petter, Galpin & Co., 1887), 46–56.

23 David Galloway, ed., *Norwich,* 256, 264.

24 Ibid., 264–5. Instead of "object" in the phrase "objecte to every kinde of injurie" Moens has "*exposed* to every kind of injury"; see Moens, *Walloons,* 43.

25 David Galloway, ed., *Norwich.*, 265.

26 Ibid., 266.

27 Ibid., 274, lines 12–13.

28 John Whitgift, *The Works of John Whitgift* (Cambridge: Cambridge University Press, 1853), 584.

29 For a full account of this less cheerful progress, see Zillah Dovey, *An Elizabethan Progress, The Queen's Journey into East Anglia, 1578* (Madison: Farleigh Dickson University Press, 1996), 88–123.

30 George Wapull, *The Tide Tarrieth No Man*, 1576 (reprint 1910; Kessinger Publishing, 2002).

31 Kermode, *Aliens*, 23–4, 49–58.
32 Ibid., 49–58.
33 See G.L. Kittredge, "The Date of *The Pedler's Prophecy*," *Harvard Studies and Notes in Philology* 16 (1934): 97–118; and Grantley, *English*, 268. See also, Laura Caroline Stevenson, *Praise and Paradox: Merchants and Craftsmen in Elizabethan Popular Literature* (Oxford: Oxford University Press, 2002), 230.
34 *The Pedlers Prophecie* (London: Thomas Creede, 1595), D2r.
35 Ibid., D2v.
36 Ibid., F3r–v.
37 I am here thinking of George Wapull's *The Tide Tarrieth No Man*, Ulpian Fulwell's *Like Will to Like*, and Robert Wilson's *Three Ladies of London* and *Three Lords of London*. For discussions of the negative representation of immigrants in these plays, see Kermode, *Aliens*, 40–76; and Hoenselaars, *Images*, 41–8.
38 Leviticus, 19:34. All Biblical citations refer to the Geneva Bible. The Bible and Holy Scriptures (Geneva: Rouland Hall, 1560).
39 Heal, *Hospitality*, 10.
40 Qtd. in Walter Howard Frere and Charles Edward Douglas, *Puritan Manifestoes: A Study of the Origins of the Puritan Revolt* (New York: B. Franklin, 1972), 148.
41 Henri Estienne, *A mervaylous discourse vpon the lyfe, deedes, and behaviours of Katherine de Medicis Queene mother: vvherin are displayed the meanes vvhich she hath practised to atteyne vnto the vsurping of the kingedome of France, and to the bringing of the estate of the same vnto vtter ruine and destruction* (London: Henry Middleton, 1575).
42 Arthur Golding, trans., *The Lyfe of the Mostly Godly, Valeant, and Noble Capteine and maintener of the Trew Christian Religion in Fraunce, Jasper Colignie Shatilion, Sometyme Greate Admirall of Fraunce* (London: Thomas Vautrollier, 1576); and *The Edict or Proclamation Set For the by the Frenche Kinge vpon the Pacifying of the Troubles in Fraunce* (London: Thomas Vautrollier, 1576). On Golding, see James Wortham, "Arthur Golding and the Translation of Prose," *Huntington Quarterly* 12.4 (1949): 339–67.
43 Richard Robinson, ed., *A poore knight his pallace of priuate pleasures Gallantly garnished, with goodly galleries of strang inuentio[n]s and prudently polished, with sundry pleasant posies* (London: W. How, 1579), D1r. Thomas Churchyard, *The Miserie of Flaunders, Calamatie of Fraunce, Misfortune of Portugall, Unquietnes of Irelande, Troubles of Scotlande, and the Blessed State of Englande* (London: Andrew Maunsell, 1579), B1r–B4v.
44 Arthur Geoffrey Dickens, "The Elizabethans and St. Bartholomew," in *The Massacre of St. Bartholomew: Reappraisals and Documents*, ed. Alfred Soman

(The Hague: Martinus Nijhoff, 1974): 52–70. See also Robert Kingdon, *Myths About the St. Bartholomew's Day Massacre, 1572–1576* (Harvard University, Press, 1988), 20–3, 125–35.
45 For a balanced view of the violence of the Wars of Religion, see Natalie Zemon Davis, "The Rites of Violence, " *Past and Present* 59 (1973): 51–91.
46 On the printing of Protestant propaganda in the wake of Louis XIV's renewed persecution of Protestants, see Elizabeth L. Eisenstein, *Grub Street Abroad: Aspects of the French Cosmopolitan Press from the Age of Louis XIV to the French Revolution* (Oxford: Oxford University Press, 1992). On the settlements established in the 1680s, see Gwynn, *Huguenot Heritage*, 129–59; Cottret, *Huguenots in England*, 185–228; and Daniel Statt, *Foreigners and Englishmen: The Controversy Over Immigration and Population 1660–1760* (Newark: University of Delaware Press, 1995), 66–120.
47 Theodore Beza [Bèze], *A Tragedie of Abrahams Sacrifice*, Trans. Arthur Golding (London: Thomas Vautrollier, 1575), A2r. On the publication history of the play, see Malcolm W. Wallace, ed., Introduction to *A Tragedie of Abraham's Sacrifice* (Toronto: University of Toronto Library, 1906), xxxvii–xxxviii. See also Marguerite Soulié and Jean-Dominque Beaudin, Introduction to *Abraham Sacrifiant* (Paris: Honoré-Champion, 2006), 9–28. On the theological concerns of the play, see Jean-Claude Carron, "Abraham sacrifiant de Théodore de Bèze: Exil et propagande évangélique au XVIe siècle," *Revue D'histoire Du Théâtre* 1–2, no. 221–2 (2004): 69–92.
48 On this and other details of Bèze's life, see David Curtis Steinmetz, *Reformers in the Wings: From Geiler von Kayserberg to Theodore Beza* (Oxford: Oxford University Press, 2001), 114–20. See also, Tadataka Maruyama, *The Ecclesiology of Theodore Beza: The Reform of the True Church* (Geneva: Droz, 1978).
49 For more about Vautrollier, see chapter 6.
50 Beza, *Tragedie*, B1r.
51 Ibid,,B3r.
52 Ibid., B3v.
53 Along similar lines, Philip Benedict notes that French Protestants in Roeun tended to give their children Old Testament names such as Abraham, Isaac, Daniel, Sara, and Judith; see Benedict, *Rouen during the Wars of Religion* (Cambridge: Cambridge University Press, 1981), 105–6; 256–60.
54 Beza, *Tragedie*, B4r, C2v, C7r.
55 Ibid., D3v.
56 On the relationship between Hugh and Anne Dowriche, see Micheline White, "Power Couples and Women Writers in Elizabethan England: The Public Voices of Dorcas and Richard Martin and Anne and Hugh Dowriche," in *Framing the Family: Narrative and Representation in the Medieval and*

Early Modern Periods, ed. Rosalynn Voaden and Diane Wolfthal (Tempe, AZ: Arizona Center for Medieval and Renaissance Studies, 2005): 119–38. On Dowriche as part of a circle of West Country Puritan literary figures, see Micheline White, "Women Writers and Literary-Religious Circles in the Elizabethan West Country: Anne Dowriche, Anne Lock Prowse, Anne Lock Moyle, Elizabeth Rous, and Ursula Fulford," *Modern Philology* 103.2 (2005): 187–214.

57 Elaine Beilin, "'Some Freely Spake Their Minde': Resistance in Anne Dowriche's *The French Historie*," in *Women, Writing and the Reproduction of Culture in Tudor and Stuart Britain*, ed. Mary E. Burke, Jane Donaworth, Linda L. Dove, and Karen Nelson (Syracuse, NY: Syracuse University Press, 2000), 127. Susanne Woods and Margaret P. Hannay, with Elaine Beilin, and Anne Shaver, "Renaissance Englishwomen and the Literary Career," in *European Literary Careers: The Author from Antiquity to the Renaissance*, ed. Patrick Cheney and Frederick A. de Armas (Toronto: University of Toronto Press, 2002), 302–24.

58 Anne Dowriche, *The French Historie*, Imprinted at London by Thomas Orwin for Thomas Man, 1589), A2r.

59 Elaine Beilin, "Writing Public Poetry: Humanism and the Woman Writer," *Modern Language Quarterly* 51.2 (1990): 258–67. Kate Chedgzoy argues that too much has been made of Dowriche's use of the modesty topos; see her "This Pleasant and Sceptered Isle: Insular Fantasies of National Identity in Anne Dowriche's *The French Historie* and William Shakespeare's *Richard II*," in *Archipelagic Identities* ed. Philip Schwyzer and Simon Mealor (Farnham: Ashgate, 2004), 25–42. On the modesty topos in women's writing, see Patricia Pender, *Early Modern Women's Writing and the Rhetoric of Modesty* (New York: Palgrave/Macmillan, 2012). On Dowriche's entry into public discourse and Tudor historiography see, Elaine Beilin, "'Some Freely Spake Their Minde'"; Danielle Clarke, *The Politics of Early Modern Women's Writing* (Harlow: Longman, 2001), 162–6; Patricia Demers, *Women's Writing in English: Early Modern England* (Toronto: University of Toronto Press, 2005), 135–7; Megan Matchinske, *Women Writing History in Early Modern England* (Cambridge: Cambridge University Press, 2009), 20–44; and Mihoko Suzuki, "Warning Elizabeth with Catherine de' Medici's Example: Anne Dowriche's *French Historie* and the Politics of Counsel," in *The Rule of Women in Early Modern Europe*, ed. Anne J. Cruz and Mihoko Suzuki (Urbana: University of Illinois Press, 2009): 174–93.

60 The acrostic is evidently a nod to her main source, Timme's translation of *The Commentaries*, A2v. There is also an acrostic dedicatory poem in Hugh Dowriche's *The Jaylor's Conversion*, to which Anne Dowriche contributed

a poem; Hugh Dowriche, *The Jaylor's Conversion* (London: John Windet, 1596), A2r.
61 Anne Dowriche, *French Historie*, A4r.
62 On Dowriche as martyrologist, see Armel Dubois-Nayt, "Anne Dowriche et l'Histoire de France ou … d'Angleterre?" *Études Épistémè* 17 (2010): 11–30; and Randall Martin, "Anne Dowriche's 'The French Historie,' Christopher Marlowe, and Machiavellian Agency," *Studies in English Literature* 39.1 (1999): 69–87. Sidney L. Sondergard cautions against too strong a comparison between Dowriche and Foxe; see Sondergard, *Sharpening Her Pen: Strategies of Rhetorical Violence by Early Modern English Women Writers* (Selinsgrove: Susquehanna University Press, 2002): 70–2.
63 Although the acrostic poem has a long tradition in Medieval literature, Dowriche and Timme's use of the acrostic may well provide another example of Protestants drawing on Jewish traditions, as their acrostics seem to have roots in the Old Testament. See, for example, David N. Freedman, "Acrostics and Metrics in Hebrew Poetry," *Harvard Theological Review* 65.3 (1972): 367–92; and Benjamin D. Giffone, "A 'Perfect' Poem: The Use of the Qatal Verbal Form in the Biblical Acrostics," *Hebrew Studies* 51 (2010): 49–72. On the use of acrostics in Puritan poetry, see Jeffrey Walker, "Anagrams and Acrostics: Puritan Poetic Wit," in *Puritan Poets and Poetics: Seventeenth-Century American Poetry in Theory and Practice*, ed. Peter White (University Park: Pennsylvania State University Press, 1985): 247–57.
64 Anne Dowriche, *French Historie*, B1v. See Deuteronomy 29: 17–18: "That there shulde not be among you man nor woman, nor familie, nor tribe, which shulde turne his heart away this day from te Lord our God, to go & serve the gods of these nations & that there shulde not be amongyou anie roote that bringeth fourth gall and wormwood."
65 Anne Dowriche, *French Historie*, C4r-v.
66 Subtitles are from Anne Dowriche, *French Historie*, A1v.
67 Anne Dowriche, *French Historie*, B1v.
68 Elaine Beilin, *Redeeming Eve: Women Writers of the English Renaissance* (Princeton: Princeton University Press, 1987), 103.
69 Hotman and de Serres are well-known sources for Dowriche's poem. For *The French Historie*'s connection to *Contre-Machiavel* see Randall Martin, "Anne Dowriche's *The French Historie* and Innocent Gentillet's *Contre-Machiavel*," *Notes and Queries* 44.1 (1997): 41.
70 Matchinske, *Women Writing*, 22, 32–5. On the expansion of the role of Satan see, for example, Beilin, "Writing Public Poetry," 260; and Sondergard, *Sharpen Her Pen*, 80–3.
71 Anne Dowriche, *French Historie*, C1v.

72 Ibid., D1v.
73 Ibid., F2v.
74 Ibid., A4r. Beilin discusses this passage in terms of Dowriche's poetics; see Beilin, "Writing Public Poetry," 260. It is striking how neatly that poetics fits Sidney's *Apology* (printed after Dowriche's poem) where poetry is lauded for its ability to participate simultaneously in history and philosophy; Sidney, *Apology*, 22–8.
75 On Acontius, see Charles Donald O'Malley, *Jacopo Acontio Traduzione di Delio Cantimori Uomini e Dottrine* (Rome: Edizioni di Storia e Letteratura 1955).
76 I am here citing John Goodwin's seventeenth-century translation, but the book was available in Latin as early as 1565; Jacobus Acontius, *Satans Stratagems or the Devils Cabinet-Councel* (London: John Macock, 1648), 7.
77 Jean Jacquot, "Acontius and the Progress of Tolerance in England," *Bibliothèque d'Humanisme et Renaissance* 16.2 (1954): 195. See also, Aart de Groot, "Acontius's Plea for Tolerance," in *From Strangers to Citizens: The Integration of Immigrant communities in Britain, Ireland and Colonial America, 1550–1750*, ed. Randolph Vigne and Charles Galton Littleton (London: Huguenot Society of Great Britain and Ireland, 2002), 48–54.
78 Dowriche, *French Historie*, A1.
79 William Russell and Thomas Man apprenticed under John Harrison in London. For more on their careers, see Cyprian Blagden, *The Stationers' Company: A History, 1403–1959* (Stanford: Stanford University Press, 1977), 78–91; and Anne Dowrichie, *The French Historie* (London: Thomas Orwin for William Russell). Interestingly, the second bookseller known to do business in Exeter was a stranger, John Gropall; see Henry Plomer, "An Exeter Bookseller, His Friends and Contemporaries," *The Library: The Transactions of the Bibliographical Society* 3.8 (1917): 128–35.
80 Micheline White, "Women Writers and Literary-Religious Circles."
81 Lart, "Huguenot Settlements and Churches."
82 On the refugee community in the West Country see, C.W. Bracken, "The Huguenot Churches," 166–7, 175. See also, Charles Edmund Lart, ed., *Registers of the French Churches of Bristol, Stonehouse, and Plymouth*, Publications of the Huguenot Society of London, vol. 20 (London: Spottiswoode, 1912).
83 The letter included a hand-drawn map and further description of possible accommodations; see Hessels, 3.1, 267–78 and 3.2, 939–40.
84 Bracken, "Huguenot Churches," 175.
85 Anne Dowriche, *French Historie*, B2v.
86 On providence in *The French Historie*, see Matchinske, *Women Writing*, 26–8.
87 Dowriche, *French Historie*, B2v.

88 Martin, "Anne Dowriche's *The French Historie*, Christopher Marlowe, and Machiavellian Agency."
89 On these texts and their influence on Marlowe, see Paul Kocher, "François Hotman and Marlowe's *The Massacre at Paris*," *PMLA* 56.2 (1941): 349–68; Paul H. Kocher, "Contemporary Pamphlet backgrounds for Marlowe's The Massacre at Paris," *Modern Language Quarterly* 8 (1947): 151–73 and 309–18; and Julia Briggs, "Marlowe's *Massacre at Paris*: A Reconsideration." Vivien Thomas and William Tydeman suggest that Marlowe's reading may not have been quite so diverse, since several of these pamphlets were excerpted in Simon Goulart's *Mémoires de l'état de France sous Charles Neuvième* (1576). Even so, the implication is a fairly deep engagement with the Huguenot perspective. See Vivien Thomas and William Tydeman, *Christopher Marlowe: The Plays and Their Sources* (New York: Routledge, 1994), 253.
90 For Ramus's influence on Marlowe, see Yuzo Yamada, *Writing under Influences: A Study of Christopher Marlowe* (Tokyo: Eihosha, 1999), 159–82. See also, John R. Glenn, "The Martyrdom of Ramus in Marlowe's Massacre at Paris," *Papers on Language and Literature* 9 (1973): 365–79; and Mishtooni Bose, "'On Kai Me On': A Tension in the Ramist Manuals," *Notes and Queries* 236.1 (1991): 29–31.
91 William Urry, *Christopher Marlowe and Canterbury* (London: Faber and Faber 1988), 2, 8, 21. See also Constance Brown Kuriyama, *Christopher Marlowe, A Renaissance Life* (Cornell: Cornell University Press, 2002), 10, 12.
92 In addition to Urry, see Joseph Meadow Cowpers, ed., *The Register Booke of the Parish of St. George the Martyr* (Canterbury: Cross and Jackman, 1891), 99. For Richardson's dwelling and denization, see William Page, *Letters of Denization and Acts of Naturalization for Aliens in England, 1550–1607* (Lymington, England: Printed for the Huguenot Society of London by C.T. King, 1891), 206. A Gerrard Richardson, listed in the 1549 Returns of Aliens as living in London and serving Protestant brewer, Giles Harrison, may be the same man relocating to Canterbury to make his way; see Kirk and Kirk, *The Returns of Aliens*, I: 177.
93 For an overview of this migration and its possible impact on a young Marlowe, see Richard F. Hardin, "Marlowe Thinking Globally," in *Christopher Marlowe, the Craftsman: Lives, Stage, and Page*, ed. Sarah K. Scott and M.L. Stapleton (Farnham: Ashgate, 2010): 24–27.
94 Anne M. Oakley, "The Canterbury Walloon Congregation from Elizabeth I to Laud." See also, Beate Magen, "The Administration of the Walloon Settlement in Canterbury 1576–1599."
95 William Somner, *The Antiquities of Canterbury* (London: John Legat, 1640), 175.

96 Oakley, "Canterbury Walloon," 62–5.
97 Ibid., 67–9.
98 David Riggs, *The World of Christopher Marlowe* (New York: Henry Holt, 2004), 31–5. See also A.D. Wraight and Virginia F. Stern, *In Search of Christopher Marlowe* (Sussex: Adam Hart, 1965): 32–5.
99 On Marlowe as witness to the will, see Riggs, *World,* 99.
100 Stephen Wright, "Copcot, John (d. 1590)," in *Oxford Dictionary of National Biography*, ed. Lawrence Goldman (Oxford University Press, 2004); online edition http://www.oxforddnb.com/view/article/6248 (accessed 22 February 2013). How "foreign" someone from Calais would have been is a complex matter: Copcot may have been born in Calais when it was still an English possession, but even so, he is said to have sometimes signed his name Copequot, emphasizing a French heritage.
101 Kuriyama, *Christopher Marlowe,* 55–6. On the debate's influence on Marlowe's *Doctor Faustus*, see G.M. Pinciss, "Marlowe's Cambridge Years and the Writing of *Doctor Faustus*," *Studies in English Literature, 1500–1900* 33.2 (1993): 253–5. On Baro, see C.S. Knighton, "Baro, Peter (1534–1599)," in *Oxford Dictionary of National Biography*, ed. H.C.G. Matthew and Brian Harrison (Oxford University Press, 2004), online edition, ed. Lawrence Goldman, September 2010, http://www.oxforddnb.com/view/article/1492.
102 Hessels, 3.1, 962–3. See also, Raingard Esser, "Immigrant Cultures," 165.
103 Kuriyama, 178–9; Kristen Poole, "*Dr. Faustus* and Reformation Theology," in *Early Modern English Drama: A Critical Companion*, ed. Garrett A. Sullivan (Oxford: Oxford University Press, 2005), 96–107, 101; Jolene Mendel, *Christopher Marlowe* (Lulu Publishing, 2008), 259. On Marlowe's reading of Calvin, see James Harmer, "Toying with Religion in the Prologue to *The Jew of Malta*," *Notes and Queries* 57 (255), no. 3 (September 2010): 352–5.
104 All in-text citations of Marlowe's plays refer to Christopher Marlowe, *The Complete Plays*, ed. Irving Ribner (New York: Odyssey Press, 1963).
105 The tale, however, appears to have been well known in England; see *Gammer Gurton's Needle* and Dekker's *If This Be Not a Good Play, The Devil Is In It*. Note also that the text most frequently cited when critics survey Marlowe's understanding of predestination is Bèze's "A Briefe Declaration of the Chiefe Points of Christian Religion."
106 Anne Lake Prescott, "English Writers and Beza's Latin Epigrams: The Uses and Abuses of Poetry," *Studies in the Renaissance* 21 (1974): 83–117.
107 This "treason of his heart" is, of course, reminiscent of Faustus's body warning him of the danger he poses to his soul: "*Homo fuge!*"
108 On the ritualistic elements of the violence see Davis, "Rites of Violence."

109 Stephen Greenblatt, "Murdering Peasants: Status, Genre and the Representation of Rebellion," in *Learning to Curse: Essays in Early Modern Culture* (New York: Routledge, 1990), 114–16. Briggs, "Marlowe's *Massacre*," 277–8.
110 Briggs, "Marlowe's *Massacre*," 266. Alan Shepard, *Marlowe's Soldiers: Rhetorics of Masculinity in the Age of the Armada* (Farnham: Ashgate, 2002), 159–60.
111 On Norreys, see David Parham, "The Mobilisation of Troops for Cross Channel Transportation: Norrey's Men, Brittany, July–December 1592," in *A Ship Cast Away about Alderney: Investigations of an Elizabethan Shipwreck*, ed. Mensun Bound and Jason Monaghan (Alderney: Alderney Maritime Trust, 2001), 157–64; and John S. Nolan, *Sir John Norreys and the Elizabethan Military World* (Exeter: University of Exeter Press, 1997), 180–90.
112 On the "Englishing" of French history in *A Massacre at Paris*, see Andrew M. Kirk, "Marlowe and the Disordered Face of French History," *Studies in English Literature 1500–1900* 35.2 (1995): 193–213.
113 Strype, *Annals*, 4: 234.
114 Francois Hotman, *A True and Plaine Report of the Furious and Outrages of Fraunce*, trans. Ernest Varamund (Striveling, Scotland, 1573), A2.
115 Strype, *Annals*, 4: 234.
116 The complete libel and an account of its impact on Marlowe and Kyd may be found in Arthur Freeman, "Marlowe, Kyd, and the Dutch Church Libel," *English Literary Renaissance* 3 (1973): 44–52.
117 On the anti-Semitic rhetoric of the libel, see Shapiro, *Shakespeare and the Jews*, 184.
118 For discussions of the libel, see Riggs, *World of Christopher Marlowe*, 319–22; Kuriyama, *Christopher Marlowe*, 131–48; Kermode, *Aliens*, 71–8.
119 Qtd. in Freeman, "Marlowe, Kyd," 45. See Yungblut, *Strangers*, 40.
120 Qtd. in Freeman "Marlowe, Kyd," 45. See also Charles Norman, *The Muses' Darling: Christopher Marlowe* (New York: Macmillan, 1960), 183–4.
121 Qtd. in Freeman, "Marlowe, Kyd," 45
122 Kermode, *Aliens*, 71–3, 77–8.
123 Robert Wilson, *The Pedlers Prophecie*, D2v.
124 Kermode, *Aliens*, 71–3, 77–8.
125 Robert Wilson, *Three Ladies of London*, B3r–v.
126 Kermode, *Aliens*, 73.
127 Selwood, *Diversity and Difference*, 25–6; Scouloudi, *Returns*, 57–8. Surveys prior to 1593 (in 1568, 1571, 1581, and 1583), like the 1593 Returns, were the result of concerns about the size and impact of the immigrant communities. For a sense of the petitions for such surveillance, see Strype, *Annals*, 2, part 1: 212.

3. Artisanal Tolerance

1. Karl Marx and Frederick Engels, *The Collected Works of Karl Marx and Frederic Engels*, vol. 42 (New York: International Publishers, 1988), 567.
2. On the English involvement in the Dutch Revolt in the 1580s, see F.G. Oosterhoff, *Leicester and the Netherlands, 1586–87* (HES Publishers, 1988). On Essex in France, see Paul E.J. Hammer, *The Polarisation of Elizabethan Politics: The Political Career of Robert Devereux, 2nd Earl of Essex, 1585–1597* (Cambridge: Cambridge University Press, 1999), 199–268.
3. Qtd. in Freeman, "Marlowe, Kyd," 45.
4. Hessels, 3.1, 819–20.
5. On the several economic troubles London faced in the 1590s, see Steve Rappaport, *Worlds within Worlds: Structures of Life in Sixteenth-Century London* (Cambridge: Cambridge University Press, 1989), 11–18.
6. The fee to the informer, at least in 1574, was one-third of the total fine the stranger had to pay. The earliest instance I have found of immigrant complaints about informers dates from 1571; see Hessels, 3.1, 126–8, 270. For more on informers, see G.R. Elton, "Informing for Profit: A Sidelight on Tudor Methods of Law Enforcement," *Cambridge Historical Journal* 11.2 (1954): 149–67; Maurice W. Beresford, "The Common Informer, The Penal Statues and Economic Regulation," *Time and Place: Collected Essay* (Leeds: Leeds University Press, 1961): 209–26; and more recently Malcolm Gaskill, *Crime and Mentalities in Early Modern England* (Cambridge: Cambridge University Press, 2000): 165–202.
7. Hessels, 3.1, 939–40. Similarly, in 1592 the Consistory of the Dutch Community of Norwich wrote to the Dutch Church of London, "Our church is greatly harassed by the Sheriffs of this City who annually demand from some of our members sums varying from five to ten pounds, which they call *mercements*." This new arbitrary tax was no doubt motivated by a combination of resentment and the need for increased city revenue; see Hessels, 3.1, 938–9.
8. Sir Edward Coke, *The Third Part of the Institutes of the Law of England Concerning High Treason and Other Pleas of the Crown, and Criminall Causes* (London: M. Flesher for W. Lee and D. Pakeman, 1644), 194.
9. Hessels 3.1, 975 and 980–1; see also 963–4.
10. Hessels, 3.1, 981, 1240–1. James issued a similar warning. In 1616 James put a temporary end to the matter when he insisted that all courts and individual subjects allow members of the "outlandish Churches" to peacefully practice their trades. See Hessels 3.1, 1263.
11. Thomas Middleton's play refers to the informers as promoters (2.2). All references to Middleton refer to Thomas Middleton, *Thomas Middleton, The*

Collected Works, ed. Gary Taylor and John Lavagnino (Oxford: Oxford University Press, 2007). "By the Queene" (London: Christopher Barker, 1594).
12 Hessels, 3.1, 1037–8, 1056–8, 1197–8.
13 See Hessels, 3.2, 2899.
14 Hessels, 3.2, 2899.
15 Hessels, 3.1, 1263.
16 Hessels 3.1, 928, 3.1, 1057.
17 Lien Luu, "Assimilation."
18 Hessels 3.1, 573–5 and 710–11; Forster, *Janus Gruter*, 4.
19 Luu, "Assimilation," 168.
20 For an excellent account of the complex status of the children of strangers, see Selwood, *Diversity*, 87–127.
21 For an example of the idiosyncrasies of early modern urban life, see William Beik, *Urban Protest in Seventeenth-century France: The Culture of Retribution* (Cambridge: Cambridge University Press, 1997), 49–51.
22 There is no definite information about Deloney's date or place of birth. Merritt Lawlis, assuming that the early ballads are the work of a young man, guesses that Deloney was born around 1560 (Introduction, xxiii), but Francis O. Mann writes, "It is impossible to give even a rough guess at the date of his birth." Still, the earliest date hazarded – 1543 – seems altogether out of keeping for a figure who appears to be of the same generation as Robert Greene (born 1558) and Thomas Nashe (born 1567), and who in 1595 was still considered a yeomen of the Weavers' Company. Deloney may have been born in Norwich, but this speculation began with a misquoting of Thomas Nashe traced by Hyder E. Rollins. If it were verifiable it would only bolster the argument in favour of Deloney's immigrant heritage; during his lifetime about 30 per cent of Norwich's population was made up of immigrants. See Merritt Lawliss, *Apology for the Middle Class: The Dramatic Novels of Thomas Deloney* (Bloomington: Indiana University Press, 1960), xxiii, and Introduction to *The Novels of Thomas Deloney* (Bloomington: Indiana University Press, 1961); Francis O. Mann, Introduction to *The Works of Thomas Deloney*, vii; Hyder E. Rollins, "Notes on Thomas Deloney," *Modern Language Notes* 32.2 (1917): 121–3.
23 Numerous French and Walloon immigrants bore variations of this surname: Dalenne, Dallene, and Dallenne all appear in the rolls for the Walloon church in Norwich, and records of denization reveal similar surnames (Delanoy, De Laune, etc.); see Kirk and Kirk, *Returns*, 2: 29, 70.
24 Lawlis, Introduction to *The Novels*, xxiv; Ole R. Reuter, *Thomas Deloney and The Mirrour of Mirth and Pleasant Conceits* (Helsinki: Societas Scientiarum Fennica, 1982), 7; Mann, "Introduction," viii. Hyder E. Rollins seems

to have taken a special delight in pointing out the limits of Deloney's formal education; see Rollins, "Notes on Thomas Deloney," *Modern Language Notes* 32.2 (1917): 121–3; "Deloney's Sources for Euphuistic Learning," *PMLA* 52.3 (1936): 399–406; "Thomas Deloney's Euphuistic Learning and the Forest," *PMLA* 50.3 (1935): 679–86.

25 Max Dorsinville, "Design in *Jack of Newbury*," *PMLA* 88.2 (1973): 233; Walter Davis, *Idea and Act in Elizabethan Fiction* (Princeton: Princeton University Press, 1969), 252. On Calvinism and the Church of England, see Richard Henry Tawney, *Religion and the Rise of Capitalism* (Gloucester, MA: Harcourt, Brace, and World, 1962), 112–13. It is interesting to note the resonance between early Calvinist social ethics, which were largely neglected by the English, and the moral economy outlined in Deloney's texts.

26 Qtd. in Eugene P. Wright, *Thomas Deloney* (Boston: Twayne Publishers, 1981), 17.

27 Thomas Nashe, *Have with you to Saffron Walden* (Menston: Scolar Press, 1971), 50.

28 The earliest extant copy of this poem is from 1618, but it is listed in the Stationers' Register in 1598.

29 George Unwin, *The Gilds and Companies of London* (New York: Barnes and Noble, 1963), 246; Eric Kerridge, *Textile Manufactures in Early Modern England* (Manchester, UK: Manchester University Press, 1985) 126–7; Luu, *Immigrants*, 175–213.

30 Details on silk weaving here are drawn from Luu, *Immigrants*, 175–213.

31 Linda Schlossberg, Introduction to *Passing: Identity and Interpretation in Sexuality, Race, and Religion*, ed. Linda Schlossberg and Maria Carla Sanchez (New York: New York University Press, 2001), 4.

32 Ernest Baker, *History of the English Novel*, vol. 2 (New York: Barnes and Noble, 1950), 174.

33 Lawlis, *Apology*, 12–13; E.P. Wright, *Thomas Deloney*, 70.

34 Rappaport, *Worlds*, 184 and passim.

35 Thomas Deloney, *The Novels of Thomas Deloney*, ed. Merritt E. Lawlis (Bloomington: Indiana University Press, 1961), 91, 173; all subsequent citations of Deloney's prose fiction refer to this edition.

36 Deloney, *The Novels*, 3.

37 For more on the precarious position of immigrants vis a vis the crown, see Yungblut, *Strangers*, 61–95.

38 Roze Hentschell, *The Culture of Cloth in Early Modern England: Textual Construction of a National Identity* (Farnham: Ashgate, 2008), 51–74; Louis B. Wright, "The Elizabethan Middle-Class Taste for History," *The Journal of Modern History* 3.2 (1931): 189; Dorsinville, "Design," 238; Merritt E. Lawlis, *Apology for the Middle Class*.

39 Mann, "Introduction," xiv.
40 Louis B. Wright, *Middle-Class Culture in Elizabethan England* (Ithaca: Cornell University Press, 1958), 128.
41 David Margolies, *Novel and Society in Elizabethan England* (London and Sydney: Croom Helm, 1985), 144.
42 E.D. Mackerness, "Thomas Deloney and the Virtuous Proletariat," *The Cambridge Journal* 5.1 (1951): 47.
43 On the complexities of categorizing Deloney, see John Carpenter, "Placing Thomas Deloney," *The Journal of Narrative Theory* 36.2 (2006): 125–62.
44 Frances Consitt, *The London Weavers' Company* (Oxford: Clarendon Press, 1933), 128.
45 Consitt, *London Weavers*, 150; see also D.C. Colman, "An Innovation and Its Diffusion: The 'New Draperies,'" *The Economic History Review* n.s. 22.3 (1969): 417–29.
46 Charles Galton Littleton, "Geneva on Threadneedle Street: The French Church of London and Its Congregation, 1560–1625," Dissertation (University of Michigan, 1995) 180; Kirk and Kirk, *Returns*, 2: 305–14; Scouloudi, *Returns*, 40–4.
47 Littleton, "Geneva," 180.
48 Alfred Plummer, *The London Weavers' Company, 1600–1970* (London and Boston: Routledge, 1972), 16–17.
49 Frederick Norwood, *Strangers and Exiles: A History of Religious Refugees* (Nashville: Abingdon Press, 1969), 362.
50 Consitt, *London Weavers*, 144–7.
51 Ibid., 147.
52 Ibid., 150.
53 Joseph P. Ward, "'[I]mployment for All Handes that Will Worke': Immigrants, Guilds and the Labour Market in Early Seventeenth-Century London," in *Immigrants in Tudor and Early Stuart England*, ed. Nigel Goose and Lien Luu (Brighton: Sussex Academic Press, 2005), 81.
54 Consitt, *London Weavers*, 148–51.
55 Ibid.,147, 316–18.
56 Freemen of the city, regardless of their particular guild membership could practice any trade; maintaining the secrets of the craft was, then, extraordinarily important. At one point, the petition complains that women were being married to craftsmen of other guilds: at issue was the fear that the women would in turn reveal craft secrets.
57 Consitt, *London Weavers,*151.
58 Ibid., 315.
59 Mihoko Suzuki, "The London Apprentice Riots of the 1590s and the Fiction of Thomas Deloney" *Criticism* 38.2 (1996): 186. See also the more abbreviated

discussion in Suzuki's revision of this article: *Subordinate Subjects: Gender, the Political Nation, and Literary Form in England, 1588–1688* (Farnham: Ashgate, 2003), 38; and Ian Archer, *The Pursuit of Stability: Social Relations in Elizabethan London* (Cambridge and New York: Cambridge University Press, 1991), 131.

60 Joseph P. Ward, *Metropolitan Communities: Trade Guilds, Identity, and Change in Early Modern London* (Stanford: Stanford University Press, 1997), 127.

61 Even a fairly light-hearted text such as Sir Thomas Overbury's *New and Choise Characters* (1615) might call into question a stranger's faith. In a caricature of a Dutch refugee, Overbury quips, "his zeale consists much in hanging his Bible in a Dutch button" while "his devotion is Obstinancy, the onley solace of his heart, Contradiction, and his maine ende, Hypocrisie." See Sir Thomas Overbury, *New and Choise Characters Together with That Exquisite and Unmacht Poem, The Wife* (London: Thomas Creede, 1615): Lr–v.

62 Qtd. in Consitt, *London Weavers*, 315–16.

63 "Complaint to Sir William Periam, chief baron, by Robert Whyte of London, silk weaver and button maker," Document ref.: SP 46/38 f.379 folio numbers: ff. 379, The National Archives, United Kingdom.

64 Consitt, *London Weavers*, 151.

65 Willington was the alleged leader of the group, according to the Mayor, but no given name is provided. The Lay Subsidy of 1598 lists three Willingtons: Walter, Paul, and Thomas. It is odd that the Mayor should give full names for the two accomplices, Deloney and Muggins, but not for the leader. Perhaps he was known well enough locally that no given name was necessary. Further, it is tempting to imagine Deloney writing the petition for his brothers in the company, as most critics assume, but it must be noted that Muggins, too, was a poet, although his only known publication appeared in 1603. The complaint was read aloud at Muggins's home before the other weavers involved, and it must be imagined that input was requested. Given that two known writers were involved and that input was likely gathered from the other weavers, I believe the complaint should be read as a collective work.

66 Consitt, *London Weavers*, 152, 316–17. The Aldermen required the drawing up of a single comprehensive document that summarized all of the guild's active ordinances so as to clarify the rights and responsibilities of the several parties involved. Subsequent petitions from "distressed weavers" in the early seventeenth century suggest that this was a short-lived victory for the native weavers; see Plummer, *The London Weavers' Company*, 144–62.

67 The connection between the episode in *Jack of Newbury* and the "Complaint of the Yeomen Weavers" has become a commonplace in Deloney scholarship.

For an early article making the connection, see G.W. Kuehn, "Thomas Deloney: Two Notes," *Modern Language Notes* 52.2 (1937): 103–5. Two recent discussions stand out: Roger A. Ladd, "Thomas Deloney and the London Weavers' Company," *The Sixteenth Century Journal* 32.4 (Winter 2001): 981–1001; and Roze Hentschell, *Culture of Cloth*, 51–74.
68 Deloney, *The Novels*, 56.
69 Roger Manning, *Village Revolts: Social Protest and Popular Disturbances in England, 1509–1640* (Oxford: Oxford University Press, 1988), 208.
70 Schlossberg, "Introduction," 3.
71 E.P. Wright, *Thomas Deloney*, 16, 68.
72 Deloney, *The Novels*, 61.
73 Ibid., 61–2.
74 Ibid., 62–3.
75 Ibid., 68.
76 Virginia Mason Vaughan, *Performing Blackness on English Stages, 1500–1800* (New York: Cambridge University Press, 2005): 74–93. This episode also contrasts with the issues of race and the bed trick explored by Celia R. Daileader in *Racism, Misogyny, and the Othello-Myth: Inter-racial Couples from Shakespeare to Spike Lee* (New York: Cambridge University Press, 2005), 40–8.
77 E.P. Wright, *Thomas Deloney*, 68.
78 Lara Bovilsky, *Barbarous Play: Race on the English Renaissance Stage* (University of Minnesota Press, 2008), 108.
79 Michael Wyatt, *Italian*, 143, 140–6.
80 Qtd. in Wyatt, *Italian*, 145.
81 See Bovilsky, *Barbarous*, 103–33; Kenneth R. Bartlett, "The Strangeness of Strangers: English Impressions of Italy in the Sixteenth Century," *Quaderni d'italianistica* 1.1 (1980): 46–63; George B. Parks, "The First Italianate Englishmen," *Studies in the Renaissance* 8 (1961): 197–216; Manfred Pfister, "*Inglese Italianato – Italiano Anglizzato*: John Florio," in *Renaissance Go-Betweens: A Cultural Exchange in Early Modern Europe*, ed. Andreas Höfele and Werner von Kopenfels (Berlin: Walter de Gruyter, 2005), 32–54.
82 Deloney, *The Novels*, 62.
83 On the relationship between Deloney and the jest book genre, see Kurt-Michael Pätzold, "Thomas Deloney and the English Jest-Book Tradition," *English Studies* 53.4 (1972): 313–28.
84 Suzuki, *Subordinate*, 46.
85 Deloney, *The Novels*, 141.
86 Ibid., 161–2.
87 Ibid., 166.

88 Julia Gasper, *The Dragon and the Dove: The Plays of Thomas Dekker* (Oxford: Oxford University Press, 1990), 18.
89 To be fair to Florence, it was not unheard of for migrants to start new marriages despite previous marriages in their homelands. One Maeyken Lupaerts, for instance, having not heard from her neglectful Dutch husband for some time, married an Englishman. The case stirred up something of a scandal in the Dutch Church of London in 1591; see Hessels, 3.1, 924–6. In fact, there are several such cases; see also Hessels, 3.1, 854 and 3.1, 909–10.
90 Deloney, *The Novels,* 51–2.
91 Ibid., 50.
92 Ibid., 71–2.
93 Ibid, 81–2.
94 Hentschell, *Culture of Cloth,* 58.
95 R.G. Howarth, *Two Elizabethan Writers of Fiction: Thomas Nashe and Thomas Deloney* (Cape Town: Editorial Board of the University of Cape Town, 1956), 40.
96 All citations of Deloney's ballads refer to Thomas Deloney, *The Works of Thomas Deloney,* ed. Francis Oscar Mann (Oxford: Clarendon Press, 1912); line numbers appear as in-text citations.
97 See Pettegree, *Foreign,* 26, 37–43, 53–4.
98 Teresa Watt, *Cheap Print and Popular Piety, 1550–1640* (Cambridge: Cambridge University Press, 1991), 91–2.
99 Mann, *Works of Thomas Deloney,* 587.
100 Forster, *Janus Gruter,* 151–2.
101 Hessels, 3.2, 144–6.

4. Language and Labour in Thomas Dekker's Provincial Globalism

1 On Dekker, canting, and rogue literature in general see Miles Taylor, "'Teach Me This Peddler's French': The Allure of Cant in *The Roaring Girl* and Dekker's Rogue Pamphlets," *Renaissance and Reform/Renaissance et Réform* 29.4 (2005): 107–24; and Laurie Ellinghausen, "Black Acts: Textual Labor and Commercial Deceit in Dekker's *Lantern and Candlelight*," in *Rogues and Early Modern Literature,* ed. Craig Dionne (Ann Arbor: University of Michigan Press, 2004), 294–311. On the various global elements of early modern life, see Jyostna Singh, ed., *A Companion to the Global Renaissance: English Literature and Culture in the Era of Expansion* (Chichester: Wiley-Blackwell, 2009); and Alison Games, "England's Global Transition and the Cosmopolitans Who Made It Possible," *Shakespeare Studies* 35 (2007): 24–31.

2 Nimrod, the instigator of the Tower of Babel in Josephus's *The Antiquities of the Jews*, is only briefly mentioned in the Bible (Genesis 10:8–9, Micah 5:6, and the First Book of Chronicles 1:10) and in the marginalia of the Geneva Bible (Genesis, 11). Although Josephus's texts were not printed in English until 1602, he was widely read throughout the early modern period. See Flavius Josephus, *The Famous and Memorable Workes of Josephus*, trans. Thomas Lodge (London: George Bishop, 1602), 9. On Josephus's influence in the early modern period, see Pauline Smith, "The Reception and Influence of Josephus's Jewish War in the Late French Renaissance with Special Reference to the Satyrre of Menippée," *Renaissance Studies* 13.2 (1999): 174–91. On the astounding number of early editions of Josephus's texts, see Heinz Schreckenberg, *Bibliographie zu Flavius Josephus* (Leiden: Brill Academic Publishing, 1968).
3 Thomas Dekker, *The Non-Dramatic Works of Thomas Dekker*, vol. 3 (London: Huth Library, 1884), 189.
4 Ibid., 190.
5 Ibid., 191.
6 Ibid., 188–9.
7 Geneva Bible, Genesis 11:1.
8 Dekker, *Non-Dramatic Works*, 188.
9 Ibid., 188.
10 Qtd. in Gabriel Harvey, *The Works of Gabriel Harvey*, vol. 1, ed. Alexander Balloch Grosart (London: Hazell, Watson, and Viney, 1884), 35. Helgerson, *Forms of Nationhood* 1–18. It should be further noted that Spenser's question is prompted by his struggle to fit English words into classical (foreign) models of quantitative verse.
11 Later in *Lanthorne* Dekker rails against gypsies as "a people more scattered then Jewes, and more hated." In addition to base prejudice, Dekker's depiction of gypsies seems fuelled by the fact that they are by definition not labourers but rather "Land-pyrates, which would seem to highlight the place of labour in Dekker's vision of community; see Dekker, *Non-Dramatic Works*, 258–64.
12 Marie-Therese Jones-Davies, *Un Peintre de la Vie Londonienne: Thomas Dekker* (Paris: Collection des Études Anglaises, 1958), 1: 29–30; Mary Leland Hunt, *Thomas Dekker, A Study* (New York: Russell and Russell, 1964), 32–4. See also Gasper, *The Dragon*, 20, 37.
13 M.L. Hunt, *Thomas Dekker*, 20–3.
14 The Janssen family, involved in the Shakespeare funeral monument, probably arrived in England in 1567; Droeshout's family arrived around 1569. Droeshout and Janssen are discussed more fully in chapter 6. See Adam White, "Johnson [Janssen] family (*per. c.*1570–*c.*1630)," *Oxford Dictionary*

of National Biography, online edition, ed. Lawrence Goldman (Oxford University Press, 2004); Mary Edmond, "Droeshout, Martin (1565x9–c.1642)," *Oxford Dictionary of National Biography*, ed. H.C.G. Matthew and Brian Harrison (Oxford University Press, 2004); online edition, ed. Lawrence Goldman, May 2008.

15 Unless otherwise indicated, references to Dekker's plays are from Thomas Dekker, *The Dramatic Works of Thomas Dekker*, 4 vols, ed. Fredson Bowers (Cambridge: Cambridge University Press, 1953).

16 On *Old Fortunatus* and travel, see Paul Frazer, "Performing Places in Thomas Dekker's *Old Fortunatus*," *Philological Quarterly* 89.4 (2010): 457–80; and Daniel Vitkus, "Labor and Travel on the Early Modern Stage: Representing the Travail of Travel in Dekker's *Old Fortunatus* and Shakespeare's *Pericles*," in *Working Subjects in Early Modern English Drama*, ed. Michelle M. Dowd and Natasha Korda (Farnham: Ashgate, 2010), 225–42.

17 On *The Whore of Babylon* in the context of the Gunpowder Plot, see Susan Krantz, "Thomas Dekker's Political Commentary in *The Whore of Babylon*," *Studies in English Literature* 35.2 (1995): 271–91.

18 Gasper, *The Dragon*, 62–108.

19 Ibid., 36–43.

20 Indeed, James had already sent letters to the stranger churches of London indicating that he intended to maintain Elizabeth's policies toward Protestant refugees; see Hessels 3.1, 1100–1.

21 Marjorie Rubright, "An Urban Palimpsest: Migrancy, Architecture, and the Making of an Anglo-Dutch Royal Exchange," *Dutch Crossings* 33.1 (2009): 23–43.

22 Gasper, *The Dragon*, 16–35.

23 On comparisons of *The Shoemaker's Holiday* to *The Gentle Craft*, see Peter Mortenson, "The Economics of Joy in *The Shoemaker's Holiday*," *Studies in English Literature, 1500–1900* 16.2 (1976): 241–52; and Ann C. Christensen, "Being Mistress Eyre in Dekker's *The Shoemaker's Holiday* and Deloney's *The Gentle Craft*," *Comparative Drama* 42.4 (2008): 451–80.

24 Pettegree, *Foreign*, 291–5.

25 Marianne Montgomery, *Europe's Languages on England's Stages, 1590–1620* (Farnham: Ashgate, 2012), 73.

26 Andrew Fleck, "Marking Difference and National Identity in Dekker's *The Shoemaker's Holiday*," *Studies in English Literature, 1500–1900* 46.2 (2006): 439–70.

27 *Letters and Papers, Foreign and Domestic, of the Reign of Henry VIII*, vol. 4.2, ed. J.S. Brewer (London: Longman and Co., and Trubner and Co., Paternoster Row, 1872), 2171.

28 Jones-Davies, 2: 72; Gasper, *The Dragon*, 19; Peter M. McCluskey, "'Shall I Betray My Brother?" Anti-Alien Satire and Its Subversion in *The Shoemaker's Holiday*," *Tennessee Philological Bulletin: Proceedings of the Annual Meeting of the Tennessee Philological Association* 37 (2000): 43–54. Joseph P. Ward, "Fictitious Shoemakers, Agitated Weavers and the Limits of Popular Xenophobia in Elizabethan London," in *From Strangers to Citizens: The Integration of Immigrant communities in Britain, Ireland and Colonial America, 1550–1750* (Brighton and Portland, OR: Sussex Academic Press, 2001), 80–7; see also Hoenselaars, *Images*, 61-4.
29 David Scott Kastan, "Workshop and/as Playhouse," in *Staging the Renaissance: Reinterpretations of Elizabethan and Jacobean Drama*, ed. David Scott Kastan and Peter Stallybrass (New York and London: Routledge, 1991): 153.
30 Christian M. Billing, "The Dutch Diaspora in English Comedy: 1598 to 1618," in *Transnational Exchange in Early Modern Theater*, ed. Robert Henke and Eric Nichols (Farnham: Ashgate, 2008), 119–40.
31 Deloney, *The Novels*, 141–2.
32 Hoenselaars, *Images*, 62.
33 See Douglas R. Bisson, *The Merchant Adventurers of England: The Company and the Crown, 1474–1564* (Newark: University of Delaware Press, 1993), 48–69.
34 *Calendar of State Papers and Manuscripts Relating to English Affairs, Existing in the Archives and Collections of Venice*, vol. 9, ed. Horatio F. Brown (London: Eyre and Spottiswoode, 1897), 284–5. For more on these tensions, see John Conybeare, "Trade Wars: A Comparative Study of Anglo-Hanse, Franco-Italian, and Hawley-Smoot Conflicts," *World Politics* 38.1 (1985): 147–72; Dollinger, *German Hansa*, 343; and T.H. Lloyd, *England*, 292–362.
35 It is tempting to assume that the nautical imagery relates to the fact that the actors were the Lord Admiral's Men, but given Charles Howard's success in defending England, "disgrace" seems hardly to be an apt adjective.
36 Note that although Lacy is the romantic hero of the plot, the money he loans to Eyre was given to him with the understanding that he was leaving to fight in France; that is, the money that was meant to support him as he served his king serves instead Lacy's artisan master. Critics sometimes point to this shift of money as an indication of a dark side to *The Shoemaker's Holiday* – that Eyre rises only because of Lacy's "embezzlement" – but the productive wealth that results from what would have supported destruction abroad may well argue that investment in citizens rather than wars abroad would be better for the realm.
37 In Deloney's *The Gentle Craft* Eyre disguises himself as an alderman to persuade the merchant that he will make good on his down payment. While this

is not entirely clear in Dekker's adaptation, Hodge and Margery's comments imply that Eyre has never before worn an Alderman's gown. Firk's comment, "My maister will be proud as a dogge in a dublet" (2.3.125–6) suggests that Eyre is disguising himself and that Dekker is here following his source. Moreover, Eyre seems especially well acquainted with the theatre: he alludes to Nicholas Udall's *Ralph Roister Doister,* the anonymous *Tamar Cham,* Kyd's *Soliman and Persida,* and Marlowe's *Doctor Faustus* and *Tamburlaine.*

38 On Hans Beerpot as a model for Hans Meulter, see Hoenselaars, *Images,* 60–1. Dekker seems to have taken Hans as a stock-name for a Dutch character, as he also uses the name for Hans van Belch in *Northward Ho!* Finally, coupled with the Dutch captain, the name Hans may allude to the Hanse merchants.

39 Gasper notes the puns Lacy/lazy and Hans/hands (*The Dragon,* 27–8). The notion of the theatre as the transformative force that makes this pun possible is my own.

40 On Tilney's role in censoring riot scenes, see Georgio Melchiori, "The Master of the Revels and the Date of the Additions to *The Book of Sir Thomas More,*" in *Shakespeare: Text, Language, Criticism, Essays in Honour of Marvin Spevack* (Zurich: Olms-Weidmann, 1987), 164–79.

41 Frank Ardolino, "Hans and Hammon: Dekker's Use of Hans Sachs and Purim in *The Shoemaker's Holiday,*" *Medieval and Renaissance Drama in England* 14 (2001): 144–67.

42 The comparison of Elizabeth to Esther persisted throughout her reign. In 1572, during debates about the fate of the Duke of Norfolk following the Ridolfi Plot, one member of Parliament compared "the wicked Haman" and "the godly Queen Hester" to Norfolk and Elizabeth; see Jennifer E. Neale, *Elizabeth I and Her Parliaments, 1559–1581* (New York: St Martin's Press, 1958), 277–8.

43 Josephus, *The Famous,* 276–83.

44 See Heinz Schreckenberg and Kurt Schubert, *Jewish Historiography and Iconography in Early and Medieval Christianity* (Haag: Van Gorcum, 1991), 7–50. On the history of Judaism's contact with Greco-Roman culture and with Josephus in particular, see Tessa Rajak, *The Jewish Dialogue with Greece and Rome* (Boston: Brill Academic Publishers, 2002). On Josephus's cosmopolitanism, see Nicole Kelley, "The Cosmopolitan Expression of Josephus's Prophetic Perspective in the Jewish War," *Harvard Theological Review* 97.3 (2004): 257–74.

45 David Novarr, "Dekker's Gentle Craft and the Lord Mayor of London," *Modern Philology* 57 (1960): 233–9; and Charles Whitney, "The Devil His

Due: Mayor John Spencer, Elizabethan Civic Antitheatricalism, and *The Shoemaker's Holiday*," *Medieval and Renaissance Drama in England: An Annual Gathering of Research, Criticism and Reviews* 14 (2001): 168–85.
46 Qtd. in Carol Chillington Rutter, ed., *Documents of the Rose Playhouse* (Manchester, UK: Manchester University Press, 1984), 86.
47 Ibid.
48 Hessels, 3.1, 852–3.
49 On the date of composition for this play, see Julia Gasper, "*The Noble Spanish Soldier, The Wonder of a Kingdom*, and *The Parliament of Bees*: A Belated Solution to This Long-Standing Dekker Problem" Durham University Journal 79.2 (1987): 223–32. On the name Balthazar and its relation to race and gender on the early modern stage, see Bovilsky, *Barbarous Play*, 103–4.

5. The "Jumbled" City

1 D'Ewes, *Compleat Journal*, 506.
2 For more on Marston's Italian background, see George L. Geckle, "John Marston," *Dictionary of Literary Biography*, vol. 58: *Jacobean and Caroline Dramatists*, ed. Fredson Bowers (Madison, VA: The Gale Group, 1987), 139–68; and Alexander B. Grosart, Introduction to *The Poems of John Marston*, ed. Alexander B. Grosart (Blackburn: Occasional Issues of Rare or Unique Books, 1879), vi–ix.
3 Hessels 3.2, 2438–9.
4 Hessels 3.1, 266.
5 Luu, "Assimilation," 160; D'Ewes, *Compleat Journal*, 506.
6 Andrew Spicer, "A Process of Gradual Assimilation," 193. Charles Littleon, "Social Interaction of Aliens in Late Elizabethan London: Evidence from the 1593 Return and the French Church Consistory 'Actes,'" in *The Strangers Progress*, 147–59. For examples of such marriages, see Hessels, 3.1, 806, 888, 932, 980, 1199.
7 Morant, "The Settlement," 210–14.
8 Judy Ann Ford, "Marginality and the Assimilation of Foreigners in the Lay Parish Community: The Case of Sandwich," in *The Parish in English Life, 1400–1600*, ed. Katherine L. French, Gary G. Gibbs, and Beat A. Kumin (Manchester: Manchester University Press, 1997): 203–16.
9 Thomas Fuller, *The Church History of Britain*, vol. 3 (London: Thomas Tegg and Son, 1837), 419.
10 Ibid.

11 Gayle Rubin, "Traffic in Women: Notes on the 'Political Economy' of Sex," in *Toward an Anthropology of Women*, ed. Raya R. Reiter (New York: Monthly Review Press, 1975), 158.
12 Linda Racioppi and Katherine O'Sullivan See, "Engendering Nation and National Identity," in *Women, States, and Nationalism: At Home in the Nation?*, ed. Sita Ranchod-Nilsson and Mary Ann Tétreault (London and New York: Routledge, 2000), 18–34. See also Anthony D. Smith and Ernest Gellner, "The Nation: Real or Imagined?: The Warwick Debates on Nationalism," *Nations and Nationalism* 2.3 (1996): 357–70; Eric Hobsbawm, *Nations and Nationalism since 1780* (Cambridge: Cambridge University Press, 1990); John Armstrong, *Nations before Nationalism* (Chapel Hill: University of North Carolina Press, 1982), especially 3–6.
13 Nira Yuval-Davis, *Gender and Nation* (London: Sage Publication, 1997), 2.
14 Floya Anthias and Nira Yuval-Davis, Introduction to *Woman – Nation – State* (New York: St Martin's Press, 1989), 7.
15 Linda Pollock, *Forgotten Children: Parent-Child Relations from 1500–1900* (Cambridge: Cambridge University Press, 1983), 235. See also her more recent contribution to this topic, "Parent-Child Relations," in *Family Life in Early Modern Times, 1500–1789*, ed. David I. Kertzer and Mazio Barbagli (New Haven: Yale University Press, 2011): 191–220.
16 Patricia Crawford, *Parents of Poor Children in England, 1500–1800* (New York: Oxford University Press, 2010), 19–20, 161.
17 Lawrence Stone, *The Family, Sex and Marriage in England 1500–1800* (New York: Harper and Row, 1977), 116. Indeed, recent scholarship suggests significant bonds between parents and children even among the upper classes that Stone thinks of as remote. See, for example, Catherine Frances, "Making Marriages in Early Modern England: Rethinking the Role of Family and Friends," in *The Marital Economy in Scandinavia and Britain, 1400–1900*, ed. Maria Agren and Amy Louise Erickson (Farnham: Ashgate, 2005), 39–56. See also Steven Ozment, *Ancestors: The Loving Family in Old Europe* (Cambridge: Harvard University Press, 2001).
18 For detailed accounts of parental involvement in courtship, see David Cressy, *Birth, Marriage, and Death: Ritual, Religion, and the Life-Cycle in Tudor and Stuart England* (Oxford: Oxford University Press, 1997), 233–84.
19 Nancy F. Cott, *Public Vows: A History of Marriage and the Nation* (Cambridge, MA and London: Harvard University Press, 2000), 5.
20 For a discussion of the date of the play, see David Crane, Introduction to *The Dutch Courtesan*, ed. David Crane (New York: W.W. Norton, 1997), xiii.
21 Jean Howard, *Theater of a City: The Places of London Comedy, 1598–1642* (Philadelphia: University Pennsylvania Press, 2009), 154–5.

22 On the association of Dutch women with prostitution see Hoenselaars, *Images*, 117; Jean Howard, *Theater of a City*, 152; and Marjorie Rubright, "Going Dutch in London City Comedy: Economies of Sexual and Sacred Exchange in John Marston's *The Dutch Courtesan* (1605)," *English Literary Renaissance* 40.1 (2010): 95–7. On the prevalence of visual representations of Dutch prostitutes, see Lotte C. van de Pol, "The Whore, The Bawd, and the Artist: The Reality and the Imagery of Seventeenth-Century Dutch Prostitution," *The Journal of Historians of Netherlandish Art* 2.1 (2010): http://www.jhna.org/index.php/past-issues/volume-2-issue-1-2/116-the-whore-the-bawd-and-the-artist.
23 Michael Scott, *John Marston's Plays* (New York: Barnes and Noble, 1978), 47. On Marston's influence on other plays by Aphra Behn, see Cynthia Cayerwood, "The Geography of Aphra Behn's City Comedies" *Literary London: Interdisciplinary Studies in the Representation of London* 5.2 (2007): http://www.literarylondon.org/london-journal/september2007/caywood.html.
24 Anne M. Haselkorn, *Prostitution in Elizabethan and Jacobean Comedy* (Troy, NY: Whitson Press, 1983), 58, 62–5.
25 Harry Keyishian, "Dekker's *Whore* and Marston's *Courtesan*," *English Language Notes* 4 (1967): 261–6.
26 Jean Dietz Moss, "Variations on a Theme: the Family of Love in Renaissance England," *Renaissance Quarterly* 31.2 (1978): 189.
27 For more on the Family of Love, see Alastair Hamilton, *The Family of Love* (Cambridge, UK: James Clarke, 1981); and Christopher Marsh, *The Family of Love in English Society: 1550–1630* (Cambridge: Cambridge University Press, 1994). Janet E. Halley further argues that the diversity of opinion regarding the Family of Love is in part attributable to the difficulty of the texts, especially those of Henrik Niclaes; see Halley, "Heresy, Orthodoxy, and the Politics of Religious Discourse: The Case of the English Family of Love," *Representations* 15 (1986): 98–120. More recently, Christopher Carter has examined the use anti-Familist rhetoric in the context of broader religious and political debates in the 1570s and 1580s; Christopher Carter, "The Family of Love and Its Enemies," *The Sixteenth-Century Journal* 37.3 (2006): 651–72.
28 James I, *Basilikon Doron* (London: Felix Kyngston for John Norton, 1603), A4v.
29 Philip J. Finkelpearl, *John Marston of the Middle Temple* (Cambridge: Harvard University Press, 1969), 197.
30 All in-text citations of *The Dutch Courtesan* refer to John Marston, *The Dutch Courtesan,* ed. David Crane (New York: Norton, 1997).
31 Crane, "Introduction," 45.
32 Rubright, "Going Dutch," 111–12.

33 Howard, *Theater of a City*, 154; "mulligrub, n." in OED online edition (Oxford University Press), http://www.oed.com/view/Entry/123498?redirectedFrom=mulligrub (accessed 14 March 2013).
34 Martin L. Wine, Introduction to *The Dutch Courtesan* (Lincoln: University of Nebraska Press, 1968), xix, note 15.
35 Hoenselaars, *Images*, 117. See also Bovilsky, *Barbarous Plays*, 108.
36 Andrew Fleck, "The Custom of Courtesans and John Marston's *The Dutch Courtesan*," *A Quarterly Journal of Short Articles, Notes, and Reviews* 21.3 (2008): 15. Marjorie Rubright, "Going Dutch," 95, 100.
37 Howard, *Theater of a City*, 154.
38 On the figure of Francesquina in *commedia dell'arte*, see Allardyce Nicoll, *The World of Harlequin: A Critical Study of the Commedia Dell' Arte* (Cambridge: Cambridge University Press, 1963), 95–7.
39 Howard, *Theater of a City*, 155–7.
40 Rubright, "Going Dutch," 107–10.
41 I am here thinking of René Girard's theorization of the scapegoat: "Ultimately, the persecutors always convince themselves that a small number of people, or even a single individual, despite his relative weakness, is extremely harmful to the whole of society." Girard goes on to explain the central crime projected on the scapegoat is "destroying the community's distinctions," precisely what is implied by the spread of Franceschina's jumbling of cultural identities; see Girard, *The Scapegoat*, trans. Yvonne Freccero (Baltimore: Johns Hopkins University Press, 1986), 15.
42 On "will" as a sexual pun, see Eric Partridge, *Shakespeare's Bawdy* (New York: Routledge, 1968), 218–19.
43 To some degree Marston's play loosely follows the structure of Dante's *Divine Comedy*: the play begins with a trip to the sinful brothel; characters pay for their sins in prison; and as Freevill "resurrects" himself for Beatrice, she asks, "Am I in heaven?" (5.2.49).
44 On the relation between Marston and Montaigne, see William M. Hamlin, "Common Customers in Marston's Dutch *Courtesan* and Florio's Montaigne," *Studies in English Literature 1500–1900* 52.2 (2012): 407–24.
45 Hamilton, *Family of Love,* 117.
46 Halley, "Heresy."
47 Amy L. Erickson, *Women and Property in Early Modern England* (London: Routledge, 1997), 150.
48 Crane, "Introduction," xx–xxix.
49 Andrew Gurr, *Playgoing in Shakespeare's London* (Cambridge: Cambridge University Press, 1996), 156.

50 For more on Haughton, see Lloyd Edward Kermode, Introduction to *Three Renaissance Usury Plays* (Manchester: Manchester University Press, 2009), 39–42.
51 Early printings spell the name Vandalle, which would appear to be a version of "van Dale." Kermode prefers "Vandal," as it suggests the way the Dutch might be thought to be causing damage to England.
52 See, for example, Hoenselaars, *Images*, 58; Howard, "Mastering," 106; Theodore B. Leinwand, *The City Staged: Jacobean Comedy, 1603–1613* (Madison: University of Wisconsin Press, 1986), 7.
53 For more on the local colour of *Englishmen for My Money*, see Howard, *Theater of a City*, 29–68; and Crystal Bartolovich, "London's the Thing: Alienation, the Market, and *Englishmen for My Money*," *Huntington Library Quarterly* 71.1 (2008): 137–56.
54 Kermode, *Aliens*, 130.
55 Tom Rutter, "*Englishmen for My Money*: Work and Social Conflict?" in *Working Subjects in Early Modern English Drama*, ed. Michelle M. Dowd and Natasha Korda (Burlington, VT: Ashgate, 2011): 99. Kermode ("Introduction," 44) similarly describes Pisaro as retaining qualities of the "noble Jew."
56 Alan Stewart, "'Every Soyl to Mee is Naturall": Figuring Denization in William Haughton's *English-Men for My Money*," *Renaissance Drama* n.s. 35 (2006): 75.
57 Campos, "Jews, Spaniards, and Portingales," 613.
58 Ibid., 613–14.
59 All citations of *Englishmen for My Money* are from William Haughton, *Englishmen for My Money*, *Three Renaissance Usury Plays*, ed. Lloyd Edward Kermode (Manchester: Manchester University Press, 2009), 164–74. Citations appear in the text.
60 On the overlapping motives of romance and finance in early modern drama, see, for example, Karen Newman, *Essaying Shakespeare* (Minneapolis: University of Minnesota Press, 2009), 59–76; and Patricia Parker, "Temporal Gestation, Legal Contracts, and the Promissory Economics of *The Winter's Tale*," in *Women, Property, and the Letters of the Law in Early Modern England*, ed. Andrew Buck, Margaret Ferguson, and Nancy E. Wright (Toronto: University of Toronto Press, 2004), 25–49. In addition to Erickson, for the social history informing these stage representations, see Barbara J. Harris, *English Aristocratic Women, 1450–1550: Marriage and Family, Property and Careers* (Oxford: Oxford University Press, 2002).
61 On this particular scene, see Bartolovich, "London's the Thing," 147–55.
62 Emma Smith, "'So Much English by the Mother': Gender, Foreigners, and the Mother Tongue in William Haughton's *Englishmen for My Money*," *Medieval and Renaissance Drama in England* (200): 165–81.

63 Elizabeth Schaffer, "William Haughton's *Englishmen for My Money*: A Critical Note," *The Review of English Studies*, n.s. 41.164 (1990): 536–8.
64 On *jus soli* ("rule of birthplace") and *jus sanguinus* ("rule of blood" or inherited belonging), see Selwood, *Diversity and Difference*, 87–128.
65 Kermode, Introduction, 44.
66 On the play's linguistic chauvinism, see Janette Dillon, *Language and Stage in Medieval and Renaissance England* (Cambridge: Cambridge University Press, 1998): 173–4.
67 Emma Smith, "So Much English, "178.
68 Kermode, *Aliens*, 128.
69 Philip Henslowe, *The Diary of Philip Henslowe from 1591 to 1611*, ed. J. Payne Collier (London: Shakespeare Society, 1845), 119, 122, 276; Arber, *A Transcript*, 3: 190.
70 On "tran-dido, dil-dido" as a ballad refrain, see Kermode, *Three Renaissance Usury Plays*, 243n56; and A.E.H. Swaen, "Notes on Ballads and Tunes in W. Sampson's *Vow-Breaker*," *Neophilologus* 3 (1918): 149–54.
71 Robert Greene, *The Dramatic Works of Robert Greene,* vol. 2, ed. Alexander Dyce (London: William Pickering, 1831), 268; and Pauline Kiernan, *Filthy Shakespeare: Shakespeare's Most Outrageous Sexual Puns* (New York: Gotham Books, 2006), 239.
72 John Ford, *The Lover's Melancholy*, ed. R.F. Hill (Manchester: Manchester University Press, 1985), 120n43. On the ballad, see Joseph Woodfall Ebsworth (Ed.), *The Roxsburghe Ballads, Illustrating the Last Years of the Stuarts,* part 26, vol. 8 (Hertford: Stephen Austin and Sons, 1899), lvi. Citations of "Love's Melancholy" are drawn from Hill's edition. Citations from *Fancies Chaste and Noble* are from John Ford, *The Works of John Ford*, vol. 2, ed. William Gifford (London: James Toovey, 1869). Finally, for more on the bawdy implications of "dido" see Gordon Williams, *A Dictionary of Sexual Language and Imagery in Shakespearean and Stuart Literature* (London: Athlone Press, 1994), 383–4.
73 See Partridge, *Shakespeare's Bawdy*, 218–19.
74 On the play's portrayal of commodification and capitalism in general, and the title of the play specifically, see Bartolovich, "London's the Thing," 155.
75 Erickson, *Women and Property*, 225.
76 Fleck, "Making Difference and National Identity," 365.
77 Rubright, "Going Dutch," 109–12.
78 This is precisely the pattern Lawrence Stone found evident in his classic *The Family, Sex and Marriage in England*, 60–1.
79 Deloney, *The Novels*, 312.
80 Cressy, *Birth, Marriage, and Death*, 233, 255–6.

6. Shakespeare, the Foreigner

1 On the authorship debate, see the recent collection of essays edited by Paul Edmondson and Stanley Wells, *Shakespeare beyond Doubt: Evidence, Argument, Controversy* (Cambridge: Cambridge University Press, 2013).
2 Richard Owen, "Shakespeare? He's one of us, say Italians," *The Times*, 8 April 2000.
3 Ernest Jones, *The Life and Work of Sigmund Freud*, vol. 1 (New York: Hogarth, 1953), 24; Frank Harris, *My Life and Loves* (New York: Grove Press, 1963), 67. One 1999 posting to *Shaksper, the Global Electronic Shakespeare Conference* went so far as to claim that Shakespeare may have been of African descent; Tim Perfect, in the same forum, likewise reports that Muammar al-Gaddafi claimed Shakespeare to be of "Middle Eastern descent"; see Perfect, "Spear-Shaking," online posting, 22 January 1999, *SHAKSPER: The Global Electronic Shakespeare Conference*, 10 Nov. 2011, http://shaksper.net/archive/1999/152-january/7547-re-spear-shaking.
4 Ania Loomba, "'Local-Manufacture Made-In-India Othello Fellows': Issues of Race, Hybridity, and Location in Post-Colonial Shakespeares," in *Post-Colonial Shakespeares*, ed. Ania Loomba and Martin Orkin (London: Routledge, 1998), 143–63; Nicholas Visser, "Shakespeare and Hanekom, *King Lear* and Land: A South African Perspective," in *Post-Colonial Shakespeares*, ed. Loomba and Orkin (London: Routledge, 1998), 205–17.
5 McEachern, *Poetics*, 32; Helgerson, *Forms of Nationhood*; Howard and Rackin, *Engendering a Nation*; Maley, *Nation, State and Empire*, 7–30; Maley "'And bloody England into England gone'"; and Schwyzer, *Literature, Nationalism and Memory*, 126–50.
6 Leslie Fiedler, *The Stranger in Shakespeare* (London: Paladin, 1974); Jonathan Burton, "'A most wily bird': Leo Africanus, *Othello* and the Trafficking in Difference," in *Post-Colonial Shakespeares*, ed. Ania Loomba and Martin Orkin (London and New York: Routledge, 1998), 43–63.
7 Graham Bradshaw, "Shakespeare's Peculiarity," *Proceedings of the British Academy* 111 (2001): 99–126; Geraldo de Sousa, *Shakespeare's Cross-Cultural Encounters* (New York: St Martin's Press, 1999), 8.
8 Richard Wilson, "Making Men of Monsters: Shakespeare in the Company of Strangers," *Shakespeare* 1.1 (2005): 8–28; B.J. Sokol, *Shakespeare and Tolerance* (Cambridge: Cambridge University Press, 2008), xiv.
9 I am by no means arguing that these are the only positions in relation to Shakespeare's plays. Bovilsky, for instance, takes a middle ground, arguing that *The Merchant of Venice* tries "to absorb desirable Jewish qualities, while disavowing Jewish manners and blood" (*Barbarous Play*, 102).

10 The details of Greene's invective against Shakespeare are discussed in many places. See, for example, Bart Van Es, "'*Johannes fac Totum*'?: Shakespeare's First Contact with the Acting Companies," *Shakespeare Quarterly* 61.4 (2010): 551–77; and Hanspeter Born, "Why Greene Was Angry at Shakespeare," *Medieval and Renaissance Drama in England* 25 (2012): 133–73.
11 Ann Thompson, "Dating Evidence for *The Taming of the Shrew*," *Notes and Queries* 29 (1982): 108–9. See also *The Norton Shakespeare*, ed. Stephen Greenblatt, Walter Cohn, Jean E. Howard, and Katharine Eisaman Maus (New York and London: W.W. Norton, 1997), 109.
12 Samuel Schoenbaum, *William Shakespeare: A Compact Documentary Life* (Oxford: Oxford University Press, 1977), 117. Unless otherwise indicated, the biographical information on Field that follows is based on A.E.M. Kirwood, "Richard Field, Printer," *The Library, Quarterly Review of Bibliography*, series 4, vol. 12 (1932): 1–27.
13 Katherine Duncan-Jones suggests that Field may have married not the widow but the daughter of the same name; see Duncan-Jones, *Ungentle Shakespeare: Scenes from His Life* (London: Arden, 2001), 114.
14 Stephen Greenblatt, *Will in the World: How Shakespeare Became Shakespeare* (New York and London: W.W. Norton, 2004), 194–5; Charles Nicholl, *The Lodger Shakespeare: His Life on Silver Street* (New York: Viking, 2007), 177; Duncan-Jones, *Ungentle*, 114–16.
15 Schoenbaum, *William Shakespeare*, 260.
16 Nicholl, *The Lodger*, 17.
17 This material is reiterated in nearly every Shakespeare biography. See especially William Portal, "Address to the Twenty-Sixth Annual General Meeting of the Huguenot Society of London," *Proceedings of the Huguenot Society of London* 9.2 (1910): 141–4; and E.A.J. Honigmann, "Shakespeare and London's Immigrant Community." More recently, a full-length study based on these episodes has been published; see Nicholl, *The Lodger*.
18 Honigmann, "Shakespeare and London's Immigrant Community," 151; Nicholl, *The Lodger*, 41–2.
19 Greenblatt, *Will in the World*, 192; Schoenbaum, *Wiliam Shakespeare*, 315.
20 June Schlueter, "Martin Droeshout, Redivivus: Reassessing the Folio Engraving of Shakespeare," *Shakespeare Survey* 60 (2007): 237–51; Mary Edmond, "It Was for Gentle Shakespeare Cut," *Shakespeare Quarterly* 42 (1990): 339–44. See also Nicholl, *The Lodger*, 335n55; and Christiaan Schuckman, "The Engraver of the First Folio Portrait of Shakespeare," *Print Quarterly* 8.1 (1991): 40–3.
21 Honigmann, "Shakespeare and London's Immigrant Community," 144–6.
22 Edmond, "It Was for Gentle Shakespeare Cut," 343–4.

23 Honigmann, "Shakespeare and London's Immigrant Community," 148.
24 Steven Mullaney, *The Place of the Stage: License, Play and Power in Renaissance England* (Chicago: University of Chicago, 1988).
25 Scouloudi, *The Returns*, 145–237; and Yungblut, *Gender*, 27.
26 Leslie Hotson, *Shakespeare's Sonnets Dated, and Other Essays* (New York: Oxford University Press, 1949), 119.
27 See Walter Cohen, "Various Poems," in *The Norton Shakespeare* (New York and London: W.W. Norton, 1997), 1991–4; *Norton Shakespeare*, 2006.
28 *Norton Shakespeare*, 2006–7.
29 Mary Edmond, "Tooley, Nicholas (1583–1623)," *Oxford Dictionary of National Biography*, Oxford University Press, 2004; online edition, January 2008.
30 Susanne Woods, *Lanyer: A Renaissance Woman Poet* (Oxford: Oxford University Press, 1999), 181. Janet Adelman suggests that contact with the Bassano family may have influenced some of Shakespeare's choices in the writing of *The Merchant of Venice*; see Adelman, *Blood Relations: Christian and Jew in Merchant of Venice* (Chicago: University of Chicago Press, 2008), 138. For a careful review of the theory that Lanyer is the Dark Lady, see David Bevington, "A.L. Rowse's Dark Lady," in *Lanyer: Gender, Genre, and the Canon*, ed. Marshall Grossman (Lexington: University of Kentucky Press, 1998), 1028. Although the most interesting thing about Lanyer is her poetry, the speculation that she is the Dark Lady persists; see Martin Green, "Emilia Lanier *IS* the Dark Lady of the Sonnets," *English Studies* 87.5 (2006): 544–76.
31 Jonathan Bate, *The Genius of Shakespeare* (Oxford: Oxford University Press, 1997), 54–8; Saul Frampton, "Who Edited Shakespeare?" The Guardian, 12 July 2013, accessed 10 August 2013, http://www.theguardian.com/books/2013/jul/12/who-edited-shakespeare-john-florio.
32 Greenblatt, *Will in the World*, 362.
33 Park Honan, *Shakespeare: A Life* (Oxford: Oxford University Press, 1998): 322–9.
34 See, for example, Sonja Fielitz, "Shakespeare and Catholicism: The Jesuits as Cultural Mediators in Early Modern Europe," *Critical Survey* 21.3 (2009): 72–86; Ralph Berry, "Shakespeare and the Catholic Network," *Contemporary Review* 286 (2005): 233–8; Richard Wilson, "Shakespeare and the Jesuits: New Connections Supporting the Theory of the Lost Catholic Years in Lancashire," *The Times Literary Supplement* (19 December 1997): 11–13; Burton Raffel, "Shakespeare and the Catholic Question," *Religion and Literature* 30.1 (1998): 35–51. For more sceptical views on the topic see, Peter Davidson and Thomas McCoog, "Unreconciled: What Evidence Links Shakespeare and the Jesuits?" *The Times Literary Supplement* (16 March 2007): 12–13;

Michael Davies, "The Transubstantial Bard: Shakespeare and Catholicism," in *The Poetics of Transubstantiation: From Theology to Metaphor*, ed. Douglas Burnham and Enrico Giaccherini (Farnham: Ashgate, 2005): 26–43; Arthur F. Marotti, "Shakespeare and Catholicism," in *Theatre and Religion: Lancastrian Shakespeare*, ed. Richard Dutton, Alison Gail Findlay, and Richard Wilson (Manchester: Manchester University Press, 2004): 218–41; and Dympna C. Callaghan, "Turning Point: Shakespeare and Religion," *Textual Practice* 16 (2001): 1–4.

35 Emma Smith has recently argued that Shylock's dilemma may have been intended as an allusion to the situation of Protestant refugees in London at the time; see Smith, "Was Shylock Jewish?" *Shakespeare Quarterly* 64.2 (213): 189–219, especially 212–19.

36 "London's Praise, or, the Glory of the City," in *The Pepys Ballads,* vol. 3, ed. W.G. Day (Wolfboro, NH: D.S. Brewer 1991), 218–22.

37 See, for example, Ian Archer, *Pursuit of Stability*, 131–40; Rappaport, *Worlds,* 29–36.

38 Patrimony (or inheriting freedom of the city from one's father) was relatively rare as it required the son to provide evidence that he was born after his father had gained the freedom of the city; see Rappaport, *Worlds,* 291–4.

39 John Michael Archer, *Citizen Shakespeare: Freemen and Aliens in the Language of the Plays* (New York: Palgrave, 2005), 17.

40 "An Act of Common Councell Prohibiting All Strangers Borne, and Forrainers, to use Any Trades" (London: John Windet, 1606). See also Hessels, 3.1, 1182–5.

41 Ian Archer, *Pursuit of Stability*, 259.

42 Interestingly, Alexandra Halasz argues that national identity is in part constructed from the figure of clowns like Richard Tarlton; see Halasz, *The Marketplace of Print: Pamphlets and the Public Sphere in Early Modern England* (Cambridge: Cambridge University Press, 1997), 68–9.

43 Helgerson, however, does work from this connection in *Adulterous Alliances: Home, State, and History in Early Modern European Drama and Painting* (Chicago: University of Chicago Press, 2003): 57–78.

44 A notable exception is Willy Maley's analysis of *Cymbeline,* but here Maley is primarily addressing multiplicity within the concept of Britishness more than he is addressing nationalism in the play; see Maley, *Nation, State and Empire,* 31–44.

45 Helgerson, *Forms of Nationhood*, 222.

46 On stage clowns and their relation to class, see Maya Mathur, "An Attack of the Clowns: Comedy, Vagrancy, and the Elizabethan History Play," *The Journal for Early Modern Cultural Studies* 7.1 (2007): 33–54.

47 Anthony D. Smith, *National Identity* (London: Penguin, 1991), 54–7.
48 Helgerson, *Adulterous Alliances*, 64. See also Wendy Wall, *Staging Domesticity: Household Work and English Identity in Early Modern Drama* (Cambridge: Cambridge University Press, 2002), 112–16.
49 The performance date was likely earlier. See, for example, Barbara Freedman, "Shakespearean Chronology, Ideological Complicity, and Floating Texts: Something Rotten in Windsor," *Shakespeare Quarterly* 45.2 (1994): 190–210.
50 Karl Marx and Frederick Engels, *The Collected Works of Karl Marx and Frederick Engels*, vol. 11 (New York: International Publishers, 1979), 103.
51 Karl Marx and Friedrich Engels, *Marx and Engels on Literature and Art* (Progress Publishers: Moscow, 1976), 260.
52 Leah Marcus, *Unediting the Renaissance: Shakespeare, Marlowe, Milton* (London: Routledge, 1996), 68–100. On *The Merry Wives* as a kind of city comedy, see Jean E. Howard, "Shakespeare and the London City Comedy," *Shakespeare Studies* 39 (2001): 1–21.
53 Hoenselaars, *Images*, 58.
54 Schoenbaum, *William Shakespeare*, 264. Nicholl, *The Lodger*, 89–110; and Portal, "Address."
55 Hoenselaars, *Images*, 115 and 283n29.
56 David Daube, "Shakespeare on Aliens Learning English," *Metamorphoses: Journal of the Five College Literary Translation Seminar* 6.2 (1998): 70–84.
57 *Norton Shakespeare*, 1227–9.
58 On the translation scene and translation in general as a theme of *The Merry Wives of Windsor*, see Patricia Parker, *Shakespeare from the Margins: Language, Culture, Context* (Chicago: University of Chicago Press, 1996), 116–48; Vanna Gentili, "A National Idiom and Other Languages: Notes on Elizabethan Ambivalence with Examples from Shakespeare," in *Italian Studies in Shakespeare and His Contemporaries*, ed. Michele Marrapodi and Giorgio Melchiori, (Cranbury, NJ: University of Delaware Press, 1999), 187–205; and Montgomery, *Europe's Languages*, 114–17.
59 See, for example, Beik, *Urban Protest*, 6.
60 On the final scene as a shaming ritual, see Frederick B. Jonassen, "The Stag Hunt in *The Merry Wives of Windsor*," *Bestia: Yearbook of the Beast Fable Society* 3 (1991): 87–101; and Soji Iwasaki, "Rough Music and Deer's Horn in *The Merry Wives of Windsor*," *Shakespeare Studies* (Shakespeare Society of Japan) 37 (1999): 1–20.
61 Jeffrey Theis, "The 'ill kill'd' Deer: Poaching and Social Order in *The Merry Wives of Windsor*," *Texas Studies in Literature and Language* 43.1 (2001): 46–73.
62 See, for example, the Bevington and Riverside editions; in contrast, the Norton and the most recent Arden editions avoid such an interpolation.

63 Hoenselaars, *Images*, 59–60.
64 On the Oldcastle controversy see James M. Gibson, "Shakespeare and the Cobham Controversy: The Oldcastle/Falstaff and Brooke/Broome Revisions," *Medieval and Renaissance Drama in England* 25 (2012): 94–132; Paul Whitfield White, "Shakespeare, the Cobhams, and the Dynamics of Theatrical Patronage," in *Shakespeare and Theatrical Patronage in Early Modern England*, ed. Paul Whitfield White and Suzanne R. Westfall (Cambridge: Cambridge University Press, 2002): 64–89; and Peter Corbin and Douglas Sedge, eds., *The Oldcastle Controversy: Sir John Oldcastle, Part 1 and The Famous Victories of Henry V* (Manchester: Manchester University Press/Revels Edition, 1991).
65 See discussions in Yungblut, *Strangers*, 50, 88.
66 Tracey Hill, "'The Cittie is in an uproare': Staging London in *the Booke of Sir Thomas More*," *Early Modern Literary Studies* 11.1 (May, 2005) 2.1–19 http://purl.oclc.org/emls/11-1/more.htm.

On authorship, see Peter W.M. Blayney, "*The Booke of Sir Thomas Moore* Re-examined," *Studies in Philology* 69 (1972): 167–91; Michael L. Hays, "Shakespeare's Hand in *Sir Thomas More:* Some Aspects of the Palaeographic Argument," *Shakespeare Studies* 8 (1975): 241–53; Thomas Merriam, "The Authorship of *Sir Thomas More*," *ALLC Bulletin* 10.1 (1982): 1–7; Charles Forker, "Webster or Shakespeare? Style, Idiom, Vocabulary, and Spelling in the Additions to *Sir Thomas More*," in *Shakespeare and* Sir Thomas More: *Essays on the Play and Its Shakespearian Interest*, ed. T.H. Howard-Hill (Cambridge: Cambridge University Press, 1989), 151–70; John Jowett, "Henry Chettle and the Original Text of *Sir Thomas More*," in *Shakespeare and* Sir Thomas More, ed. T.H. Howard-Hill (Cambridge: Cambridge University Press, 1989), 131–49; Thomas Merriam, "Did Munday Compose Sir Thomas More?" *Notes and Queries* 37 (1990): 175–8; Paul Ramsey, "The Literary Evidence for Shakespeare as Hand D in the Manuscript Play *Sir Thomas More*: A Re-re-reconsideration," *Upstart Crow* 11 (1991): 131–55; M.W.A. Smith, "Shakespeare, Stylometry, and *Sir Thomas More*," *Studies in Philology* 89 (1992): 434–44; Thomas Merriam, "Some Further Evidence for Shakespeare's Authorship of Hand D *in Sir Thomas More*," *Notes and Queries* 53 (2006): 65–6; Timothy Irish Watt, "The Authorship of the Hand-D Addition to *The Book of Sir Thomas More*," in *Shakespeare, Computers, and the Mystery of Authorship*, ed. Hugh Craig and Arthur F. Kinney (Cambridge: Cambridge University Press, 2012), 134–61; and Macdonald P. Jackson, "Is 'Hand D' of *Sir Thomas More* Shakespeare's? Thomas Bayes and the Elliott-Valenza Authorship Tests," *Early Modern Literary Studies* 12.3 (2007): 1: 1–36 http://purl.oclc.org/emls.

On the date of composition, revision, and performance, see Karl P. Wentersdorff, "The Date of the Additions in *The Booke of Sir Thomas More*," *Shakespeare-Jahrbuch* 101 (1965): 305–25; D.J. Lake, "The Date of the *Sir Thomas More* Additions by Dekker and Shakespeare," *Notes and Queries* 24 (1977): 114–16; Giorgio Melchiori, "*The Booke of Sir Thomas Moore:* A Chronology of Revision," *Shakespeare Quarterly* 37 (1986): 291–308; William B. Long, "The Occasion of *The Book of Sir Thomas More,*" in *Shakespeare and* Sir Thomas More, ed. T.H. Howard-Hill (Cambridge: Cambridge University Press, 1989), 45–56; Scott McMillin, "*The Book of Sir Thomas More:* Dates and Acting Companies," in *Shakespeare and* Sir Thomas More, ed. T.H. Howard-Hill (Cambridge: Cambridge University Press, 1989), 57–76; Giorgio Melchiori, "The Master of the Revels and the Date of the Additions to *The Book of Sir Thomas More,*" in *Shakespeare: Text, Language, Criticism: Essays in Honour of Martin Spevack*, ed. Bernhard Fabian, 164–79 (New York: Lubrecht & Cramer, 1987); Giorgio Melchiori, "Hand D in *Sir Thomas More*: An Essay in Misinterpretation," *Shakespeare Survey* 38 (1985): 101–14.

67 For a critique of this practice, see Jeffrey Masten, "More or Less: Editing the Collaborative," *Shakespeare Studies* 29 (2001): 109–31.
68 Chris Hopkins, "Review of *Sir Thomas More,* by Anthony Munday, William Shakespeare and Others," *Early Modern Literary Studies* 11.2 (September, 2005) 13.1–6 http://purl.oclc.org/emls/11-2/revmore.htm; Melchiori, "*The Booke of Sir Thomas Moore:* A Chronology of Revision," 291–308, especially 296.
69 Alfred W. Pollard, Introduction to *Shakespeare's Hand in* The Play Sir Thomas More, ed. Alfred W. Pollard and John Dover Wilson (Cambridge: Cambridge at the University Press, 1923), 17–32; McMillin, "*The Book of Sir Thomas More:* Dates and Acting Companies"; G. Harold Metz, "'Voice and Credyt': The Scholars and *Sir Thomas More,*" in *Shakespeare and* Sir Thomas More, ed. T.H. Howard-Hill (Cambridge: Cambridge University Press, 1989), 25–9.
70 Qtd. in Vittorio Gabrieli and Giorgio Melchiori, eds., *Sir Thomas More: A Play by Anthony Munday, and Others* (Manchester, UK, and New York: Manchester University Press, 1990), 17.
71 See for example, David M. Bevington, *Tudor Drama,* 133–4.
72 Geoffrey Rudolph Elton, *The English* (Cambridge, MA: Blackwell, 1992), 120; Rappaport, *Worlds,* 17.
73 Pettegree, *Foreign,* 282.
74 Edward Hall, *The Lives of the Kings: The Triumphant Reign of Henry VIII,* vol. 1, ed. Charles Whibley (London: T.C. & E. Jack, 1904), 159–61.
75 See Thomas Wyatt, "Aliens," 75.

76 Hall, *Lives*, vol. 1, 159; *Letters and Papers* ii.2, p. 1031, letter 32–4.
77 Wyatt, "Aliens," 75.
78 John Stow, *The Survey of London*, ed. H.B. Wheatley (London: Everyman's Library, 1987), 152.
79 Hall, *Lives*, vol. 1, 156.
80 Martin Holmes, "Evil May-Day, 1517: The Story of a Riot," *History Today* 15 (1965): 642–3; Hall, *Lives*, vol. 1, 153–5.
81 Susan Dwyer Amussen, "Punishment, Discipline, and Power: The Social Meanings of Violence in Early Modern England," *The Journal of British Studies* 34.1 (1995): 6.
82 Hall, *Lives*, 228.
83 Ibid., 227.
84 See Manning, 204.
85 Pollard, Introduction to *Shakespeare's Hand*, 4.
86 Citations of *Sir Thomas More* refer to the Arden edition: John Jowett, ed., *Sir Thomas More* (London: Methuen Drama, 2011).
87 Hall, *Lives*, 272.
88 Jehan Scheyfve, "Advices sent by…" 21 April 1551, Vienna, Imp. Arch. E. 19 in *Calendar of Letters, Despatches, and State Papers Relating to the Negotiations Between England and Spain*, vol. 10, Edward VI 1550–1552, ed. Royall Tyler (London: The Hereford Times Limited, 1914), 279.
89 Ibid.
90 See, for example, Alexander Neville, *Norfolkes Furies, or a View of Ketts Campe* (London: Printed by William Stansby for Edmund Casson, 1615), especially H2–K3. For more on Kett's Rebellion, see Andy Wood, *The 1549 Rebellions and the Making of Early Modern England* (Cambridge: Cambridge University Press, 2007).
91 Compare Hall, *Lives*, 230 to *Sir Thomas More*, 1.118–34.
92 Manning, *Village Revolts*, 188.
93 As early as 1923 R.W. Chambers pronounced the comparison "a commonplace of criticism"; see Chambers, "The Expression of Ideas – Particularly Political Ideas – in the Three Pages and in Shakespeare," in *Shakespeare's Hand in* The Play Sir Thomas More, ed. Alfred W. Pollard and John Dover Wilson (Cambridge: Cambridge University Press, 1923), 144. Recently Simon Hunt has drawn attention to the way in which rebellion is associated with stage clowns in Shakespeare, drawing on *2 Henry VI, Sir Thomas More,* and *Jack Strawe*, but Lincoln does not seem to me to be a very likely stage clown, and there is very little clowning on the whole in *Sir Thomas More*; see Hunt, "'Leaving out the insurrection': Carnival Rebellion, English History Plays, and a Hermeneutics of Advocacy," *Renaissance Culture and the Everyday* (Philadelphia: University of Pennsylvania, 1999), 299–314. See also Walter

William Greg, ed., *The Book of Sir Thomas More* (Oxford: Malone Society Reprints, 1911), xiii; Melchiori, "*The Book of Sir Thomas More*: Dramatic Unity," 94; John Velz, "*Sir Thomas More* and the Shakespeare Canon: Two Approaches," in *Shakespeare and* Sir Thomas More, ed. T.H. Howard-Hill (Cambridge: Cambridge University Press, 1989), 172–3.

94 Velz, "*Sir Thomas More,*" 173. We would do well to remember that Cade is not without his sympathetic moments. See, for example, Thomas Cartelli, "Jack Cade in the Garden: Class Consciousness and Class Conflict in *2 Henry VI*" in *Enclosure Acts: Sexuality, Property, and Culture in Early Modern England,* ed. Richard Burt and John Michael Archer (Ithaca: Cornell University Press, 1994), 48–67.

95 There may, in addition, be a play on words, with the English mercy and the French *merci*: "we accept of the king's mercy [*merci*/thanks], but we will show no mercy upon the strangers."

96 During Kett's Rebellion of 1549, for instance, the king granted pardons to all who dispersed, but days later authorities gathered many rebels together for execution; see Neville, *Norfolkes Furies*, K4v–r.

97 See, for example, discussions in Yungblut, *Strangers*, 10–13.

98 Sir Thomas More, *Utopia*, trans. Ralph Robynson (Cambridge: Cambridge University Press, 1956), 33; E.A.J. Honigmann, "*The Play of Sir Thomas More* and Some Contemporary Events," *Shakespeare Survey* 42 (1990): 77–87. See also, *Sir Thomas More*, ed. Jowett, 189.

99 Nina Levine, "Citizen's Games: Differentiating Collaboration in *Sir Thomas More*," *Shakespeare Quarterly* 58.1 (2007): 31–64, especially 57–9.

100 D'Ewes, *Compleat Journal*, 507.

101 On this debate see Yungblut, *Strangers*, 31–2.

102 Melchiori, "*The Book of Sir Thomas More*: Dramatic Unity," in *Shakespeare and* Sir Thomas More, ed. T.H. Howard-Hill (New York and Cambridge: Cambridge University Press, 1989), 77.

103 Hall, *Lives*, vol. 1, 162.

104 Ibid., 163.

105 Ibid., 162.

106 Anthony D. Smith, *The Antiquity of Nations* (Cambridge: Polity Press, 2004), 16–17.

107 Helgerson, *Forms of Nationhood*, 234.

Conclusion: The Return of Hans Beer-Pot

1 Dabridgcourt Belchier, *Hans Beer-Pot, His Invisible Comedie of See Me, and See Me Not* (London: Bernard Alsop, 1618).

2 Matthew Steggle, "Belchier, Dabridgcourt (bap. 1581, d. 1621)," in *Oxford Dictionary of National Biography*, online edition, ed. Lawrence Goldman (Oxford University Press, 2004).
3 Shortly after the printing of the play Ogle was replaced by Horace Vere; see D.J.B. Trim, "Ogle, Sir John (bap. 1569, d. 1640)," in *Oxford Dictionary of National Biography*, online edition, ed. H.C.G. Matthew and Brian Harrison (Oxford University Press, 2004).
4 Belchier, *Hans Beer-Pot*, F2v. On the conflict between Calvinist and Arminian doctrine, see Jan Rohls, "Calvinism, Arminianism, and Socinianism in the Netherlands until the Synod of Dort," in *Socinianism and Arminianism: Antitrinitarians, Calvinists and Cultural Exchange in Seventeenth-Century Europe*, ed. Martin Muslow and Jan Rohls (Leiden: Brill, 2005), 3–48; and Charles H. Parker, "To the Attentive, Nonparitsan Reader: The Appeal to History and National Identity in the Religious Disputes of the Seventeenth-Century Netherlands," *The Sixteenth Century Journal* 28.1 (1997): 57–78.
5 Demmy Verkbeke, "Swag-Bellied Hollanders and Dead-Drunk Almaines: Reputation and Pseudo-Translation in Early Modern England," *Dutch Crossing* 34.2 (2010): 187; Alison A. Chapman, "'Met I With an Old Mare': Lust, Misogyny, and the Early Modern Walsingham Ballads," in *Walsingham in Literature and Culture form the Middle Ages to Modernity*, ed. Dominic Janes and Gary Waller (Franham: Ashgate, 2010), 223. George Evans Light casts some doubt on this idea, however; see Light, "All Hopped Up: Beer, Cultivated National Identity, and Anglo-Dutch Relations, 1524–1625," *Journal X* 2.2 (1998): 168. On the requests for troops to keep the peace at this time, see Maarten Prak, *The Dutch Republic in the Seventeenth Century* (Cambridge: Cambridge University Press, 2005), 32–3.
6 Belchier, *Hans Beer-Pot*, A4v. Note that a printer's error occurred on this page, which is listed as A3v. Belchier apparently wrote the "Epistle Dedicatory" on 14 November 1617. Although the war had not technically begun, it was clear by this time that tensions were rising, as Protestant nobility rejected Ferdinand II as Bohemia's Crown Prince.
7 On the Twelve Years' Truce, see Paul C. Allen, *Philip III and the Pax Hispanica, 1598–1621* (New Haven: Yale University Press, 2000), 203–33.
8 Belchier, *Hans Beer-Pot*, C1v, B4v–C1r. Cornelius, incidentally, was the namesake of Ogle's father-in-law, Cornelius de Vries.
9 Belchier, *Hans Beer-Pot*, F4v.
10 Ibid., D1r, D4r,
11 Light, "All Hopped Up," 168–71.
12 Belchier, *Hans Beer-Pot*, B3r.
13 Ibid., D4v.

14 Rolf Soellner, *Timon of Athens: Shakespeare's Pessimistic Tragedy* (Columbus: Ohio State University Press, 1979), 121–2.
15 Belchier, *Hans Beer-Pot*, F3r.
16 Ibid., B4r.
17 Ibid., B4r.
18 Ibid., G4r–v.
19 On the tensions between James's policy and militant Protestantism, see Jason White, *Militant Protestantism and British Identity, 1603–1642* (London: Pickering and Chatto, 2012), 39–63.
20 Belchier, *Hans Beer-Pot*, H1r.
21 Ibid., B3v.
22 On moderate masculinity, see Todd W. Reeser, *Moderating Masculinity in Early Modern Culture* (Chapel Hill: University of North Carolina Press, 2006).
23 Thomas Middleton, *Collected Works*, 1311.
24 Ibid., 1306–7. On the pamphlet's attribution to James, see Susan Dwyer Amussen, "The Peacemaker; or Great Britain's Blessing," in *Thomas Middleton, The Collected Works*, ed. Gary Taylor and John Lavagnino (Oxford: Oxford University Press, 2007), 1303–4.
25 Thomas Middleton, *Collected Works*, 1311, 1306.
26 Ibid., 1307.
27 Constantijn Huygens, *A Selection of the Poems of Sir Constantijn Huygens (1596–1687)*, trans. Peter Davidson and Adriaan van de Weel (Amsterdam: Amsterdam University Press, 1996), 65.
28 On Huygens' pastoral poetry, see Jan Leopold Peter Blommendaal, "Huygens als hoofdketter: De versvorm in vertaalde Italiaanse herdersspelen," *Spiegel Der Letteren: Tijdschrift Voor Nederlandse Literatuurgeschiedenis En Voor Literatuurwetenschap* 31.4 (1989): 257–77; and Wim Vermeer, "Pastorale poëzie van Huygens," *Utrecht Renaissance Studies* 1 (1982): 79–101.
29 On Hensius in England, see Paul Sellin, *Daniel Heinsius and Stuart England* (Leiden: Leiden University Press, 1968), 69–122 passim. On Huygens' connections to Britain, see A.G. Bachrach, *Sir Constantine Huygens and Britain, 1597–1619* (Oxford: Oxford University Press 1962).
30 Huygens, *Selection*, 67.
31 Gwynn, *Huguenot Heritage*, 50. For an example of James's positive correspondence with stranger churches, see Hessels, 1.1240.
32 Ole Peter Grell, *Dutch Calvinists in Early Stuart London: The Dutch Church in Austin Friars, 1603–1642* (Leiden and New York: E.J. Brill, 1989), 42–5. See also Luu, "Alien Communities in Transition," 1570–1650," in *Immigrants in Tudor and Early Stewart England*, ed. Nigel Goose and Lien Bich Luu (Brighton: Sussex Academic Press, 2005), 199.

33 Qtd. in Moens, *The Walloons*, 59.
34 My translation of the passage in Fernand David Georges de Schickler, *Les Églises due Refuge en Angleterre* (Paris: Librarie G. Fischbacher, 1892), 1: 368–9.
35 Cottret, *The Huguenots in England*, 84, 92.
36 James I, *The Essayes of a Prentise in the Divine Art of Poesie* (Edinburgh: Thomas Vautrollier, 1584), D1r–G1r. Guillaume de Salluste Du Bartas, *The Historie of Judith*, trans. Thomas Hudson (Edinburgh: Thomas Vautrollier, 1584), A4r.
37 Hugh Trevor-Roper, *Europe's Physician: The Life of Sir Theodore de Mayerne, 1573–1655* (New Haven: Yale University Press, 2006), 162–208 passim.
38 Hessels, 3.1, 1240–4 and 3.1, 1263. On this period in Colchester, see Jeffrey R. Hankins, "Crown, County, and Corporation in Seventeenth-Century Essex," *The Sixteenth Century Journal* 38.1 (2007): 27–47; and Nigel Goose, "The 'Dutch' at Colchester."
39 Hessels, 3.1, 1263.
40 Hessels, 3.1, 1267–8.
41 Grell, *Dutch Calvinists*, 42. See also Luu, "Alien Communities," 199.
42 Sir Henry Middleton, *The Last East-Indian Voyage* (London: Thomas Purfoot for Walter Burre, 1606), 70.
43 John Skinner, *A True Relation of the Cruell, and Barbarous Proceedings against the English at Amboyna* (London: H. Lownes for Nathaniel Newbury, 1624).
44 On these events and English responses, see Karen Chancy, "The Amboyna Massacre in English Politics, 1624–1635," *Albion: A Quarterly Journal Concerned with British Studies* 30.4 (1998): 583–98. For an exploration of how popular perceptions of events abroad could inform attitudes in England, see Steven C.A. Pincus, "From Butterboxes to Wooden Shoes: The Shift in Popular Sentiment from Anti-Dutch to Anti-French in the 1670s," *The Historical Journal* 38.2 (1995): 333–61. On the early history of the East India Company, see Philip J. Stern, *The Company-State: Corporate Sovereignty and the Early Modern Foundations of the British Empire in India* (Oxford: Oxford University Press, 2011).
45 Alastair Bellany and Andrew Mcrae, *Early Stuart Libels: An Edition of Poetry from Manuscript Sources*, Early Modern Literary Studies, Text Series 1 (2005), http://www.earlystuartlibels.net, 544.
46 Edmund Bolton, *Hypercritica, or a Rule of Judgment for Writing or Reading our History's*, in *Ancient Critical Essays on English Poets and Poesy*, vol. 2, ed. Joseph Haslewood (London: Triphook, 1815), 254. *Hypercritica* was not printed until 1722, and its date of composition has proved somewhat difficult to determine. Thomas H. Blackburn notes that it can be dated no earlier than

1616 but ultimately argues for 1621 as the date of composition with possible emendations in 1625; see Blackburn, "The Date and Evolution of Edmund Bolton's 'Hypercritica,'" *Studies in Philology* 63.2 (1966): 196–202.
47 Grafton and Weinberg, *I Have Always Loved*, 177–83.
48 Cottret, *The Huguenots in England*, 90.
49 On James and Du Moulin, see Cottret, *The Huguenots in England*, 87–93; and W. Brown Patterson, "James I and the Huguenot Synod of Tonneins of 1614," *The Harvard Theological Review* 65.2 (1972): 241–70.
50 George Benson, *A Sermon Preached at Paules Crosse* (London: H.L. for Richard Moore, 1609), 1, 34, 35, 40, 45, 51, 56.
51 Ibid., 26.
52 Ibid., 27.
53 Thomas Adams, *The Blacke Devill or Apostate* (London: William Jaggard, 1615), 23. Thomas Adams, *Eirenopolis: The Citie of Peace* (London: Augustus Matthews for John Grismand, 1622), 59–60.
54 Dalechamp, *Christian Hospitalitie*, 124–7.
55 I am here following the title offered by the editors of *The Complete Works*.
56 Montgomery, *Europe's Languages*, 64–5.
57 Ibid., 65.
58 Billing, "The Dutch Diaspora," 134.
59 Linda Pollock, "The Practice of Kindness in Early Modern Elite Society," *Past and Present* 211.1 (2011): 121–58.
60 Hoenselaars, *Images*, 140.
61 David Nicol, "Citizens, Gentry, and the Double Ending of Rowley and Middleton's A Fair Quarrel," *Studies in English Literature* 51.2 (2011): 427–45.
62 On the stranger churches conflict with Laud, see Grell, *Dutch Calvinists*, 74–97; Cottret, *The Huguenots in England,* 112–17; and Gwynn, *Huguenot Heritage*, 54–7.
63 Grell, *Dutch Calvinists*, 64–5.
64 Hessels, 3.2, 1905.
65 Grell, *Dutch Calvinists*, 135–6.
66 Daniel Statt, *Foreigners and Englishmen: The Controversy Over Immigration and Population 1660–1760* (Newark: University of Delaware Press, 1995).
67 *The Grand Concern of England Explained in Several Proposals* (London: 1673), 13.
68 Statt, *Foreigners*, 121–65.
69 Qtd. in Statt, *Foreigners*, 115–19.
70 Statt, *Foreigners*, 136, 199–201. See also W.R. Owens and P.N. Furbank, "Defoe and the Dutch Alliance: Some Attributions Examined," *British Journal for Eighteenth-Century Studies* 9.2 (1986): 169–82.

71 Daniel Defoe, *The True-Born Englishman in Satire*, in *Fantasy and Writings on the Supernatural by Daniel Defoe*, vol. 1, ed. W.R. Owens (London: Pickering and Chatto, 2003), 7980. Lines from the poem appear in in-text parenthetical citations. For a reading of Defoe's *Robinson Crusoe* in terms of xenophobia and a counterbalancing xenodochia, see Rajani Sudan, *Fair Exotics: Xenophobic Subject in English Literature, 1720–1850* (Philadelphia: University of Pennsylvania Press, 2002), 1–13.

72 On the Vaudois, see Evan Cameron, *The Reformation of the Heretics: The Waldenses of the Alps, 1480–1580* (Oxford: Oxford University Press, 1984). On Valtelline, see G. Parker, *The Thirty Years' War*, 64–5.

73 Wolfram Schmidgen argues that Defoe's defense of immigration and intermixing of peoples is part of a larger pattern of valuing mixture as a generative force; see Wolfram Schmidgen, *Exquisite Mixture: The Virtues of Impurity in Early Modern England* (Philadelphia: University of Pennsylvania Press, 2013), 6–12.

Bibliography

Achinstein, Sharon. "John Foxe and the Jews." *Renaissance Quarterly* 54.1 (2001): 86–120.
Acontius, Jacobus. *Satans Stratagems or the Devils Cabinet-Councel*. London: John Macock, 1648.
"An Act of Common Councell Prohibiting All Strangers Borne, and Forrainers, to use Any Trades." London: John Windet, 1606.
Adams, Thomas. *The Blacke Devill or Apostate*. London: William Jaggard, 1615.
– *Eirenopolis: The Citie of Peace*. London: Augustus Matthews for John Grismand, 1622.
– *The Happiness of the Church*. London: G.P. for John Grismand, 1619.
Adelman, Janet. *Blood Relations: Christian and Jew in Merchant of Venice*. Chicago: University of Chicago Press, 2008.
Allen, Paul C. *Philip III and the Pax Hispanica, 1598–1621*. New Haven: Yale University Press, 2000.
Amussen, Susan Dwyer. "The Peacemaker; or Great Britain's Blessing." In *Thomas Middleton: The Collected Works*. Ed. Gary Taylor and John Lavagnino, 1303–6. Oxford: Oxford University Press, 2007.
– "Punishment, Discipline, and Power: The Social Meanings of Violence in Early Modern England." *The Journal of British Studies* 34.1 (1995): 1–34.
Anderson, Benedict. *Imagined Communities: Reflections on the Origin and Spread of Nationalism*. Rev. ed. London and New York: Verso, 1991.
Anglo, Sydney. *Spectacle, Pageantry, and Early Tudor Policy*. 2nd ed. Oxford: Clarendon Press, 1997.
Anthias, Floya, and Nira Yuval-Davis. Introduction. *Woman – Nation – State*. New York: St Martin's Press, 1989. 1–16.
Appiah, Kwame Anthony. *Cosmopolitanism: Ethics in a World of Strangers*. New York: W.W. Norton, 2006.

Arber, Edward, ed. *A Transcript of the Registers of the Company of Stationers of London, 1554–1640*. 5 vols. London: 1875–94.
Archer, Ian. *The Pursuit of Stability: Social Relations in Elizabethan London*. Cambridge and New York: Cambridge University Press, 1991.
Archer, John Michael. *Citizen Shakespeare: Freemen and Aliens in the Language of the Plays*. New York: Palgrave, 2005.
Ardolino, Frank. "Hans and Hammon: Dekker's Use of Hans Sachs and *Purim* in *The Shoemaker's Holiday*." *Medieval and Renaissance Drama in England* 14 (2001): 144–67.
Armstrong, John. *Nations before Nationalism*. Chapel Hill: University of North Carolina Press, 1982.
Arnold, Janet. *Queen Elizabeth's Wardrobe Unlock'd*. Leeds: W.S. Maney and Sons, 1988.
Asch, Ronald G. *The Thirty Years War: The Holy Roman Empire and Europe, 1618–48*. New York: Palgrave, 1997.
Bachrach, Alfred Gustave. *Sir Constantine Huygens and Britain, 1597–1619*. Oxford: Oxford University Press 1962.
Backhouse, Marcel. *The Flemish and Walloon Communities at Sandwich During the Reign of Elizabeth I, 1561–1603*. Brussel: Koninklijke Academie voor Wetenschappen, Letteren en Schone Kunsten, 1995.
Baker, Ernest. *The History of the English Novel*. Vol. 2. New York: Barnes and Noble, 1950.
Bartlett, Kenneth R. "The Strangeness of Strangers: English Impressions of Italy in the Sixteenth Century." *Quaderni d'italianistica* 1.1 (1980): 46–63.
Bartolovich, Crystal. "London's the Thing: Alienation, the Market, and *Englishmen for My Money*." *Huntington Library Quarterly* 71.1 (2008): 137–56.
Baskerville, Charles Read. *Elizabethan and Stuart Plays*. New York: H. Holt, 1934.
Bate, Jonathan. *The Genius of Shakespeare*. Oxford: Oxford University Press, 1997.
Beik, William. *Urban Protest in Seventeenth-Century France: The Culture of Retribution*. Cambridge: Cambridge University Press, 1997.
Beilin, Elaine. *Redeeming Eve: Women Writers of the English Renaissance*. Princeton: Princeton University Press, 1987.
– "'Some Freely Spake Their Minde': Resistance in Anne Dowriche's *The French Historie*." In *Women, Writing and the Reproduction of Culture in Tudor and Stuart Britain*. Ed. Mary E. Burke, Jane Donaworth, Linda L. Dove, and Karen Nelson, 119–40. Syracuse, NY: Syracuse University Press, 2000.
– "Writing Public Poetry: Humanism and the Woman Writer." *Modern Language Quarterly* 51.2 (1990): 249–71.
Belchier, Dabridgcourt. *Hans Beer-Pot, His Invisible Comedie of See Me, and See Me Not*. London: Bernard Alsop, 1618.

Bellany, Alastair, and Andrew Mcrae, *Early Stuart Libels: An Edition of Poetry from Manuscript Sources*, Early Modern Literary Studies, Text Series 1 (2005). http://purl.oclc.org/emls/texts/libels.

Benedict, Philip. *Rouen during the Wars of Religion.* Cambridge: Cambridge University Press, 1981.

Benson, George. *A Sermon Preached at Paules Crosse.* London: H.L. for Richard Moore, 1609.

Beresford, Maurice W. "The Common Informer, The Penal Statues and Economic Regulation." In *Time and Place: Collected Essays.* Leeds: Leeds University Press, 1961: 209–26.

Bergeron, David M. *English Civic Pageantry, 1558–1642.* London: Edward Arnold, 1971.

Berry, Ralph. "Shakespeare and the Catholic Network." *Contemporary Review* 286 (2005): 233–8.

Bevington, David M. "A.L. Rowse's Dark Lady." In *Lanyer: Gender, Genre, and the Canon.* Ed. Marshall Grossman, 10–28. Lexington: University of Kentucky Press, 1998.

– *Tudor Drama and Politics: A Critical Approach to Topical Meaning.* Cambridge: Harvard University Press, 1968.

Beza [Bèze], Theodore. *A Tragedie of Abrahams Sacrifice.* Trans. Arthur Golding. London: Thomas Vautrollier, 1575.

Billing, Christian M. "The Dutch Diaspora in English Comedy: 1598 to 1618." In *Transnational Exchange in Early Modern Theater.* Ed. Robert Henke and Eric Nichols, 119–40. Farnham: Ashgate, 2008.

Bisson, Douglas R. *The Merchant Adventurers of England: The Company and the Crown, 1474–1564.* Newark: University of Delaware Press, 1993.

Blackburn, Thomas H. "The Date and Evolution of Edmund Bolton's 'Hypercritica.'" *Studies in Philology* 63.2 (1966): 196–202.

Blagden, Cyprian. *The Stationers' Company: A History, 1403–1959.* Stanford: Stanford University Press, 1977.

Blayney, Peter W.M. "*The Booke of Sir Thomas Moore* Re-examined." *Studies in Philology* 69 (1972): 167–91.

Blommendaal, Jan Leopold Peter. "Huygens als hoofdketter: De versvorm in vertaalde Italiaanse herdersspelen." *Spiegel Der Letteren: Tijdschrift Voor Nederlandse Literatuurgeschiedenis En Voor Literatuurwetenschap* 31.4 (1989): 257–77.

Bolton, Edmund. *Hypercritica, or a Rule of Judgment for Writing or Reading our History's.* In *Ancient Critical Essays on English Poets and Poesy*, vol. 2. Ed. Joseph Haslewood, 221–54. London: Triphook, 1815.

Bolton, James L. *The Alien Communities of London in the Fifteenth Century: The Subsidy Rolls of 1440 and 1483–4.* Stamford: Brepols, 1998.

- "Irish Migration to England in the Late Middle Ages: The Evidence of 1394 and 1440." *Irish Historical Studies* 32.125 (2000): 1–21.
Bonney, Richard. *The Thirty Years' War, 1618–1648.* Oxford: Osprey, 2002.
Born, Hanspeter. "Why Greene Was Angry at Shakespeare." *Medieval and Renaissance Drama in England* 25 (2012): 133–73.
Bose, Mishtooni. "'On Kai Me On': A Tension in the Ramist Manuals." *Notes and Queries* 236.1 (1991): 29–31.
Bovilsky, Lara. *Barbarous Play: Race on the English Renaissance Stage.* University of Minnesota Press, 2008.
Brachtel, M.E. "Regulation and Group-Consciousness in the Later History of London's Italian Merchant Colonies." *Journal of European Economic History* 9.3 (1980): 585–610.
Bracken, C.W. "The Huguenot Churches of Plymouth and Stonehouse." *Report and Transactions of the Devonshire Association for the Advancement of Science, Literature and Art* 66 (1934): 163–79.
Bradshaw, Brendan, Andrew Hadfield, and Willy Maley, eds. *Representing Ireland: Literature and the Origins of Conflict, 1534–1660.* Cambridge: Cambridge University Press, 1993.
Bradshaw, Graham. "Shakespeare's Peculiarity." *Proceedings of the British Academy* 111 (2001): 99–126.
Brennan, Gillian E. "The Cheese and the Welsh: Foreigners in Elizabethan Literature." *Renaissance Studies* 8.1 (1994): 40–64.
Briggs, Julia. "Marlowe's *Massacre at Paris*: A Reconsideration." *Review of English Studies* n.s. 34 (1983): 257–78.
Brady, Ciaran, and Jane H. Ohlmeyer, eds. *British Interventions in Early Modern Ireland.* Cambridge: Cambridge University Press, 2005.
Brown, Keith M. "Scottish Identity in the Seventeenth Century." In *British Consciousness and Identity: The Making of Britain, 1533–1707.* Ed. Brendan Bradshaw and Peter Roberts, 236–58. Cambridge: Cambridge University Press, 1998.
Brooke, C.F. Tucker. *The Tudor Drama: A History of English National Drama to the Retirement of Shakespeare.* Boston and New York: Houghton Mifflin, 1911.
Brooke, Thomas. *Certayne Versis Written by Thomas Brooke, Gentleman.* Norwich: Anthony de Solemne, 1570.
Burton, Jonathan. "'A most wily bird': Leo Africanus, *Othello* and the Trafficking in Difference." In *Post-Colonial Shakespeares.* Ed. Ania Loomba and Martin Orkin, 43–63. London and New York: Routledge, 1998.
"By the Queene." London: Christopher Barker, 1594.
Caball, Marc. "Faith Culture, and Sovereignty: Irish Nationality and Its Development, 1558–1625." In *British Consciousness and Identity: The Making of*

Britain, 1533–1707. Ed. Brendan Bradshaw and Peter Roberts, 112–39. Cambridge: Cambridge University Press, 1998.
Calendar of Letters, Despatches, and State Papers Relating to the Negotiations between England and Spain. Ed. Royall Tyler. Vol. 11 London: Hereford Times, Limited, 1916.
Calendar of Letters, Despatches, and State Papers Relating to the Negotiations between England and Spain. Ed. Royall Tyler. Vol. 12. London: His Majesty's Stationery Office, 1949.
Calendar of State Papers, Domestic Series, of the Reigns of Edward VI, Mary, Elizabeth, 1547–1580. Ed. Robert Lemon. London: Longman, 1856.
Calendar of State Papers and Manuscripts Relating to English Affairs, Existing in the Archives and Collections of Venice. Vol. 9. Ed. Horatio F. Brown. London: Eyre and Spottiswoode, 1897.
Calendar of State Papers: Spanish: Calendar of Letters and State Papers Relating to English Affairs. Vol. 2: *Elizabeth, 1568–1579*. Ed. Martin A.S. Hume. London: Eyre and Spottiswoode, 1894.
Callaghan, Dympna C. "Turning Point: Shakespeare and Religion." *Textual Practice* 16 (2001): 1–4.
Cameron, Evan. *The Reformation of the Heretics: The Waldenses of the Alps, 1480–1580*. Oxford: Oxford University Press, 1984.
Campos, Edmund Valentine. "Jews, Spaniards, and Portingales: Ambiguous Identities of Portuguese *Marranos* in Elizabethan England." *English Literary History* 69.3 (2002): 599–616.
Carpenter, John. "Placing Thomas Deloney." *The Journal of Narrative Theory* 36.2 (2006): 125–62.
Carrol, Stuart. *Martyrs and Murderers: The Guise Family and the Making of Europe*. Oxford: Oxford University Press, 2009.
Carron, Jean-Claude. "*Abraham sacrifiant* de Théodore de Bèze: Exil et propaganda évangélique au XVIe siècle." *Revue d'histoire du théâtre* 1–2, no. 221–2 (2004): 69–92.
Cartelli, Thomas. "Jack Cade in the Garden: Class Consciousness and Class Conflict in *2 Henry VI*." In *Enclosure Acts: Sexuality, Property, and Culture in Early Modern England*. Ed. Richard Burt and John Michael Archer, 48–67. Ithaca: Cornell University Press, 1994.
Carter, Christopher. "The Family of Love and Its Enemies." *The Sixteenth Century Journal* 37.3 (2006): 651–72.
Cayerwood, Cynthia. "The Geography of Aphra Behn's City Comedies." *Literary London: Interdisciplinary Studies in the Representation of London* 5.2 (2007). http://www.literarylondon.org/londonjournal/september2007/caywood.html.
Chambers, R.W. "The Expression of Ideas – Particularly Political Ideas – in the Three Pages and in Shakespeare." In *Shakespeare's Hand in* The Play Sir

Thomas More. Ed. Alfred W. Pollard and John Dover Wilson, 142–88. Cambridge: Cambridge University Press, 1923.

Chancy, Karen. "The Amboyna Massacre in English Politics, 1624–1635." *Albion: A Quarterly Journal Concerned with British Studies* 30.4 (1998): 583–98.

Chapman, Alison, A. "'Met I With an Old Mare": Lust, Misogyny, and the Early Modern Walsingham Ballads." In *Walsingham in Literature and Culture form the Middle Ages to Modernity*. Ed. Dominic Janes and Gary Waller, 217–32. Farnham: Ashgate, 2010.

Chedgzoy, Kate. "This Pleasant and Sceptered Isle: Insular Fantasies of National Identity in Anne Dowriche's *The French Historie* and William Shakespeare's *Richard II*." In *Archipelagic Identities*. Ed. Philip Schwyzer and Simon Mealor, 25–42. Farnham: Ashgate, 2004.

Chitty, Charles W. "Aliens in England in the Sixteenth Century." *Race* 8 (1966–67): 129–45.

Christensen, Ann C. "Being Mistress Eyre in Dekker's *The Shoemaker's Holiday* and Deloney's *The Gentle Craft*." *Comparative Drama* 42.4 (2008): 451–80.

Christopherson, John. *An exhortation to all menne to take hede and beware of rebellion where in are set forth the causes, that commonlye moue men to rebellion, and that no cause is there, that ought to moue any man there vnto.*[etc.]. London: John Cawood, 1554.

The Chronicle of Queen Jane, and of Two Years of Queen Mary, and Especially of the Rebellion of Sir Thomas Wyat. Ed. John Gough Nichols. London: Camden Society, 1850.

Churchyard, Thomas. *The Miserie of Flaunders, Calamatie of Fraunce, Misfortune of Portugall, Unquietnes of Irelande, Troubles of Scotlande, and the Blessed State of Englande.* London: Andrew Maunsell, 1579.

Clair, Colin. "Refugee Printers and Publishers in Britain during the Tudor Period." *Proceedings of the Huguenot Society of London* 22 (1970–76): 115–26.

Clanchy, Michael T. *England and Its Rulers, 1066–1272*. Oxford: Blackwell, 1998.

Clarke, Danielle. *The Politics of Early Modern Women's Writing*. Harlow: Longman, 2001.

Cohen, Walter. "Various Poems." In *The Norton Shakespeare*. Ed. Stephen Greenblatt, et al., 1991–4. New York and London: W.W. Norton, 1997.

Coke, Sir Edward. *The Third Part of the Institutes of the Law of England Concerning High Treason and Other Pleas of the Crown, and Criminall Causes.* London: Miles Flesher for W. Lee and D. Pakeman, 1644.

Collinson, Patrick. *Godly People: Essays on English Protestantism and Puritanism*. London: Hambledon Press, 1983.

Colman, D.C. "An Innovation and Its Diffusion: The 'New Draperies.'" *The Economic History Review* n.s. 22.3 (1969): 417–29.
Colson, Justin. "Alien Communities and Alien Fraternities in Later Medieval London." *The London Journal* 35.2 (2010): 111–43.
Commendone, Giovanni. Francesco. "Events of the Kingdom of England Beginning with King Edward VI until the Wedding of the Most Serene Prince Philip of Spain and the Most Serene Queen Mary." In *The Accession Coronation and Marriage of Mary Tudor as Related in Four Manuscripts of the Escorial*, translated by C.V. Malfatti. Barcelona: Published by C.V. Malfatti, 1956.
"Complaint to Sir William Periam, chief baron, by Robert Whyte of London, silk weaver and button maker." Document ref.: SP 46/38 f.379 Folio numbers: ff. 379, The National Archives, United Kingdom.
Connolly, Sean J. *Contested Island: Ireland, 1460–1630*. Oxford: Oxford University Press, 2007.
Consitt, Frances. *The London Weavers' Company*. Oxford: Clarendon Press, 1933.
Conybeare, John. "Trade Wars: A Comparative Study of Anglo-Hanse, Franco-Italian, and Hawley-Smoot Conflicts." *World Politics* 38.1 (1985): 147–72.
Cooper, William Durrant. *Lists of Foreign Protestants and Aliens Resident in England, 1618–1688, from Returns in the State Paper Office*. Westminster: Camden Society, 1862.
Corbin, Peter and Douglas Sedge, eds. *The Oldcastle Controversy: Sir John Oldcastle, Part 1 and The Famous Victories of Henry V*. Manchester: Manchester University Press/Revels Edition, 1991.
Cott, Nancy F. *Public Vows: A History of Marriage and the Nation*. Cambridge, MA, and London: Harvard University Press, 2000.
Cottret, Bernard. *The Huguenots in England: Immigration and Settlement c. 1550–1700*. Cambridge: Cambridge University Press, 1991.
Cowell, H. J. "The French-Walloon Church at Glastonbury 1550–1553." *Proceedings of the Huguenot Society* 13 (1923–29): 483–515.
Cowpers, Joseph Meadow, ed. *The Register Booke of the Parish of St George the Martyr*. Canterbury: Cross and Jackman, 1891.
Craik, Thomas Wallace. "The Political Interpretation of Two Tudor Interludes: *Temperance And Humility* and *Wealth and Health*." *The Review of English Studies*. New series 4.14. (1953): 98–108.
– *The Revels History of Drama in English*. Vol. 2. New York: Barnes and Noble, 1977.
Crane, David. Introduction to *The Dutch Courtesan*. Ed. David Crane. New York: W.W. Norton, 1997.

Crawford, Patricia. *Parents of Poor Children in England, 1500–1800*. New York: Oxford University Press, 2010.
Cressy, David. *Birth, Marriage, and Death: Ritual, Religion, and the Life-Cycle in Tudor and Stuart England*. Oxford: Oxford University Press, 1997.
Cross, F.W. *History of the Walloon and Huguenot Church at Canterbury*. Publications of the Huguenot Society 15. London: 1898.
Cunningham, William. *Alien Immigrants to England*. 2nd ed. London: Frank Cass, 1969; 1st ed. 1897.
Crouzet, Denis. *Dieu en ses royaumes: Une histoiredes guerres de religion*. Seyssel, France: Champ Vallon, 2008.
Daileader, Celia R. *Racism, Misogyny, and the Othello-Myth: Inter-racial Couples from Shakespeare to Spike Lee*. New York: Cambridge University Press, 2005.
Dalechamp, Caleb. *Christian Hospitalitie Handled Common-place-wise*. Cambridge: Thomas Buck, 1632.
Dathenus, Petrus. *De C.L. Psalmen Dauids. Wt den Francoyschen dichte in Nederlantschen overghesett door Petrum Dathenum*. Norwich: Anthony de Solemne, 1568.
Daube, David. "Shakespeare on Aliens Learning English." *Metamorphoses: Journal of the Five College Literary Translation Seminar* 6.2 (1998): 70–84.
Davidson, Peter and Thomas McCoog. "Unreconciled: What Evidence Links Shakespeare and the Jesuits?" *The Times Literary Supplement* (16 March 2007): 12–13.
Davies, Michael. "The Transubstantial Bard: Shakespeare and Catholicism." In *The Poetics of Transubstantiation: From Theology to Metaphor*. Ed. Douglas Burnham and Enrico Giaccherini, 26–43. Farnham: Ashgate, 2005.
Davies, R.R. *The First English Empire: Power and Identities in the British Isles, 1093–1343*. Oxford: Oxford University Press, 2000.
Davis, Natalie Zemon. "The Rites of Violence." *Past and Present* 59 (1973): 51–91.
Davis, Walter. *Idea and Act in Elizabethan Fiction*. Princeton: Princeton University Press, 1969.
Defoe, Daniel. *The True-Born Englishman*, in *Satire, Fantasy and Writings on the Supernatural by Daniel Defoe*, vol. 1. Ed. W.R. Owens. London: Pickering and Chatto, 2003.
De Groot, Aart. "Acontius's Plea for Tolerance." In *From Strangers to Citizens: The Integration of Immigrant Communities in Britain, Ireland and Colonial America, 1550–1750*. Ed. Randolph Vigne and Charles Galton Littleton, 48–54. Proceedings of a conference convened in London, 5–7 May 2000, by the Huguenot Society of Great Britain and Ireland. Brighton and Portland, OR: Sussex Academic Press, 2001.

Dekker, Thomas. *The Dramatic Works of Thomas Dekker*. 4 vols. Ed. Fredson Bowers. Cambridge: Cambridge University Press, 1953–61.
– *The Non-Dramatic Works of Thomas Dekker*. Vol. 3. London: Huth Library, 1884.
Deloney, Thomas. *The Novels of Thomas Deloney*. Ed. Merritt E. Lawlis. Bloomington: Indiana University Press, 1961.
– *The Works of Thomas Deloney*. Ed. Francis Oscar Mann. Oxford: Clarendon Press, 1912.
Demers, Patricia. *Women's Writing in English: Early Modern England*. Toronto: University of Toronto Press, 2005.
D'Ewes, Simonds. *A Compleat Journal of the Votes, Speeches, and Debates, Both of the House of Lords and House of Commons throughout the Whole Reign of Queen Elizabeth*. London: Paul Bowes, 1693.
Dickens, Arthur Geoffrey. "The Elizabethans and St. Bartholomew." In *The Massacre of St. Bartholomew: Reappraisals and Documents*. Ed. Alfred Soman, 52–70. The Hague: Martinus Nijhoff, 1974.
Diefendorf, Barbara. "Memories of the Massacre: Saint Bartholomew's Day and Protestant Identity in France." In *Voices of Tolerance in an Age of Persecution*. Ed. Vincent P. Carey, 45–62. Washington, DC: Folger Shakespeare Library, 2004.
Dillon, Janette. *Language and Stage in Medieval and Renaissance England*. Cambridge: Cambridge University Press, 1998.
Dollinger, Philippe. *The German Hansa*. Trans. and ed. D.S. Ault and S.H. Steinberg. Stanford, CA: Stanford University Press, 1970.
Dorman, Thomas. "The Foreign Element in the Parishes of St. Peter, Holy Cross and Canterbury, 1575–1684." *Proceedings of the Huguenot Society of London* 2 (1886–7): 197–204.
– "Notes on the Dutch, Walloons, and Huguenots at Sandwich in the Sixteenth and Seventeenth Centuries." *Proceedings of the Huguenot Society of London* 2 (1886–7): 205–62.
Dorsinville, Max. "Design in *Jack of Newbury*." *PMLA* 88.2 (1973): 233–9.
Dovey, Zillah. *An Elizabethan Progress: The Queen's Journey into East Anglia, 1578*. Madison: Farleigh Dickson University Press, 1996.
Dowriche, Anne. *The French Historie*. London: Thomas Orwin for Thomas Man, 1589.
Dowriche, Anne. *The French Historie*. London: Thomas Orwin for William Russell, 1589.
Dowriche, Hugh. *The Jaylor's Conversion*. London: John Windet, 1596.
Du Bartas, Guillaume de Salluste. *The Historie of Judith*. Trans. Thomas Hudson. Edinburgh: Thomas Vautrollier, 1584.
Dubois-Nayt, Armel. "Anne Dowriche et l'Histoire de France ou … d'Angleterre?" *Études Épistémè* 17 (2010): 11–30.

Duke, Alistair. "Martyrs with a Difference: Dutch Anabaptist Victims of Elizabethan Persecution." *Nederlands Archief voor Kerkgeschieddenis* 80 (2000): 263–81.
– *Reformation and Revolt in the Low Countries*. London: Continuum Press, 2003.
Duncan-Jones, Katherine. *Sir Philip Sidney: Courtier Poet*. New Haven: Yale University Press, 1991.
– *Ungentle Shakespeare: Scenes from His Life*. London: Arden, 2001.
Ebsworth, Joseph Woodfall, ed. *The Roxsburghe Ballads, Illustrating the Last Years of the Stuarts*. Part 26, vol. 8. Hertford: Stephen Austin and Sons, 1899
Edmond, Mary. "Droeshout, Martin (1565x9–c.1642)." *Oxford Dictionary of National Biography*. Ed. H.C.G. Matthew and Brian Harrison. Oxford: Oxford University Press, 2004. Online edition, ed. Lawrence Goldman, May 2008.
– "It Was for Gentle Shakespeare Cut." *Shakespeare Quarterly* 42 (1990): 339–44.
– "Tooley, Nicholas (1583–1623)." *Oxford Dictionary of National Biography*, Oxford University Press, 2004; online edition, Jan. 2008.
Edmondson, Paul, and Stanley Wells, eds. *Shakespeare Beyond Doubt: Evidence, Argument, Controversy*. Cambridge: Cambridge University Press, 2013.
Eisenstein, Elizabeth L. *Grub Street Abroad: Aspects of the French Cosmopolitan Press from the Age of Louis XIV to the French Revolution*. Oxford: Oxford University Press, 1992.
Ellinghausen, Laurie. "Black Acts: Textual Labor and Commercial Deceit in Dekker's *Lantern and Candlelight*." In *Rogues and Early Modern Literature*. Ed. Craig Dionne, 294–311. Ann Arbor: University of Michigan Press, 2004.
Elton, Geoffrey Rudolph. *The English*. Cambridge, MA: Blackwell, 1992.
– "Informing for Profit: A Sidelight on Tudor Methods of Law Enforcement." *Cambridge Historical Journal* 11.2 (1954): 149–67.
Ephraim, Michelle. *Reading the Jewish Woman on the Elizabethan Stage*. Farnham: Ashgate, 2008.
Erickson, Amy L. *Women and Property in Early Modern England*. London: Routledge, 1997.
Es, Bart Van. "*'Johannes fac Totum'*?: Shakespeare's First Contact with the Acting Companies." *Shakespeare Quarterly* 61.4 (2010): 551–77.
Escobedo, Andrew. *Nationalism and Historical Loss in Renaissance England: Foxe, Dee, Spenser, Milton*. Ithaca: Cornell University Press, 2004.
Esser, Raingard. "Germans in Early Modern Britain." In *Germans in Britain since 1500*. Ed. Panikos Panayi, 17–28. Hambledon: Continuum, 1996.
– "Immigrant Cultures in Tudor and Stuart England." In *Immigrants in Tudor and Early Stuart England*. Ed. Nigel Goose and Lien Bich Luu, 161–74. Brighton: Sussex Academic Press, 2005.

- "News across the Channel: Contact and Communication between the Dutch and the Walloon Refugees in Norwich and their Families in Flanders." *Immigrants and Minorities* 14.2 (1995): 31–46.
- *Niederländische Exulanten im England des späten 16. und frühen 17. Jahrhundert: Die Norwicher Fremdengemeinden*. Berlin: Duncker & Humblot, 1996.
- "Social Concern and Calvinistic Duty: The Norwich Strangers' Community." In *Het Beloofde Land, Acht Opstellen Over Werken, Geloven en Vluchten Tijdens de XVIe en XVIIe Eeuw, Bijdragen tot de geschiedenis van de Westhoek*. Ed. Jaak Decaestecker, 172–84. Dikkebus, Westhoek, 1992.

Estienne, Henri. *Ane Mervaylous Discourse Upon the Lyfe, Deedes and Behaviors of Katherine de Medicis Queen Mother*. London: Henry Middleton, 1575.

Evans, Charles Blakemore. *The Riverside Shakespeare*. Boston and New York: Houghton Mifflin, 1997.

Evans, Kathryn J. "Jacques Grévin's Religious Attitude and The Family of Love." *Bibliothèque d'Humanisme et Renaissance* 47.2 (1985): 357–65.

Fagel, Raymond. "The Netherlandish Presence in England Before the Coming of the Stranger Churches, 1480–1560." In *From Strangers to Citizens: The Integration of Immigrant Communities in Britain, Ireland and Colonial America, 1550–1750*. Ed. Randolph Vigne and Charles Galton Littleton, 7–16. Proceedings of a conference convened in London, 5–7 May 2000, by the Huguenot Society of Great Britain and Ireland. Brighton and Portland, OR: Sussex Academic Press, 2001.

Farmer John S., ed. *Recently Recovered "Lost" Tudor Plays*. London: Early English Drama Society, 1907.

Fiedler, Leslie. *The Stranger in Shakespeare*. London: Paladin, 1974.

Fielitz, Sonja. "Shakespeare and Catholicism: The Jesuits as Cultural Mediators in Early Modern Europe." *Critical Survey* 21.3 (2009): 72–86.

Finkelpearl, Philip J. *John Marston of the Middle Temple*. Cambridge: Harvard University Press, 1969.

Fleay, Frederick Gard. *A Chronicle History of the London Stage*. London: Reeves and Turner, 1893.

Fleck, Andrew. "The Custom of Courtesans and John Marston's *The Dutch Courtesan*." *A Quarterly Journal of Short Articles, Notes, and Reviews* 21.3 (2008): 11–19.

- "Marking Difference and National Identity in Dekker's *The Shoemaker's Holiday*." *Studies in English Literature 1500–1900* 46.2 (2006): 349–70.

Fleming, Arnold J. *Flemish Influence in Britain*. Vol. 1. Glasgow: Jackson, Wylie, 1930.

Floyd-Wilson, Mary. *English Ethnicity and Race in Early Modern Drama*. Cambridge: Cambridge University Press, 2003.

Ford, John. *The Lover's Melancholy*. Ed. R.F. Hill. Manchester, UK: Manchester University Press, 1985.
– *The Works of John Ford*. Vol. 2. Ed. William Gifford. London: James Toovey, 1869.
Ford, Judy Ann. "Marginality and the Assimilation of Foreigners in the Lay Parish Community: The Case of Sandwich." In *The Parish in English Life, 1400–1600*. Ed. Katherine L. French, Gary G. Gibbs, and Beat A. Kumin, 203–16. Manchester: Manchester University Press, 1997.
Forker, Charles. "Webster or Shakespeare? Style, Idiom, Vocabulary, and Spelling in the Additions to *Sir Thomas More*." In *Shakespeare and* Sir Thomas More: *Essays on the Play and Its Shakesperian Interest*. Ed. T.H. Howard-Hill, 151–70. Cambridge: Cambridge University Press, 1989.
Forster, Leonard. *Janus Gruter's English Years: Studies in the Continuity of Dutch Literature in Exile in Elizabethan England*. London: Oxford University Press, 1967.
Foxe, John. *Acts and Monuments*. 12 vols. Albany, OR: Hartland Publications, 1997.
Frampton, Saul. "Who Edited Shakespeare?" *The Guardian*, 12 July 2013, http://www.theguardian.com/books/2013/jul/12/who-edited-shakespeare-john-florio.
Frances, Catherine. "Making Marriages in Early Modern England: Rethinking the Role of Family and Friends." In *The Marital Economy in Scandinavia and Britain, 1400–1900*. Ed. Maria Agren and Amy Louise Erickson, 39–56. Farnham: Ashgate, 2005.
Frazer, Paul. "Performing Places in Thomas Dekker's *Old Fortunatus*." *Philological Quarterly* 89.4 (2010): 457–80vi.
Freedman, Barbara. "Shakespearean Chronology, Ideological Complicity, and Floating Texts: Something Rotten in Windsor." *Shakespeare Quarterly* 45.2 (1994): 190–210.
Freedman, David N. "Acrostics and Metrics in Hebrew Poetry." *Harvard Theological Review* 65.3 (1972): 367–92.
Freeman, Arthur. "Marlowe, Kyd, and the Dutch Church Libel." *English Literary Renaissance* 3 (1973): 44–52.
Frere, Walter Howard, and Charles Edward Douglas. *Puritan Manifestoes: A Study of the Origins of the Puritan Revolt*. New York: B. Franklin, 1972.
Fuller, Thomas. *The Church History of Britain*. Vol. 3. London: Thomas Tegg and Son, 1837.
Gabrieli, Vittorio, and Giorgio Melchiori, eds. *Sir Thomas More: A Play by Anthony Munday, and Others*. Manchester, UK, and New York: Manchester University Press, 1990.

Galloway, David. *Norwich: 1540–1642*. Records of Early English Drama 5. Toronto: University of Toronto Press, 1984.
Galloway, James A. "Scottish Migration to England, 1400–1560." *Scottish Geographical Magazine* 112.1 (1996): 29–38.
Games, Alison. "England's Global Transition and the Cosmopolitans Who Made It Possible." *Shakespeare Studies* 35 (2007): 24–31.
Gaskill, Malcolm. *Crime and Mentalities in Early Modern England*. Cambridge: Cambridge University Press, 2000.
Gasper, Julia. *The Dragon and the Dove: The Plays of Thomas Dekker*. Oxford: Oxford University Press, 1990.
– "*The Noble Spanish Soldier, The Wonder of a Kingdom*, and *The Parliament of Bees*: A Belated Solution to This Long-Standing Dekker Problem." *Durham University Journal* 79.2 (1987): 223–32.
Geckle, George L. "John Marston." *Dictionary of Literary Biography*. Vol. 58: *Jacobean and Caroline Dramatists*. Ed. Fredson Bowers, 139–68. Madison, VA: Gale Group, 1987.
Geneva Bible. The Bible and Holy Scriptures. Geneva: Rouland Hall, 1560.
Gentili, Vanna. "A National Idiom and Other Languages: Notes on Elizabethan Ambivalence with Examples from Shakespeare." In *Italian Studies in Shakespeare and His Contemporaries*. Ed. Michele Marrapodi and Giorgio Melchiori, 187–205. Cranbury, NJ: University of Delaware Press, 1999.
Gibson, James M. "Shakespeare and the Cobham Controversy: The Oldcastle/Falstaff and Brooke/Broome Revisions." *Medieval and Renaissance Drama in England* 25 (2012): 94–132.
Giffone, Benjamin D. "A 'Perfect' Poem: The Use of the Qatal Verbal Form in the Biblical Acrostics." *Hebrew Studies* 51 (2010): 49–72.
Girard, René. *The Scapegoat*. Trans. Yvonne Freccero. Baltimore: Johns Hopkins University Press, 1986.
Glenn, John R. "The Martyrdom of Ramus in Marlowe's Massacre at Paris." *Papers on Language and Literature* 9 (1973): 365–79.
Golding, Arthur, trans. *The Edict or Proclamation Set For the by the Frenche Kinge vpon the Pacifying of the Troubles in Fraunce*. London: Thomas Vautrollier, 1576.
– *The Lyfe of the Mostly Godly, Valeant, and Noble Capteine and maintener of the Trew Christian Religion in Fraunce, Jasper Colignie Shatilion, Sometyme Greate Admirall of Fraunce*. London: Thomas Vautrollier, 1576.
Goodman, Godfrey. *The Fall of Man, or the Corruption of Nature, Proved by the Light of Our Naturall Reason*. London: Felix Kingston for Richard Lee, 1616.
Goose, Nigel. "The 'Dutch' in Colchester: The Economic Influence of an Immigrant Community in the Sixteenth and Seventeenth Centuries." *Immigrants and Minorities*. 1.3 (1982): 261–80.

– "Immigrants and English Economic Development in the Sixteenth and Early Seventeenth Centuries." In *Immigrants in Tudor and Early Stuart England*. Ed. Nigel Goose and Lien Bich Luu, 136–60. Brighton: Sussex Academic Press, 2005.
– "'Xenophobia' in Elizabethan and Early Stuart England: An Epithet Too Far." In *Immigrants in Tudor and Early Stuart England*. Ed. Nigel Goose and Lien Bich Luu, 110–35. Brighton: Sussex Academic Press, 2005.
Goose, Nigel, and Lien Bich Luu, eds. *Immigrants in Tudor and Early Stuart England*. Brighton: Sussex Academic Press, 2005.
Gosart, Alexander B. Introduction, *The Poems of John Marston*. Ed. Alexander Grosart, v–lv. Blackburn: Occasional Issues of Rare or Unique Books, 1879.
Grafton, Anthony and Joanna Weinberg. *"I Have Always Loved the Holy Tongue": Isaac Casaubon, The Jews, and a Forgotten Chapter in Renaissance Scholarship*. Cambridge, MA: Harvard University Press, 2011.
Grantley, Darryll. *English Dramatic Interludes, 1300–1580: A Reference Guide*. Cambridge and New York: Cambridge University Press, 2004.
– *Wit's Pilgrimage: Drama and the Social Impact of Education in Early Modern England*. Farnham: Ashgate, 2000.
The Grand Concern of England Explained in Several Proposals. London: 1673.
Greg, Walter William, ed. *The Book of Sir Thomas More*. Oxford: Malone Society Reprints, 1911.
Green, Martin. "Emilia Lanier IS the Dark Lady of the Sonnets." *English Studies* 87.5 (2006): 544–76.
Greenblatt, Stephen. "Murdering Peasants: Status, Genre, and the Representation of Rebellion." In *Learning to Curse: Essays in Early Modern Culture*, 99–130. New York: Routledge, 1990.
– *Will in the World: How Shakespeare Became Shakespeare*. New York and London: W.W. Norton, 2004.
Greene, Robert. *The Dramatic Works of Robert Greene* Vol. 2. Ed. Alexander Dyce. London: William Pickering, 1831.
Greenfeld, Liah. *Nationalism: Five Roads to Modernity*. Cambridge: Harvard University Press, 1992.
Grell, Ole Peter. *Calvinist Exiles in Tudor and Stuart England*. Farnham: Ashgate, 1996.
– *Dutch Calvinists in Early Stuart London: The Dutch Church in Austin Friars, 1603–1642*. Leiden and New York: E.J. Brill, 1989.
– "Exile and Tolerance." In *Tolerance and Intolerance in the European Reformation*. Ed. Ole Peter Grell and Bob Scribner, 164–81. Cambridge: Cambridge University Press, 1996.
Grévin, Jacques. *Jacques Grévin, 1538–1570*. Ed. Lucien Pinvert. Paris: Ancienne Librairie Thorin et Fils, 1899.

Griffiths, Jane. "Counterfeit Countenance: (Mis)representation and the Challenge to Allegory in Sixteenth-Century Morality Plays." *Yearbook of English Studies* 38.1–2 (2008): 17–33.
Gurr, Andrew. *Playgoing in Shakespeare's London*. Cambridge: Cambridge University Press, 1996.
Gwynn, Robin D. *Huguenot Heritage: The History and Contribution of the Huguenots in Britain*. London: Routledge, 1985.
Habib, Imtiaz. *Black Lives in the English Archives, 1500–1677*. Farnham: Ashgate, 2008.
Hadfield, Andrew. *Edmund Spenser's Irish Experience: 'Wild Fruite and Savage Soyl.'* Oxford: Oxford University Press, 1997.
– *Literature, Politics and National Identity: Reformation to Renaissance*. Cambridge: Cambridge University, 1994.
Hadfield, Andrew, and John McVeagh, eds. *Strangers to That Land: British Perceptions of Ireland from the Reformation to the Famine*. Gerrards Cross: Colin Smythe, 1994.
Halasz, Alexandra. *The Marketplace of Print: Pamphlets and the Public Sphere in Early Modern England*. Cambridge: Cambridge University Press, 1997.
Hall, Edward. *The Lives of the Kings: The Triumphant Reign of Henry VIII*. Vol. 1. Ed. Charles Whibley. London: T.C. & E.C. Jack, 1904.
Halley, Janet E. "Heresy, Orthodoxy, and the Politics of Religious Discourse: The Case of the English Family of Love." *Representations* 15 (1986): 98–120.
Hamilton, Alastair. *The Family of Love*. Cambridge, UK: James Clarke, 1981.
Hamlin, William M. "Common Customers in Marston's Dutch *Courtesan* and Florio's Montaigne." *Studies in English Literature 1500–1900* 52.2 (2012): 407–24.
Hammer, Paul E. J. *The Polarisation of Elizabethan Politics: The Political Career of Robert Devereux, 2nd Earl of Essex, 1585–1597*. Cambridge: Cambridge University Press, 1999.
Hankins, Jeffrey R. "Crown, County, and Corporation in Seventeenth-Century Essex." *The Sixteenth Century Journal* 38.1 (2007): 27–47.
Hardin, Richard F. "Marlowe Thinking Globally." In *Christopher Marlowe, the Craftsman: Lives, Stage, and Page*. Ed. Sarah K. Scott and M.L. Stapleton, 23–32. Farnham: Ashgate, 2010.
Hardy, William J. "Foreign Refugees at Rye." *Proceedings of the Huguenot Society of London* 2 (1886–7): 406–27.
– "Foreign Settlers and Colcheser and Halstead." *Proceedings of the Huguenot Society of London* 2 (1887–8): 182–96.
Harmer, James. "Toying with Religion in the Prologue to *The Jew of Malta*." *Notes and Queries* 57 (255), no. 3 (September 2010): 352–5.

Harris, Barbara J. *English Aristocratic Women, 1450–1550: Marriage and Family, Property and Careers*. Oxford: Oxford University Press, 2002.
Harris, Frank. *My Life and Loves*. New York: Grove Press, 1963.
Harvey, Gabriel. *The Works of Gabriel Harvey*. Vol. 1. Ed. Alexander Balloch Grosart. London: Hazell, Watson, and Viney, 1884.
Haselkorn, Anne M. *Prostitution in Elizabethan and Jacobean Comedy*. Troy, NY: Whitson Press, 1983.
Hastings, Anthony. *The Construction of Nationhood: Ethnicity, Religion and Nationalism*. Cambridge: Cambridge University Press, 1997.
Hauben, Paul J. "A Spanish Calvinist Church in Elizabethan London, 1559–65." *Church History* 34.1 (1965): 50–65.
Haughton, William. *Englishmen for My Money*. In *Three Renaissance Usury Plays*. Ed. Lloyd Edward Kermode. Manchester, UK: Manchester University Press, 2009.
Haynes, Alan. "Italian Immigrants in England, 1558–1603." *History Today* 27.8 (1977): 485–534.
Hays, Michael L. "Shakespeare's Hand in *Sir Thomas More:* Some Aspects of the Palaeographic Argument." *Shakespeare Studies* 8 (1975): 241–53.
Heal, Felicity. *Hospitality in Early Modern England*. Oxford: Clarendon Press, 1990.
Helgerson, Richard. *Forms of Nationhood: The Elizabethan Writing of England*. Chicago: University of Chicago Press, 1992.
– *Adulterous Alliances: Home, State, and History in Early Modern European Drama and Painting*. Chicago: University of Chicago Press, 2003.
Henslowe, Philip. *The Diary of Philip Henslowe from 1591 to 1611*. Ed. J. Payne Collier. London: Shakespeare Society, 1845.
Hentschell, Roze. *The Culture of Cloth in Early Modern England: Textual Construction of a National Identity*. Aldershot, UK: Ashgate, 2008.
Hessels, Joannes Henricus. *Ecclesiae Londino-Batavae Archivum*. 3 vols. Cambridge: Typis Academiae, 1887–97.
Highley, Christopher. *Catholics Writing the Nation in Early Modern Britain and Ireland*. Oxford: Oxford University Press, 2008.
Hill, Tracey. "'The Cittie is in an uproare': Staging London in *The Booke of Sir Thomas More*." *Early Modern Literary Studies* 11.1 (May 2005) 2.1–19. http://purl.oclc.org/emls/11-1/more.htm.
Hobsbawm, Eric J. *Nations and Nationalism since 1780*. Cambridge: Cambridge University Press, 1990.
Hoenselaars, A.J. *Images of Englishmen and Foreigners in the Drama of Shakespeare and His Contemporaries*. Rutherford, NJ: Farleigh Dickinson University Press, 1992.

Holmes, Martin. "Evil May-Day, 1517: The Story of a Riot." *History Today* 15 (1965): 642–50.
Holt, Mack P. *The French Wars of Religion, 1562–1629*. Cambridge: Cambridge University Press, 2005.
Holthausen, Ferdinand. Einleitung to An Interlude of Welth and Helth: *Eine Englische Moralität des XVI. Jahrhundrets*. 53–66. Kiel: Universität Kiel, 1908.
Honan, Park. *Shakespeare: A Life*. Oxford: Oxford University Press, 1998.
Honigmann, E.A.J. "*The Play of Sir Thomas More* and Some Contemporary Events." *Shakespeare Survey* 42 (1990): 77–87.
– "Shakespeare and London's Immigrant Community circa 1600." *Elizabethan and Modern Studies, Presented to Professor Willem Schrickx on the Occasion of His Retirement*. Ed. J.P. Vander Motten, 143–53. Gent: Seminarie voor Engelse en Amerikaanse Literatuur, R.U.G., 1985.
Hopkins, Chris. "Review of *Sir Thomas More,* by Anthony Munday, William Shakespeare and Others." *Early Modern Literary Studies* 11.2 (September 2005) 13.1–6. http://purl.oclc.org/emls/11-2/revmore.htm.
Hotman, Francois. *A True and Plaine Report of the Furious and Outrages of Fraunce*. Trans. Ernest Varamund. Striveling, Scotland, 1573.
Hotson, Leslie. *Shakespeare's Sonnets Dated and Other Essays*. New York: Oxford University Press, 1949.
Howard, Jean. "Shakespeare and the London City Comedy." *Shakespeare Studies* 39 (2001): 1–21.
– *Theater of a City: The Places of London Comedy, 1598–1642*. Philadelphia: University Pennsylvania Press, 2009.
Howard, Jean E., and Phyllis Rackin. *Engendering a Nation: A Feminist Account of Shakespeare's English Histories*. London: Routledge, 1997.
Howarth, R.G. *Two Elizabethan Writers of Fiction: Thomas Nashe and Thomas Deloney*. Cape Town: Editorial Board of the University of Cape Town, 1956.
Howard-Hill, T.H., ed. *Shakespeare and* Sir Thomas More: *Essays on the Play and Its Shakesperian Interest*. Cambridge: Cambridge University Press, 1989.
Hughes, Paul L., and James F. Larkin, eds. *Tudor Royal Proclamations*. 3 vols. New Haven: Yale University Press, 1964–9.
Hunt, Alice. *The Drama of Coronation: Medieval Ceremony in Early Modern England*. Cambridge: Cambridge University Press, 2008.
Hunt, Mary Leland. *Thomas Dekker, A Study*. New York: Russell and Russell, 1964.
Hunt, Simon. "'Leaving out the insurrection': Carnival Rebellion, English History Plays, and a Hermeneutics of Advocacy." In *Renaissance Culture and the Everyday*. Ed. Patricia Fumerton and Simon Hunt, 299–314. Philadelphia: University of Pennsylvania, 1999.

Hunter, Mark. "Notes on the *Interlude of Wealth and Health.*" *Modern Language Review* 3.4 (1907): 366–9.
Huygens, Constantijn. *A Selection of the Poems of Sir Constantijn Huygens (1596–1687).* Trans. Peter Davidson and Adriaan van de Weel. Amsterdam: Amsterdam University Press, 1996.
Interlude of Wealth and Health, The. Ed. W.W. Greg. Malone Society Reprints. London: Chiswick Press, 1907.
Israel, Jonathan I. *The Dutch Republic: Its Rise: Its Rise, Greatness, and Fall, 1477–1806.* Oxford: Oxford University Press, 1995.
Ivic, Christopher. "Mapping British Identities: Speed's *Theatre of the Empire of Great Britain.*" In *British Identities and English Renaissance Literature*. Ed. David J. Baker and Willy Maley, 135–55. Cambridge: Cambridge University Press, 2002.
Iwasaki, Soji. "Rough Music and Deer's Horn in *The Merry Wives of Windsor.*" *Shakespeare Studies* (Shakespeare Society of Japan) 37 (1999): 1–20.
Jackson, Macdonald P. "Is 'Hand D' of *Sir Thomas More* Shakespeare's? Thomas Bayes and the Elliott-Valenza Authorship Tests." *Early Modern Literary Studies* 12.3 (2007): 1: 1–36. http://purl.oclc.org/emls/12-3.jackbaye.htm.
Jacquot, Jean. "Acontius and the Progress of Tolerance in England." *Bibliothèque d'Humanisme et Renaissance* 16.2 (1954): 192–206.
James I. *Basilikon Doron.* London: Felix Kyngston for John Norton, 1603.
– *The Essayes of a Prentise in the Divine Art of Poesie.* Edinburgh: Thomas Vautrollier, 1584.
Jonassen, Frederick B. "The Stag Hunt in *The Merry Wives of Winsdor.*" *Bestia: Yearbook of the Beast Fable Society* 3 (1991): 87–101.
Jones, Ernest. *The Life and Work of Sigmund Freud.* Vol. 1. New York: Hogarth, 1953.
Jones, J. Gwynfor. *Wales and the Tudor State.* Cardiff: University of Wales Press, 1989.
Jones-Davies, Marie-Therese. *Un Peintre de la Vie Londonienne: Thomas Dekker.* 2 vols. Paris: Collection des Études Anglaises, 1958.
Josephus, Flavius. *The Famous and Memorable Workes of Josephus.* Trans. Thomas Lodge. London: George Bishop, 1602.
Jowett, John. "Henry Chettle and the Original Text of *Sir Thomas More.*" In *Shakespeare and* Sir Thomas More: *Essays on the Play and Its Shakesperian Interest.* Ed. T.H. Howard-Hill, 131–49. Cambridge: Cambridge University Press, 1989.
Kastan, David Scott. "Workshop and/as Playhouse." In *Staging the Renaissance: Reinterpretations of Elizabethan and Jacobean Drama.* Ed. David Scott Kastan and Peter Stallybrass, 151–63. New York and London: Routledge, 1991.

Kelley, Nicole. "The Cosmopolitan Expression of Josephus's Prophetic Perspective in the Jewish War." *Harvard Theological Review* 97.3 (2004): 257–74.

Kelly, Donald R. "Martyrs, Myths, and Massacre: The Background of St. Bartholomew." *American Historical Review* 77.5 (1972): 1323–42.

Kermode, Lloyd Edward. *Aliens and Englishness in Elizabethan Drama*. Cambridge: Cambridge University Press, 2009.

– Introduction to *Three Renaissance Usury Plays*. Ed. Lloyd Edward Kermode, 1–78. Manchester: Manchester University Press, 2009.

Kerridge, Eric. *Textile Manufactures in Early Modern England*. Manchester, UK: Manchester University Press, 1985.

Keyishian, Harry. "Dekker's *Whore* and Marston's *Courtesan*." *English Language Notes* 4 (1967): 261–6.

Kidd, Colin. *British Identities before Nationalism: Ethnicity and Nationhood in the Atlantic World, 1600–1800*. Cambridge: Cambridge University Press, 1999.

Kiernan, Pauline. *Filthy Shakespeare: Shakespeare's Most Outrageous Sexual Puns*. New York: Gotham Books, 2006.

Kim, Keechang. *Aliens in Medieval Law: The Origins of Modern Citizenship*. Cambridge: Cambridge University Press, 2001.

Kingdon, Robert. *Myths about the St. Bartholomew's Day Massacre, 1572–1576*. Cambridge, MA: Harvard University Press, 1988.

Kinney, Arthur, F., ed. *Renaissance Drama, an Anthology of Plays and Entertainments*. Oxford: Blackwell Publishers, 1999.

Kirk, Andrew M. "Marlowe and the Disordered Face of French History." *SEL: Studies in English Literature 1500–1900* 35.2 (1995): 193–213.

Kirk, R.E.G., and Ernest Kirk, eds. *Returns of Aliens Dwelling in the City and Suburbs of London, 1525–1571*. Huguenot Society of London. Aberdeen: University Press, 1900.

Kirwood, A.E.M. "Richard Field, Printer." *The Library: Quarterly Review of Bibliography*, series 4, vol. 12 (1932): 1–27.

Kittredge, George L. "The Date of *The Pedler's Prophecy*." *Harvard Studies and Notes in Philology* 16 (1934): 97–118.

Knighton, C.S. "Baro, Peter (1534–1599)." In *Oxford Dictionary of National Biography*. Ed. H.C.G. Matthew and Brian Harrison. Oxford: Oxford University Press, 2004. Online edition, ed. Lawrence Goldman, Sept. 2010.

Kocher, Paul H. "Contemporary Pamphlet Backgrounds for Marlowe's *The Massacre at Paris*." *Modern Language Quarterly* 8 (1947): 151–73 and 309–18.

– "François Hotman and Marlowe's *The Massacre at Paris*." *PMLA* 56.2 (1941): 349–68.

Kramnick, Jonathan Brody. "The Making of the English Canon." *PMLA* 112.5 (1997): 1087–1101.

Krantz, Susan. "Thomas Dekker's Political Commentary in *The Whore of Babylon*." *Studies in English Literature* 35.2 (1995): 271–91.
Kuehn, George W. "Thomas Deloney: Two Notes." *Modern Language Notes* 52.2 (1937): 103–5.
Kuriyama, Constance Brown. *Christopher Marlowe: A Renaissance Life*. Ithaca: Cornell University Press, 2002.
Ladd, Roger A. "Thomas Deloney and the London Weavers' Company." *The Sixteenth Century Journal* 32.4 (Winter 2001): 981–1001.
Lake, David J. "The Date of the *Sir Thomas More* Additions by Dekker and Shakespeare." *Notes and Queries* 24 (1977): 114–16.
Lanquet, Thomas. *An epitome of chronicles Conteyninge the whole discourse of the histories as well of this realme of England, as al other cou[n]treys, with the succession of their kinges, the time of their reigne, and what notable actes they did [etc]*. London: William Seres, 1559.
Lart, Charles E. "The Huguenot Settlements and Churches in the West of England." *Proceedings of the Huguenot Society of London* 7 (1901–4): 286–303.
Lart, Charles E., ed. *Registers of the French Churches of Bristol, Stonehouse, and Plymouth*. Publications of the Huguenot Society of London, Vol. 20. London: Spottiswoode, 1912.
Laslett, Peter. *The World We Have Lost: England before the Industrial Age*. New York: Charles Scribner's Sons, 1965.
Lawlis, Merritt E. *Apology for the Middle Class: The Dramatic Novels of Thomas Deloney*. Bloomington: Indiana University Press, 1960.
– Introduction to *The Novels of Thomas Deloney*. Bloomington: Indiana University Press, 1961.
Leinwand, Theodore B. *The City Staged: Jacobean Comedy, 1603–1613*. Madison: University of Wisconsin Press, 1986.
Letters and Papers, Foreign and Domestic of the Reign of Henry VIII. Vol. 4.2. Ed. J.S. Brewer. London: Longman and Co., and Trubner and Co., Paternoster Row, 1872.
Levine, Nina. "Citizen's Games: Differentiating Collaboration in *Sir Thomas More*." *Shakespeare Quarterly* 58.1 (2007): 31–64.
Lewis, C.S. *The Allegory of Love: A Study in Medieval Tradition*. London, Oxford, and New York: Oxford University Press, 1973.
Light, George Evans. "All Hopped Up: Beer, Cultivated National Identity, and Anglo-Dutch Relations, 1524–1625." *Journal X* 2.2 (1998): 159–78.
Lindeboom, Johannes. *Austin Friars: History of the Dutch Reformed Church in London, 1550-1950*. The Hague: Martinus Nijhoff, 1950.
Lipson, Ephraim. *The Economic History of England*. Vol. 2. New York: Barnes and Noble, 1959.

Littleton, Charles Galton. "Geneva on Threadneedle Street: The French Church of London and Its Congregation, 1560–1625." Dissertation. University of Michigan, 1995.
- "Social Interaction of Aliens in Late Elizabethan London: Evidence from the 1593 Return and the French Church Consistory 'Actes.'" In *The Strangers' Progress: Integration and Disintegration of the Huguenot and Walloon Refugee Community, 1567–1889. Essays in Memory of Irene Scouloudi.* Ed. Randolph Vigne and Graham C. Gibbs, 147–59. London: Huguenot Society of Great Britain and Ireland, 1995.

Lloyd, T.H. *England and the German Hanse, 1157–1611.* London: Macmillan, 1991.

Loades, David M. "The Press under the Early Tudors: A Study of Censorship and Sedition." *Transactions of the Cambridge Bibliographic Society.* 4.1 (1964): 29–50.
- *The Reign of Mary Tudor: Politics, Government and Religion in England, 1553–58.* London and New York: Longman, 1991.

"London's Praise, or, the Glory of the City." In *The Pepys Ballads,* vol. 3. Ed. W.G. Day. Wolfboro, NH: D.S. Brewer 1991.

Long, William B. "The Occasion of *The Book of Sir Thomas More.*" In *Shakespeare and* Sir Thomas More: *Essays on the Play and Its Shakesperian Interest.* Ed. T.H. Howard-Hill, 45–56. Cambridge: Cambridge University Press, 1989.

Loomba, Ania. *Gender, Race, Renaissance Drama.* Manchester University Press, 1989.
- "'Local-Manufacture Made-In-India Othello Fellows': Issues of Race, Hybridity, and Location in Post-Colonial Shakesepares." In *Post-Colonial Shakespeares.* Ed. Ania Loomba and Martin Orkin, 143–63. London: Routledge, 1998.

Luu, Lien Bich. "Alien Communities in Transition, 1570–1650." In *Immigrants in Tudor and Early Stuart England.* Ed. Nigel Goose and Lien Bich Luu, 192–210. Brighton: Sussex Academic Press, 2005.
- "Assimilation or Segregation: Colonies of Alien Craftsmen in Elizabethan London." In *The Strangers' Progress: Integration and Disintegration of the Huguenot and Walloon Refugee Community, 1567–1889. Essays in Memory of Irene Scouloudi.* Ed. Randolph Vigne and Graham C. Gibbs, 160–72. London: Huguenot Society of Great Britain and Ireland, 1995.
- *Immigrants and the Industries of London, 1500–1700.* Farnham: Ashgate, 2005.
- "'Taking the Bread Out of Our Mouths': Xenophobia in Early Modern London. *Immigrants and Minorities* 19.2 (July 2000): 1–22.

Mac Cuarta, Brian, ed. *Reshaping Ireland, 1550–1700: Colonization and its Consequences.* Dublin: Four Courts Press, 2011.

Machyn, Henry. *The Diary of Henry Machyn, Citizen and Merchant-Taylor of London, from A.D. 1550 to A.D. 1563.* Ed. John Gough Nichols. Camden Society, New York: AMS Press, 1968.
Mackerness, Eric D. "Thomas Deloney and the Virtuous Proletariat." *The Cambridge Journal* 5.1 (1951): 34–50.
Magen, Beate. "The Administration of the Walloon Settlement in Canterbury 1576–1599." *Proceedings of the Huguenot Society of London* 22 (1970–76): 307–17.
Maley, Willy. "'And bloody England into England gone': Empire, Monarchy, and Nation in *King John*." In *This England, That Shakespeare: New Angles on Englishness and the Bard*. Ed. Willy Maley and Margaret Tudeau-Clayton, 49–62. Farnham: Ashgate, 2010.
– *Nation, State and Empire in English Renaissance Literature: Shakespeare to Milton*. New York: Palgrave/Macmillan, 2003.
Maley, Willy, and Philip Schwyzer, eds. *Shakespeare and Wales: From the Marches to the Assembly*. Farnham: Ashgate, 2010.
Malfatti, C.V., ed. and trans. *Two Italian Accounts of Tudor England: A Journey to London In 1497; A Picture of English Life under Queen Mary*. Barcelona: Itinerarium Britanniae, 1953.
Mann, Francis O. Introduction. *The Works of Thomas Deloney*. Oxford: Clarendon Press, 1912.
Manning, Roger. *Village Revolts: Social Protest and Popular Disturbances in England, 1509–1640*. Oxford: Oxford University Press, 1988.
Marcus, Leah. *Unediting the Renaissance: Shakespeare, Marlowe, Milton*. London: Routledge, 1996.
Mares, Francis Hugh. "The Origin of the Figure Called 'the Vice' in Tudor Drama." *Huntington Library Quarterly* 22.1 (1958): 11–29.
Margolies, David. *Novel and Society in Elizabethan England*. London and Sydney: Croom Helm, 1985.
Marlowe, Christopher. *The Complete Plays*. Ed. Irving Ribner. New York: Odyssey Press, 1963.
Marotti, Arthur F. "Shakespeare and Catholicism." In *Theatre and Religion: Lancastrian Shakespeare*. Ed. Richard Dutton, Alison Gail Findlay, and Richard Wilson, 218–41. Manchester: Manchester University Press, 2004.
Marsh, Christopher. *The Family of Love in English Society: 1550–1630*. Cambridge: Cambridge University Press, 1994.
Marston, John. *The Dutch Courtesan*. Ed. David Crane. New York: Norton, 1997.
Martin, Randall. "Anne Dowriche's *The French Historie* and Innocent Gentillet's *Contre-Machiavel*." *Notes and Queries* 44.1 (1997): 40–2.

- "Anne Dowriche's *The French History*, Christopher Marlowe, and Machiavellian Agency." *SEL: Studies in English Literature 1500–1900* 39.1 (1999): 69–87.
Maruyama, Tadataka. *The Ecclesiology of Theodore Beza: The Reform of the True Church*. Geneva: Droz, 1978.
Marx, Karl, and Frederick Engels. *The Collected Works of Karl Marx and Frederick Engels*. Vol. 11. New York: International Publishers, 1979.
- *The Collected Works of Karl Marx and Frederick Engels*. Vol. 42. New York: International Publishers, 1988.
- *Marx and Engels on Literature and Art*. Progress Publishers: Moscow, 1976.
Masten, Jeffrey. "More or Less: Editing the Collaborative." *Shakespeare Studies* 29 (2001): 109–31.
Matchinske, Megan. *Women Writing History in Early Modern England*. Cambridge: Cambridge University Press, 2009.
Mathur, Maya. "An Attack of the Clowns: Comedy, Vagrancy, and the Elizabethan History Play." *The Journal for Early Modern Cultural Studies* 7.1 (2007): 33–54.
McCall, R.A. "The Huguenot in Kent." *Proceedings of the Huguenot Society of London* 12 (1924–29): 18–36.
McEachern, Claire. *The Poetics of English Nationhood, 1590–1612*. Cambridge: Cambridge University Press, 1996.
McCluskey, Peter M. "'Shall I Betray My Brother?' Anti-Alien Satire and Its Subversion in *The Shoemaker's Holiday*." *Tennessee Philological Bulletin: Proceedings of the Annual Meeting of the Tennessee Philological Association* 37 (2000): 43–54.
McMillin, Scott. "*The Book of Sir Thomas More:* Dates and Acting Companies." In *Shakespeare and* Sir Thomas More: *Essays on the Play and Its Shakesperian Interest.* Ed. T.H. Howard-Hill, 57–76. Cambridge: Cambridge University Press, 1989.
McGurk, John. *The Elizabethan Conquest of Ireland: The 1590s Crisis.* London: St. Martin's Press, 1997.
Mealor, Simon. "*O Belle Tamise*: The Development of a Huguenot Pastoral Mode in Elizabethan England." In *Archipelagic Identities: Literature and Identity in the Atlantic Archipelago, 1550–1800.* Ed. Philip Schwyzer and Simon Mealor, 180–194. Aldershot, UK: Ashgate, 2004.
Melchiori, Giorgio. "*The Book of Sir Thomas More*: Dramatic Unity." In *Shakespeare and* Sir Thomas More: *Essays on the Play and Its Shakesperian Interest.* Ed. T.H. Howard-Hill, 77–100. Cambridge: Cambridge University Press, 1989.
- "*The Booke of Sir Thomas Moore:* A Chronology of Revision." *Shakespeare Quarterly* 37 (1986): 291–308.

- "Hand D in *Sir Thomas More*: An Essay in Misinterpretation." *Shakespeare Survey* 38 (1985): 101–14.
- "The Master of the Revels and the Date of the Additions to *The Book of Sir Thomas More*." In *Shakespeare: Text, Language, Criticism. Essays in Honour of Marvin Spevack*. Ed. Bernhard Fabian, 164–79. Zurich: Olms-Weidmann, 1987.

Mendel, Jolene. *Christopher Marlowe*. Lulu Publishing, 2008.

Merriam, Thomas. "The Authorship of *Sir Thomas More*." *ALLC Bulletin* 10.1 (1982): 1–7.

- "Did Munday Compose Sir Thomas More?" *Notes and Queries* 37 (1990): 175–8.
- "Some Further Evidence for Shakespeare's Authorship of Hand D *in Sir Thomas More*." *Notes and Queries* 53 (2006): 65–6.

Metz, G. Harold. "'Voice and Credyt': The Scholars and *Sir Thomas More*." In *Shakespeare and* Sir Thomas More: *Essays on the Play and Its Shakesperian Interest*. Ed. T.H. Howard-Hill, 11–44. Cambridge: Cambridge University Press, 1989.

Middleton, Sir Henry. *The Last East-Indian Voyage*. London: Thomas Purfoot for Walter Burre, 1606.

Middleton, Thomas. *Thomas Middleton: The Collected Works*. Ed. Gary Taylor and John Lavagnino. Oxford: Oxford University Press, 2007.

Modood, Tariq. *Multiculturalism: A Civic Idea*. New York: Polity Press, 2007.

Moens, W.J.C. *The Walloons and their Church at Norwich, 1565–1832*. Lymington: Huguenot Society of London, 1887–8.

Montgomery, Marianne. *Europe's Languages on England's Stages, 1590–1620*. Farnham: Ashgate, 2012.

Montrose, Louis. *The Subject of Elizabeth: Authority, Gender, and Representation*. Chicago: University of Chicago Press, 2006.

Morant, Valerie. "The Settlement of Protestant Refugees in Maidstone during the Sixteenth Century." *Economic History Review* 4 (1951): 210–14.

More, Sir Thomas. *Utopia*. Trans. Ralph Robynson. 1551. Cambridge: Cambridge University Press, 1956.

Mortenson, Peter. "The Economics of Joy in *The Shoemakers' Holiday*." *SEL: Studies in English Literature, 1500–1900* 16.2 (1976): 241–52.

Moss, Jean Dietz. "Variations on a Theme: The Family of Love in Renaissance England." *Renaissance Quarterly* 31.2 (1978): 186–95.

Mulcaster, Richard. *The Queen's Majesty's Passage*. In *Renaissance Drama: An Anthology of Plays and Entertainements*. Ed. Arthur F. Kinney, 243–86. Malden, MA: Blackwell, 2001.

Mullaney, Steven. *The Place of the Stage: License, Play and Power in Renaissance England*. Chicago: University of Chicago, 1988.

Nashe, Thomas. *Have with you to Saffron Walden.* Menston: Scolar Press, 1971.
Neale, Jennifer E. *Elizabeth I and Her Parliaments, 1559–1581.* New York: St Martin's Press, 1958.
Neville, Alexander. *Norfolkes Furies, or a View of Ketts Campe.* London: Printed by William Stansby for Edmund Casson, 1615.
A New Interlude No Lesse Wittie than Pleasant, Entitled New Custom. London: William How for Abraham Veale, 1573.
Newman, Karen. *Essaying Shakespeare.* Minneapolis: University of Minnesota Press, 2009.
Nicholl, Charles. *The Lodger Shakespeare: His Life on Silver Street.* New York: Viking, 2007.
Nolan, John S. *Sir John Norreys and the Elizabethan Military World.* Exeter, UK: University of Exeter Press, 1997.
Nicol, David. "Citizens, Gentry, and the Double Ending of Rowley and Middleton's *A Fair Quarrel.*" *Studies in English Literature* 51.2 (2011): 427–45.
Nicoll, Allardyce. *The World of Harlequin: A Critical Study of the Commedia Dell' Arte.* Cambridge: Cambridge University Press, 1963.
Norman, Charles. *The Muses' Darling: Christopher Marlowe.* New York: Macmillan, 1960.
Norwood, Frederick Abbott. *Strangers and Exiles: A History of Religious Refugees.* Nashville: Abingdon Press, 1969.
Novarr, David. "Dekker's Gentle Craft and the Lord Mayor of London." *Modern Philology* 57 (1960): 233–9.
Oakley, Anne M. "The Canterbury Walloon Congregation from Elizabeth I to Laud." In *Huguenots in Britain and Their French Background, 1550–1800.* Ed. Irene Scouloudi, 56–71. Totowa, NJ: Barnes and Noble Books, 1987.
O'Malley, Charles Donald. *Jacopo Acontio Traduzione di Delio Cantimori Uomini e Dottrine.* Rome: Edizioni di Storia e Letteratura 1955.
Oosterhoff, F.G. *Leicester and the Netherlands, 1586–87.* HES Publishers, 1988.
Osherow, Michelle. *Biblical Women's Voices in Early Modern England.* Farnham: Ashgate, 2009.
Overbury, Sir Thomas. *New and Choise Characters Together with That Exquisite and Unmacht Poem, The Wife.* London: Thomas Creede, 1615.
Owen, Richard. "Shakespeare? He's one of us, say Italians." *The Times.* 8 April 2000.
Owens, W.R., and P.N. Furbank. "Defoe and the Dutch Alliance: Some Attributions Examined." *British Journal for Eighteenth-Century Studies* 9.2 (1986): 169–82.
Ozment, Steven. *Ancestors: The Loving Family in Old Europe.* Cambridge: Harvard University Press, 2001.

Page, William. Preface to *Letters of Denization and Acts of Naturalization for Aliens, 1509–1603.* Publications of the Huguenot Society of London vol 8. Lymington, UK: 1893.

Page, William, ed. *Letters of Denization and Acts of Naturalization for Aliens in England, 1550–1607.* Lymington, England: Printed for the Huguenot Society of London by C.T. King, 1891.

Palmer, Patricia. *Language and Conquest in Early Modern Ireland: Renaissance Literature and Elizabethan Imperial Expansion.* Cambridge: Cambridge University Press, 2001.

Parham, David. "The Mobilisation of Troops for Cross Channel Transportation: Norrey's Men, Brittany, July–December 1592." In *A Ship Cast Away about Alderney: Investigations of an Elizabethan Shipwreck.* Ed. Mensun Bound and Jason Monaghan, 157–64. Alderney: Alderney Maritime Trust, 2001.

Parker, Charles H. "To the Attentive, Nonparitsan Reader: The Appeal to History and National Identity in the Religious Disputes of the Seventeenth-Century Netherlands." *The Sixteenth Century Journal* 28.1 (1997): 57–78.

Parker, Geoffrey. *The Dutch Revolt.* Ithaca: Cornell University Press, 1977.

– *The Thirty Years' War.* New York: Military Heritage Press, 1988.

Parker, Patricia. *Shakespeare from the Margins: Language, Culture, Context.* Chicago: University of Chicago Press, 1996.

– "Temporal Gestation, Legal Contracts, and the Promissory Economics of *The Winter's Tale.*" In *Women, Property, and the Letters of the Law in Early Modern England.* Ed. Andrew Buck, Margaret Ferguson, and Nancy E. Wright, 25–49. Toronto: University of Toronto Press, 2004.

Parks, George B. "The First Italianate Englishmen." *Studies in the Renaissance* 8 (1961): 197–216.

Partridge, Eric. *Shakespeare's Bawdy.* New York: Routledge, 1968.

Patterson, W. Brown. "James I and the Huguenot Synod of Tonneins of 1614." *The Harvard Theological Review* 65.2 (1972): 241–70.

Pätzold, Kurt-Michael. "Thomas Deloney and the English Jest-Book Tradition." *English Studies* 53.4 (1972): 313–28.

The Pedlers Prophecie. London: Thomas Creede, 1595.

Pender, Patricia. *Early Modern Women's Writing and the Rhetoric of Modesty.* New York: Palgrave/Macmillan, 2012.

Perfect, Tim. "Re: SHK 10.0113 Spear-shaking." Online posting. 22 January 1999.

Pettegree, Andrew. *Emden and the Dutch Revolt: Exile and the Development of Reformed Protestantism.* Oxford: Oxford University Press, 1992.

– *Foreign Protestant Communities in Sixteenth-Century London.* Oxford: Clarendon Press, 1986.

- "The Stranger Community in Marian London." *Proceedings of the Huguenot Society* 24.5 (1987): 390–402.
- "'Thirty Years On': Progress toward Integration amongst the Immigrant Population of Elizabethan London." In *English Rural Society, 1500–1800: Essays in Honour of Joan Thirsk*. Ed. John Chartres and David Hey, 297–312. Cambridge: Cambridge University Press, 1990.

Pfister, Manfred. "*Inglese Italianato – Italiano Anglizzato*: John Florio." In *Renaissance Go-Betweens: A Cultural Exchange in Early Modern Europe*. Ed. Andreas Höfele and Werner von Koppenfels. 32–54. Berlin: Walter de Gruyter, 2005.

Pinciss, G.M. "Marlowe's Cambridge Years and the Writing of *Doctor Faustus*." *Studies in English Literature, 1500–1900* 33.2 (1993): 249–64.

Pincus, Steven C.A. "From Butterboxes to Wooden Shoes: The Shift in Popular Sentiment from Anti-Dutch to Anti-French in the 1670s." *The Historical Journal* 38.2 (1995): 333–61.

Pineas, Rainer. "The Revision of *Wealth and Health*." *Philological Quarterly* 44 (1965): 560–2.

Platt, Jasper, Jr. "'Drowse'=Devil." *Notes and Queries* 116 (6 July 1907): 6.

Plomer, Henry. "An Exeter Bookseller, His Friends and Contemporaries." *The Library: The Transactions of the Bibliographical Society* 3.8 (1917): 128–35.

Plummer, Alfred. *The London Weavers' Company, 1600–1970*. London and Boston: Routledge, 1972.

Pollard, Alfred W. Introduction to *Shakespeare's Hand in the Play of Sir Thomas More*. Ed. Alfred W. Pollard and John Dover Wilson, 1–36. Cambridge: University Press, 1923.

Pollard, Alfred W., and John Dover Wilson, eds. *Shakespeare's Hand in the Play of Sir Thomas More*. Cambridge: University Press, 1923.

Pollitt, Ronald. "'Refuge of the Distressed Nations': Perceptions of Aliens in Elizabethan England." *The Journal of Modern History* 52.1. On demand supplement (1980): D1001–D1019.v.

Pollock, Linda. *Forgotten Children: Parent–Child Relations from 1500–1900*. Cambridge: Cambridge University Press, 1983.

- "Parent-Child Relations." In *Family Life in Early Modern Times, 1500–1789*. Ed. David I. Kertzer and Mazio Barbagli, 191–220. New Haven: Yale University Press, 2011.
- "The Practice of Kindness in Early Modern Elite Society." *Past and Present* 211.1 (2011): 121–58.

Poole, Kristen. "*Dr. Faustus* and Reformation Theology." In *Early Modern English Drama: A Critical Companion*. Ed. Garrett A. Sullivan, 96–107. Oxford: Oxford University Press, 2005.

Portal, William W. "Address to the Twenty-Sixth Annual General Meeting of the Huguenot Society of London." *Proceedings of the Huguenot Society of London* 9.2 (1910): 136–44.
Prak, Maarten. *The Dutch Republic in the Seventeenth Century*. Cambridge: Cambridge University Press, 2005.
Prescott, Anne Lake. "English Writers and Beza's Latin Epigrams: The Uses and Abuses of Poetry." *Studies in the Renaissance* 21 (1974): 83–117.
Prestwich, Menna. "Calvinism in France, 1555–1629." In *International Calvinism 1541–1715*. Ed. Menna Prestwich, 71–107. Oxford: Clarendon Press, 1985.
Prior, Roger. "A Second Jewish Community in Tudor London." *Jewish Historical Studies* 31 (1988–90): 137–52.
Proctor, John. *The historie of wyates rebellion with the order and maner of resisting the same, wherunto in the ende is added an earnest conference with the degenerate and sedicious rebelles for the serche of the cause of their daily disorder*. London: Robert Caly, 1555.
Quinn, Robert. Respondent. "What's New in Arcadia? Property, Dissonance, and Naming." 41st Annual International Congress on Medieval Studies. Kalamazoo, MI, 5 May 2006.
Racioppi, Linda, and Katherine O'Sullivan See. "Engendering Nation and National Identity." In *Women, States, and Nationalism: At Home in the Nation?* Ed. Sita Ranchod-Nilsson and Mary Ann Tétreault, 18–34. London and New York: Routledge, 2000.
Raffel, Burton. "Shakespeare and the Catholic Question." *Religion and Literature* 30.1 (1998): 35–51.
Rajak, Tessa. *The Jewish Dialogue with Greece and Rome*. Boston: Brill Academic Publishers, 2002.
Ramsey, Paul. "The Literary Evidence for Shakespeare as Hand D in the Manuscript Play *Sir Thomas More*: A Re-re-reconsideration." *Upstart Crow* 11 (1991): 131–55.
Rappaport, Steve. *Worlds within Worlds: Structures of Life in Sixteenth-Century London*. Cambridge: Cambridge University Press, 1989.
Redstone, V.B. "The Dutch and Huguenot Settlements of Ipswich." *Proceedings of the Huguenot Society* 12 (1917–23): 183–204.
Reeser, Todd W. *Moderating Masculinity in Early Modern Culture*. Chapel Hill: University of North Carolina Press, 2006.
Reuter, Ole R. *Thomas Deloney and The Mirrour of Mirth and Pleasant Conceits*. Helsinki: Societas Scientiarum Fennica, 1982.
Reynolds, Matthew. *Godly Reformers and their Opponents in Early Modern England: Religion in Norwich c. 1560–1643*. Woodbridge, UK: Boydell Press, 2005.

Richards, Judith M. "Mary Tudor as 'Sole Quene'? Gendering Tudor Monarchy." *The Historical Journal* 40.4 (1997): 895–924.
Rickwood, Douglas. "The Norwich Strangers, 1565–1643: A Problem of Control." *Proceedings of the Huguenot Society* 24 (1984): 119–28.
Riggs, David. *The World of Christopher Marlowe.* New York: Henry Holt, 2004.
Roberts, Peter R. "The Welsh Language, English Law and Tudor Legislation." *Transactions of the Honourable Society of Cymmrodorion* (1989): 19–75.
Robinson, Richard, ed. *A poore knight his pallace of priuate pleasures Gallantly garnished, with goodly galleries of strang inuentio[n]s and prudently polished, with sundry pleasant posies.* London: W. How, 1579.
Rohls, Jan. "Calvinism, Arminianism, and Socinianism in the Netherlands Until the Synod of Dort." In *Socinianism and Arminianism: Antitrinitarians, Calvinists and Cultural Exchange in Seventeenth-Century Europe.* Ed. Martin Muslow and Jan Rohls, 3–48. Leiden: Brill, 2005.
Rollins, Hyder E. "Deloney's Sources for Euphuistic Learning." *PMLA* 52.3 (1936): 399–406.
– "Notes on Thomas Deloney." *Modern Language Notes* 32.2 (1917): 121–3.
– "Thomas Deloney's Euphuistic Learning and the Forest." *PMLA* 50.3 (1935): 679–86.
Rubin, Gayle. "Traffic in Women: Notes on the 'Political Economy' of Sex." In *Toward an Anthropology of Women.* Ed. Raya R. Reiter, 157–210. New York: Monthly Review Press, 1975.
Rubright, Marjorie. "Going Dutch in London City Comedy: Economies of Sexual and Sacred Exchange in John Marston's *The Dutch Courtesan* (1605)." *English Literary Renaissance* 40.1 (2010): 88–112.
– "An Urban Palimpsest: Migrancy, Architecture, and the Making of an Anglo-Dutch Royal Exchange." *Dutch Crossings* 33.1 (2009): 23–43.
Russell, Conrad. "The British Problem and the English Civil War." *History* 72.236 (1987): 395–415.
Rutter, Carol Chillington, ed. *Documents of the Rose Playhouse.* Manchester, England: Manchester University Press, 1984.
Rutter, Tom. "*Englishmen for My Money*: Work and Social Conflict?" In *Working Subjects in Early Modern English Drama.* Ed. Michelle M. Dowd and Natasha Korda, 87–100. Farnham: Ashgate, 2011.
Sadler, Ralph. *The State Papers and Letters of Sir Ralph Sadler.* Vol 1. Edinburgh: James Ballantyne, 1809.
Samuels, Edgar. "London's Portuguese Jewish Community, 1540–1753." In *From Strangers to Citizens: The Integration of Immigrant Communities in Britain, Ireland and Colonial America, 1550–1750.* Ed. Randolph Vigne and Charles Galton Littleton, 239–46. Proceedings of a conference convened in London,

5–7 May 2000, by the Huguenot Society of Great Britain and Ireland. Brighton and Portland, OR: Sussex Academic Press, 2001.

Sauer, Elizabeth. "The Peculiar Status of Early Modern England." In *Reading the Nation in English Literature: A Critical Reader*. Ed. Elizabeth Sauer and Julia M. Wright, 144–54. New York: Routledge, 2010.

Schaffer, Elizabeth. "William Haughton's *Englishmen for My Money*: A Critical Note." *The Review of English Studies*, n.s. 41.164 (1990): 536–8.

Scheyfve, Jehan. "Advices sent by..." 21 April 1551. Vienna, Imp. Arch. E. 19. In *Calendar of Letters, Despatches, and State Papers Relating to the Negotiations between England and Spain*. Vol 10: Edward VI 1550–1552. Ed. Royall Tyler. London: The Hereford Times Limited, 1914.

Schickler, Fernand David Georges de. *Les Églises due Refuge en Angleterre*. Paris: Librarie G. Fischbacjer, 1892.

Schlossberg, Linda. Introduction to *Passing: Identity and Interpretation in Sexuality, Race, and Religion*. Ed. Linda Schlossberg and Maria Carla Sanchez, 1–12. New York: New York University Press, 2001.

Schlueter, June. "Martin Droeshout, Redivivus: Reassessing the Folio Engraving of Shakespeare." *Shakespeare Survey* 60 (2007): 237–51.

Schmidgen, Wolfram. *Exquisite Mixture: The Virtues of Impurity in Early Modern England*. Philadelphia: University of Pennsylvania Press, 2013.

Schoenbaum, Samuel. *William Shakespeare: A Compact Documentary Life*. Oxford: Oxford University Press, 1977.

Schreckenberg, Heinz. *Bibliographie zu Flavius Josephus*. Leiden: Brill Academic Publishing, 1968.

Schreckenberg, Heinz and Kurt Schubert. *Jewish Historiography and Iconography in Early and Medieval Christianity*. Haag: Van Gorcum, 1991.

Schuckman, Christiaan. "The Engraver of the First Folio Portrait of Shakespeare." *Print Quarterly* 8.1 (1991): 40–3.

Schwyzer, Philip. *Literature, Nationalism, and Memory in Early Modern England and Wales*. Cambridge: Cambridge University Press, 2004.

Scott, Michael. *John Marston's Plays*. New York: Barnes and Noble, 1978.

Scouloudi, Irene. "Notes on Strangers in the Precinct of St. Katherine-by-the-Tower c. 1500–1687, and on the 'Flemish Cemetery.'" *Proceedings of the Huguenot Society* 25.1 (1989): 75–82.

– *Returns of Strangers in the Metropolis 1593, 1627, 1635, 1639: A Study of an Active Minority*. Quarto Series (Huguenot Society of London), vol. 57. London: Huguenot Society of London, 1985.

Sellin, Paul. *Daniel Heinsius and Stuart England*. Leiden: Leiden University Press, 1968.

Selwood, Jacob. *Diversity and Difference in Early Modern London*. Farnham: Ashgate, 2010.
Shakespeare, William. *The Norton Shakespeare*. Ed. Stephen Greenblatt, Walter Cohn, Jean E. Howard, and Katharine Eisaman Maus. New York and London: W.W. Norton, 1997.
Shapiro, James. *Shakespeare and the Jews*. New York: Columbia University Press, 1996.
Sharpe, Kevin. *Selling the Tudor Monarchy: Authority and Image in Sixteenth-Century England*. New Haven: Yale University Press, 2009.
Shepard, Alan. *Marlowe's Soldiers: Rhetorics of Masculinity in the Age of the Armada*. Farnham: Ashgate, 2002.
Sidney, Sir Philip. *An Apology for Poetry*. Ed. Forest G. Robinson. Indianapolis: Bobbs-Merrill Educational Publishing, 1970.
– *The Correspondence of Sir Philip Sidney*. Vol. 1. Ed. Roger Kuin. Oxford: Oxford University Press, 2012.
Singh, Jyostna, ed. *A Companion to the Global Renaissance: English Literature and Culture in the Era of Expansion*. Chichester: Wiley-Blackwell, 2009.
Sir Thomas More. Original text by Anthony Munday and Henry Chettle ... Ed. John Jowett. Arden Shakespeare. London: Methuen Drama, 2011.
Sisson, C.J. "A Colony of Jews in Shakespeare's London." *Essays and Studies* 23 (1938): 37–52.
Skinner, John. *A True Relation of the Cruell, and Barbarous Proceedings against the English at Amboyna*. London: H. Lownes for Nathaniel Newberry, 1624.
Smith, Anthony D. *The Antiquity of Nations*. Cambridge: Polity Press, 2004.
– *National Identity*. London: Penguin, 1991.
Smith, Anthony D., and Ernest Gellner. "The Nation: Real or Imagined? The Warwick Debates on Nationalism." *Nations and Nationalism* 2.3 (1996): 357–70.
Smith, Emma. "'So Much English by the Mother': Gender, Foreigners, and the Mother Tongue in William Haughton's *Englishmen for My Money*." *Medieval and Renaissance Drama in England* (200): 165–81.
– "Was Shylock Jewish?" *Shakespeare Quarterly* 64.2 (213): 189–219.
Smith, M.W.A. "Shakespeare, Stylometry, and *Sir Thomas More*." *Studies in Philology* 89 (1992): 434–44.
Smith, Pauline. "The Reception and Influence of Josephus's Jewish War in the Late French Renaissance with Special Reference to the Satyrre of Menippée." *Renaissance Studies* 13.2 (1999): 174–91.
Smuts, Malcolm. "Public Ceremony and Royal Charisma: The English Royal Entry in London, 1485–1642." In *The First Modern Society: Essays in English*

History in Honour of Lawrence Stone. Ed. A.L. Beier, David Cannadine, and James M. Rosenheim, 65–95. Cambridge: Cambridge University Press, 1989.

Soellner, Rolf. *Timon of Athens: Shakespeare's Pessimistic Tragedy*. Columbus: Ohio State University Press, 1979.

Sokol, B.J. *Shakespeare and Tolerance*. Cambridge: Cambridge University Press, 2008.

Somner, William. *The Antiquities of Canterbury*. London: John Legat, 1640.

Sondergard, Sidney L. *Sharpening Her Pen: Strategies of Rhetorical Violence by Early Modern English Women Writers*. Selinsgrove, PA: Susquehanna University Press, 2002.

Soulié, Marguerite, and Jean-Dominque Beaudin. Introduction to *Abraham Sacrifiant: tragédie françoise*, 9–28. Paris: Honoré-Champion, 2006.

Sousa, Geraldo de. *Shakespeare's Cross-Cultural Encounters*. New York: St Martin's Press, 1999.

Spicer, Andrew. *The French-Speaking Reformed Community and Their Church at Southampton, 1567–1620*. London: Huguenot Society of Great Britain and Ireland, new series, 1997.

– "'Le Quatriesme Ordre': The Diaconate in the French-Walloon Churches of London and Sandwich, c. 1568–1573." *Proceedings of the Huguenot Society*, 29 (2008): 1–13.

– "A Process of Gradual Assimilation: The Exile Community in Southampton, 1567–1635." In *The Strangers' Progress: Integration and Disintegration of the Huguenot and Walloon Refugee Community, 1567–1889. Essays in Memory of Irene Scouloudi*. Ed. Randolph Vigne and Graham C. Gibbs, 186–98. London: Huguenot Society of Great Britain and Ireland, 1995.

Spohnholz, Jesse. *Strangers and Neighbors: The Tactics of Toleration in an Early Modern German Town*. Newark: University of Delaware Press, 2010.

Statt, Daniel. *Foreigners and Englishmen: The Controversy over Immigration and Population 1660–1760*. Newark: University of Delaware Press, 1995.

Steggle, Matthew. "Belchier, Dabridgcourt (bap. 1581, d. 1621)." In *Oxford Dictionary of National Biography*. Online edition. Ed. Lawrence Goldman. Oxford University Press, 2004.

Steinmetz, David Curtis. *Reformers in the Wings: From Geiler von Kayserberg to Theodore Beza*. Oxford: Oxford University Press, 2001.

Stern, Philip J. *The Company-State: Corporate Sovereignty and the Early Modern Foundations of the British Empire in India*. Oxford: Oxford University Press, 2011.

Stevenson, Laura Caroline. *Praise and Paradox: Merchants and Craftsmen in Elizabethan Popular Literature*. Oxford: Oxford University Press, 2002.

Stewart, Alan. "'Every Soyl to Mee is Naturall': Figuring Denization in William Haughton's *English-Men for My Money*." *Renaissance Drama* n.s. 35 (2006): 55–81.
Stone, Lawrence. *The Family, Sex and Marriage in England 1500–1800*. New York: Harper and Row, 1977.
Stow, John. *The Survey of London*. Ed. H.B. Wheatley. London and Melbourne: Everyman's Library, 1987.
Streitberger, W.R. *Court Revels, 1485–1559*. Toronto: University of Toronto Press, 1994.
Strong, Roy. *The Cult of Elizabeth: Elizabethan Portraiture and Pageantry*. Berkeley: University of California Press, 1977.
– *Gloriana: The Portraits of Queen Elizabeth I*. London: Thames and Hudson, 1987.
Strype, John. *Annals of the Reformation*, 4 vols. Oxford: Clarendon Press, 1824.
Sudan, Rajani. *Fair Exotics: Xenophobic Subject in English Literature, 1720–1850*. Philadelphia: University of Pennsylvania Press, 2002.
Suzuki, Mihoko. "The London Apprentice Riots of the 1590s and the Fiction of Thomas Deloney." *Criticism* 38.2 (1996): 181–217.
– *Subordinate Subjects: Gender, the Political Nation, and Literary Form in England, 1588–1688*. Farnham: Ashgate, 2003.
– "Warning Elizabeth with Catherine de' Medici's Example: Anne Dowriche's *French Historie* and the Politics of Counsel." In *The Rule of Women in Early Modern Europe*. Ed. Anne J. Cruz and Mihoko Suzuki, 174–93. Urbana: University of Illinois Press, 2009.
Swaen, A.E.H. "Notes on Ballads and Tunes in W. Sampson's *Vow-Breaker*." *Neophilologus* 3 (1918): 149–54.
– "*Wealth and Health*." *Englische Studien* 41 91910): 456.
Swithin, St. "'Drowse'=Devil." *Notes and Queries* 116 (27 July 1907): 73.
Tawney, Richard Henry. *Religion and the Rise of Capitalism*. Gloucester, MA: Harcourt, Brace, and World, 1962.
Tawney, Richard Henry, and Eileen Power. *Tudor Economic Documents*. 3 vols. London: Lowe and Brydone Printers, 1924; 1963.
Tedeschi, John, "Italian Reformers and the Diffusion of Renaissance Culture." *The Sixteenth Century Journal* 5.2 (1974): 79–94.
Theis, Jeffrey. "The 'ill kill'd' Deer: Poaching and Social Order in *The Merry Wives of Windsor*." *Texas Studies in Literature and Language* 43.1 (2001): 46–73.
Thomas, Vivien, and William Tydeman, *Christopher Marlowe: The Plays and Their Sources*. New York: Routledge, 1994.

Thompson, Ann. "Dating Evidence for *The Taming of the Shrew*." *Notes and Queries* 29 (1982): 108–9.
Thomson, J.A.F. "Scots in England in the Fifteenth Century." *The Scottish Historical Review* 79.207 (2000): 1–16.
Thrupp, Sylvia L. "A Survey of the Alien Population of England in 1440." *Speculum* 32.2 (1957): 262–73.
Tittler, Robert. *The Reign of Mary I*. London and New York: Longman, 1983.
Tracy, James D. *The Founding of the Dutch Republic: War, Finance, and Politics in Holland, 1572–1588*. Oxford: Oxford University Press, 2007.
Trevor-Roper, Hugh. *Europe's Physician: The Life of Sir Theodore de Mayerne, 1573–1655*. New Haven: Yale University Press, 2006.
Trim, D.J.B. "Ogle, Sir John (*bap.* 1569, *d.* 1640)." *Oxford Dictionary of National Biography*. Ed. H.C.G. Matthew and Brian Harrison. Oxford University Press, 2004. Online edition, ed. Lawrence Goldman, Jan. 2008.
Two London Chronicles from the Collections of John Stow. Ed. Charles Lethbridge Kingsford. Camden Miscellany, 12.1. London: Camden Society, 1910.
Underhill, Edward. "The History of Wyatt's Rebellion." In *Tudor Tracts, 1532–1588*. Edited by Alfred F. Pollard, 170–98. New York: E.P. Dutton, 1903.
Unwin, George. *The Gilds and Companies of London*. New York: Barnes and Noble, 1963.
Urry, William. *Christopher Marlowe and Canterbury*. London: Faber and Faber 1988.
Valente, Claire. *The Theory and Practice of Revolt in Medieval England*. Farnham: Ashgate, 2003.
van de Pol, Lotte C. "The Whore, The Bawd, and the Artist: The Reality and the Imagery of Seventeenth-Century Dutch Prostitution." *The Journal of Historians of Netherlandish Art* 2.1 (2010). http://www.jhna.org/index.php/past-issues/volume-2-issue-1-2/116-the-whore-the-bawd-and-the-artist.
Vane, Christine. "The Walloon Community in Norwich: The First Hundred Years." *Proceedings of the Huguenot Society* 24 (1984): 129–37.
Vaughan, Virginia Mason. *Performing Blackness on English Stages, 1500–1800*. Cambridge: Cambridge University Press, 2005.
Velz, John. "*Sir Thomas More* and the Shakespeare Canon: Two Approaches." In *Shakespeare and* Sir Thomas More: *Essays on the Play and Its Shakesperian Interest*. Ed. T.H. Howard-Hill, 171–96. Cambridge: Cambridge University Press, 1989.
Verkbeke, Demmy. "Swag-Bellied Hollanders and Dead-Drunk Almaines: Reputation and Pseudo-Translation in Early Modern England." *Dutch Crossing* 34.2 (2010): 182–91.

Vermeer, Wim. "Pastorale poëzie van Huygens." *Utrecht Renaissance Studies* 1 (1982): 79–101.
Villani, Stefano. "The Italian Protestant Church of London in the Seventeenth Century." In *Exiles, Emigrés and Intermediaries: Anglo-Italian Cultural Transactions*. Ed. Barbara Schaff, 217–36. New York: Rodopi, 2010.
Visser, Nicholas. "Shakespeare and Hanekom, *King Lear* and Land: A South African Perspective." In *Post-Colonial Shakespeares*. Ed. Ania Loomba and Martin Orkin, 205–17. London: Routledge, 1998.
Vitkus, Daniel. "Labor and Travel on the Early Modern Stage: Representing the Travail of Travel in Dekker's *Old Fortunatus* and Shakespeare's *Pericles*." In *Working Subjects in Early Modern English Drama*. Ed. Michelle M. Dowd and Natasha Korda, 225–42. Farnham: Ashgate, 2010.
– *Turning Turk: English Theater and the Multicultural Mediterranean, 1570–1630*. New York: Palgrave, 2003.
Wall, Wendy. *Staging Domesticity: Household Work and English Identity in Early Modern Drama*. Cambridge: Cambridge University Press, 2002.
Wallace, Charles William. *The Evolution of the English Drama up to Shakespeare*. Port Washington, NY: Kennikate Press, 1968.
Wallace, Malcolm W., ed. Introduction to *A Tragedie of Abraham's Sacrifice, Written in French by Theodore Beza and Translated into English by Arthur Golding*. xi–lxi. Toronto: University of Toronto Library, 1906.
Walsham, Alexandra. *Charitable Hatred: Tolerance and Intolerance in England, 1500–1700*. Manchester: Manchester University Press, 2006.
– *The Reformation of the Landscape: Religion, Identity, and Memory in Early Modern Britain and Ireland*. Oxford: Oxford University Press, 2011.
Walker, Jeffrey. "Anagrams and Acrostics: Puritan Poetic Wit." In *Puritan Poets and Poetics: Seventeenth-Century American Poetry in Theory and Practice*. Ed. Peter White, 247–57. University Park: Pennsylvania State University Press, 1985.
Wapull, George. *The Tide Tarrieth No Man*, 1576. (reprint 1910; Kessinger Publishing, 2002).
Ward, Joseph P. "Fictitious Shoemakers, Agitated Weavers and the Limits of Popular Xenophobia in Early Modern London." In *From Strangers to Citizens: The Integration of Immigrant Communities in Britain, Ireland and Colonial America, 1550–1750*. Proceedings of a conference convened in London, 5–7 May 2000, by the Huguenot Society of Great Britain and Ireland. Brighton and Portland, OR: Sussex Academic Press, 2001.
– "'[I]mployment for All Handes that Will Worke': Immigrants, Guilds and the Labour Market in Early Seventeenth-Century London." In *Immigrants in*

Tudor and Early Stuart England. Ed. Nigel Goose and Lien Bich Luu, 76-94. Brighton: Sussex Academic Press, 2005.
- *Metropolitan Communities: Trade Guilds, Identity, and Change in Early Modern London*. Stanford: Stanford University Press, 1997.

Watt, Teresa. *Cheap Print and Popular Piety, 1550–1640*. Cambridge: Cambridge University Press, 1991.

Watt, Timothy Irish. "The Authorship of the Hand-D Addition to *The Book of Sir Thomas More*." In *Shakespeare, Computers, and the Mystery of Authorship*. Ed. Hugh Craig and Arthur F. Kinney, 134–61. Cambridge: Cambridge University Press, 2012.

Wentersdorff, Karl P. "The Date of the Additions in *The Booke of Sir Thomas More*." *Shakespeare-Jahrbuch* 101 (1965): 305–25.

White, Adam. "Johnson [Janssen] family (*per. c.1570–c.1630*)." *Oxford Dictionary of National Biography*. Online edition, ed. Lawrence Goldman. Oxford University Press, 2004.

White, Jason. *Militant Protestantism and British Identity, 1603-1642*. London: Pickering and Chatto, 2012.

White, Micheline. "Power Couples and Women Writers in Elizabethan England: The Public Voices of Dorcas and Richard Martin and Anne and Hugh Dowriche." In *Framing the Family: Narrative and Representation in the Medieval and Early Modern Periods*. Edited by Rosalynn Voaden and Diane Wolfthal, 119–38. Tempe, AZ: Arizona Center for Medieval and Renaissance Studies, 2005.
- "Women Writers and Literary-Religious Circles in the Elizabethan West Country: Anne Dowriche, Anne Lock Prowse, Anne Lock Moyle, Elizabeth Rous, and Ursula Fulford." *Modern Philology* 103.2 (2005): 187–214.

White, Paul Whitfield. "Patronage, Protestantism, and Stage Propaganda in Early Elizabethan England." *The Yearbook of English Studies* 21 (1991): 39–52.
- "Shakespeare, the Cobhams, and the Dynamics of Theatrical Patronage." In *Shakespeare and Theatrical Patronage in Early Modern England*. Ed. Paul Whitfield White and Suzanne R. Westfall, 64–89. Cambridge: Cambridge University Press, 2002.

Whitgift, John. *The Works of John Whitgift*. Cambridge: Cambridge University Press, 1853.

Whitney, Charles. "The Devil His Due: Mayor John Spencer, Elizabethan Civic Antitheatricalism and *The Shoemaker's Holiday*." *Medieval and Renaissance Drama in England: An Annual Gathering of Research, Criticism and Reviews* 14 (2001): 168–85.

Wiggins, Martin, in association with Catherine Richardson. *British Drama, 1533–1642: A Catalogue. Vol. 2: 1567–1589*. Oxford: Oxford University Press, 2012.

Williams, Glanmor. *Wales and the Reformation*. Cardiff: University of Wales Press, 1997.
Williams, Gordon. *A Dictionary of Sexual Language and Imagery in Shakespearean and Stuart Literature*. London: Athlone Press, 1994.
Williams, William Meade, ed. *Annals of the Worshipful Company of Founders of the City of London*. Privately printed, 1867.
Wilson, Frank Percy. *The English Drama, 1485–1585*. New York: Oxford University Press, 1969.
Wilson, Richard. "Making Men of Monsters: Shakespeare in the Company of Strangers." *Shakespeare* 1.1 (2005): 8–28.
– "Shakespeare and the Jesuits: New ConnectioHuguns Supporting the Theory of the Lost Catholic Years in Lancashire." *The Times Literary Supplement* (19 December 1997): 11–13.
Wilson, Robert. *The Pedlar's Prophecy*. Ed. John S. Farmer. New York: AMS Press, 1970.
– *The Three Ladies of London*. London: Printed by Roger Warde, 1584.
Wine, Martin. L. Introduction. *The Dutch Courtesan*. i–xxviii. Lincoln: University of Nebraska Press, 1968.
Wolf, Lucien. *Jews in Elizabethan England*. London: Spottiswoode, Ballantyne, 1929.
Wood, Andy. *The 1549 Rebellions and the Making of Early Modern England*. Cambridge: Cambridge University Press, 2007.
Woods, Susanne. *Lanyer: A Renaissance Woman Poet*. Oxford: Oxford University Press, 1999.
Woods, Susanne, and Margaret P. Hannay with Elaine Beilin and Anne Shaver. "Renaissance Englishwomen and the Literary Career." In *European Literary Careers: The Author from Antiquity to the Renaissance*. Ed. Patrick Cheney and Frederick A. de Armas, 302–24. Toronto: University of Toronto Press, 2002.
Worman, Ernest James. *Alien Members of the Book-trade during the Tudor Period*. London: Printed for the Bibliographical Society by Blades, East, and Blades, 1906.
Wortham, James. "Arthur Golding and the Translation of Prose." *Huntington Quarterly* 12.4 (1949): 339–67.
Wraight, A.D. *Shakespeare: New Evidence*. London: Adam Hart, 1996.
Wraight, A.D., and Virginia F. Stern. *In Search of Christopher Marlowe*. Sussex: Adam Hart, 1965.
Wright, Eugene P. *Thomas Deloney*. Boston: Twayne Publishers, 1981.
Wright, Louis B. "The Elizabethan Middle-Class Taste for History." *The Journal of Modern History* 3.2 (1931): 175–97.

- *Middle-Class Culture in Elizabethan England*. Ithaca: Cornell University Press, 1958.
Wright, Stephen. "Copcot, John (*d.* 1590)." In *Oxford Dictionary of National Biography*. Online edition. Ed. Lawrence Goldman. Oxford University Press, 2004.
Wriothesley, Charles. *A Chronicle of England during the Reigns of the Tudors from A.D. 1485 to 1559*. Vol. 2. Ed. William Douglas Hamilton. London: Camden Society, 1877.
Wyatt, Michael. *The Italian Encounter with Tudor England: A Cultural Politics of Translation*. Cambridge: Cambridge University Press, 2005.
Wyatt, Thomas. "Aliens in England before the Huguenots." *Proceedings of the Huguenot Society of London.* 19 (1953): 74–94.
Wylie, James Aitken. *The History of Protestantism*. 3 vols. London: Cassell, Petter, Galpin & Co., 1887.
Yamada, Yuzo. *Writing under Influences: A Study of Christopher Marlowe*. Tokyo: Eihosha, 1999.
Yungblut, Laura Hunt. *'Strangers Settled Here Among Us': Policies, Perceptions and the Presence of Aliens in Elizabethan England*. London and New York: Routledge, 1996.
Yuval-Davis, Nira. *Gender and Nation*. London: Sage Publication, 1997.

Index

Abbot, George, archbishop of Canterbury, 48–9
Acontius, Jacob, 59
Adams, Thomas, 21, 180
aliens: as a term, 3–4, 185n4; anti-alien proclamations, 24, 29–30, 31, 34, 40, 42, 51–3; churches of, 4, 9, 14–15, 16, 30, 32, 41, 45, 48, 51, 60, 61, 62, 63, 76–7, 79, 84–5, 86, 95, 117–18, 142, 144, 151, 177, 182–3, 203n1, 214n7, 222n20; complaints about, 14, 15, 17, 29, 30, 48, 66, 68–70, 75–6, 83–4, 86, 115, 135, 147, 158, 165, 179, 204n14, 214n7, 218nn65–6; demographics, 4, 8, 9, 23, 30–1, 48, 75, 147, 158, 165, 179, 186n11, 188n28, 192n50, 204n12; economic need for, 17–18, 42, 45, 63, 82, 186n6, 203n3; informers on (*see* informers); integration/assimilation of, 14, 15, 77, 79, 115, 144, 193n69; merchant strangers, 3, 4, 12, 23, 26, 28, 29, 30, 69, 86–7, 89, 91, 92, 104, 105, 108, 113, 127, 154, 158, 177 (*see also* Hanseatic League); neighbourhoods associated with, 11, 32, 37, 143, 145, 193n65, 201n47; outside of London, 4, 14, 17–18, 28, 45, 50–1, 60–1, 62–4, 75, 79, 82, 84, 96, 118, 177, 182, 194–5n73, 207n82, 211n92, 214n7, 215n22; place in guild system, 4, 12, 13, 16, 33, 34, 82–6, 104, 107, 113, 146, 147, 157, 196n9 (*see also* guilds); printers and booksellers, 18, 55, 141–2, 151, 163, 196n9, 197–8n14, 210n79; taxes on, 14, 42–3, 47, 77, 214n7
Amussen, Susan Dwyer, 158
anabaptists, 9, 45, 52
Anderson, Benedict, 119, 193–4n71
Anglo, Sydney, 27
Anthias, Floya, 119
Archer, Ian, 147
Archer, John Michael, 147

Barnaud, Nicolas, 62
Bate, Jonathan, 145
beer and brewing, 24, 33, 37, 38, 42, 81, 144, 169, 196–7n10, 211n92
Behn, Aphra, 122, 227n23
Beilin, Elaine, 57, 210n74
Belchier, Dabridgecourt, 173, 175, 178; *Hans Beer-Pot*, 173–6, 178, 184, 240n6

Bellot, Stephen, 142, 145
Benson, George, 179–80
Bèze, Theodore, 55–7, 64, 67, 207n48, 212n105; *A Tragedie of Abrahams Sacrifice*, 55, 64, 67, 207n47
Bible. *See* Old Testament
Billing, Christian, 107–8
Bolton, Edmund, 179, 242–3n46
Bonner, Edmund, bishop of London, 32–3, 34
Bovilsky, Lara, 88
Bradshaw, Graham, 139
Briggs, Julia, 66, 67
Brooke, Henry, 154
Burton, Jonathan, 139

Campos, Edmund, 128, 132, 136
Casaubon, Isaac, 179
Chettle, Henry, 127, 168
Christopherson, John, 24, 43–4, 196n6, 199–200n31
Chronicle of Queen Jane, 26, 27, 28, 199n24
Churchyard, Thomas, 54
citizens and citizenship, 7, 108, 111–12, 121, 147, 149, 150, 152, 153, 157, 160, 169, 170, 171, 180, 182. *See also* freedom of the city
Coke, Sir Edward, 76
Colynet, Antony, 62
Commendone, Giovanni Francesco, 26, 28, 199n24
Consitt, Frances, 82, 84
coronation pageantries. *See under individual monarchs*
Cott, Nancy, 120
Crane, David, 123
Crawford, Patricia, 120
Cressy, David, 137

Dalechamp, Caleb, 9–10, 12–14, 83 169–70, 180
Dante, 125, 228
Daube, David, 151
Davis, Walter, 78–9
Defoe, David, 183–4, 244nn71, 73
Dekker, Thomas, 17, 113–14, 121, 123, 127, 168, 220n1; immigrant heritage of, 100–1; *The Honest Whore*, 123; *Lanthorne and Candle-light*, 99–100, 221n11; *The Magnificent Entertainment* (*see* James I: coronation pageantry for); *The Noble Spanish Soldier*, 112, 225n49; *Northward Ho!*, 100; *Old Fortunatus*, 101–2, 105; *The Shoemaker's Holiday*, 99, 100–1, 104–12, 113–14, 123, 127, 134, 135, 156, 223nn35, 36, 223–4n37; *The Whore of Babylon*, 102–3, 104, 105, 165, 175, 222n17
Delenus, Peter, 30
Deloney, Thomas, 17, 78–98, 100, 113–14, 140, 215n22, 218n65, 218–19n67, 219n83; immigrant heritage of, 78–9; *Canaan's Calamity, Jerusalem's Misery*, 79; *The Gentle Craft, Part One*, 79, 90–1, 92, 93, 96, 97, 105, 108, 115, 223n37; *The Gentle Craft, Part Two*, 79, 92, 115, 136–7; *Jack of Newbury*, 18, 79, 86–90, 91–2, 93, 94, 113–14, 135, 175, 218n67; *Les contes ou les nouvelles recreations et joyeux devis*, 78; *Strange Histories*, 81, 92–8, 184; *Thomas of Reading*, 18
denizens and denization, 15, 24, 29, 30–3, 62, 76, 77, 147, 193n68, 200n40, 201n48, 211n92, 215n23
Dickens, Arthur, 54

Ditchley Portrait of Queen Elizabeth, 6–7, 145, 188n24
Dorsinville, Max, 78–9, 81
Dowriche, Anne, 16, 57–62, 67, 208n59, 208–9n60, 209nn62–4, 69, 210n74; family of, 57, 60–1, 207–8n56; *The French Historie,* 16, 57–62, 67, 68, 184
Droeshout, Martin, 101, 143, 145, 221–2n14
Du Bartas, Guillaume de Salluste, 177
Du Moulin, Pierre, 179, 243n49
Dutch, 7, 8, 9, 10, 11, 14, 18, 28, 29, 32, 36, 38, 42, 49, 60, 71, 75, 76, 96, 97, 100–1, 102, 103, 104, 112, 114, 117, 118–19, 128, 136, 137, 168, 173, 174–5, 176, 177, 178, 182, 183, 220n89, 227n22; acrobat, 27–9, 199n24; Amboyna Massacre, 178, 242n44; artists, 4, 7, 143; as a broad term, 10, 202n67; candle-makers, 76, 159; causes of immigration, 7, 8, 54; Dutch Churches in England, 14, 30, 32, 45, 51, 60, 61, 69–70, 76, 77, 84, 117–18, 144, 214nn7, 10, 220n89 (*see also* aliens: churches of); literary representations of, 11, 34–41, 90, 92, 98, 100–1, 103–4, 105–12, 117, 121–8, 136, 137, 173–5, 176, 180–2, 218n61, 224n38, 229n51; ministers, 14, 45, 50, 117; shoemakers, 32, 33, 37, 105–7, 112, 117
Dutch Church Libel, 69–70, 75, 213n116
Dutch Revolt, 8, 24, 48, 75, 101, 102–3, 114, 173–6, 190n35, 214n2

Edgecombe, Pearse, 57, 60–1, 210n83
Edict of Nantes, 8, 54
Edmond, Mary, 143, 144
Edward VI, 8, 9, 26, 45, 82, 96, 182; coronation pageantry for, 26
Elizabeth I, 4, 8, 15, 18, 31, 45–6, 49, 54, 57, 59, 68, 76, 82, 93, 96, 101, 102, 103, 108, 110, 111, 175, 177, 184, 203n1, 204n14, 222n20, 224n42; coronation pageantry for, 25, 26, 205n20; Ditchley portrait of, 6–7, 145, 188n24; entertainment at Norwich, 49–51, 57, 60
Elton, G.R., 157
Englishness, 4–5, 11, 23, 35, 46, 53–4, 77, 89, 92, 96–7, 118, 119, 124–5, 128, 129–31, 135, 137, 145, 149, 154, 184, 188n25. *See also* nationhood and nationalism
Erickson, Amy L., 126, 133
Estienne, Henri, 62
Evans, Kathryn J., 47

Family of Love, 31, 123, 126, 227n27
Fiedler, Leslie, 139
Field, Richard, 140–2, 232nn13, 17
Finkelpearl, Philip J., 123
Fischer, Kuno, 138
Fleck, Andrew, 106, 124–5, 134
Flemings and Flemish, 7, 10–11, 28, 38, 60, 69, 111, 112, 114, 145, 176, 183, 196–7n10, 201n49, 202n67; literary representations of, 4, 34, 36–41, 196n10
Florio, John, 145
Ford, John, 132
foreigners (non-free English), 7, 146–7, 150, 151, 152, 153, 163, 164, 168, 169, 170, 189n30
Foxe, John, 28–30, 32, 55, 57, 93, 95, 201n49, 204n12

Frampton, Sue, 145
France and the French, 3, 4, 7, 10–11, 18, 24, 28, 29, 30–1, 32, 36, 47, 54, 56, 57–62, 63, 64, 65, 68, 69, 71, 77, 78, 79, 80, 81, 85, 86, 93, 94, 97, 104, 114, 118, 124, 125, 137, 138, 142, 145, 153, 157, 159, 165, 172, 176, 184, 207n53, 212n100, 215n23; as a term, 10, 202n67; causes of immigration, 8, 48, 54; fashions from, 7, 90; French churches in England, 14, 45, 51, 60, 76, 77, 79, 84, 87, 117, 118, 142, 151, 177; literary representations of, 11, 90, 96, 98, 108, 112, 117, 123, 125, 127, 128, 129–30, 149, 150–1, 159; preachers, 28, 65; silk-weavers, 6–7, 79–80, 87, 97, 114, 142; Wars of Religion, 8, 16, 48, 54, 55, 57–8, 61, 62, 63, 65–9, 75, 175 190n38, 207n53 (*see also* Saint Bartholomew's Day Massacre)
freedom of the city, 83, 86, 141, 146–8, 153, 168, 170, 217n56, 234n38. *See also* citizens and citizenship
Freud, Sigmund, 138
Fuller, Nicholas, 12, 15
Fuller, Thomas, 118–19, 136

Gardiner, Stephen, 31–2, 33
Gasper, Julia, 90, 101, 104, 175, 224n39
Gellner, Ernest, 119
Gentillet, Innocent, 59
Gheerarts the Younger, Marcus, 7, 143, 145
Golding, Arthur, 54, 55
Goose, Nigel, 5, 14, 15
Goulart, Simon, 62
Grantley, Darryll, 36
Greenblatt, Stephen, 65–6, 142, 145

Greene, Robert, 132, 140, 215n22, 232n10
Grell, Ole Peter, 8, 177, 178, 193n70
Grévin, Jacques, 47–8, 204n8
Griffiths, Jane, 42
Grindal, Edmund, archbishop of Canterbury, 45, 203n2
Gruter, Janus, 18, 96
guilds, 4, 12, 13, 16, 33, 34, 77, 79, 80–6, 94, 97, 99, 104, 107, 113, 137, 146–8, 157, 217n56, 218n66. *See also* aliens: place in the guild system; *individual crafts (beer and brewing, weavers, shoemakers)*
Gwynn, Robin D., 176–7

Hadfield, Andrew, 5, 6
Haemstede, Adrian van, 45, 96, 203nn1–2
Hall, Edward, 158–60, 161, 167
Halley, Janet E., 126
Hamilton, Alastair, 126
Hannay, Maragret P., 57
Hanseatic League, 26–7, 29, 37–8, 107, 108, 111, 198n19, 224n38. *See also* aliens: merchant strangers
Harvey, Gabriel, 100
Haselkorn, Ann, 122
Haughton, William, 17, 120, 127, 128, 129, 130, 131, 135, 229n50; *Englishmen for My Money*, 17, 54, 69, 73, 120, 127–37, 153, 175, 229nn51–2, 54, 230nn65, 69, 73
Heal, Felicity, 54
Helgerson, Richard, 5, 6, 92, 100, 139, 148–50, 170, 234n43
Henry VIII, 4, 5, 9, 42, 86, 107, 163, 167, 178
Henslowe, Philip, 111, 127, 132, 170

Hentschell, Roze, 81, 92
Heywood, John, 28, 35
Highley, Christopher, 23
Hobsbawm, Eric, 119
Hoenselaars, A.J., 40–1, 124, 150–1, 153–4, 182
Holinshed, Raphael, 92–5
Holmes, Martin, 158
Honan, Park, 145
Honigmann, E.A J., 142, 143, 164
Hotman, François, 54, 59, 62, 209n69
Howard, Jean, 4, 121, 125, 139
Huguenots. See France and the French
Hurault, Michel, 62
Huygens, Sir Constantijn, 176–7, 241nn28–9

immigrants. See aliens
Impacyente Pouertye, A New Interlude of, 3
informers, 75–6, 83, 177–8, 214nn6–7, 214n10, 214–15n11
Ireland and the Irish, 7, 112, 183, 189–90n31
Italy and Italians, 7, 10, 26, 27, 59, 60, 88, 89, 112, 117, 124, 125, 128, 145, 172, 176, 179, 184, 191n49, 225n2; literary representations of, 87–9, 91, 92, 97, 114, 127

James, Elias, 144, 145
James I, 7, 8, 76, 123, 175–7, 178, 179, 180, 184, 214n10, 222n20, 241nn19, 31, 243n49; coronation pageantry for, 25, 26, 103–4, 105
Janssen, Gheerart, 101, 143, 145, 221–2n14
Jews, 49–50, 56, 69, 109–10, 128, 129, 132, 136, 139, 146, 171, 204–5n18, 205n19, 209n63, 213n117, 221n11, 224n44, 229n54, 231n9
Jonson Ben, 101, 103, 127
Josephus, Flavius, 99, 110, 221n2, 224n44

Kastan, David Scott, 107, 111
Kermode, Lloyd Edward, 5, 35, 37, 52, 54, 70, 128, 131, 201n55, 206n37, 229nn50–1, 54
Kerridge, Eric, 79
Keyishian, Harry, 122–3
Kiernan, Paul, 132
Kirwood, A.E.M., 141
Kott, Jan, 140
Kyd, Thomas, 70, 213n116, 223–4n37

Lanquet, Thomas, 26, 28
Lanyer, Amelia, 145, 233n30
Laud, William, archbishop of Canterbury, 8, 118, 182–3
Levine, Nina, 165
Light, George Evans, 174
Like Will to Like, 3
Littleon, Charles, 117
Loades, David M., 30, 36, 196n10, 198n14
Locke, Anne, 60
Luu, Lien Bich, 8, 15, 77, 79, 178

Machyn, Henry, 26, 28, 197–8n14, 199n24
Maley, Willy, 6, 8, 139, 234n44
Mann, Francis O., 78, 81, 92, 95
Manning, Roger, 87, 161
Marcus, Leah, 150
Marlowe, Christopher, 62–70; connections to immigrant communities, 62–4, 211nn89, 93; *Doctor Faustus*, 64, 212n107, 223–4n37;

288 Index

The Jew of Malta, 62, 63, 64, 66; *The Massacre at Paris,* 16, 17, 62–8, 69, 70; *Tamburlaine,* 63, 223–4n37
Marston, John, 17, 115, 125, 135, 225n2, 227n23, 228n44; *The Dutch Courtesan,* 17, 120, 121–7, 133, 136, 179, 226n20, 228nn33, 38, 43
Marx, Karl, 150
Mary I, 8, 16, 23–34, 36, 40–4, 45, 49, 57, 65, 95, 96, 165, 184, 196–7n10, 197–8n14, 199–200n31, 200n40, 201n49; coronation pageantry for, 24, 25–8, 34, 37, 44, 184, 199n24
masculinity, 175–6, 241n22
Matchinske, Megan, 59
May Day riot (1517), 85, 155, 156–7, 166
McCluskey, Peter M., 107
McEachern, Claire, 5, 6, 139
Mealor, Simon, 47
Melchiori, Georgio, 156, 162, 166
Middleton, Thomas, 76, 127, 175; *Anything for a Quiet Life,* 123; *A Chaste Maid on Cheapside,* 76, 132; *A Fair Quarrel,* 181–2; *No Wit/ Help Like a Woman's,* 180–1, 182; *The Peacemaker,* 175–6, 177, 184
Modet, Herman, 50, 205n22
Montaigne, Michel de, 125
Montgomery, Marianne, 106, 180–1
More, Sir Thomas, 164. *See also* Shakespeare, William: *The Play Sir Thomas More*
Moss, Jean Dietz, 123
Mountjoy, Christopher, 142, 145, 151, 163
Muggins, William, 85–6, 218n65
Mullaney, Steven, 143
Munday, Anthony, 168

Nashe, Thomas, 79, 215n22
nationhood and nationalism, 4–7, 9, 11, 15, 17–18, 23–5, 33–4, 44, 48, 53, 89–90, 92, 97, 99, 100, 107, 113–14, 119–21, 124, 127, 128, 131, 135, 137–40, 147–8, 149, 161, 162, 170, 171, 173, 179, 182, 183, 187n20, 193–4n71, 234nn42, 44; literary canons and, 17. *See also* Englishness; self-other paradigm; xenophobia
New Custom, A New Interlude No Lesse Wittie than Pleasant, Entitled, 46, 51, 203n4
New Interlude of Impacyente Pouertye, A, 3
Nicholl, Charles, 142
Nicol, David, 182
Norwich, 4, 18, 49–51, 56, 57, 60, 64, 77, 79, 82, 84, 96, 110, 182, 194, 205n20, 214n7, 215n22

Oakley, Anne M., 63
Old Testament, 49–50, 55–7, 65, 177, 204–5n18, 205n20, 207n53, 209n63, 221n2, 224n42

Pettegree, Andrew, 5, 15, 30–1, 33, 106, 157, 193
Pollock, Linda, 119, 181–2
Portuguese, 10, 49, 178, 191; literary representations of, 127–32, 133, 135
Prescott, Anne Lake, 64

Racioppi, Linda, 119
Rackin, Phyllis, 4, 139, 187, 231
Ramus, Peter, 54, 62, 211n90
Rappaport, Stephen, 79, 157
Renard, Simon, 30, 36
Richards, Judith M., 27
Riggs, David, 63

Robinson, Richard, 54
Rowley, William, 181
Rubin, Gayle, 119
Rubright, Marjorie, 103, 124, 136
Rutter, Tom, 128

Saint Bartholomew's Day Massacre, 3, 8, 48, 54, 58, 62–9, 185n3, 204n12. *See also* France and the French: Wars of Religion
Schaffer, Elizabeth, 130
Scheyfve, Jehan, 160–1
Schlossberg, Linda, 79, 86
Schlueter, June, 143
Schoenbaum, Samuel, 140, 142
Schwyzer, Philip, 5, 139, 188
Scotland and the Scottish, 7, 69, 125, 142, 183, 184, 189n31
Scott, Michael, 122
See, Katherine O'Sullivan, 119
self-other paradigm, 4–5, 11, 23, 35, 53, 92, 118, 125, 138–9, 148, 161. *See also* aliens: complaints about; nationhood and nationalism; xenophobia
Serres, Jean de, 54, 56, 59, 62
Shakespeare, William, 4, 17, 120, 138–72, 221; connections to immigrant communities, 140–8; authorship question, 3, 138, 236n66, 239n93; *All Is True/Henry VIII*, 148, 155, 171; *All's Well That Ends Well*, 142; *The Comedy of Errors*, 146, 170–1; *Cymbeline*, 148, 234n44; *1 Henry IV*, 150, 156, 167; *2 Henry IV*, 150; *Henry V*, 112, 150, 167; *1 Henry VI*, 112, 156, 167; *2 Henry VI*, 162, 167, 238n93; *3 Henry VI*, 140; *King John*, 148; *Measure for Measure*, 142; *The Merchant of Venice*, 146, 171, 234n35; *The Merry Wives of Windsor*, 7, 140, 148–55, 160, 169–71, 175, 235nn49, 58; *Othello*, 125, 146, 171; *The Play Sir Thomas More*, 110, 140, 148, 155–71, 236–7n66, 238n93, 239n96; *Twelfth Night*, 146, 151, 153, 171; *Two Gentlemen of Verona*, 140; *Two Noble Kinsmen*, 155
shoemakers, 32, 33, 37, 39, 62, 80, 90, 107. *See also* Dekker, Thomas: *The Shoemakers' Holiday*
Sidney, Sir Philip 3, 4, 65, 141, 174, 175, 185n3, 204n10, 210n74
Smith, Anthony D., 119, 149, 170
Smith, Emma, 129, 131
Soellner, Rolf, 174–5
Sokol, B.J., 139
Sousa, Geraldo de, 139
Spenser, Edmund, 100, 102, 221n10
Spicer, Andrew, 115
Statt, Daniel, 183–4
Stewart, Alan, 128
Stone, Lawrence, 120
strangers. *See* aliens
Strype, John, 48, 51, 53, 55
Suzuki, Mihoko, 85, 88, 89, 91
Sympson, Gabriel, 84

Theis, Jeffrey, 153
Titler, Robert, 24
Tooley, Nicholas, 145

Underhill, Edward, 26, 27, 199n24
Unwin, George, 79

Vautrollier, Jacqueline, 141–2, 145, 151
Vautrollier, Thomas, 55, 141–2, 163
Velz, John, 162
Vulcob, Jean de, 47, 204n10

Wales and the Welsh, 7, 124, 149–52, 188n29
Walloons, 7, 10, 60, 63, 78, 112, 114, 118, 183, 202n67, 215n23
Walsingham, Sir Francis, 75, 185n3
Wapull, George, 51; *The Tide Tarrieth No Man*, 51, 70
Ward, Joseph P., 83–4, 85, 107
Watt, Teresa, 95
Wealth and Health, An Interlude of, 3, 16, 24–5, 34–44, 71, 109, 173, 174, 181, 201nn55, 63, 202nn68–70, 202n74, 202–3n75, 224n38; dates of composition and performance, 37, 196–7n10
weavers, 6, 79, 80, 82–6, 87, 91, 92, 93, 96, 159, 216n30, 218nn65–6
White, Micheline, 60
Wilson, Mary Floyd, 11
Wilson, Richard, 139
Wilson, Robert, 3, 65; *Pedlers Prophecie*, 52–3, 70; *Three Ladies of London*, 70

Wine, Martin L., 124, 125
Wolf, Lucien, 49
Wolley, Sir John, 12
Woods, Susanne, 57, 145
Wright, Eugene P., 87–8, 91
Wright, Louise B., 81
Wriothesley, Charles, 26, 28, 199n24
Wyatt, Michael, 89
Wyatt, Sir Thomas, 29, 30, 43, 199–200n31
Wyatt, Thomas (historian), 157

xenophobia, 4–5, 12, 13, 24–5, 29, 30–3, 34, 36, 38, 43, 44, 48, 52, 53, 54, 69, 85, 87–90, 107–11, 113, 114, 137, 156–61, 162, 163, 165, 167, 168, 173, 178, 179, 182, 184, 186n12, 190n40, 199–200n31, 206n37, 244n71. *See also* aliens: complaints about

Yuval-Davis, Nira, 119–20, 135

www.ingramcontent.com/pod-product-compliance
Lightning Source LLC
Chambersburg PA
CBHW030307080526
44584CB00012B/471